FROM INSIDE OUT

FROM INSIDE OUT: WRITING FROM SUBJECTIVE TO OBJECTIVE

PAULINE GRABILL CHRISTIANSEN
Bellevue Community College

WINTHROP PUBLISHERS, INC.
Cambridge, Massachusetts

Library of Congress Cataloging in Publication Data

Christiansen, Grabill Pauline.
    From inside out.

    Includes index.
    1.   Report writing.   2.   English language—Rhetoric.
I. Title.
LB2369.C494   808'.042   77–16378
ISBN 0–87626–293–0

Copyright © 1978 by Winthrop Publishers, Inc.
    17 Dunster Street, Cambridge, Massachusetts 02138

*To Finn who encouraged me to write the book,
and Gregg who I hope one day can use it.*

Contents

CHAPTER FOUR

Expanded Analysis: Contrast and Comparison Writing   215

CHAPTER FIVE

Thinking Logically   253

CHAPTER SIX

Toward Complete Objectivity   307

To the Student

This book demonstrates the two controlling concepts of writing: subjectivity (writing focused inside yourself) and objectivity (writing focused outside yourself) to help you fit different approaches and techniques to different writing purposes.

As you progress through the chapters, you will be writing and moving from inside out. You will experience and see the different effects you achieve in both subjective and objective writing. You will start with writing a subjective form of personal experience in chapter 1, and as you continue, your writing will become increasingly objective as succeeding chapters lead your focus progressively outside yourself.

Each chapter follows roughly the same format so you can easily scan it for the kind of information you find most useful. In each chapter, boxes set off definitions of terms and brief descriptions of writing type, approach needed, and purpose intended for each writing assignment. Self-descriptive subheadings throughout the book also make information quick to find.

If you learn best from examples, start by scanning the student examples at the end of each assignment. If you want a quick review of suggestions in list form that have helped others with a particular type of writing, look for the sections entitled "Check Lists." For additional help on any points on the check list, an expanded version of that list follows with detailed explanations, examples, and referrals to related material in other sections of the book.

Each chapter takes you through the entire writing process for each assignment from topic finding and prewriting suggestions to final editing and polishing techniques.

This book will make the writing process clearer, easier, and more enjoyable for you. I hope it not only helps you to write, but also makes you want to write.

This book resulted from feedback from previous students on what suggestions worked best in helping them improve their writing. I would also like your responses to which ideas helped you the most. Please use the response sheet at the end of this book to send me your ideas and suggestions. A book is only effective if it meets your needs.

To the Instructor

Using the concepts of subjectivity and objectivity as controlling frameworks, *From Inside Out* presents six different writing approaches starting with personal experience and ending with various forms of analysis.

Each chapter includes:

1. *Topic Ideas* to help students get involved and want to write because they have something to say.

2. *Prewriting Suggestions* to help students organize their material and see the advantages and disadvantages of different approaches and formats.

3. *Check Lists* to provide a quick overview of techniques that have helped others with the assignments.

4. *Expanded Check Lists* to give more extensive explanations and examples for each point on the overview check lists.

5. *Style Exercises* to call attention to writing techniques that improve, clarify, and tighten each form of writing.

6. *Student Example Papers* to illustrate effective writing for each assignment and to help elicit further writing topics and ideas.

Since we all have individual teaching styles and preferences, *From Inside Out* presents information in a format that offers maximum flexibility of approach. As presented, each chapter guides the student through the various stages of writing a paper, starting with finding a topic and ending with student example papers. You may present the material, however, in any order you find effective. For example, you may want to read and discuss some example papers before you present the assignment, or you may want to begin by calling attention to check lists items that you feel are crucial. You may also begin with any chapter you prefer, rather than following the subjective to objective progression of the book.

From Inside Out uses a practical, straightforward approach to writing that provides concrete directions and examples, while retaining variety and scope in possible assignments and topic choices. It has produced equally effective student writing for each writing style and has removed much of the fear students often experience in learning to write by making writing approachable and tangible. It has produced powerful results for those of us who use its techniques. If, after using it, you have any suggestions for improving its effectiveness for you, please fill in and send me the response sheet at the end of the book. I look forward to your replies.

Acknowledgments

First, I would like to acknowledge my students whose needs created the book and whose many fine writing examples are included in the book to help others struggling with similar assignments.

A new maxim in my life might read, "To learn who one's friends are, try writing a book." The constant help and support of many friends make up the marrow of this book. I thank them all and would like to identify the following in specific areas:

Contributions: Linda Bennett, Connie Freeland, Sue Gibson-Breda, Jackie Hartwich, and Gary McGlocklin, of the English department at Bellevue Community College, all contributed possible student example papers. Don Distad of the history department and Kae Hutchison of the music department also searched their areas for possible analytical examples.

Linda Bennett, Connie Freeland, Jackie Hartwich, Jerrie Kennedy, Gary McGlocklin, and Craig Sanders also helped me evaluate possible student example papers to decide which to include when the manuscript needed cutting.

My greatest debt in this area, however, goes to Connie Freeland. To her I owe the original idea for reaction paper writing, as well as many strong student example papers and useful ideas on format and layout.

Reviews: Dorothy Bestor reviewed my pilot chapters and encouraged me at a strategic moment. Connie Freeland critiqued these same chapters and offered many fine ideas.

My greatest debt in this area, however, goes to Jackie Harwich, Jerry Howard, and Jerrie Kennedy. All have read and critiqued the book from its inception and contributed much to its final form.

Editing: Craig Sanders edited the original version, and Julie Seeman edited the revised version. Both worked under the same time pressures I faced and often had to decipher a handwritten manuscript. I owe to their discerning eyes and incisive pens the book's final clean and tight form.

Proofing: Tracy Zacharias proofed the final manuscript and caught the errors we all missed.

Guidance: Cary Jensen guided me through the first steps in writing a book, and Ken Symes answered many questions and offered good advice.

Research: Margaret Johnston and Shirley Johnson of our library department found information needed on short notice.

Typing: Betty Ramsey typed the original pilot chapters, and Marty Bienz and Gail Smith also helped type portions of the first version. Susan Carlson typed most of the instructor's manual, and my husband, Finn Christiansen, helped finish typing it when time ran out.

My greatest debt in this area, however, is to my mother, Priscilla Yeager. She typed and retyped all versions of this book meeting impossible time limits, deciphering a messy manuscript, proofing as she went. Without her dedication and support, I would never have met my deadlines.

FROM INSIDE OUT

Chapter One

Writing from the Inside Out

Some Preliminary Definitions

Subjective writing   Writing that focuses on the inside of you, the writer; writing in which you reflect and emphasize your feelings and emotions as you present your material.

Objective writing   Writing that focuses outside of you; writing in which you seek to eliminate or at least to minimize any show of personal bias or emotion as you present your material.

Focus   A writer's emphasis or center of attention.

Focal point   The incident that pinpoints your paper's main idea.

Subjective and Objective Writing: A Matter of Focus

Subjective writing focuses inside the self. You become your own main topic. You emphasize feeling: how you felt at a given time, what produced those feelings, and how they influenced what you said or did. In writing subjectively, you re-create the feelings you experienced during an incident for your reader.

Objective writing focuses outside the self. Some observable aspect of the outside world becomes your main topic. You focus on fact: on what a person said or did rather than on your feelings toward that person. In writing objectively, you attempt to present information free from emotional distortion.

Whether you should write subjectively or objectively depends upon your purpose. If you want to re-create an experience the way you felt it for another person to feel and share, choose the subjective approach. If you want to focus on information and separate it from personal bias, choose a more objective format.

A Professional Example

The suicide attempt scene in Sylvia Plath's autobiographical novel, *The Bell Jar*, illustrates the different effects produced by objective and subjective writing.[1]

The news clippings of the event give a relatively objective view of the incident, for while the reporters might have been interested in the story's sensational aspects, at least they were not personally or emotionally involved with the story's subject, Ms. Plath. Under headings like "Scholarship Girl Missing, Mother Worried," "Sleeping Pills Feared Missing with Girl," and "Girl Found Alive," the articles retell mostly observable facts as they follow the course of the incident.

They report that Sylvia disappeared on August 17, that she was wearing a green skirt and a white blouse, and that she had left her mother a note saying she was going for a long walk. Excerpts from the articles read: "When Miss Greenwood had not returned by midnight . . . her mother called the town police." "Mrs. Greenwood asked that this picture be printed in hopes that it will encourage her daughter to return home." "Bloodhounds used in search for missing girl. Police Sgt. Bill Hindley says: 'It doesn't look good.'" Nowhere are the reporters' feelings or involvement detailed or emphasized.

In the subjective account, Sylvia's mother is down in the cellar washing clothes when she hears faint groans coming from an old breezeway hole and upon investigating finds her daughter drugged and disoriented. Unlike the objective report, you actually experience the scene from inside of Sylvia as she re-creates it from a subjective point of view.

> It was completely dark.
>
> I felt the darkness, but nothing else, and my head rose, feeling it, like the head of a worm. Someone was moaning. Then a great, hard weight smashed against my cheek like a stone wall and the moaning stopped.
>
> The silence surged back, smoothing itself as black water smooths to its old surface calm over a dropped stone.
>
> A cool wind rushed by. I was being transported at enormous speed down a tunnel into the earth. Then the wind stopped. There was a rumbling, as of many voices, protesting and disagreeing in the distance. Then the voices stopped.
>
> A chisel cracked down on my eye, and a slit of light opened, like a mouth or a wound, till the darkness clamped shut on it again. I tried to

---

[1]Sylvia Plath, *The Bell Jar* (New York: Harper & Row, Publishers, 1971), pp. 192–3.

roll away from the direction of the light, but hands wrapped round my limbs like mummy bands, and I couldn't move.

I began to think I must be in an underground chamber, lit by blinding lights, and that the chamber was full of people who for some reason were holding me down.

Then the chisel struck again, and the light leapt into my head, and through the thick, warm, furry dark, a voice cried,

"Mother!"

In reading the subjective account you experience the rescue as Sylvia does: in a drugged state of dazed semi-consciousness. Her cries for "mother" and her moans are heard as voices coming from outside herself. You know that she is rescued only by the light and wind breaking into the hole as the wood is removed before disembodied hands and voices carry her off.

Subjective writing limits itself to the speaker's conscious awareness. If that consciousness is dazed, frightened, or confused, the writing reflects and re-creates that state. An event is reproduced first; explanations, if needed, come later.

Writing from the Inside: Personal Experience

A math teacher I once had always presented new or difficult material to the class with the advice, "Start with something you know. Ask yourself a question you can answer. Always work from the known to the unknown." His advice also works for writing. "Start with something you know."

In looking for something to write about, start with the subjective, start with yourself. You have accumulated a store of memories, feelings, and reactions. Explore your past for its topic potential. Examine your present: people, places, incidents, accidents, emergencies, celebrations, and your reactions to them can all provide starting points for good subjective writing.

Personal Experience Writing, Its Purpose and Approach

> **Type of writing** Personal experience
> **Approach** Subjective
> **Purpose** To re-create an event so your reader can experience it from "inside your skin"

Effective personal experience writing shows rather than tells, re-creates rather than relates, substitutes scenes for summaries.

The following paragraph, flashing back to a childhood memory, contains the germ of a personal experience topic even though it is general and unspecific in its present form:

> We always went to Aunt Martha's on special occasions and had a big dinner. She lived in a neat old house, and she always gave us lots to eat. I liked going to Aunt Martha's. She was my favorite aunt.

If you want to take the memory of a feast at Aunt Martha's and work it into an effective personal experience paper, you will re-create the experience complete with the sights, sounds, tastes, and smells of that special event.

Reconstruct the eating scene itself, if that was the highlight of the event for you: What foods were present? How were they served? What did they look like, smell like, taste like? What family rituals did you observe in serving them? Who was present? What did people talk about? What did they act like? What were your thoughts while the scene was taking place?

If Aunt Martha is your central character, detail a visual image of her. Include her size, her outstanding facial features, her way of dressing, her gestures, and the way she moves. Add to the visual image a sound track of her voice, her special laugh, the expressions she used, and the questions she always asked. Add to these descriptions at intervals comments on how her various characteristics made you feel, and your paper will come alive.

A portion of the paper might read as follows:

> When I was eight or nine, my favorite holidays were the ones spent at Aunt Martha's. Aunt Martha lived on Poplar Street in a three-storied house with peeling paint and a big old green and red striped lawn swing on its front porch. The smell of freshly baked bread, jams, cookies, and other secret goodies hidden in old coffee cans greeted me even before Aunt Martha's tiny, energetic form appeared in the doorway.
>
> Aunt Martha was slightly hard of hearing, and her voice always was a little louder than normal, especially when she got excited. She'd pop out the front door, throw an arm around me, and shout in my ear, "There's something waiting for ya in the kitchen, Joey," and I'd squirm loose and let my nose lead me to the special pie, or cake, or apple tart she'd made for me with the ingredients left over from the "official" after-dinner dessert. . . .

In personal experience writing, you pump life into an experience rather than deflate it into a series of dead facts. You put the reader inside your skin, let him or her see what you saw, feel what you felt, think what you thought, and react as you reacted, literally living through the event described.

Topic Finders

Successful Topics

Some people have the mistaken idea that only "glamorous" people live "exciting" lives and have experiences worth writing about. Ever thought, "But nothing ever happened to me. I have nothing to write about"? Each of us is unique. Only you have experienced a particular emotion under the specific conditions present at some point in your life and that makes it worth writing about.

Consider the following examples on two seemingly mundane subjects: suffering from a cold and battering chicken thighs at Chicken Delight. The cold sufferer re-created misery in repulsive but accurate detail, at one point writing:

> My nose is filling up again after just having sniffed and sucked all the snot out of it. I've given up blowing the lousy thing, because blowing does absolutely nothing. I blow and blow and blow until my ears plug up and my eyes swell only to find I have blown a hole clean through the tissue and everything is all over my hand.

The Chicken Delight worker described the agonies of the nightly battle with chicken fat with equally accurate detail:

> The thighs of chickens, as any chef *cordon bleu* knows, have fatty deposits. Customers do not seem to like fried chicken fat; therefore, it must be removed. Removing the fat is part of my job. It is slimy. It is slippery, and it is not easy to remove. I grasp the chicken thigh in my left hand while with my right hand I grasp the fat and pull. If I'm lucky, the fat will come off. If not, I have to use my thumb and gouge it out.

While good topics can be found in seemingly trivial events, a topic usually will not work for you unless you have some kind of emotional involvement with it. After being told that all good writing was concrete, one student wrote a personal experience paper describing his grandmother's garden. He took you through the garden row by row, first the peas, then the cabbage, then the squash. He described each plant, its height, color, shape, and exact location. By the end of the third row, you wanted out. The paper was mechanically correct but emotionally dead. When I asked how he happened to choose the garden for his topic and whether he had any particular attachment to it, he replied, "I really couldn't care less about the place, but it was the only thing I could think of to describe in detail."

When he zeroed in on a place that produced a strong emotional reaction in him, however, the result was a personal experience paper on his mud bunker in Vietnam. The student had a fear of small enclosed places, and the grave-like bunker with its dank smell terrified him. During a surprise attack by the Vietcong, the bunker collapsed and became an actual grave for one of his buddies. His paper created the sense of place so powerfully, it was painful to read. His topic worked, and the incident proved an important point: if a topic is going to mean something to your reader, it must first mean something to you.

Association Technique for Finding Topics

Since good personal experience topics are often ones you associate with some emotion, try scanning the following list of emotions and see what incidents they bring to mind.

Association Exercise

Fold a piece of paper in half lengthwise to produce two columns. In one column copy the emotions from the following list that trigger a strong, immediate reaction in you. Add any others that come to mind as you go along. Leave the other column blank for your reactions.

Labels of Emotions or States of Being

threatened	rewarded	afraid	irritated
angry	snubbed	brave	crabby
lost	cruel	cowardly	disappointed
betrayed	tricked	confused	amused
welcome	vindicated	childish	astounded

unwelcome	unattractive	safe	silly
impressed	attractive	rejected	anxious
proud	fat	misunderstood	crushed
jealous	skinny	relieved	sorrowful
hate	wet	nostalgic	exhausted
love	tense	curious	bewildered
sad	judged	bitter	used
happy	foolish	bored	colorful
sick	shy	tired	hysterical
in pain	stupid	inspired	hopeful
embarrassed	smart	honored	immature
homesick	overconfident	unprotected	panicky
foreign	disgusted	protected	frustrated
guilty	lonely	included	tense
		zealous	patronized

Slowly now, go over each term on your list and try to remember a time when you felt that way. Whenever an incident comes to mind, try to associate it with a specific scene or group of scenes and then jot down a brief description of those scenes in the column next to the term. When you are finished, go over your descriptions and see which incident is clearest in your mind and evokes a specific emotional memory. That incident probably has the most potential for your personal experience topic.

Alternative Lists for Topic Finding

Make three lists: one starting with "I am . . . ," one starting with "I like . . . ," and one starting with "I dislike . . . ." Complete the sentences in each of the lists with statements that are true about yourself. For example one student wrote:

I am	I like	I dislike
a girl	people	exams
19-years-old	chocolate	rude people
a full-time student	skiing	homework
a psychology major	sailing	drizzly weather
a part-time waitress	scuba diving	pressure
a daughter	tennis	greasy foods
a sister	cats	being criticized
single	peace and quiet	loud noises
an American	sunny days	working late hours

a Democrat	being unpressured	not hearing from
a vegetarian	learning new things	my boyfriend
slightly overweight	feeling healthy	cleaning my apartment
shy	feeling loved	

Good personal experience topics combine firsthand information with personal feeling; they join what you are or what you have been with how you feel about it.

The student who produced the above lists, for example, might combine her job as a waitress with her dislike of "rude people" and come up with an incident that made her feel that dislike. She might couple her love for "peace and quiet" with "learning new things" by re-creating her reactions on her first scuba dive. When you link specific emotions with specific events, you will find the topics you need.

Sports Topics

If you feel uncomfortable revealing your private emotions, try describing a sports activity. These subjects lend themselves well to writing that re-creates an event since they often include a lot of sensory awareness. They are not, however, as intimate or as revealing as topics about personal relationships because they focus on physical events rather than on emotional situations. Write about a sport activity only if you're a participant since you need to have experienced actual involvement to re-create effective sensory detail.

Follow the same format as before. Scan the following list for topics. Add any other sports or physical activities the list brings to your mind and test them as well:

skiing	sky diving	football
hiking	skin diving	hockey
swimming	hang gliding	wrestling
sailing	mountain climbing	gymnastics
water skiing	baseball	pole vaulting
diving	volleyball	long distance running
tennis	basketball	sprinting
ping-pong	soccer	bicycling

You can't go through an entire game or track meet without exhausting your reader or falling away from concrete detail into a general summary. Focus your paper on a single memorable incident, scene, or high point within a game or event. If you're a pitcher, focus on the winning or losing pitch, your thoughts during it, and the crowd's reaction to it. If you're hiking, reproduce only the last part of the hike, the view that rewards you, and whether you're in any condition to enjoy it. If you're injured during an event, begin your paper right before the injury occurs. If you limit your focus, these events can produce good writing topics. For further help in selecting and shaping your material see "Jogging," "Penalty Kick," and "First Run" in the Student Example Papers in this chapter.

Further Topic Ideas

Natural disasters, operations, accidents, and jobs can also produce topics (not meaning to imply that the above are related to each other). If you have lived through an earthquake, flood, blizzard, fire, tornado, hurricane, or avalanche, you have the material for a powerful topic.

Operations and accidents are also good topics because they have definite beginnings and endings. A paper about a car accident could begin with a description of what you were aware of immediately before the crash occurred, including where you were going, what song was on the radio, who you were talking to, what you were thinking about. Then you would re-create the images, sights, sounds, and sensations of the accident as it occurred, and end at the point where you knew you were all right and help was on the way.

Jobs can often provide topics. Think through jobs you have held, both paid or unpaid: how you got them, what you liked and disliked about them, what scenes they bring to mind. Then pick the scene you remember most clearly and try to reproduce it for your topic.

Prewriting Suggestions and Ideas

Try Freewriting on Potential Topics

> **Freewriting**   Writing done, as rapidly as possible, without worrying about grammar or mechanical correctness; to record your normal speaking or thinking voice rather than a more self-conscious or premeditated writing style.

Freewriting is unstructured without rules or restraints, a way to loosen up your writing gears, to get the words to flow before too many do's and don't's dry up your creative juices. It allows you to try out topics and see which ones generate the most details, and it can help you find your best focal point before you begin your paper. Freewriting is particularly helpful in preparing to write personal experience papers, since these are best told in your natural voice. Above all, freewriting is a nonthreatening way to pick up your pen and actually start writing.

Unfocused and Focused Freewriting

> **Unfocused freewriting** Freewriting without a controlling subject or thought, putting down anything that comes to mind; skipping from topic to topic, thought to thought; having no subject limitations.
>
> **Focused freewriting** Freewriting on one idea, memory, thought, or reaction as long as the words come; remaining free from mechanical concerns but limiting yourself to a chosen subject or area.

Your freewrites can be either unfocused or focused. If you are undecided on a topic and uptight about writing in general, try unfocused freewriting first. Use the association list exercise (see the section on "Association Technique for Finding Topics," p. 6) to generate ideas. and feel free to skip from topic to topic, wherever your ideas take you. If you hit upon a topic that gives you more to say, stick with it, and you are already doing a focused freewrite. Freewriting can produce the germ of a writing idea or, in some cases, generate large portions of description or dialogue that can be reworked into your final paper.

When freewriting, put down whatever comes to mind. Don't worry about spelling, sentence structure, punctuation, or vocabulary at this time. These you can rework later. Try to recapture the event by writing it as it happened, putting down any dialogue you can "hear" as you remember. Write rapidly to avoid becoming self-conscious. Let the ideas and language flow.

Try doing focused freewrites for ten to fifteen minutes on three or four topic possibilities. Find the topic that is easiest for you. When the subject takes over and ideas pour out faster than you can write them down, you know you've found your topic. Keep your other choices in reserve.

Don't struggle with topics that are too distant in time to be remembered clearly or too complicated to be handled successfully in a short paper. Sometimes the best topics turn out to be offshoots of your main idea; in exploring one subject, you often find others along the way.

Ideas on Beginnings

Keep your beginnings tight. While all experiences might be said to begin with your getting up in the morning, such openings often start too far away from the actual focal point of your paper and cause you to include too much unnecessary information.

Successful beginnings start close to your paper's focal point. For example, if you write about the time you broke your leg skiing, begin the paper on the run where the accident occurred. Don't build up to the event by giving your "getting up in the morning" routine, the details of the ride to the resort, or a complete rerun of the day's activities before the accident. A possible opening for your paper might read, "I quickly checked the ski slope for signs of my skiing buddy, Jan, who had called to me from the chairlift, 'Bet I beat you down!'"

A good beginning gives enough of the "who, what, when, where, and why" of your situation to put your reader inside your skin. Indicate who you are, what your age is (if it's relevant), where you are, why you're there, and whom you're with so your reader can start to relive the incident as if he or she were you. Work this information in naturally so your beginning doesn't end up sounding like a list of vital statistics.

Ideas on Endings

A good ending makes your paper feel finished. Don't give your reader the urge to keep on reading if there's nothing more to read. Stop when your situation or conflict is resolved. If you're writing about your ski accident, for example, you can't end your paper at the point where you black out because your reader will want to know what happened to you.

This doesn't mean that you have to take your reader through three years of operations and therapy, if that's what your full recovery entailed, before you can end your paper. It does mean that you must at least regain consciousness and be free of immediate danger before your reader can relax. Your ski incident might end, "I saw Jan place my new skis over her shoulder as they loaded me onto the stretcher. 'Maybe,' I thought with some bitterness to myself, 'they'll slow her down so much that I'll still be the first one down.'"

When you've reached your end point, stop. Dragged out endings suffer the same fate as T. S. Eliot's world in "The Hollow Men." They end, "Not with a bang but a whimper."[2]

Check Lists

How to Use the Check Lists

When you have found a topic, tried freewriting on it, and are ready to write a rough draft, the next step is to go over the following check list for ideas and to return to the check list at various stages of your writing for further help. The shortened form of the list summarizes points already made and includes suggestions to help you avoid problems and produce a better final product.

Scan the list before you write your first draft. If some point needs further clarification, read the extended discussion of it in the expanded version of the check list. After you have written your paper and let it "cool" for a period of time, go back and reread the check list. Rereading it should help you find still more ways to expand, edit, polish, and reshape your paper as you continue working it into its most effective form.

List Disclaimer

Remember that all check lists in this book are intended for guidance purposes only. Most good writers break guidelines or rules at some time or another, but you should break a rule only when you gain more than you lose by doing so. Make sure that what you purchase in effect is not costing too much in clarity. Break rules intentionally, never out of ignorance.

Each list in this book is geared to help you with a specific type of writing. The approaches and suggestions given in the list for subjective personal experience writing will differ and at times contradict the suggestions given in a later list for more objective analytical writing.

While some aspects of good writing (clarity and specificity, for example) remain constant for all types of material, other techniques

---

[2]T. S. Eliot, "The Hollow Men," as reprinted in *Adventures in English Literature*, eds. J. B. Priestley and Josephine Spear (New York: Harcourt, Brace & World, 1963), p. 688.

(whether to focus on or away from telling the event in the first person, the "I," for example) change according to your purpose.

Check List for Personal Experience Writing

1. *Choose a topic that moves you, one that you can recall in specific detail.*
2. *Use an "I" point of view.*
3. *Focus on a high point or some controlling reaction or effect.*
4. *Show, don't tell; create, don't dictate.*
5. *Create miniscenes.*
6. *Use all five senses.*
7. *Use colorful verbs.*
8. *Add dialogue, if you can reproduce it naturally.*
9. *Identify your speakers with "tag lines" and punctuate dialogue correctly.*
10. *Stick to one tense; usually past tense is easiest to maintain.*
11. *Don't call attention to the act of writing the paper, announce your writing plans, or flash ahead to information the reader learns at a later time.*
12. *Eliminate clichés whenever possible; replace them with specifics.*
13. *Avoid adopting a forced flippant tone or limiting the paper to a conversation with yourself.*
14. *Paragraph to clarify the focus of your paper.*
15. *Vary your sentence structure to avoid a monotonous or choppy effect.*
16. *Check for unnecessary fragments and run-on sentences.*
17. *Don't withhold information to create a false surprise ending.*
18. *End on a tension-release point.*

Expanded Check List for Personal Experience Writing with Explanations, Examples, and Referrals to Related Material

1. *Choose a topic that moves you, one that you can recall in specific detail.* (Review sections on "Purpose of Personal Experience Writing," "Successful Topics," "Association Technique for Finding Topics," and "Further Topic Ideas" for help in finding suitable topics.)

A good personal experience topic is one that you experienced firsthand and felt strongly about. You can remember it in enough detail to be able to recapture what you said, thought, observed, heard, and felt as you experienced it. A good topic re-creates itself as you write it. As you investigate your topic, be aware of the power of a specific effective detail. Good details make your writing appealing. Look for the odd or unusual detail you associate with an event. Does your dentist have hairy fingers? Did you wear your track suit backwards to the championship meet? Is the image you retain of a plane's forced landing the hideous turquoise blue seat in front of you? Was death a heavy straight black line on a heart monitor? Were you lost in reverie with one eyelash on, the other looking like a centipede in your damp palm? Is craziness wearing green house slippers to your analyst's office? Each of these details appeared in different students' papers and helped make those papers interesting and unique. Details are the stuff life is made of.

2. *Use an "I" point of view.*

Point of view   Whose head you're inside of in viewing an event; the person whose mind re-creates an event.

While you may have been told in the past to avoid focusing on yourself in writing, in personal experience writing, the "I" is usually the preferred focus. Stick consistently to "I" and avoid switching to a "we" or "you" approach. You can know what is going on in your own head, but if you use a "we" approach, you risk remaining too general since you can't always tell what the "we" is thinking or feeling. For example, compare the following "we" telling of an event to the "I" telling that follows it.

"We" telling:

Last weekend, Emmy, Molly, and I were driving home from a movie when we noticed that a car was following us too closely using its high beams. This made us angry, so we started to flash our lights and step on our brakes to warn him. He not only persisted but started to ram us at intervals from behind. We got more frightened and speeded up.

"I" telling:

I was driving my friends, Emmy and Molly, home from a movie last weekend, when a car started following me too closely using its high beams. His lights reflected off my rear-view mirror with a blinding effect.

"Hey, what's that guy trying to prove," Molly squeaked in the high voice she always uses when she is nervous. I tried to hide my own irritation when I said in my "calming Molly down voice," "I don't know, but it sure makes it hard to see."

Emmy, who was sitting next to me, turned around but turned back quickly when the lights hit her.

"Boy, those lights are really bright," she said in a voice that seemed to imply I should do something about it.

I started to flash my lights and step on my brakes to catch the guy's attention, when suddenly I felt the car jolted from the rear.

He was actually ramming my car. I flashed hot with anger, but my next reaction was to step on the gas and run for it. Whoever he was, I had no desire to meet him.

Notice how the "I" telling is longer—and more detailed than the "we" version. In a "we" telling, the reactions of separate individuals are lost by combining them in one "we" reaction. Using the "I" approach, you can differentiate each person, tell what he or she does and says, and give your interpretation and reactions to each one. By focusing the reader's attention on your reactions, you re-create the incident's impact on you.

A "you" approach is used to directly address your audience. In personal experience writing, however, it can break the ongoing illusion of an incident and should be used sparingly. At its worst, it can lapse into a lazy style that substitutes the expression "you know what I mean" for the hard work of actually creating the desired effect.

Using a "you" or "we" approach also increases the tendency to switch pronouns, to hop from "you" to "I" to "we," creating confusion for your reader. For flexibility, consistency, and clarity, in personal experience writing, the "I's" definitely have it.

3. *Focus on a high point or some controlling reaction or effect.* (Review sections on "Ideas on Beginnings" and "Ideas on Endings" for how to start a paper close to a high point.)

Don't dilute your paper's effect by trying to cover too many incidents. It's better to see a series of incidents as separate topic possibilities than to try to cram them all into one short paper.

Focus your paper on one high point of an experience (for example, the last stretch of a climb rather than an entire hiking trip, the last part of a ball game rather than all nine innings), or on one central feeling or reaction a person evokes in you and detail several scenes that explain why. (See the student example paper "Jackie" (p. 32), which uses multiple scenes to reinforce a single reaction.)

Begin in the midst of what you're doing, identifying briefly what you're doing, where, and with whom, then build directly to the high point or significant reaction.

4. *Show, don't tell; create, don't dictate.* Portray a word before you use it. Make your reader feel your fear, sense your nervousness, experi-

ence your embarrassment, rather than tell him you felt that way. "Tell" words on the following list dictate emotions to your reader; avoid them:

beautiful	unbelievable	majestic
breathtaking	indescribable	vivid
lovely	wonderful	incredible
memorable	magnificent	fantastic
idyllic	awe-inspiring	grand

Make your details earn the response on their own. Instead of saying something general like "the beauty of the scene influenced us," the student in the paragraph below created the effect with careful choice of detail:

> Margie and I were slowly trolling in the waterway which connects Ross Lake to Lake Diablo. During the brief periods when the sun was not obscured by the morning mists, the waterfalls, cascading from towering rock faces, displayed an endless variety of multicolored rainbows. The deep-blue water, sparkling with reflected sunlight, lapped against the boulder-encrusted cliffs. The slow, gentle roll of the boat caused us to be overcome by a sense of well-being and listlessness.

A student searching for a hotel in an unknown European city reproduces her exhaustion for us in the following scene:

> Chris, who is five feet tall and fairly weak, couldn't carry her suitcase any more, and now I was carrying both suitcases. My arms were shaking from the weight; I stooped over because my back wouldn't hold up any longer, and my sweaty, stiff hands felt like they had been born gripping suitcase handles.

In the student example paper "Licorice" at the end of this chapter, the author writes an entire episode re-creating the effect of guilt without once mentioning the word itself.

Good writing makes details speak. (See "Replacing 'Tell' Words Exercise" at the end of this chapter.)

5. *Create miniscenes.* To show an event effectively, reproduce it either in one continuous scene or in a series of miniscenes. Personal experience writing is like presenting a dramatic presentation. Your reader needs to see the setting, hear the dialogue, and picture the movement and action taking place. Scan the example papers at the end of this chapter and notice the prevalence of miniscenes in the writing. "Licorice" takes you from the store to the sidewalk to the tree with

filter-specked ground at the end. "My Last Autopsy" centers on the scene with the towel-draped figure on a metal table. "Jackie" builds effect by using a series of scenes from being edged off a porch to being splattered with beans across a lunchroom table. In the longer professional example, "Not Another Word," Richard Thurman shows Paul's reactions to Robert through a series of scenes: Paul's admiring Robert's courageous breakfast report before the gluttonous teacher, his helping Robert get "Buddy," the dog, drunk, his falling in love with Robert's mother who baked good things and openly showed affection, his showing-off his sled-load of Christmas gifts only to end up coveting Robert's gyroscope and Chinese-beheading sword, and ending with his fighting Robert to deny the plain facts about Robert's parents' naps.[3] Each writer creates his event by detailing effective scenes.

6. *Use all five senses.* Seeing is just one of your senses. You also hear, feel, smell, and taste. When you re-create any event, try to involve all your sensory reactors.

Good writers have keen sensory recall. The student example papers at the end of this chapter evoke a variety of sensory reactions. Nobuko Sasaki's first reaction to the United States is a combination of feel and smell: "Everything seemed to be cool. Suddenly the cool air blew through my whole body. I could smell people's lives every place in Japan, but I couldn't smell them there in the airport, because everything was too neat, too cool." Gene Hovis's memory of intense fever in polio is strongly tactile: "Its warmth was streaking up my neck into my cheeks like hot wine. My lips burned. My eyelids caught fire like leaves. I felt my brain fill with boiling mercury." To Pat Hughbanks, the memory of guilt and betrayal is associated with the taste of licorice "far down my throat."

Say you are standing by the seashore. The experience is more than simply watching breakers roll onto shore. You also hear the water as it crashes and recedes, you take in the sounds of people, dogs, and seagulls along the beach. You feel the salt spray stinging your face and the hot sand oozing between your toes. A pungent smell of kelp, wet logs, and mud flats mixes with a salty coolness you can almost taste. If you concentrated on only one sense in the above scene to the exclusion of all others, you'd blunt its effect and deprive your reader of the wealth of details actually present.

In his book, *I'm OK—You're OK: A Practical Guide to Transactional Analysis*, Dr. Thomas A. Harris describes Dr. Wilder Penfield's

---

[3]Richard Thurman, "Not Another Word," © 1957 *The New Yorker Magazine*, Inc., 25 May 1957, pp. 37–44.

research on the human brain and how it remembers an event.[4] Using a local anesthetic and electrodes, Dr. Penfield stimulated a patient's brain at a specific point in the cerebral cortex. While the point was being stimulated, the patient actually relived an experience from his past with complete sensory recall.

One patient re-experienced walking down a specific street and identified the buildings on the street as the Seven-Up Bottling Company and the Harrison Bakery, places from his past. Another hummed and sang along with the song "Oh, Marie, Oh, Marie" he was hearing on a radio station. When the electrode stimulus was removed, the patient's re-experiencing stopped. Under questioning, however, the patient could usually identify the scenes experienced as a part of his past.

Dr. Harris summarized Penfield's findings by comparing the human brain to a high fidelity tape recorder that stored memories complete with sight, sound, smell, touch, and taste tracks. The brain not only stored past events in detail but also the feelings those events evoked.

The significance of these findings for you as a writer is what they reveal about how your brain stores memories. Your brain has recorded sensory detail plus feeling as part of the memory of an event. To communicate that event fully, this same detail must be restored. When you say in frustration, "I know how it was, but I just can't explain it in words," it may be that you are leaving out part or all of the sensory detail stored in your memory bank. Draw upon that bank; it pays large dividends in writing effectiveness and reader interest. For further help, see the "Use All Five Senses" exercise at the end of this chapter.

7. *Use colorful verbs.* Strong verbs enrich and enliven your writing. Verbs appeal to the senses and produce instant images. Verbs like splash, sparkle, flutter, glimmer, glisten, twinkle, crash, scurry, bluster, and bellow convey image, sound, action, and emotion. A good verb is your most economical way to create an effect.

Experiment with the verbs in the final draft of your paper. Try to find verbs that reproduce the effect of what you're describing. Have old ladies *clump* from stores, buses *chug* to a stop, electric doors *hiss* open, outdoor engines *thump-whine* their way home. Let verb choice reflect the intensity and pitch of a vocal response.

Personify your body parts and use verbs to express their response to physical strain. In describing his first ride on a hydroplane, a student wrote, "My teeth shook; my back ached; and my liver cried." Let your

---

[4]Thomas A. Harris, *I'm OK–You're OK: A Practical Guide to Transactional Analysis* (New York: Harper & Son, Publishers, 1969), pp. 4–12.

body speak for itself. (See the verb exercises at the end of this chapter for further help in developing verb awareness.)

8. *Add dialogue, if you can reproduce it naturally.* Dialogue can pump life into a scene. If people are present in an event, they usually speak. If you can capture how they speak, their inflections, word choice, gestures, and tone, you are that much closer to making the scene real.

Good dialogue can recapture a personality or provide the high point of a scene. For many readers, the high point of Richard Thurman's "Not Another Word" (see professional example at the end of this chapter) is Robert's honest reply to Miss Devron's question of what he had for breakfast, "I had a cup of coffee and a snail, Ma'am."[5]

Effective dialogue sounds natural. Practice reading your paper out loud to see if the dialogue reads easily and sounds right. Forced dialogue can make a paper sound artificial or stilted and ruin your intended effect. If you have a poor ear for dialogue, it's better to leave it out.

9. *Identify your speaker with "tag lines" and punctuate dialogue correctly.*

Tag line   The identification of who is speaking or thinking in a direct quotation, indicated by expressions such as "I said," "he replied," "I thought to myself."

Be sure your reader knows who is speaking in a conversation and whether quoted material is said out loud or is part of your thoughts. Experiment with using tag lines that go beyond "he said" or "she said." Use descriptive verbs to indicate the voice inflection, volume, tone, or mood of your speaker.

You don't have to have a tag line for every quotation, if you're sure it's obvious to your reader who is speaking. A tag line for every speaker in short conversation can sound choppy and repetitious. Paragraph to show each change in speaker in dialogue give and take, even if it means reparagraphing every other line.

If you're not sure how to punctuate direct quotations, scan the following rules and examples for a quick review:

Rules for Punctuating Quoted Material

a. Enclose in quotation marks only the parts of the sentence that

---

[5]Thurman, p. 38.

reproduce direct speech or are actual quotations. Tag lines are *not* put in quotation marks.

Example:

He said,   "My tooth hurts."

tag line   direct speech

b. Indirect quotations (usually introduced by "that") require *no* quotation marks.

Example:
He said *that* his tooth hurt.

c. Commas and periods always go *inside* the closing quotation marks whether they're part of the quoted material or not.

Examples:
"My tooth hurts," he wailed.
He wailed, "My tooth hurts."

d. Semicolons (;) and colons (:) go *outside* the quotation marks.

Examples:
Constantly complaining, he wailed, "My tooth hurts"; it was enough to make you want to hit him.
"My tooth hurts": this cry was all we heard from him.

e. Question marks, exclamation marks, and dashes go *inside* the quotation marks if they refer to the quoted material, *outside* the quotation marks if they refer to the sentence as a whole.

Examples:
"Does your tooth hurt?" he asked.

inside because it refers to the quoted material

Did he say, "My tooth hurts"?

outside because it refers to the sentence as a whole

f. If rule e would produce two final punctuation marks (one for the quotation and one for the entire sentence), use only the first one.

Example:
Did he say, "Are you hungry?"

technically the sentence would have two question marks; use only the first one.

g. Use single quotation marks (typewritten as apostrophes) for quotations inside of quotations.

Example:
"I'm sick of his always saying 'My tooth hurts,'" Jack said.

10. *Stick to one tense; usually the past tense is easiest to maintain.*

> **Verb tense** Any of the forms of a verb that show the time of its action; English has six tenses: present, past, future, perfect, past perfect, and future perfect.

Use verb tense consistently. Change verb tense only to indicate actual time distinctions (whether an event is completed, ongoing, or about to happen), otherwise choose one tense and stick to it.

Writing an entire paper in the present tense can be difficult to maintain and often increases the danger of your switching tenses in midstream, thus breaking your continuity. Usually the past tense is easier to maintain. You don't have to write in the present tense to achieve the effect of reliving an event as it happened.

The following example takes a present tense telling and rewrites it in past tense. Notice how the immediacy and flow of the incident are retained in the past tense example:

Present tense:
I *walk* into the room and *look* around. Not seeing anyone that *looks* familiar, I *go* to the back row, and *find* a seat where I *can be* relatively anonymous.

I *sit* back and *wait* for the teacher to come in, wondering what she or he *will be* like. All I *have is* the name Christiansen to go by.

Past tense:
I *walked* into the room and *looked* around. Not seeing anyone that *looked* familiar, I *went* to the back row, and *found* a seat where I *could be* relatively anonymous.

I *sat* back and *waited* for the teacher to come in, wondering what she or he *would be* like. All I *had was* the name Christiansen to go by.

11. *Don't call attention to the act of writing the paper, announce your writing plans, or flash ahead to information the reader learns at a*

later time. To sustain the illusion of experiencing an event from inside your skin, refrain from comments that take a reader's attention away from the immediate event and focus it on the act of writing the paper instead. Avoid statements like "I am going to write about the most exciting event in my life." Start with the event itself. Also avoid statements like "as I was soon to discover" or "as I found out later." They destroy the tension a reader experiences in reliving an event with you and break the illusion of immediacy. By breaking tension, you lose the powerful grip a paper can have on your reader's attention and interest.

12. *Eliminate clichés whenever possible; replace them with specifics.*

Cliché   A worn-out expression that has lost its originality, specificity, and impact through overuse.

A cliché is an expression that has been used so often, it has lost all freshness and uniqueness for your reader. If you start an expression like "deep sigh of . . ." and your reader can finish it for you automatically, you have probably written a cliché.

Clichés are catchall expressions that can be applied to almost any situation. They are "dead-weight" in your paper since they add no new thought or original detail. Clichés are appropriate if they are part of someone's directly quoted speech or if your intention is to characterize or satirize your speaker's lack of imagination. If your paper is nothing more than a collection of clichés, however, you should review your approach.

Usually a cliché detracts more than it adds to your paper. Scan your paper for possible clichés, and if you find any, try one of the following options.

A. Throw it out.

B. Retain the information part, but change the overused word pattern.
(For example, "broke into a cold sweat" becomes "I started to sweat.")

C. Replace the cliché with specifics.
(For example, I was "in sad shape" becomes "My hair was in tangles; my arms were bleeding; my clothes were torn and wrinkled.")

D. Replace it with a comparison unique to your own past experience.
(Thus, "Empty feeling in my stomach" becomes "I felt like I did the time my mother told me my dog, Jeff, had died.")

(See the cliché exercise at the end of this chapter for more practice in recognizing and reworking clichés out of your writing.)

13. *Avoid adopting a flippant tone or limiting the paper to a conversation with yourself.* A writer who sounds like "Mr. Cool" and who writes mainly in slang, clichés, and current "in" expressions risks sounding forced and artificial. A paper that begins "Last weekend my buddies and I boogied down to Main Street to do some cruisin' and, like, you know, to hustle some chicks and get in on the action" may sound "in," but it lacks all the specifics of the situation. It could apply to any number of adolescents, on any number of weekends, on many main streets. There is nothing original or unique in the writing. The attempt to appear disinterested, detached, or "cool" in relating an event often sounds phony, conceited, and callous and keeps your reader from seeing you as a sensitive human being. Effective personal experience writing requires an honest, detailed, and concrete reaction to a specific situation, which a false sophisticated tone suppresses.

In a self-talk approach, the writer talks to himself during an event rather than describing it and re-creating it. As a result, the writer often leaves out what is actually seen, done, and reacted to, being too wrapped up in his own personal conversation to notice.

14. *Paragraph to clarify idea focus.* Paragraphing is the equivalent of "thought punctuation." Just as a period indicates the end of a sentence, so should a paragraph indicate the end of one thought or emphasis and the beginning of another. When your attention switches to a new idea, person, or thought, paragraph to show the change.

In many cases paragraphing can be a matter of opinion, but be sure to avoid the extremes either of writing large blocks of material with no paragraphs or of stringing together pages of one or two sentence paragraphs. While one-sentence paragraphs are needed to show change of speaker in dialogue, in most writing they should be used sparingly and saved for situations where you want to emphasize an idea by making it stand alone. If you write a series of short paragraphs, check each one carefully to see if it can be combined with other material, expanded by adding support details, or simply thrown out.

Accurate paragraphing reflects your control of your material. If you have difficulty paragraphing, chances are you need to clarify your focus.

15. *Vary your sentence structure to avoid a monotonous or choppy effect.* Overreliance on one-sentence patterns can be monotonous. Use a variety of lengths and vary your pattern so you don't have a series of all long or all short sentences. Notice the improvement the writer gained by rewriting the following sentences.

Example using too many short sentences of the same pattern.
    I woke up. I rolled over. I fumbled to turn off the alarm. It was raining outside. I wondered what Mom would make for breakfast. I stuck one foot out of bed to test the floor temperature.

Same example rewritten to achieve sentence variety.
    Hearing the alarm, I woke up, rolled over, and fumbled to turn it off. It was raining outside. I wondered what Mom would make for breakfast as I stuck one foot out of bed to trial test the floor temperature.

16. *Check for unnecessary fragments and run-on sentences.*

Fragment   Part of a sentence written as if it were a complete sentence.
Run-on   Two or more sentences written as one.

Personal experience writing gives you a lot of license to break grammatical rules and write in fragments, since it often reflects or quotes spoken language in which fragments are quite acceptable. They are an effective way to capture a confused or emotional state of mind. Be careful, however, to avoid overusing them, especially in straight descriptions. Since fragments are incomplete statements, they leave your reader hanging in the air and can interfere with clarity. Make sure your sentences have clear subjects and verbs. Attach descriptions of actions to a person or an object for greater clarity.

Fragment example:
    Skiing furiously down the hill, unaware of my surroundings, or other people on the slope.

Corrected fragment example:
    Skiing furiously down the hill, unaware of my surroundings or other people on the slope, I collided suddenly with a large man in a blue parka.

Run-ons or "fused sentences" are largely a matter of punctuation oversight. Be sure to check your quoted material and separate the sentences in it just as you would if they were written outside the quotation marks.

Example of a run-on in dialogue:
    "I waited and waited, he never showed up, he just left me," she wailed.

Corrected run-on example:
"I waited and waited; he never showed up; he just left me," she wailed.

17. *Don't withhold information to create a false surprise ending.* In personal experience writing, you aim to have your reader relive an incident with you. To achieve this effect, you must give your reader all the information you were reacting to during the event. Your reader can't experience your reactions unless he or she knows clearly who you are, where you are, why you're there, what you're doing, and how you feel about it. When you withhold significant information, your reader is more apt to be irritated than intrigued.

18. *End on a tension-release point.* Composing a paper is similar to composing music; both use tension and release points. Music builds tension by moving away from basic tonal centers and resolves tension by returning to its home chords. A piece sounds unfinished until the tension is resolved. The same is true of writing. A tension point is created in writing whenever participants are unsure of the situation or face a real or imagined danger or problem. Musically speaking, they are "away from their tonal centers," off home base. Knowing the outcome, whether it be positive or negative, resolves the tension by returning your reader to the known.

An incident can have one main tension or focal point or build a series of tension points as it goes. Imagine that your paper re-creates a serious ski injury that required surgery. The accident and your injury create the paper's major tension, and successful surgery provides its final resolution. However, you may find that retelling an entire event up to this ending would create too long a paper for your purposes. The next thing to explore would be minor tension-release points within the incident, any one of which could be developed into a possible ending.

Minor tension-release points in the ski incident could include being found by the ski patrol after the accident, being carried down the hill successfully in the rescue toboggan, having your friends come to comfort you in the ski patrol hut, completing the ride into the hospital and meeting the emergency doctor, or finally waking up from the completed operation.

Any time one of these tension-release points is reached, the paper has a potential stopping place. You can manipulate the length of your paper by deciding how many release points you want to include, but you must end on some release point if your paper is to sound finished.

Style Exercises for Personal Experience Writing

Not "To Be"

The verb "to be" in its many forms ("is," "was," "are," "were," and the like) simply states that someone or something exists. It neither produces a visual image nor creates a sense of action. Other verbs ("lunge," "bounce," "sputter," "flash," "grapple," "grovel," "spit," among others) paint pictures, imitate sounds, and produce a variety of effects.

Scan any piece of your writing for use of the verb "to be." Circle its use. Now go back and see if any of these "to be" forms can be replaced with more accurate and colorful verb choices.

Description Exercise

Try writing a description without using any form of the verb "to be." Share descriptions with other class members to create a master list of evocative verb choices. Add to the list as you encounter effective verbs. While you will not need to eliminate "to be" entirely from your writing, this exercise can increase your awareness of better verb choices. A careful use of verb power can add immeasurably to your descriptive impact.

Creating Images with Verbs

Write a simple sentence containing at least two verbs such as: He *sat* on the couch and *laughed* at her father's jokes.

Take the two italicized verbs in the example sentence and make exploratory lists of all the verbs you can think of that describe the action of either sitting or laughing.

Example Lists

sat	*laughed*
slouched	guffawed
slumped	snickered
perched	twittered

sprawled	roared
lounged	giggled
fidgeted	smirked

Now experiment with replacing the original verbs and creating different images of men sitting on that couch. Obviously, one who "slouches" and "guffaws" produces a different effect than one who "perches" and "twitters." Write and experiment with other verb sentences and possible replacement combinations. Verbs can create entire personality sketches in miniature. They provide one of your most powerful descriptive tools. Use them to your advantage.

Sensory Awareness Exercise

Pick a place you are familiar with (such as your kitchen, a favorite beach, the school cafeteria, a classroom, a park, a ski area, or any other spot) and describe it in detail. Then list your five senses (seeing, hearing, smelling, tasting, feeling). Check your description for any senses that are not used. If all are present, think back over which senses you used most easily and which ones you had to add consciously. Note the senses you are most likely to overlook. Try to create scenes that would rely heavily on these particular senses to increase your awareness of them.

Point of View Exercise

Pick a location such as a park, classroom, garage, or yard. Imagine yourself as a different person in a different mood with different interests in the location than your own and write various descriptions of it. Let your assumed point of view control your focus, mood, word choice, tone, and selection of detail.

For example, describe the same park, as it would be seen by a botanist doing a field study, an old man returning to it full of memories, a small boy looking it over for its play potential, or young lovers seeking it for a place to be alone.

Cliché Replacement Exercise

Take the list of clichés below and reduce each to its basic message, discarding the old word pattern or rewording it using a fresh comparison.

Keep a list of clichés to increase your awareness of them.

felt like an eternity.
my head swirled.
coast was clear.
went on my merry way.
nice golden brown tan.
sent chills up and down
   my spine.
streak to the rescue.
it seemed like hours.
my heart was beating like
   a drum.
my mind raced back and forth.
had to see it to believe it.
it didn't faze me.
if I had to die sometime, it
   might as well be now.
ten seconds flat.
couldn't back out now.
slow but sure.
somewhere deep inside.
it frightened me out of my wits.
hair-raising experience.
safe to say.
I felt no pain.
I couldn't quite put my finger
   on it.
in close pursuit.
to no avail.
kept my fingers crossed.
I thought I would die of
   embarrassment.
you can't win them all.
cold cruel world.
get away from it all.
in one fell swoop.
point with pride at.
by leaps and bounds.
busy as a bee.

slim chances.
hold your chin up high.
beat around the bush.
in high hopes.
my heart skipped a beat.
hoping against hope.
a long way to go.
get the hell out of there.
jumped two feet out of
   my chair.
deafening sound.
much to my dismay.
supreme test.
everything I thought it would
   be and more.
head straight for home.
now or never.
not even daring to move a
   muscle.
I was in sad shape.
my life passed in front of my
   eyes.
I wanted to make the most of it.
caused my hair to stand on end.
played my cards right.
felt like sinking into the floor.
spine tingling.
suddenly out of nowhere.
a cloud seemed to lift.
feeling deep down inside.
scared the hell out of me.
mustered up enough courage.
the silence was deafening.
point of no return.
empty feeling in my stomach.
never to be seen again.
I shivered at the thought.
flying every which way.

dull throb.

cold sweat.

clear blue sky.

deep sigh of relief.

enough to make my mouth
water.

to break the ice (with someone).

bring him out of his shell.

here to stay.

made a mad dash.

suddenly without warning.

sent my head spinning.

tearing us to shreds.

whole blessed ordeal.

better late than never.

face turned red as a beet.

cold sweaty palms.

sadder but wiser.

last but not least.

Cliché Awareness Exercise

Increase your awareness of clichés by writing a short story or description using as many clichés as possible. If others participate in the same exercise, share your results and add to your cliché list any additional examples found in other papers.

Example beginning for cliché story:
I woke up with a head-splitting headache. There was no denying it. Today was the day. I told myself "to hold my chin up high," but my heart was beating like a drum, my sweaty palms were cold and clammy, shivers were running up and down my spine, and my mind was racing back and forth. Somewhere deep inside, I had this funny feeling, but I couldn't quite put my finger on it, even though it scared me out of my wits. All I could do was keep my fingers crossed and hope for the best.

Replacing "Tell" Words Exercise

Replace each of the "tell" words in the following sentences with precise, accurate "show" descriptions.

Example: It was a *magnificent* view.
Replacement no. 1: We looked down on a valley of patchwork farms and curving rivers, where rolling patterns glinted gold in the noonday sun.
Replacement no. 2: Two small lakes nestled like eggs within the grey boulder cliffs.

Further "tell" words to replace:

She gave a *fantastic* speech.

The cabin was located in an *idyllic* spot.

She had on a *lovely* dress.

His music was *unbelievable*.

What a *magnificent* voice!

My graduation was a *memorable* occasion.

He made an *incredible* leap.

Her dance performance was *awe-inspiring*.

Hang gliding is an *indescribable* experience.

She has a *vivid* memory.

Group Exercise for Personal Experience Writing

Filming Approach

Form groups of five or six people. Each person should bring the rough draft of a personal experience paper and additional paper for note taking. (If you are writing on your own, find a friend, member of the family, or any willing ear and ask them to help you with this exercise.)

As each volunteer reads a rough draft, each listener takes notes on the personal experience as if it were a working script for a film. The listener-producer envisions where to shoot the film and whom to cast for the various roles in the film. Listeners imagine themselves playing the lead role (the writer's part) and see if they can visualize what the main character is doing and feeling during each part of the incident.

The listeners then tell the writer which parts of the paper they easily visualize and which parts need further clarification or information. The writer should note their comments for use in further revisions and also ask for help on difficult or unclear sections.

Student Example Papers for Personal Experience Writing

LICORICE

Rocky, Johnny, and I slouched nervously outside the old store. Occasionally Rocky sauntered over to the thick green window and pressed his face close to the glass to search the wooden aisles inside. Johnny and I sat cross-legged on the curb, Johnny playing with his jacket zipper, while I stared at an ancient wad of gum between my knees.

God, I hated the idea of stealing cigarettes from the old man. There was nothing wrong with swiping from Safeway or something, but why did they have to steal from Mr. Walkey.

"The old lady's coming out!" flashed Rocky. "Marlboros, right?"

"Yeah, O.K.," I muttered as I watched the door open to an elderly lady in a shin-length coat and grandmother-style shoes. She clumped from the store and made her way down the walk, clutching her groceries.

Sometimes Mr. Walkey would let me buy six or seven five-cent things for a quarter instead of just five, and he always asked how my brothers were and why hadn't he seen my Mother lately. I'd tell him about the game I'd pitched Saturday, that my brothers were fine and Mother, too. And I hated to steal from Mr. Walkey.

We shuffled into the store, and the old man peered at us over the rim of his spectacles from his three-posted stool behind the counter. Then he rocked himself to his feet, straightened his vest, and smiled his greetings behind his bristly moustache.

"We were just around, so I thought I'd stop by and tell you we won Saturday," I explained rather unconvincingly.

The old man dropped his pencil, and Rocky slipped a long red carton beneath his coat and under his arm. When Mr. Walkey appeared from behind the counter, Rocky only stood with his arms at his side, and Johnny played with the zipper on his jacket.

"Well . . . I, I guess I got to go; lunch is pretty soon," I stuttered.

"Can't I help you with anything today?" he offered.

"No, that's all right. I don't get my allowance 'til Monday, anyway," I said.

The old man thought, then brightened and said, "Tell you what. Why don't you get something now, and you can pay me on allowance day. You're good for the credit, I think."

"Well, yeah, thanks, but, O.K.," I said as I hurriedly picked out two long giant strands of licorice—48 inches for 10¢—and showed it to Mr. Walkey. He smiled approvingly.

"Thanks a lot, but we really should go now," I murmured.

"O.K., but remember you've got responsibilities now, and I gave you credit, so don't forget me on allowance day," he grinned at me. "I don't even give your parents credit."

"Yeah, O.K. Thanks again," I said, almost to myself.

The three of us split the licorice and left the store. As we walked down the street, Rocky and Johnny joked about what a sucker "Old Soggy" was and how funny it was that Rocky had the weeds under his coat the whole time. The two of them pitched over their stomachs with laughter and hung onto each other's shoulders, but I only watched a stream of tiny pebbles flow between my feet.

So the three of us climbed our smoking tree and divided Mr. Walkey's cigarettes. I sat on a crooked branch and stared at the filter-specked ground beneath me. The smoke filled the tree and choked me, and when I coughed, I could taste licorice far down in my throat.

—Pat Hughbanks

Questions on "Licorice"

1. What is the dominant emotion the writer feels? Does he ever label it for you? How does he reproduce the feeling?

2. What descriptions show how the boys are feeling at different times in the story? Why does Johnny repeatedly play with his jacket zipper? Where does the writer focus his attention as he walks? What details reflect this? How does this action help portray his mood?

3. List colorful verbs used throughout the essay. Which come through most effectively and why?

4. What is Mr. Walkey like? How does the writer create the feeling of his personality for you?

5. Identify the miniscenes present in the story. What senses does the ending scene rely on? What does the taste of licorice come to mean at the end?

JACKIE

Jackie was hideously fat. Her pasty white skin was blotched with scaling sores which she picked in a nervous habit, causing them to be constantly in the process of bleeding and scabbing. Her fingernails were filthy with a thin coating of blood to which the scabs adhered. She wore her black hair short, chopped off level with her ears and unnoticed behind her flabby, pus-oozing, sore covered face. Her expression was always one of pleading, of "Please like me; I like you."

In the summer of my junior year, I started a food gathering group of neighborhood kids to get food for a local relief program, and Jackie heard about it. She asked to be allowed to help. I remembered how once when I was about twelve years old there was a spider in the bathroom sink. I wanted to wash my face but didn't want to get close to so ugly a creature, so I put in the plug and filled the sink with water. The spider swam in circles but failed to die. I did not wash my face that night. He was still alive, scraggly and caught in soap-scum the next morning. Jackie reminded me of the spider, looking with resignation and accusation from many faceted eyes at an inhuman world. I accepted her help.

When the other kids learned of my invitation, they nearly walked out on me until, in a moment of self-punishment, I volunteered to be her partner. Always, she stood too close. If I rang a door bell and then stepped back to leave room for an opening door, I would find myself standing on her. If she rang the door bell, she would edge over to stand closer to me, until, to gain room from the horror, I would find myself edged off the porch. When I pulled the food-laden wagon up a hill, her hand would suddenly be firmly clasped over mine, helping to pull, pressing her scabs and warts against my imprisoned fingers. She touched me when she talked, a hand on the arm, an elbow resting on my shoulder until she seemed to be spinning a cocooning web about me prior to sucking me dry. Eventually, I let the group die rather than continue as her victim.

Mom said to allow for Jackie because she was mentally retarded. I felt guilt at my dislike for so helpless a creature, but the prejudice continued.

It got so when I heard Jackie's high pitched whine in the school halls, I would try to hide, but always it ended in a lips-pulled-away-from-the-teeth smile, and "Hi."

In the lunch room, she would plunk her tray down opposite me, shovel in a spoonful of beans, and begin to blabber happily, spraying fragments of beans over my food. I took to bringing sack lunches and eating directly from the sack, holding it over my sandwich on each journey to my mouth. Still, there was the table becoming speckled as she ate and sprayed. I stopped eating lunch entirely and spent the hour in the aloneness of the library, reading or writing.

Then Jackie found my refuge. Her hand would clamp onto my upper arm to draw my attention from the book to her, and she would whisper a conversation, the quietness of her hissing seeming to send her spittle that much farther.

I hated her until my skin tightened and my throat contracted at just the mention of her name. But the more I rejected her, the more guilt I felt. And always there was Mom:

"You have to remember that Jackie hasn't any friends," Mom would remind me. "I was talking with her mother yesterday, and she said Jackie was always being tormented at school.

It was true. There was something so inhuman about Jackie, it drew a response from even the elite kids. The kids who were above most of us in high school would lower themselves to taunting her, until, unable to stand by and watch, I would tell them to "go to hell" and "grow up." These conflicts would often send Jackie to a restroom in tears, but i savored them, for by my angry protection of her I felt less guilty at my own more furtive evasions and rejections.

I think by my senior year at high school, Jackie realized I really didn't like her. The clique that every institution has, the one where all the outcasts and rejects take refuge in thinking themselves better and more noble than anyone else, had adopted her. I asked some of them if they really liked her, and the answer was "No, not really. No one does, or can. But we can't just LEAVE her, you know."

And of course they couldn't, for like an innocent spider, her web of guilt was strong and sticky.

—Louise Anderson

Questions on "Jackie"

1. What image helps tie the paper together? How does returning to the image help end the paper?

2. What specific details and miniscenes come across most powerfully in making Jackie real for you?

3. What conflict does the writer have about Jackie? Is the conflict ever resolved?

MY LAST AUTOPSY

I arrived at the Coroner's Office at about 7:30 A.M. A low rolling fog gave the building a cold and deserted appearance, and when I entered, it felt as chilled inside as it looked outside. The walls were cracked and faded in spots, showing their age. I ran into a little old man in work-clothes as I entered the hallway. With a grin on his face, he asked me if I wanted to know where the autopsy was. He seemed rather ghoulish being so eager to direct me to the autopsy room. I probably looked no different than any other zoology student or nurse anticipating nausea.

After entering the autopsy room, I first noticed a human shape. It was covered mysteriously with a sheet and stretched out on a large metal table. It seemed like a pretty strange thing to get up at six-thirty in the morning to look at. Around the edge of the table were trays resembling rain-gutters with a hose at one end; I prayed that this thing wouldn't be too bloody. Most of the other students looked fairly calm; I was hoping that my nervousness wouldn't show in front of these seemingly collected people.

A large man walked briskly into the room wearing a long white cotton jacket. He introduced himself casually and proceeded to explain a few things about the morning's autopsy victim. It was a woman who had died from an ulcer that had broken through her stomach. We were told to quit drinking, if we didn't want to end up like this lady.

He picked up a scalpel and made an incision from the armpits to just above the bellybutton forming a "V." A nauseating stench poured out of the cadaver's incision. I quickly covered my nose and mouth; my vision blurred from my watering eyes. After my vision cleared a bit, I could see other students with their hands clasped around their mouths and noses too. I felt little desire to watch him make the other incisions; it reminded me of the way I always got when a gory part was coming up in a horror movie. An eerie, crackling sound filled the room as he separated the flap of skin from the rib cage and left it lying over the woman's face.

My stomach contents surged upward toward my throat. I walked tightly out of the room holding my breath. I had no intention of returning to that room. I sat down on a bench in the hallway hoping to get myself back together again. The little old man shuffled around the corner with a smirk on his face. "Is this your first autopsy, Miss?" he queried.

"Yes, it is," I said, "and it's my last."

—Nancy Ausman Hansen

Questions on "My Last Autopsy"

1. An "envelope effect" in writing is achieved when an opening detail or description is returned to in closing a paper to help make it all "tie together" and sound finished. What or who provides the "envelope effect" in this paper? How does it create a natural end point for the paper?

2. How does the use of specific detail add to the tension and anticipation in the paper?

3. What thoughts and observations make it easy to identify with the writer?

POLIO

At four in the morning, I was still awake in my small black room. The bed was damp under my head and back. I was too warm. I looked at the vast black ceiling squares with insane concentration. For awhile I had screamed and thrashed, but now I was too weak and too hoarse to continue. The nurse had come in a couple of times to wipe the sweat from my forehead with a wet towel. Now I was silent, my hands strapped to my legs.

I felt the walls of my body change, the organs shift, the lungs catch fire like burning bellows of pure alcohol. The disease had eaten my body and reproduced itself in feverish duplication.

Its warmth streaked up my neck into my cheeks like hot wine. My lips burned. My eyelids caught fire like leaves. My brain filled with boiling mercury. My left eye clenched in upon itself, and like a snail, withdrew, twisted, and shifted until it was blind. It no longer belonged to me. My tongue was gone, cut out. Now my left cheek was numb. My left ear stopped hearing. This thing that was being born, this mineral thing, this disease replacing healthy animal cells was what was left.

I tried to scream and was able to scream once, loudly. Just as my brain flooded down, my right eye and right ear were extinguished. I was blind, and deaf: all fire, all terror, all pain. "Is this death?" I thought. My scream faded as the nurse came through the door and hurried to my side to give whatever reassurance her presence could provide.

—Gene Hovis

Questions on "Polio"

1. The writer, who had polio as a child, is trying to capture the intensity of a moment that for him seemed to have neither beginning nor end. In what ways did he succeed in doing this?

2. What descriptions effectively treat the disease like a living but subhuman thing?

3. To re-create how the disease felt, the writer uses artistic overstatement. For example, when he says, "My eyelids caught fire like leaves," it isn't that they are actually burning, but they feel like they are to him. Find other places where the writer uses "artistic overstatement" in his essay.

4. How does the title add to the paper's horror effect?

MY FIRST DAY IN A FOREIGN COUNTRY

When I arrived at the Sea-Tac airport from Japan, my heart was beating with fear and expectation.

I came through the routine work of customs' formalities. Everything was new to me. For example, there were people who weren't Japanese. I felt that even the walls of the buildings, because they were really wide and high, clean and neat compared to the walls of the buildings in my small country of Japan, were interesting to me. Everything seemed to be cool. Suddenly the cool air blew through my whole body. I could smell people's lives every place in Japan, but I couldn't smell them there in the airport, because everything was too neat, too cool.

I was sitting down on the chair in the hall, and I was waiting for

Mrs. King, who was supposed to be my sponsor. I was looking for a lady who looked like Mrs. King, but what I knew about her appearance was only that, according to her letter, she was short, had short red hair, and was about fifty years old. I didn't have her picture with me, but she had a picture of me. She was supposed to find me first, so I had to wait until she saw me.

There were not many people here compared to the airport in Japan. Some people were walking around looking for someone or waiting for someone, and some people were waiting for their baggage. I had picked up my baggage already. It was really heavy for one tired girl. I brought two suitcases from Japan: one was a medium-sized suitcase in which I packed many clothes, as many as I could, that I needed for this coming year; the other one was a rather small-sized suitcase with my camera, some presents for Mrs. King, and some other important things like my passport. I had to pay attention especially to this small suitcase, but I was so tired that I just put it carelessly in front of me.

I was just waiting for whoever would pick me up from the airport and take me to stay in her home. What kind of person would she be? Would I be able to get along well with her? I was thinking what I should say when she came, "How do you do? I'm Nobuko from Sapporo. It's nice to meet you." I wondered whether I would say only these words.

One lady was coming toward me, looking directly at me, but she was rather old. Was Mrs. King supposed to be that old? No, she was not. The woman turned out to be a relative of a young boy behind me. The two started talking about how their family had been.

Outside, it was getting dark. People were going their ways little by little. I was watching the clock on the wall over and over, looking at every lady that passed to see if she was Mrs. King. I started to think, "She might not come, or she might have forgotten that I was coming. What should I do then?"

I was really tired. My head was dropping down little by little. Soon I was looking down at my feet and at the small bits of litter around them. The litter stood out because everything else was so clean. I was just watching, thinking about taking the litter to the wastebasket, but not doing it.

Suddenly I heard a voice. "Are you . . . ?" I turned my head toward this lady. For awhile I couldn't say anything. "Are you Nobuko?" This time I could hear that she was saying my name; although she didn't pronounce it correctly, it was quite close. It was my name.

"Yes, I am," I said. I stood up from the chair and said, "I'm Nobuko from Sapporo. How do you do? Nice to meet you."

Then she started speaking fast. Her lips were moving; her mouth was opening, and her hands were moving. I was just watching her, hearing some noise. Suddenly she stopped talking and said to me, "Do you understand? Did I talk too fast to you?"

I knew what to say to this kind of question. "No, I don't understand. Could you speak more slowly?"

She answered rapidly. "O.K! I'll try." She started speaking slowly this time, but as soon as she got excited, she went fast again.

Even though I didn't understand her talking, I had to nod somehow because she seemed to want me to give her my nodding. I was nodding several times without knowing what she was saying.

Suddenly she stopped speaking again, because I had nodded. "Did you. . . ?" This time she was saying it with a strange face. She kept her eyes directly on me.

She asked again, "Did you have much trouble on the way here?"
I got it. "Oh! No, I didn't have any trouble."

"You said, 'yes.'"

"I'm sorry, I didn't understand it."

"Oh! Well, I have to speak more slowly to you, don't I?"

"Yes, please," I answered with a very small voice.

Her voice became really loud. She was concerned about my ability to hear. Some people were watching us with strange faces, and they were smiling at me. I smiled back at them.

She took one of my suitcases and said something to me, and started to walk to the exit. I just followed her hoping, "Maybe, she is going to take me to her house now."

We went out to the road. The air was blowing, and it was fresh. Outside, it was dark already. Suddenly I stopped and asked her, "Are you really Mrs. King?" She laughed and laughed and laughed. She repeated, "Yes. Yes."

We got to her house after driving for thirty minutes. Mrs. King's daughter was waiting for us and preparing dinner. I didn't feel I was hungry at that time, but I ate as much as I could because I felt sorry for them since they had gone to all the trouble of fixing a large meal to welcome me.

After dinner Mrs. King asked me, "Do you want to go to bed soon?" Of course, I did. Immediately I answered, "Yes." I had been waiting for these words from Mrs. King. As soon as I took a hot shower, I went to bed. For awhile I found myself thinking again with natural fright and anticipation of how my life would be from now on. Then I fell into a welcome deep, deep sleep.

—Nobuko Sasaki

Questions on "My First Day in a Foreign Country"

1. How do Nobuko's first impressions of America contrast with her memories of Japan? What senses does she use to show the differences?

2. What details show her fatigue?

3. How is dialogue used to show the problems with communication on both sides? What description best captures Mrs. King's way of talking, and the effect it has on Nobuko? Why does Nobuko keep nodding? Why does Mrs. King speak loudly? Why are the people passing by smiling at the scene?

4. How is the same communication problem also reflected in the Kings' preparation of a large welcoming dinner?

FIRST RUN

I walked towards the dock and gazed at the *Valu-Mart*, an unlimited hydroplane with a bright orange base, black trim, and yellow lettering. On the deck were the numbers "U-Twenty-one" in big block letters and numerals. The boat looked quite a bit more dangerous to me than it had before, since this time I knew I'd soon be in it. This would be my first ride in an unlimited.

When I did reach the boat, I met the driver, Bill Wurster. He was somewhat taller than most drivers, about six feet one. His brown hair was combed back, and he had a serious look on his face. As I was introduced by my uncle, we shook hands and said "Hello." He shook with such a vise grip that my knuckles cracked loudly. I felt a sudden rush of blood to my face, but I knew his grip had to be strong or on every bounce he would fly out of the boat. He asked me if I had ever been in an unlimited before. I tried to answer, but my words came out all jumbled.

Before we stepped into the boat, Bill said, "There isn't much to worry about." He paused, and then added, "Cans and floating pieces of wood can put a hole in the boat." His ending remark was, "And a submerged log can shatter it into a thousand pieces."

Bill told me to jump in but to watch my step since the deck was slippery. I lowered myself carefully into the cockpit while Bill threw the tow rope back to the dock. Everything was ready. Bill got in the boat, and with two of us in there, it became a tight fit. I had just enough room to get my arms out and grab on to the side of the cockpit. My head stuck up over Bill's, and it must have looked kind of funny, but I did have plenty of room for my legs.

Inside the cockpit there was a steering wheel with gauges for fuel, oil pressure, water temperature, r.p.m.'s, and time surrounding it on a metal frame. On the right hand side of the gauges were the switches. Underneath the gauges and switches was the foot pedal. Hydroplanes have no brakes. Fortunately, Bill would be in complete control of everything. I was just there for the ride.

Suddenly, there was a pop, like that of ten firecrackers going off all at once. I nearly jumped out of my stomach, as all the needles on the gauges jerked upward. He had just turned over the engine, but it had failed to start. Once again Bill flipped the switches. This time the engine started. As we took off onto the Lake Washington course, I looked back at the crew that was standing on the dock of the Stan Sayres pit area. They raised one arm with a clenched fist, acting as if we were out to set some record. But this was only a test run, and fortunately, no record setting was planned.

At the start, we were going forty m.p.h. We didn't work up to that speed; we started there. As the speedometer rose, so did the roar of the engine. My teeth shook; my back ached; and my liver cried. Behind us, we were shooting up a roostertail of water fifty feet high and about 100 yards long. It was impossible to look at the water, and even the distant shoreline looked like a shimmering, bouncing blur.

Suddenly we were doing 150 m.p.h., and the lake seemed smaller than a goblet. As we flew down the lake, my ears were ringing, and my butt was bouncing like a kernel in a popcorn popper, and this was only the straightaway. I knew there had to be a corner, and I dreaded the moment when it would come. Quickly the entrance buoy whooshed by, and I could feel the harried look on my face. The boat spun sideways around the buoys at about ninety m.p.h.

I was sure we were going to hit the log boom, but Bill turned the wheel sharply, and we came into a straight position once again. Now I felt a little at ease knowing the worst must be over, until we suddenly hit a wake. The boat bounced violently, came down on its nose, and started bouncing from sponson to sponson. I came out of the seat about a foot, hit the dash with my thighs quite hard, and was slammed back with the same force. My back bent like a bow with the arrow drawn back. We both looked at each other as he backed off the gas a little. I was gasping for air after that. As we continued down the straightaway, I glanced at the needles which were somewhat erratic because of all the bouncing. I tried to get my mind sidetracked from the current situation, but the ringing in my ears and the smell of methanol kept me aware of what was going on. I felt like I was in a cocktail shaker, and I prayed it would end soon.

Then as we approached the pit area, Bill cut the engine, and we glided toward the dock. They threw the tow rope to us and pulled us in. My body was bruised, and my psyche felt scrambled. When I stepped out of the boat, I did an uncontrollable cha-cha-cha. Bill said, "Everyone shakes on the first trip, but after a couple of times out, you become used to it." I shook his hand, said "Thanks," and took off running. I didn't stop until I was out of sight of anything called or resembling a boat.

Questions on "First Run"

1. How does the writer give you a feeling for the boat driver: his looks, actions, and slightly wry sense of humor? How do the driver's remarks add to the writer's nervousness? How do you know the writer is both nervous and embarrassed?

2. Find effective use of verbs in this paper.

JOGGING

A flock (group? bunch? herd?) of gnats greeted me as I started my first night of jogging, decked out in the full regalia—my Buffalo Braves No. 1 sweatshirt, old jeans, and red, white, and blue sneakers with fish blood on the toes. "I must learn to jog with my mouth closed," I resolved as I swallowed three gnats. My route started level; I had wings. Who can tell me I'm out of shape?

I met a dog who wanted to race—he pulled up beside me and barked out his challenge, "Wanna drag?" I might have beaten him had I not stepped in a souvenir left on the sidewalk by one of his colleagues. I had to make a pit stop and scrape off my shoe. When I looked up, he was nowhere in sight.

I lumbered onward alone. "Watch out for muggers and rapists," my helpful neighbor had warned as I left the house. This warning came back in full force as I approached a corner on which stood six young men smoking cigarettes and looking generally mean. "This is it. I'm going to get raped and mutilated, and they won't find my body for fourteen years." As I held my breath and zoomed by, I heard one of them say to the other, "Is that a boy or a girl?" "Damned if I know," was the reply. I was insulted—I felt like going back and stripping off all my clothes and showing them.

Deciding against this, I carried on until I was stopped by a traffic light. Waiting with me was an old lady dressed in an ankle length grey skirt, an old black cloth raincoat, "sensible shoes" with white anklets, and a grey pillbox hat. "Young lady (at least she could tell what I was), I couldn't help noticing that your form is all wrong. This is the proper way." With that, she set down her bag of groceries and proceeded to jog down the street. I leaned against a telephone pole and watched. She had great form. Arms bent at the elbows, pumping like pistons, each step—heel, ball, heel, ball—raising her knees in crankshaft fashion—a real running machine. I was impressed. She returned, reclaimed her bag, said, "Like that," and ambled off.

Using my new-found form, I lumbered on until I got to a freeway overpass. Being a future engineer, I have an interest in aerodynamics. I stopped on the overpass for a rest. Most cars were traveling at sixty miles per hour; I was probably twenty feet up; my spit travels maybe ten miles per hour; and $E = MC^2$. I looked down the freeway for a likely target. A red pick-up was approaching. I waited, ready to strike. My tension mounted as he came closer. I thought, "Boy, won't he be surprised." Just at the crucial moment, my mouth went dry. The red truck passed safely, totally ignorant of what had almost transpired. Then I realized just what I had almost done—twenty-six-year-old girls do not stand on freeway overpasses spitting at cars. "Maintain a little decorum," I decided.

Remembering the proper form I had just been taught, I thundered on. I arrived at an intersection where one road went uphill and one down. I had to halt to make a decision. "If I go uphill, I'll get tired faster, but on the way back, it'll be downhill. Downhill now would be pleasant, but on the other hand, if I went downhill now, maybe someone I know will come by and give me a ride." Banking on this, I went downhill toward the marina where I looked at boats, had a bottle of pop, threw rocks in the water, and waited for my ride. No one came.

Half an hour later, I was jogging up the hill. My stomach gurgled from the pop with every footfall; I began to sweat; my deodorant gave out. I ached all over; my legs weighed one hundred pounds each.

Panting and puffing, I staggered into my house just in time to answer the phone. "Hi, it's such a nice night, I thought you'd like to go jogging." I explained, between breaths, that I had just run five miles. The following day with legs so sore I could barely work the clutch of my car, I retraced my route to see how far it was. According to my odometer, I had run nine-tenths of one lousy mile.

—Nancy Nichols

Questions on "Jogging"

1. Find examples in the essay where an element of surprise adds to the humor.

2. What verbs in the paper create humor through overstatement?

3. Underline the use of specifics in one of the paper's descriptions. How do they create their effect?

4. Which details are returned to in telling the incident? What does this repetition achieve?

THE PROMISE

I pulled the comb through Mom's short brown grey streaked hair, unwillingly. I disliked combing her hair as much as I hated to have someone else mess with mine. I did it anyway. I had made myself a promise, hadn't I?

I remembered the day I made that promise. It was the day that Dad told my brother and I that Mom had cancer, again. In 1967 or '68, Mom had had a radical mastectomy. Now, seven years later, she was back in the hospital for tests to see if the irritation of her scar was cancerous or not. The day after the biopsy, Dad called Jon and me into the living room.

I could tell by the tone of his voice when he called us that he was going to report something bad, and that it was about Mom. He told us to sit down. The quietness of the room overwhelmed me. Dad spoke in an unusually subdued voice, "Your mom has to stay in the hospital for a while. They . . . they found some more cancer. It is on the same side as before, and they can't get it all." He had begun to cry before he finished his last sentence.

My mind and body parted; the body stayed in the chair, and my mind was somewhere above looking down on this strange scene. I had never seen my Dad cry before. Jon remained slumped in his chair and didn't say anything; he didn't even look upset. I wanted to yell at him; didn't he realize that Mom might die, my Mom, HIS Mom? Instead of yelling, my body walked into the kitchen, put its back against the refrigerator, and slid to the floor. Mind and body once again united.

Dad had just said that my Mom was going to die. She couldn't do that; I needed her; if she was gone, I would have to take care of everybody, and at sixteen, I wasn't ready for that. I realized how much we all needed her, how many things she did that went unnoticed and unappreciated.

My tailbone was getting numb; it always did that when I sat on the floor. Something inside of me wanted to burst out; the lump in my throat felt like it was going to strangle me. Tears gushed out of my eyes, ran down my cheeks, and dripped from my chin onto my shirt. I picked up the cat as she stepped over my outspread legs. I held her warm body to me and squeezed her so tight that she squeaked. I buried my face in her short cream-colored fur and wept. Her fur smelled like Fritos and tickled my nose every time I gasped for air.

My Mom liked to have me do things like play with her hair, and I liked to do it 'til a few years ago, when I outgrew it. She didn't ask much of me, so I made myself promise to do what she asked, without a complaint or argument, for the rest of her life, and that included combing her hair.

My Dad was sobbing in the other room. I realized just how much he loved Mom. If she died, I would lose my Mom, but he would lose his lifetime companion. I choked down my tears and shuffled into the living room. Jon hadn't moved. Dad seemed small and alone on the couch. I wrapped my arms around him, and he held onto me like he was never going to let me go.

I put more love and tenderness into combing Mom's hair. She didn't look sick; she even looked a bit more perky than usual. It was easy to forget that anything was wrong and hard to remember my promise.

Questions on "The Promise"

1. What sensory detail adds to the paper's effectiveness?
2. What device does the writer use to provide a beginning and ending for her paper?

PENALTY KICK

A shrill whistle from the referee sent me stumbling off the soccer field in disbelief. We had actually tied Newport, the defending state champions. My water-soaked sweats clung to my numbed legs as I slogged to the bench with my jubilant teammates. I grabbed a pair of sweats and yelled at my coach that I was going to change. No one had counted on this late February snow that now covered the field, making it into a huge ice rink.

As I fumbled into my dry sweats, I thought back to the beginning of the season, and how we joked about winning the state championship. In reality, Sammamish was a team that few expected to be in the running. Even at the end of the season with a record of three wins, four losses and five ties, people were wondering why we were still vying for the state title. What we did have was a team that was built on hustle, desire, and teamwork. With all of this behind us plus the luck of the draw, we arrived at this moment.

The crowd's clamoring followed us back out onto the field for the deciding two ten-minute sudden death overtime periods. I jogged out and took my position between the two metal posts, which at the moment seemed farther than the regulation twenty-four feet. As the game began to flow back and forth, I lost all sense of time, and before I realized it, the whistle sounded signaling the end of the twenty minutes. Neither team had scored.

After giving everything I had for 110 minutes, I wondered if I would last. Penalty kicks were now the last test. The team that scored the most after five kicks would walk away as the state champs. Once in the goal box, I turned my back on my opponents and prayed for God's mercy. Slowly I turned around and brushed the snow away very deliberately, making sure I had gotten it all.

With my heels on the line, I crouched between the posts like a cobra ready to strike out at its prey. Every muscle in my body was ready to spring. I concentrated, focusing my eyes on the ball resting twelve yards away. It sat teasingly, ready to be sent hurtling towards me. My first opponent approached the ball slowly, then "bang" with a quick sure motion of his foot he sent the ball screaming to my left. Without a second thought, I threw my body to my left, stretching, straining, clawing for every inch of ground. My fingers tense, waiting for the impact of the ball, I landed, rolled, and with relief watched it go wide of the post.

As we traded shots and goal keepers, the score remained even. After five shots on me, I was both mentally and physically exhausted. The score was still tied 3 to 3—sending us into sudden death overtime. In the sixth round of shots, both teams made their shots making it 4 to 4. The seventh round ended with us still tied at 5 to 5. In the next round, both teams missed at 6 to 6. I was so mentally and physically fatigued that I was responding only by instinct. I faced the next kicker and recognized him as the Newport goalie. I gambled that he would try to blast it through me. I stood my ground and watched the ball as it went flying into the top left hand corner. I looked up the field to see who was our next penalty kicker. I turned slowly towards the ref and saw him motioning towards ME. Stunned, I walked out to the ball and faced the goal box I'd just left. I was the 22nd and last kicker. With this kick would go my team's bid for the state championship. I could feel the pressure on me as I approached the ball still unsure of where I was going to kick it. My stomach churned. I ran. Contact! Wide! The crowd groaned. I stood a moment with my head down, then slowly walked back to my teammates as the snow swirled around my head.

—Mark Mauren

Questions on "Penalty Kick"

1. How does the writer use the weather in his paper?
2. How do penalty kicks provide a focal point for the paper?
3. Are scores used too often in the paper's last paragraph, or do they help the writer achieve his effect?
4. What detail helps the ending work?

A BLESSED EVENT

Pop became the official wine expert in the Italian section of New Haven. He was known as the "wine midwife." He could predict with great accuracy when the homemade "blood thinner" was ready to be transferred from the huge vats into gallon jugs. It was a critical time. It meant either a year of happy drinking or a year of vinegar selling. Pop took numerous samples to determine the exact moment of "birth." The house-to-house tour was a yearly pilgrimage and although some neighbors, at times, doubted his sagacity, they didn't dare take a chance on inviting misfortune. (Pop's accuracy was nothing more than figuring the exact number of days of fermentation according to the completion of lunar months, somewhat similar to an obstetrician's forecast.)

Now the season was over, and when Momma announced that she wanted to go to the Franciscan Monastery in Washington to make her own special pilgrimage, Pop inwardly enjoyed a weakening of the senses. Momma worked every year campaigning for special collections and selling the seminarians' relics. Now, after all the years of devotion, she felt the time was ripe for a personal appearance. Besides, she had made thirteen novenas, and she wanted some special plenary indulgence bestowed upon her. She was adamant. He was tickled. It was settled. Off we went.

Immediately upon entering the grounds, Momma fell victim to the aura surrounding the monastery. She retreated from reality and succumbed to its spiritual force. Pop took his cue, and with me in tow, he found his way to the cool corridors of the monastery. The monks who greeted Pop were dressed in brown cassocks which blended with the walls. At times, it seemed as though they disappeared into them. Each waist was cinctured with a thick leather belt and a strand of beads. The strong and familiar smell of fermenting wine permeated the air. A solid wooden table with matching chairs occupied the center of the wine cellar. Small but well-used tasting glasses littered the table.

After Pop presented them with a bottle of his best red wine, he and the monks fell into a long discourse about grapes, color, quality, and bouquet. These subjects required much sampling. Each category had to be reinforced with a sampling, and each difference of opinion had to be doubly reinforced. Only after the wine had passed this stiff criticism, and only after the monks had passed this criticism stiff, did Pop emerge from the cellars, singing benediction in Latin, and wearing a rosary strand around his neck. His voice was deep and mellow; his grey-white moustache was tinged with red. He blessed everything in sight with his hand. Coming up behind him was a defrocked brother swinging Pop's necktie like an incense burner.

Momma gasped at the sight of this procession. She clasped her

arthritic hands together, raised her pleading eyes to heaven, and be-
seeched God to forgive this "insect" who called himself a man. She
begged God not to withdraw His blessings and to grant her the special
favor she had asked, especially now when the Lord could "See what I
mean!"

Through all the years, though, Momma never believed that God
ever listened to her. She said He was always too busy keeping track of
and protecting Pop.

—Maria Budak

Questions on "A Blessed Event"

1. The writer has a good ear for language and delights in using puns and
extended comparisons. Find some effective example of these techniques in the
paper. How many ways can the title be taken?
2. Which scene creates the high point of the story?
3. How does the reversal of roles between Pop and the monk as they
leave the wine cellars add to the humor of the situation?
4. What descriptions create the blend of warmth and humor in the story?

Professional Examples of Personal Experience Writing

While the following two excerpts are actually episodes from Sylvia
Plath's autobiographical novel, *The Bell Jar*, they can also be read as
separate examples of personal experience papers.

Read and enjoy these excerpts along with the news article and
longer essay that follow as professional examples that illustrate and
refine many of the writing techniques presented in this chapter.

"WATCHING THE BIRTH OF A BABY SCENE" FROM *THE BELL JAR*

SYLVIA PLATH[6]

Sylvia Plath (1932–1963) first published her autobiographical
novel *The Bell Jar* in London using the pseudonym Victoria

---

[6]Plath, pp. 69–74.

Lucas, since she feared hurting the feelings of people close to her who were portrayed in the book. Sick and suffering from depression following a broken marriage, she took her own life on February 11, 1963, during one of London's coldest winters.

I had kept begging Buddy to show me some really interesting hospital sights, so one Friday I cut all my classes and came down for a long weekend and he gave me the works.

I started out by dressing in a white coat and sitting in a room with four cadavers, while Buddy and his friends cut them up. These cadavers were so unhuman-looking they didn't bother me a bit. They had stiff, leathery, purple-black skin and they smelt like old pickle jars.

After that, Buddy took me out into the hall where they had some big glass bottles full of babies that had died before they were born. The baby in the first bottle had a large white head bent over a tiny curled-up body the size of a frog. The baby in the next bottle was bigger and the baby next to that one was bigger still and the baby in the last bottle was the size of a normal baby and he seemed to be looking at me and smiling a little piggy smile.

I was quite proud of the calm way I stared at all these gruesome things. The only time I jumped was when I leaned my elbow on Buddy's cadaver's stomach to watch him dissect a lung. After a minute or two I felt this burning sensation in my elbow and it occurred to me the cadaver might just be half alive since it was still warm, so I leapt off my stool with a small exclamation. Then Buddy explained the burning was only from the pickling fluid, and I sat back in my old position.

In the hour before lunch Buddy took me to a lecture on sickle-cell anemia and some other depressing diseases, where they wheeled sick people out onto the platform and asked them questions and then wheeled them off and showed colored slides.

One slide I remember showed a beautiful laughing girl with a black mole on her cheek. "Twenty days after that mole appeared the girl was dead," the doctor said, and everybody went very quiet for a minute and then the bell rang, so I never really found out what the mole was or why the girl died.

In the afternoon we went to see a baby born.

First we found a linen closet in the hospital corridor where Buddy took out a white mask for me to wear and some gauze.

A tall fat medical student, big as Sydney Greenstreet, lounged nearby, watching Buddy wind the gauze round and round my head until my hair was completely covered and only my eyes peered out over the white mask.

The medical student gave an unpleasant little snicker. "At least your mother loves you," he said.

I was so busy thinking how very fat he was and how unfortunate it must be for a man and especially a young man to be fat, because what woman could stand leaning over that big stomach to kiss him, that I didn't immediately realize what this student had said to me was an insult. By the time I figured he must consider himself quite a fine fellow and had thought up a cutting remark about how only a mother loves a fat man, he was gone.

Buddy was examining a queer wooden plaque on the wall with a row of holes in it, starting from a hole about the size of a silver dollar and ending with one the size of a dinner plate.

"Fine, fine," he said to me. "There's somebody about to have a baby this minute."

At the door of the delivery room stood a thin, stoop-shouldered medical student Buddy knew.

"Hello, Will," Buddy said. "Who's on the job?"

"I am," Will said gloomily, and I noticed little drops of sweat beading his high pale forehead. "I am, and it's my first."

Buddy told me Will was a third-year man and had to deliver eight babies before he could graduate.

Then he noticed a bustle at the far end of the hall and some men in lime-green coats and skull caps and a few nurses came moving toward us in a ragged procession wheeling a trolley with a big white lump on it.

"You oughtn't to see this," Will muttered in my ear. "You'll never want to have a baby if you do. They oughtn't to let women watch. It'll be the end of the human race."

Buddy and I laughed, and then Buddy shook Will's hand and we all went into the room.

I was so struck by the sight of the table where they were lifting the woman I didn't say a word. It looked like some awful torture table, with these metal stirrups sticking up in mid-air at one end and all sorts of instruments and wires and tubes I couldn't make out properly at the other.

Buddy and I stood together by the window, a few feet away from the woman, where we had a perfect view.

The woman's stomach stuck up so high I couldn't see her face or the upper part of her body at all. She seemed to have nothing but an enormous spider-fat stomach and two little ugly spindly legs propped in the high stirrups, and all the time the baby was being born she never stopped making this unhuman whooing noise.

Later Buddy told me the woman was on a drug that would make her forget she'd had any pain and that when she swore and groaned she really didn't know what she was doing because she was in a kind of twilight sleep.

I thought it sounded just like the sort of drug a man would invent.

Here was a woman in terrible pain, obviously feeling every bit of it or she wouldn't groan like that, and she would go straight home and start another baby, because the drug would make her forget how bad the pain had been, when all the time, in some secret part of her, that long, blind, doorless and windowless corridor of pain was waiting to open up and shut her in again.

The head doctor, who was supervising Will, kept saying to the woman, "Push down, Mrs. Tomolillo, push down, that's a good girl, push down," and finally through the split, shaven place between her legs, lurid with disinfectant, I saw a dark fuzzy thing appear.

"The baby's head," Buddy whispered under cover of the woman's groans.

But the baby's head stuck for some reason, and the doctor told Will he'd have to make a cut. I heard the scissors close on the woman's skin like cloth and the blood began to run down—a fierce, bright red. Then all at once the baby seemed to pop out into Will's hands, the color of a blue plum and floured with white stuff and streaked with blood, and Will kept saying, "I'm going to drop it, I'm going to drop it, I'm going to drop it," in a terrified voice.

"No, you're not," the doctor said, and took the baby out of Will's hands and started massaging it, and the blue color went away and the baby started to cry in a lorn, croaky voice and I could see it was a boy.

The first thing that baby did was pee in the doctor's face. I told Buddy later I didn't see how that was possible, but he said it was quite possible, though unusual, to see something like that happen.

As soon as the baby was born the people in the room divided up into two groups, the nurses tying a metal dog tag on the baby's wrist and swabbing its eyes with cotton on the end of a stick and wrapping it up and putting it in a canvas-sided cot, while the doctor and Will started sewing up the woman's cut with a needle and a long thread.

I think somebody said, "It's a boy, Mrs. Tomolillo," but the woman didn't answer or raise her head.

"Well, how was it?" Buddy asked with a satisfied expression as we walked across the green quadrangle to his room.

"Wonderful," I said. "I could see something like that every day."

I didn't feel up to asking him if there were any other ways to have babies.

Questions on "Watching the Birth of a Baby Scene" from Sylvia Plath's The Bell Jar

1. What do all the scenes in the excerpt have in common?
2. What is the tone of Sylvia's comments? How do they compare with her actual feelings? How do you account for her ending line?
3. What images remain in Sylvia's mind as she retells the incident?

"WORKING AS A HOSPITAL VOLUNTEER EPISODE" FROM *THE BELL JAR*[7]

SYLVIA PLATH

The flowers nodded like bright, knowledgeable children as I trundled them down the hall.

I felt silly in my sage-green volunteer's uniform, and superfluous, unlike the white-uniformed doctors and nurses, or even the brown-uniformed scrubwomen with their mops and their buckets of grimy water, who passed me without a word.

If I had been getting paid, no matter how little, I could at least count this a proper job, but all I got for a morning of pushing round magazines and candy and flowers was a free lunch.

My mother said the cure for thinking too much about yourself was helping somebody who was worse off than you, so Teresa had arranged for me to sign on as a volunteer at our local hospital. It was difficult to be a volunteer at this hospital, because that's what all the Junior League women wanted to do, but luckily for me, a lot of them were away on vacation.

I had hoped they would send me to a ward with some really gruesome cases, who would see through my numb, dumb face to how I meant well, and be grateful. But the head of the volunteers, a society lady at our church, took one look at me and said, "You're on maternity."

So I rode the elevator up three flights to the maternity ward and reported to the head nurse. She gave me the trolley of flowers. I was supposed to put the right vases at the right beds in the right rooms.

But before I came to the door of the first room I noticed that a lot of the flowers were droopy and brown at the edges. I thought it would be discouraging for a woman who'd just had a baby to see somebody plonk down a big bouquet of dead flowers in front of her, so I steered the trolley to a washbasin in an alcove in the hall and began to pick out all the flowers that were dead.

Then I picked out all those that were dying.

There was no wastebasket in sight, so I crumpled the flowers up and laid them in the deep white basin. The basin felt cold as a tomb. I smiled. This must be how they laid the bodies away in the hospital morgue. My gesture, in its small way, echoed the larger gesture of the doctors and nurses.

I swung the door of the first room open and walked in, dragging my trolley. A couple of nurses jumped up, and I had a confused impression of shelves and medicine cabinets.

---

[7]Plath, pp. 182–4.

"What do you want?" one of the nurses demanded sternly. I couldn't tell one from the other, they all looked just alike.

"I'm taking the flowers round."

The nurse who had spoken put a hand on my shoulder and led me out of the room, maneuvering the trolley with her free, expert hand. She flung open the swinging doors of the room next to that one and bowed me in. Then she disappeared.

. I could hear giggles in the distance till a door shut and cut them off.

There were six beds in the room, and each bed had a woman in it. The women were all sitting up and knitting or riffling through magazines or putting their hair in pin curls and chattering like parrots in a parrot house.

I had thought they would be sleeping, or lying quiet and pale, so I could tiptoe round without any trouble and match the bed numbers to the numbers inked on adhesive tape on the vases, but before I had a chance to get my bearings, a bright, jazzy blonde with a sharp, triangular face beckoned to me.

I approached her, leaving the trolley in the middle of the floor, but then she made an impatient gesture, and I saw she wanted me to bring the trolley too.

I wheeled the trolley over to her bedside with a helpful smile.

"Hey, where's my larkspur?" A large, flabby lady from across the ward raked me with an eagle eye.

The sharp-faced blonde bent over the trolley. "Here are my yellow roses," she said, "but they're all mixed up with some lousy iris."

Other voices joined the voices of the first two women. They sounded cross and loud and full of complaint.

I was opening my mouth to explain that I had thrown a bunch of dead larkspur in the sink, and that some of the vases I had weeded out looked skimpy, there were so few flowers left, so I had joined a few of the bouquets together to fill them out, when the swinging door flew open and a nurse stalked in to see what the commotion was.

"Listen, nurse, I had this big bunch of larkspur Larry brought last night."

"She's loused up my yellow roses."

Unbuttoning the green uniform as I ran, I stuffed it, in passing, into the washbasin with the rubbish of dead flowers. Then I took the deserted side steps down to the street two at a time, without meeting another soul.

Questions on "Working as a Hospital Volunteer Episode" from Sylvia Plath's The Bell Jar

1. What effect does the dialogue in this excerpt help achieve?

2. How do Sylvia's comparisons help make a comment on the scenes they describe?

3. Explain the appropriateness of Sylvia's actions in ending the episode.

"GET OUT OF THE BUILDING . . . IT'S ON FIRE![8]"

STEVE JOHNSTON
P-I Staff

A couple of weeks ago I covered a story about a couple who died in a house fire. The man's body was found in a closet in the bedroom. I asked a fireman why someone would go into a closet when their house was on fire.

"People get confused in the smoke," he said.

Saturday night I found out just what he meant.

The first sound was breaking glass, a sort of dull, far-away sound like someone busting bottles in the alley. It was the windows in apartment 304—my next door neighbor—blowing out.

Then footsteps in the hallway. Someone beating on my door, screaming, "Get out of the building . . . the building's on fire!"

I opened the door. There was a thick oily smell in the hallway and a little smoke curling out from under the door of apartment 304. The guy who lives there wasn't home.

I went back into my apartment, turned off the radio and put on my shoes. Just in case I had to go outside I put on a sweater. Things didn't look too serious. A little smoke and that oily smell.

A girl came running by my open door and asked if I would call the fire department. I started to dial 911 when I heard something like a roaring wind in the hallway and more glass breaking.

The lights started to go out in the hall, but not before I saw a cloud of ink-black smoke go rolling by my door. It turned into my apartment and I watched it roll along my ceiling as the phone rang.

Now things were beginning to look serious.

It seemed the phone rang an hour before someone answered 911. I told them I wanted to report a fire. A man said I reached the police line and would I hold on a minute?

My living room was starting to fill with smoke.

The smoke looked like the cloud an octopus leaves behind. It rolled past the bathroom and started to drop as the phone rang for the fire department.

---

[8]Steve Johnston, "Get Out of the Building . . . It's on Fire!" *Seattle Post-Intelligencer* (24 January 1974).

Professional Examples of Personal Experience Writing

"Fire department."

"I would like to report a fire at 221 East Belmont." I was still calm enough to remember where I lived.

"Is that 221 Belmont East?" he asked.

I couldn't remember if it was Belmont East or East Belmont. At the time it didn't seem very important. The lights in my apartment were starting to dim and hiss and crackle. The room was filled with smoke. "Yeah, third floor," I said.

All this time, my cat was running around my legs, wondering what was going on. I picked him up and started for the door.

Then the lights went out.

A person can live in an apartment for years, but when something like this happens you find out you don't really know where your door is after all. I couldn't find my door.

Now I suddenly realized that things were getting really serious.

Imagine standing in a pitch-black room filled with oily choking smoke, a frightened cat clawing under your left arm and trying to find the door.

After tripping over a coffee table, I found my way out to the hallway. The smoke was worse out there and I started to choke. The lights started to flicker back on, then went off again. I couldn't see my hand in front of my face. I reached out for a wall, felt it and started to grope my way.

Now my cat was panicking and jumped out of my grasp. I couldn't get enough air to call him back.

It's about 50 feet from my door to the stairs. Saturday night it was no less than a mile. As I felt my way along the wall, a nagging thought kept coming up that I was going the wrong way and that I was heading for the fire.

I remembered the fireman and what he said about people getting confused in the smoke. I could never remember that hallway being that long before.

But then I could hear the fire behind me and shouting in front of me. Finally I saw some light and made a rush for it. By the time I stumbled down three flights of stairs, the fire department was pulling up in front.

The whole thing took less than three minutes from the time I made the call. Someone timed the firemen and said it took them nine minutes to put the fire out.

Somehow in all that smoke and flame, a fireman managed to find my cat. When he brought him outside, the cat looked more dead than alive. He just laid on the wet grass, panting.

Someone from the aid car offered to give him oxygen. They stuck a thin plastic tube in front of the cat's face and in a few minutes he was scratching and fighting, and on the way to a full recovery.

After the fire was out, I went back to my place. The door was still open and a large fan was in an open window, sucking the smoke out. It was hard to see because of the smoke and soot covering the light bulbs.

The walls, once white, were now completely black. My books, pictures, clothes, typewriter, everything was covered with greasy black soot. The smell made my eyes water.

A man in a hard hat came in and said he was from the Seattle Fire Buffs. He asked if I knew what I was going to do now. I didn't have the faintest idea.

He said his organization could put me up in a hotel if I wanted. He also asked if I had enough money to see me through and if I needed any transportation. He gave me some phone numbers to call if I needed any help. Then he disappeared, apparently to help some of the other people.

Five firemen came in, looked the damage over and set to work. Some started wiping down the walls while others cleaned out the kitchen—sink included—and the bathroom. They even cleaned the tub and sink in there. The rug was vacuumed and everything was stacked in neat piles.

When I asked about this clean-up project (I figured cleaning up the mess was my problem), one fireman said they do it all the time. "Sort of a maid service," he called it.

By the time I left for my parents' home, the apartment was still looking grim, but not as bad as when I first walked in.

About 90 minutes had passed since the fire started.

Questions on "Get Out of the Building . . . It's on Fire!"

1. What incident introduces the article? How is this incident returned to later in the article to help produce an effect?

2. Trace the use of sensory impressions as the fire develops. Which comparisons are most effective for you? Which details? What miniscenes stick in your mind?

3. There are three clichés in the article: "couldn't see my hand in front of my face," "more dead than alive," and "on the way to a full recovery." Evaluate the use of these clichés. Do they work? Why or why not? Can you replace them with new word patterns?

4. What effect do the time references throughout the article help the writer achieve? What point does he stress by ending with a time reference?

NOT ANOTHER WORD[9]

RICHARD THURMAN

> Richard Thurman (1921–) was born in Salt Lake City, Utah, and majored in English at Utah State University. He has published in *Harper's*, the *Atlantic, Reader's Digest*, and *The New Yorker*. In 1956, he received the O. Henry Award for best short stories published in American magazines.

Because I was one of the bigger, healthier boys in the class—and also one of the biggest, smoothest liars, and thus apt to set an inspiring example for the others—Miss Devron would often begin the morning's inquisition with me. "Paul Adam," she would say, beaming down upon me, "would you be kind enough to tell us what you had for breakfast this morning?"

Even in the third grade, we were perceptive enough to sense that Miss Devron's inquiries into our daily breakfast menus sprang from something deeper than a mere interest in keeping us healthy. One look at her size and you knew what supreme importance food had in her life, and since we were her children—those she would never have herself, because of age, temperament, and general appearance—she apparently found it necessary to feel her way into our souls by following a glass of fruit juice and an egg and a slice of ham down our throats each morning. It wasn't just her zeal to know us personally through the food we ate that made us guard against her with a series of outrageous lies; she also wanted to know our families—their general way of life, their social and economic status in our small Utah town, and whether or not they lived in accordance with the Mormon doctrines, which were as inseparable from our lives as the mountain air we breathed. And she had a nasty way of pointing out any deviation from her set of standards by interrupting the stream of breakfast reports. "Hominy grits!" I remember her saying on one of the first mornings we were in her class. "Did you hear, class? Ronald Adair had hominy grits for breakfast."

She smiled her closed smile of wisdom and commiseration at Ronald, and placed the index finger of her left hand like a hot dog between her second and third chins while waggling her free hand scoldingly in his direction. "It's a lucky thing for you, young man, that your parents somehow had the energy to come out West, where you can get a new start in life," she said. "It's food like hominy grits that has kept the South backward so long. Out *here* we eat bacon and ham-and-eggs and hot cereal and fresh fruit juices and good buttered toast with jam.

---

[9]Richard Thurman, "Not Another Word," reprinted by permission; © 1957 *The New Yorker Magazine,* Inc.

You're very lucky, young man! My, yes."

With such tactics she soon taught us to lie, and regardless of what each of us had eaten at home, there in Miss Devron's class we began to share a breakfast as monotonous as it was sumptuous. It was only a variation in quantity that crept into our diets from the first student's report to the last, for if one egg and a modest piece of ham were enough to start Miss Devron's fingers strolling contentedly over the terraces of her chins, it took considerably more than this to keep them happy and moving by the time the class was half through its recital, and by the time the last student's turn came, Miss Devron's wolfish appetite responded to nothing less than a gorge. Lila Willig was the last student on our class list. She looked as if she were made from five laths, and in the hectic flush of her unhealthiness—perhaps caused by near-starvation at home—she would sometimes get a little hysterical and report that she had eaten twenty-five eggs and a whole ham. I'm sure now that this was not because of any native waggishness in Lila, but we thought it was then, and we always laughed until Miss Devron had to pound the desk with her ruler.

"Now, stop that foolishness, Lila," she would say briskly. "Tell the class right out how many eggs you had for breakfast."

"Five," Lila would say, nervously scratching her frizzled yellow curls until they stood out like coiled wires. She could have said nothing else. The boy in front of her had just reported a breakfast of five eggs; anything less from Lila would have been picked up by Miss Devron as an example of parental neglect.

"That's better," the teacher would say, her fingers resuming their stroll "And as I look over your faces this morning, class, I can already see the differences that good eating habits can make in one's life. How much brighter your eyes! How much stronger your backs!"

We simpered back at her, only vaguely and uneasily aware that she was a tyrant who was flattening our individuality with the weight of her righteous self-assurance. In less than a month under her, we were reduced to a spineless group of sycophantic ham, egg, and cereal eaters, with only Lila's occasional lapses to show us what a dull mold we had been crushed into. And then our integrity was rescued in an unexpected way.

The new boy who turned up in our class a month after the opening of school certainly looked like no hero. He was smaller than most of us, and while all of us boys were proudly wearing corduroy knickers, he still wore the short pants we scorned, and in the sharp air of that October morning his thin legs were mottled with a network of blue. We welcomed this pathetic figure with a fine generosity of spirit. "Where you from?" one of us asked him as we walked up to where he was standing, at the edge of the playground.

"New York."

"New York!" we said, and I now had an explanation of why he was such a puny-looking little rat. From the handful of Western movies and cowboy books I had already absorbed, I knew the kind of magic that enters into a man's blood when he is born west of the Mississippi River. His eye is clearer, his nerves are truer, his gait is more tireless, his aim is steadier, and in the very heart of his manliness there is a dimension that effete Easterners know nothing about. All this I knew as I looked down at the new boy's skinny blue legs.

"New York, eh?" I said menacingly, moving up to him until I could have rested my chin on top of his head.

"That's right," he said, lounging against the top rail of the playground fence and casually lifting one foot to rest it on the lower rail.

I eyed him with a steely coldness I had learned from a story about a man who had built the Union Pacific Railroad across the plains and who could drive a spike into a tie with two hammer blows. I put my fingers into my belt, just above where my six-shooters should have been. "Who's your old man voting for?" I asked. "Al Smith or Hoover?"

"Al Smith."

"Well, then, I guess I'll have to beat you up."

Perhaps nowadays, what with the broadened horizons brought on by the Second World War, Korea, UNESCO, and the stress on social-adjustment patterns in modern education, a new student from, say, Siam or Afghanistan can take his place unobtrusively in an American schoolroom. I don't know. But I do know that in my part of America in 1928 a new student had to fight his way into school, particularly if he had come to us from more than five blocks away. It will be understood, then, that I had no unusual political precocity or passion at the age of eight, and that this difference in our fathers' political views was only a pretext for me to beat up the new boy, who had offended every one of us by coming all the way from New York, with his short pants and blue skin.

We sized each other up for a second. Then he shrugged his thin shoulders and said "O.K.," and the quickness with which he squared away for battle gave me a little turn. We circled around each other, with everyone urging me to get in there and show him what was what. But just then the bell rang, and I felt a surge of relief that was just a bit disconcerting to anyone born as far west as I had been.

"I'll finish with you later," I said.

"O.K.," he said, with that same unnerving readiness.

Something more immediate than our fathers' political inclinations operated to bring us closer together that morning. Miss Devron put the new boy in the empty seat just in front of me, and I spent the first few minutes of class watching his blue neck turn pink in the warm room, while the pupils drearily went through their recital of breakfasts eaten that morning.

"And now the new boy, Robert Bloom," said Miss Devron, smiling down at him. "What did you have this morning?"

He had been listening carefully to what was going on, and once, when he turned his profile to me, I could see that he was enjoying himself. The rest of the pupils had answered from their seats, but he stood up in the aisle. He stood at attention like a soldier.

"I had a cup of coffee and a snail, Ma'am."

There was a stony quiet for a second, and then the dazzling irreverence of what he had said burst through us with shock waves of pure delight. Miss Devron pounded on the desk with the ruler, and her red chins trembled in front of her like molten lava. "Class!" she cried. "Class, we'll have order here! Come to order. Come to order this instant!"

But she was trying to calm down a madhouse.

"A cup of coffee and a snail, please!" somebody shouted.

"Give me a worm with mine!" somebody yelled back.

And on we went, up that enticing road of suggestibility, until we were eating snakes on muffins. The special delight, of course, was the coffee. *There* was the alluring evil and joy of what he had said, because most of us in that room, including Miss Devron, were Mormons, who felt, in a way beyond reason, that murder was no more than a high-spirited lark compared to drinking coffee or smoking. It wasn't until Miss Devron and her ruler and the powers of light finally triumphed over the dark joy in us that we began to realize the outrageousness of what he had said. We slunk back from debauchery to righteousness under Miss Devron's glowering eye, and finally he was left standing there, all alone before the glare of our joint indignation.

"We should never laugh at those who don't know better, class," Miss Devron began, in a carefully controlled voice. "We must share our knowledge with those less fortunate, and help them to know the truth. Robert comes from a part of the country where they don't know about health. Now then, Robert, that can't be all you had for breakfast, can it?" She looked at him with the pity, the heart-spoken prayer, and the tenderness of a missionary meeting with a cannibal for the first time.

"No, Ma'am," he said. "I had two cups of coffee."

The tight breath gathered in our throats again, but Miss Devron was in control now, and aside from a few blown cheeks and red faces there was no sign that we were not with her in spirit.

"Now, class," she continued, "I want to ask Robert's pardon for what I'm about to do, but I think we can all learn a great deal from what he has told us and from what we can see. Very soon now Robert will be as big and strong as any of you, because he will soon be eating the right foods. But look at him now. See how small he is? *This* is what comes from not eating the right foods and from drinking coffee."

We looked him over, almost seeming to pass him from desk to

desk, as if he were a mounted disease-carrying bug we were studying. But what a happy, smiling bug! To judge from his face, he considered the attention we gave him an unexpectedly hearty welcome to his new school.

"I don't think it's the coffee, Ma'am," he suddenly added. "My dad says I steal too many of his cigarettes."

During the next couple of minutes, Miss Devron could have fired salvos of cannon shells over our heads without getting our attention. We were like an oppressed people hailing with insane joy the coming of a revolutionary leader. Even the girls in the room were caught up in the exultation of our victory. All the cigars, cigarettes, or drinking straws filled with grains of coffee that any of us had smoked in secret, all our uneasy past abandonments to appetite, curiosity, and lawlessness were suddenly recalled and made more glorious by Robert's cheerful confession. We worshipped him instantly, and at the end of the day a lot of us walked with him, proud to be seen with such a man. We were walking along with him, swearing, talking about smoking, and making faces at the girls on the other side of the street, when he stopped and tapped me on the arm.

"How about this place?" he said, pointing to a strip of grass between two houses.

"What do you mean?" I asked.

"Your old man's voting for Hoover, isn't he?"

"Sure, but . . ."

"Well, let's fight."

I wanted no part of the fight now, but Robert insisted. He proceeded to support his political views with a ferocity I couldn't seem to match, and it wasn't until he hit me a hard one in the eye that I brought any personal enthusiasm to the fight. From then on, my size and strength started getting the better of him, but no one in the group around us was shouting for me. Those who had been beside me that morning were now yelling for Robert to kill me, and I must say that he did his best. But I finally knocked him down and sat on top of him, and kept his shoulders pinned to the grass until he admitted that Hoover would win the election. When he was up again, he expressed some strong reservations about his opinion, but the election a few days later proved I was right, and, with our political differences out of the way, we became the best of friends.

For the next two or three weeks, Miss Devron tried her best to change Robert's breakfast habits, or at least to get him to lie a little in the interests of classroom harmony. But his incorruptible honesty soon inspired the rest of us to tell what we had really had for breakfast. Variety returned to the menu, and Miss Devron's discovery that some of the larger, healthier children, like me, frequently ate what tasted good for breakfast, instead of simply what was good for them, seemed to undermine her spirit. She acknowledged defeat one morning when she opened class by reading aloud to us from a book of dog stories by Albert Payson Terhune. Subsequently, she read to us whenever there were spare minutes in the day, and the breakfast lists were forgotten. From that time on, she was one of our favorite teachers.

My first idea about Robert's father was that he was a sailor in the United States Navy. Robert showed me pictures of him in a sailor suit—pictures in which he was leaning against a palm tree; laughing, with his arm around two girls; pulling a rope; scrubbing the deck of a ship; or standing on his hands, with a distant and smoking volcano framed between his spread legs. Then I learned that he was no longer in the Navy but was selling something—"selling something out on the road," as Robert described it. With only that imagination-tickling description, I developed the permanent expectation of turning a corner in the city someday and seeing Robert's father selling something right in the middle of the road. What he would be selling I couldn't imagine, nor had I a clear idea of how he would be doing it. Salesmen were never allowed in my own neighborhood, and the only prototype of Mr. Bloom I could conjure up was a man I had seen at the circus the year before. He had been standing outside one of the tents—a man with a dark face and a croaking voice, who kept urging us to come in, trying to scoop us up over his shoulder and into the dark tent with a dipping swing of his straw hat. "Selling, selling, selling!" my mother had said to my father. "It's plain disgusting." And so the man with the straw hat became Mr. Bloom, and I always had the feeling that Robert's house, too, was somehow disgusting. But it was also the most exciting house I had ever been in.

The excitement would hit me as soon as I entered the front door—usually in the form of Robert's dog, an overgrown mongrel lummox called Buddy. I think he was mostly a police dog, but any remnants of purebred respectability had worn thin through long association with the underworld of back alleys and garbage cans, and through personal vice, for the dog was a hopeless drunkard. At least once a week, Robert and I would take a bottle of beer from his refrigerator (and how thrilling it was for me to be in a house containing anything so illegal and wicked as a bottle of beer!) and pour some of it out into a saucer for the dog. He would go at it with a ravenous thirst, frothing the beer with slaps from his scooping tongue until the white suds were all over the floor and his muzzle. He looked as if he were mad, and soon he would act mad. He would lurch around the house, bumping into chairs and tables, and endangering ashtrays and bric-a-brac in his weaving course. I would hold him by the collar at one end of the living room while Robert called him from the other end, and negotiating those fifteen feet of open rug held for him all the peril and adventure of a walk on a slippery deck in a typhoon. Once he made it to safety, he would sit down, brace himself against a chair, and look at us triumphantly. We would never get him drunk when Robert's mother was around, of course. That was the one thing I ever saw her really angry about. But she was a person of such unquenchable joy and good cheer that even the sight of Buddy drunk that one time didn't keep her angry for long.

She came home from town unexpectedly that day. Buddy's flank had just crashed into a floor lamp and Robert was juggling it back to equilibrium when his mother walked in the front door.

"Robert, have you got that dog drunk again?" she asked, after one look.

"Yes, Mom."

His truthfulness, both at school and at home, always amazed me. For me the truth was usually a fearful thing; my telling it often seemed to hurt my father or my mother, or someone else. But Robert was dauntless before it.

"I've *told* you not to, Robert," Mrs. Bloom said. "You know I have. Poor Buddy! Just look at him. That's no way to treat a dog."

We all looked at him, and I, at least, was conscience-stricken at what we had done. But none of us could remain remorseful for long. Deep in his cups, Buddy had misgauged the size and slipperiness of the low black leather hassock in front of the rocking chair, and though he managed to plant one haunch on it, it kept sliding off. He would edge it back momentarily, his happy face conveying to all of us his certainty that he was seated there four-square and in perfect dignity. I don't know what there was about him—perhaps a certain slack-jawed serenity—but we all started laughing helplessly at the same time. Robert's mother threw herself onto the couch, and Robert and I rolled on the floor in our laughter, while Buddy watched us out of one open eye.

She recovered enough after a time to continue her scolding, but she couldn't get more than a few words out without looking at Buddy, and then she would laugh again. Finally, she gave us some cookies and milk, and poured out a big saucerful of thick cream for Buddy, which she said would sober him faster than anything else. While Robert was drinking his milk at the kitchen table, she came up behind him and slipped her arms under his and clasped her hands on his chest. She kissed him on his neck and on his cheek and up into his hair, and all this time he went on eating his cookies and drinking his milk. I hardly dared to look at them, but I *had* to see the way she kissed him. She was a young woman, with long, dark hair, and black eyes that opened very suddenly at times, then closed very slowly, the lids seeming to take great pleasure in their long trip back down. The nails of her fingers, clasped on Robert's chest, were buffed to a high polish, and her lips were full and red, and looked wonderfully soft against Robert's cheek. I was the fifth, and youngest, child in my family, and I had only been pecked at gingerly by thin lips pulled tight against clenched teeth, and now I could almost feel that cushioned touch of Robert's mother's kiss on my own cheek. I had no name for the feeling it gave me. I was simply fascinated.

She straightened up, put her hand to the back of her hair, and walked to the refrigerator again. "Boys, boys, boys!" she said, "Little devils, all of you. Little heartless devils, getting dogs drunk, pulling girls' hair, fighting, swearing. You're no good, any of you." As she said it, she dug two big scoops of applesauce out of a bowl and slapped them into two dishes.

"So why do I like you so much?" she said to me as she leaned over the table to put a dish in front of me. She was wearing the kind of low dress she usually wore, but I didn't dare to look away from her face. I just looked at her smile, and that was everywhere. Then she leaned over and kissed my forehead.

By the time I left for home, Buddy was on his feet and feeling well enough to walk to the corner with Robert and me.

"I like your mother," I said.

"Ah, she's all right," he said, leveling his toe at a rock and kicking it out into the street.

"You bet she's all right. I'd like to marry her when I grow up."

"She's already married."

"I know she is. My gosh, don't I know that? I just said I'd like to, that's all."

We stood on the corner and kicked a few more rocks into the street. And then we were just standing there. Suddenly there was between us a strip of that infinite desolation that surrounds and crisscrosses life, which children must face without the comfort of philosophy or the retreat of memory.

Robert slapped the dog on the side as hard as he could. "Come on, you," he said to him, and I stood and watched them run down the street. I wondered why he never seemed to like the dog except when we got him drunk. I would have given anything for him, but it had been made clear to me at home long before that our yard was too beautiful to be ruined by a "dirty dog."

Besides Buddy, and Robert's mother, with whom I fell more and more in love as I sampled her cakes, home-canned fruit, dill pickles, candy, sandwiches, and lemonade, there were other charms at Robert's house that made my own seem intolerably dreary. Although it was nearly Christmas and I had known Robert for more than two months, I still hadn't met his father, and yet I had come to feel that I knew him as well as my own, or even better. My father's actual physical arrival at home, after a day spent seeing patients in his office or operating at the hospital or attending a church meeting, was the main thing that impressed his existence upon me. He was so neat, so disciplined in his habits, and so completely without vices, eccentricities, or hobbies that he carried himself completely with him wherever he went. But Robert's father lay scattered about the house in the form of pipes, fishing equipment, shotguns, whiskey bottles locked in a glass-front cabinet, a tennis racket, a set of rusty golf clubs, and a three-foot-long Chinese beheading sword, with a dragon engraved on the length of the blade and a dull, pewtery stain on the bright steel, which Robert said was blood. His father had brought the sword home from China when he was in the Navy, and it hung, with its handle wrapped in cords of scarlet silk, above the bed that he and Robert's mother slept in. I was so taken by the sword at the time that I thought anyone would die of pride to have it hanging above his bed, but I now see what a generous concession to his male taste it was for her to have it there. I remember the room as delicately feminine in decor, but it was his room, too, and he had chosen the exact thing to put his mark on it that I would have chosen if I had been married to Robert's mother.

Mr. Bloom did come home occasionally, but even then I didn't get to see him. He was sleeping, Robert would say, going on to explain how tired a salesman becomes after several weeks on the road. On two or three such afternoons, Robert's mother was also not to be seen, and he told me that she, too, was taking a nap and that we were to tiptoe carefully when we went past the closed door to their bedroom.

Christmas morning came and I was downstairs at 5 A.M., tearing into my carefully wrapped presents with impatient, greedy hands. The unexpected child of my parents' middle age, with all my brothers and sisters grown up and living away from home, I had spent my early hours of the past three Christmases all by myself, and I am certain that the pain of a child getting up on Christmas morning to find nothing under the tree cannot be much worse than the pain of one who finds everything there but has no one to show it to. It was not that my parents were really unfeeling. Indeed, they carefully kept my belief in Santa Claus alive beyond the customary age of disillusionment, perhaps because I *was* the last and much youngest child—even telling me that all my Christmas presents, except for some clothing from my mother, had come from Santa Claus. But it never occurred to them to get up early on Christmas morning in order to share my excitement, and I can still remember the sick emptiness of the hour and a half between my discovery of my presents and the first sound of someone else stirring in the house. That year, as usual, I finally heard the maid come upstairs from her basement room, and for the next ten minutes I held her captive while I gloated over each new addition to my wealth.

"Santa was certainly generous to you," she said, and it was so true that I didn't at all mind her saying it in the middle of a yawn.

"Look what Santa Claus left me!" I was able to say to my parents at last, when they came down for breakfast. I had been particularly struck that year by the great number of things he had given me compared to what my mother had given me, and I emphasized this difference by putting his gifts to me and hers in two piles, side by side. But a peck on the cheek and a cursory smile were all the tribute my parents paid to me, Christmas, and Santa Claus's generosity before they opened their own small presents from me, with an air of rather hasty embarrassment, and then turned to the newspaper and to breakfast.

Still, this year I knew someone who would take a second look at what I had received. It took some tight crowding, but I managed to tie all my presents onto my new sled with my new lariat, and I departed for Robert's house. I wasn't disappointed. Not only did Robert's eyes pop at some of the individual presents and at the sheer mass of what I had been given but his mother and, yes, his father, too, were as excited as Robert himself. Mr. Bloom, who got down on the floor to play with my new hook-and-ladder fire engine, turned out to be just the sort of man I had expected. He liked the fire engine so much that I wanted to give it to him, except that the idea of giving it up hurt too much. Out of this dilemma came a sudden inspiration to ask him if he would like to trade his sword for my fire engine. I was circling carefully about this idea, trying to approach it in the best way, when something happened to destroy the notion utterly.

It was not surprising that none of us had paid much attention to Robert's gifts during the first few minutes I was there. All three of the Blooms were too polite not to have gone all out to admire a sledful of gifts dumped into the middle of their living room by a guest as greedy for appreciation as I was. They would have done this even if my presents had come from the ten-cent store. But my gifts were both costly and impressive, and the Blooms, in their modest circumstances, had no need to be just polite; quite simply, they all gave in to the dream of having enough money to buy what I spread out before them, and wholly enjoyed themselves with my presents. I was too far lost in their appreciation to remember that Robert had also had a Christmas that day. But he soon reminded me of it.

"Look!" he said to me. He held in his cupped hands a bright, gold-colored wheel, suspended on a silver axle within a framework of two intersecting wire circles.

"What the heck *is* it?" I asked.

Robert's mother and father were both down on the floor with us, and while Robert threaded a length of green string through a hole in the axle and then wound it carefully along the axle's length, I could feel their eyes looking from me to the wheel and back, excitedly waiting for my reaction. Then Robert gave the wound-up string a sudden vigorous pull, putting the muscles of his back and arm and the tension of his clenched teeth and closed eyes into it, and brought the top spinning to life. The golden wheel hummed softly within its unmoving world of wire circles. Robert placed the top carefully on the smooth surface of a box lid, and there it rested, poised on its projecting tip like a dancer on one leg.

"Watch," he said, and he picked up the wonderful toy and rested its cupped tip on the point of a pencil his father held up. Once the top was spinning there, Robert pushed it, a fraction of an inch at a time, until it was no longer a continuation of the pencil's length but was hanging horizontally out over space, held from falling only by the quiet humming and the touch of the pencil point on the cup.

"My *gosh!*" I said. "Where'd you get that?"

"Mom gave it to me."

"It's called a gyroscope," she said.

For the next five or ten minutes, we shared the excitement of watching the gyroscope ignore gravity in every position we could devise. I was ready to trade Robert all the solid excitement of my presents for the magic that I could feel spring to life when I pulled the green string. I held the gyroscope in my hand and laughed to feel that quiet, determined will fighting mine as I tipped the wheel away from the path it had chosen in the air. And then, suddenly, the magic would be gone and I would be left holding the toy dead in my hands.

"And what did your father give you?" I asked, staring down at the wheel.

"That Chinese beheading sword."

I gave him back the top, but I couldn't look at him. I could feel the cold, sharp edge of that sword in me.

"Where is it?" I asked at last.

"He hung it over my bed."

"Let's see it."

We stepped around the scattered toys and went into his bedroom. There it was, hanging over his bed, just as I had dreamed it might hang over mine.

"I'm not to touch it until I'm older, but she's all mine," Robert said.

I could easily have cried. My mother had given me ties, socks, gloves, shirts, pants, shoes, underwear—all the things a boy could easily do without. But Robert's mother had given him a gyroscope! And the sword had come from his father, while I didn't even think that my father had given me anything! I seemed to have only one real friend right then.

"What did Santa Claus bring you?" I asked.

"Santa Claus? *Santa Claus?*" He hooted. "There isn't any Santa Claus, you big dummy!"

I had heard there wasn't—but only speculatively, never with this final, crushing authority. I could think of only one way to defend myself against Robert's having everything and my not having even Santa Claus. I hit him twice, once on the chest and once in the face, and then I tied all my presents onto my sled with my lariat and started out of the living room, refusing to answer any of the questions his parents asked me. Robert followed me onto the porch and when I was half a block away he called out to me, "What did you hit me for?"

"Shut up!" I yelled back, and I went home and put my presents under the tree for my relatives to see when they came around later.

Most of the rifts of childhood are as troubled, as tearing, and as quickly smoothed over as the wake of a small motorboat, and by the time Christmas vacation came to an end I had accepted the death of another illusion and Robert had forgotten my naïveté. We went on as before, with the abrasive honesty of his life wearing away at the hypocrisy of my own until I, too, occasionally knew some emotional truths. With that encouragement of truth which had been given him at home, he was quite free to say, for example, that he liked or disliked this or that person, this or that book, or a threatening gray or a clear blue sky. But I knew no such freedom. Caught within the attitude that this world was God's green acre and too sacred to be regarded critically by the likes of me, I wasn't free to decide whether I liked a dog better than a cat, or a mountain better than a rosebush. Any expression of vital choice on my part was seen as a blasphemous elevation and denigration of two aspects of the divine order, and, pressed down by the weight of my blasphemy, I lost the power to make any choice. But Robert restored this power during the next year of our friendship. He restored it with a series of shocks that showed me that what he said about something and what I felt about it, way down, were often related. How exhilarating it was to have him come out with a truth that my bones knew but my tongue could not say!

"What do you think of Miss Brown?" I might ask him, speaking about the elementary-school art teacher.

"She's a nice lady," he answered, "but she doesn't know anything about art."

My heart pounded with the truth of what he had said. I half knew she didn't know anything about art, but she had been put in our classroom by authority as an art teacher, so it was certain that I must be wrong about her. "What do you mean, she doesn't know anything about art?" I asked—on his side, of course, but still fearful.

"All she draws is mountains," he said disgustedly. "Never people, or dogs, or flowers, or trees, or boats, or water, or houses, or clouds, or *anything* but mountains. And it's always the same mountain. You should have seen the teacher I had in New York. She could draw a face on the board in two seconds and everyone knew who it was. Boy, was she an artist!"

If I was impressed at the time by the fearlessness of what Robert knew and said, it is only now that I can appreciate the full miracle of his freshness surviving the hothouse atmosphere of souls under cultivation for adulthood that existed in our third- and fourth-grade classrooms. Having known Robert, I now seriously believe that the right sort of parents can emotionally equip a child to survive the "civilizing" process of education. But my real appreciation of Robert came mostly in retrospect, and most of whatever I now know about truth I had to learn the hard way, for in the late winter of our fourth-grade year—about a year and a half after our friendship started—I cut myself off from the hope that Robert would go on indefinitely helping me to find truth.

It was one of those false spring days that sometimes appear toward the end of winter—a sad, nostalgic day, when the air teased our bodies with the promise of games and picnics, and the earth was still locked up and unavailable for our use, beneath two feet of grimy snow. Robert and I were walking home together. "Mom just put up some more dill pickles last night," he said, and suddenly the day came alive.

"First one who gets there gets the biggest," I said, and, with my longer legs, I was on the porch while Robert was still pounding up the sidewalk. We pushed the living-room door open, and when we weren't hit in the chest by a flying, dancing Buddy, we both understood the sign. Whenever Robert's father was out of town, his mother tried to keep Buddy in the house as a watchdog—I suppose on the theory that he might possibly trip up an intruder and break his neck as he frisked about him in indiscriminate welcome. But when Buddy was absent— off on some disreputable scavenging trip, no doubt—it usually meant that Mr. Bloom was home. Robert and I now peered out the back living-room window and saw the car in front of the garage, and he lifted his fingers to his lips. "Come on," he whispered. "Let's go into the kitchen."

We tiptoed past the closed door of his parents' bedroom and past the open door of his own bedroom. As usual, I looked in and saw the sword still hanging over his bed. The sharp pain of Robert's ownership of that sword had been replaced in me by a kind of dull wonder at his exasperating sense of honor. "No, I can't touch it until I'm twelve," he had insisted a dozen or more times that past year—times when nothing in the world but a three-foot-long Chinese beheading sword was appropriate to the game at hand. Now, in the kitchen, Robert whispered, "We better not have any pickles without asking Mom. Boy, was she ever mad the last time we ate them all! How about some apricot jam and bread?"

"Swell," I whispered back.

"Hey, would you rather have apricot or strawberry?" he whispered from the depths of the icebox.

"Let's have both," I said, regaining some of the excitement I had lost in my disappointment over the pickles.

He brought out the two jam jars, spooned large helpings of each kind into a bowl, and began whipping them together with a fork. I stared, hypnotized, at the clean colors as they ran together and faded to a pinkish tan. "Boy are you ever lucky!" I said. "Eating any old thing you want when you want! Do you think my mother, or that old maid of ours, would let me eat *anything* between meals? No, sir! Our maid says you're spoiled because you're an only child and your mother doesn't know any better."

"Well, maybe," he said, shaking fist-size globs of jam onto the bread. "But Mom told me they're going to try and get me a baby brother or a baby sister pretty soon."

"A baby brother or sister? Which kind would you rather have?"

"Oh, I don't care. They're both O.K., I guess." He returned the jars to the icebox, and came back to the table and picked up his bread and jam. "How about taking these out on the front porch to eat?"

"O.K."

We crept past the closed bedroom door again and went out on the porch, being careful not to let the door slam behind us. When we were comfortably settled on the front steps, with our mouths full of bread and jam, I suddenly decided to ask him a question that had occurred to me many times. "Robert, is there something wrong with your mother and father?"

"What do you mean, 'something wrong'?" he asked.

"Well, you know. The way they're always resting when we come here. Are they sick?"

It seemed to me that they must certainly be sick, or something more than sick. For me, bed was a concept that changed entirely with the time of day. Bed at night was a completely respectable thing, both for myself and for my parents—so respectable, in fact, that I usually put up a spirited fight against going to it. But after the sun rose over the high, gray mountains east of town, bed instantly became something slack and irresponsible, even on weekend mornings, when there was no immediate reason for getting out of it. "What?" my father would say, standing over me at seven o'clock on a rainy Saturday morning. "Not up yet?" He never said it harshly but always with a friendly smile, kept just thin enough to give me the message that bed simply wasn't the place to be at that hour. So grave was this obscure crime that even when I was sick enough to stay in bed all day, I dreaded the long morning and afternoon hours there, and never wholly relaxed until it was 8 P.M. again and really time for bed. If there was one aspect of the irregularity of Robert's house that I did not enjoy, it was this matter of bed in the afternoon. There *was* something sick about it.

"Heck, no, they're not sick," Robert said. "Dad gets tired out on the road. I *told* you that. And Mom likes to be with him. They're just taking a nap. Or maybe they're trying to find me that baby brother."

I stopped in the middle of a bite and stared at him. If he had spoken the last words in Latin he could not have lost me more completely.

"They're trying to find a baby? In *there?*"

"Well, of course," he said, stuffing the last of his bread and jam into his mouth. And then the full extent of my darkness must have shown on my face. He swallowed with a little choking cough. "Oh, my gosh!" he said. "You don't know about *that*, either, do you?"

"Of course, I know about it," I said angrily. "I just didn't know what you meant."

But I couldn't cover up my ignorance or my need to know the truth, for he proceeded to tell me all about it. He told me in adequate detail and finished by saying that all babies were "found" in just this way.

"*All* babies?"

"Yep—me, you, everybody. That's the way everybody's parents get their children."

I jumped up, and, seeing the expression on my face, Robert stood up, too, and then I hit him twice—once on the chest to knock him down and once on the nose as he was falling. In its most impersonal sense, the idea he had given me was just barely tolerable, but in relation to my parents it was an unthinkable blasphemy. After all they had done for me, hitting him seemed the very least I could do. I stood over him, breathing hard and with my fists clenched. He looked up at me from the top step, where he had fallen, and slowly rubbed his nose.

"You big damn dumb!" he said at last. "I'll never tell you another thing as long as I live!"

"You just better not," I said. "You just better never say another word to me if you know what's good for you!"

And he never did. From that day forward, I was on my own.

Questions and Exercises on "Not Another Word"

1. Through his character, Paul Adam, Richard Thurman both looks back on a child's world from an adult's perspective and re-creates that world as the child experienced it. Trace the skillful blend of writing techniques that enables him to achieve this dual effect. For example, words like "inspiring ," "inquisition," "perceptive," "inquiries," and "commiseration" in the first scene,

definitely reflect an adult's vocabulary and indirect analysis of the situation. Which scenes reproduce the child's vocabulary and perspective? Can you find examples that show the child's reaction within the larger framework of the adult looking back on the scene with added awareness?

2. Note the original use of images and detail in the writing. Miss Devron places "the index finger of her left hand like a hot dog between her second and third chins"; Lila scratches her "frizzled yellow curls until they stood out like coiled wires." Robert is summed up as being the kid from New York with "short pants" and "blue skin." Find other examples of images and details that add life to the writing.

3. Note the skillful use of sentence variety. How does the writer get long sentences to read clearly?

4. Separate the essay into its dominant scenes. Outline the writing techniques (dialogue, images, and comparisons among others) present in each scene. How are the scenes connected? What devices does the writer use to move smoothly from one scene to the next? How does the writer build to a scene's high point much as a good joke teller builds to his punch line?

5. How many places in the essay does Paul hit Robert? Why does he do it? What point is the adult writer making in producing these "fight" scenes in similar contexts?

6. What does the writer both envy and admire about Robert? How does this characteristic lead to the key idea behind the essay? How does it relate to the essay's title, "Not Another Word"? What larger comment does the essay make about society in general and human nature in particular?

Chapter Two

Writing from the Outside In

The Process Reversed

In personal experience writing, you wrote from the inside. You were the topic, focus, and stimulus for the writing, and your goal was to re-create your inside experience for the outside world.

The reverse of this process can also produce writing topics and ideas. For example, if a friend tells you of a grinding chemistry exam he has just suffered through or of a breakup with his girlfriend, his misery may trigger memories of similar experiences in your own life. If you re-capture both his experience and your own in a single paper, you will produce a paper with two focal points: one outside yourself (the re-creation of his experience) and one inside yourself (the memory of your own experience). You will be writing from the outside in.

Writing a Reaction Paper

Type of writing   Reaction paper
Approach   Combines objectivity (focused outside yourself) with sub-jectivity (focused inside yourself)
Purpose   To summarize, highlight, or explain an idea or event "out-side" yourself, and then to give your subjective reaction to that event or to explore similar incidents from your own experience.

Possible Reaction Topics and Format Ideas

How to Find a Topic

Choose material that moved, enraged, delighted, inspired, repelled, or frustrated you so much you wanted to discuss or share it with someone. Use a newspaper article, essay, short story, novel, poem, live performance, or song if it produces a strong reaction in you or evokes specific memories and scenes. Plays, movies, television shows, documentaries, radio programs, and interviews also provide possible source materials. Find material that crystallizes an emotion for you, something you can identify with, or that makes you remember yourself in a similar situation or predicament.

Once you have selected and freewritten about your topic, you will need to organize your material:

1. In the objective portion of your paper, focus on the part of the work that produced the strongest response in you. Be careful to show its relationship to the entire piece and avoid distorting its original meaning. If your source triggers a reaction or memory that differs from the original author's intention, detail that difference as part of your subjective response. Don't try to twist the original to fit your experience.

2. When you apply an incident to your personal situation in your paper's subjective half, use the same techniques as you did in personal experience writing. Whether you use one extended example or a series of related examples for your subjective part, re-create the incidents with detail and sensory impressions; show rather than tell.

Possible Formats for the Objective and Subjective Portions of Your Paper

Objective Portion	Subjective Portion
1. Summarize the incident.	1. Give your reaction.
2. Highlight a scene.	2. Reproduce a parallel event in your own life.
3. Explain a dominant theme or idea.	3. Use a series of examples to support your understanding or interpretation of the idea presented.

You can create effective reaction papers by combining any of these formats. Scan the following section for ways to develop each one:

Objective Formats

1. *Summarize.* To summarize the original work in the objective portion of your paper, use the following procedure:

   A. Begin your summary with the main point or idea in the source material.
   B. Use your own language, but preserve the spirit and intention of the original.
   C. Save interpretation and judgment for the subjective portion of your paper.
   D. Introduce your material by giving clear credit to the original source. Student example papers in this chapter that use a summary format are:

      "Styling in Style Naturally"
      "Life's Little Pains"
      "The Light"
      "From Famous to Forgotten"
      "Ti's Redemption"
      "Bananafish Days"
      "A Slap on the Back and a Smile"

2. *Highlight a scene.* A camera technique often used in modern films first captures the audience's attention with a close-up shot and then pulls back for a wide angle vision that puts the original close-up into perspective. The highlight technique in writing uses a similar approach. First you zero in on a specific scene in the work you're responding to. When the scene has produced its effect, you pull back and explain it in context.

Each of the student example papers, "The Suffragettes" and "I'm a Barbarian at Heart," uses a highlight approach. "The Suffering Suffragettes" starts with the brutal forced feeding scene from a television documentary on women's fight for the vote. "I'm a Barbarian at Heart" focuses on the scene from "One Flew Over the Cuckoo's Nest" where McMurphy tries to strangle Nurse Ratched. Both papers create impact through these specific scenes before they begin their more general summaries.

3. *Explain a controlling theme or idea.*

> **Theme**   Abstract concept, message, moral, or idea implicit in a work; feeling or interpretation of life presented by a work.

Sometimes what you react to in a work is not its plot or action but what that plot or action means. The underlying point of a work, its special view or interpretation of life, constitutes its *theme*. A theme approach can be used with any material that produces a message or moral either directly or indirectly. First, pinpoint the work's theme in the objective portion of your paper; then give a clear explanation of it and back that up with specifics that detail the main idea for your reader.

The student paper "The Light" reacts to the moments of self-discovery in the essay, "The Endless Streetcar Ride into the Night, and the Tinfoil Noose," and compares such moments to "a light." The objective portions of the student papers on "Miss Brill" detail the theme of our society's cruel and indifferent treatment of the elderly.

Subjective Portion Formats

1. *Give your reaction.* Create the subjective portion of your paper by clarifying your reaction to a specific event or by investigating the meanings of your reaction. What did your reaction tell you about yourself? Did your reaction surprise you? Did it change the way you saw others? New insights often come from emotional reactions. Was this the case with you?

The student papers "Memories of Bitter Times," "My Roots, " "The Suffering Suffragettes," and "I'm a Barbarian at Heart" all detail strong reactions and show how these reactions affected the writers.

2. *Reproduce a parallel event.* If an incident triggers a particular memory from your own life, you already have two specific scenes to shape your paper around. After you summarize the "outside" incident, show how it is different or similar to your own experiences in the subjective portion of your paper.

Increase the connections between the two events by using the language of one to present the other. For example, both students' reactions to "Miss Brill," repeat the story's image of old people as "forgotten cups in a china cupboard" in their personal experience parallels.

The following student example papers all use parallel examples in their subjective portions:

"Helplessness"
"Styling in Style Naturally"
"Life's Little Pains"
"A Leave-Taking"
"'Hello in There,' Old Woman"
"The China Cupboard"
"Sunday's Best"

3. *Use a series of examples.* Sometimes an incident can bring to mind a series of examples around a common theme rather than one parallel experience. Both "Bananafish Days" and "A Slap on the Back and a Smile" use multiple examples. In "Bananafish Days," the writer details two separate occasions where she experienced that emotionally mauled state she labels a "bananafish day." In "A Slap on the Back and a Smile," the writer recalls a series of incidents in which he, like the character in his "trigger" story, sought desperately for someone who would share his joy.

Use Transitions to Link the Objective and Subjective Sections of Your Paper

Link the objective portion of your paper to the subjective part with a transitional sentence that clearly reflects the relationship between the two parts. For example, if you're reacting to an article, use sentences that indicate your switch from summary to response such as, "Reading Paul Phillip's article on the neglect of our elderly made me feel . . ." or "Paul Phillip's article reminded me of. . . ." You might try combining the two parts in other arrangements, like starting with your reaction, then presenting the material you reacted to, and finally returning to your reactions at the end. The student essay "Bananafish Days" uses this approach. Whatever organization you choose, make sure your paper reads smoothly as a single unit. Carefully link parts with sentences that clearly show their relationships and connections.

Check Lists

Check List for Reaction Paper Writing

1. *Choose a work that produced a strong reaction in you, one you can identify with easily.*
2. *Focus on the work itself in the objective portion of your paper. Summarize, highlight a scene, or explain a theme in the work, but be faithful to the work's original tone and intention.*
3. *Keep your paper unified by using transitional statments and where applicable, by following the same organizational pattern in both halves.*
4. *Keep your reactions and applications specific; use concrete examples and scenes; avoid hazy generalities.*
5. *Reflect both parts of your paper in your ending.*

Expanded Check List for Reaction Paper Writing

1. *Choose a work that produced a strong reaction in you, one you can identify with easily.* (See section on "Possible Reaction Topics.")

Think back to the last time you read, saw, or heard a work that really affected you, something that still comes to mind when you think about a certain feeling or idea. How did the work make you feel? Why did you identify with it so strongly? Is there a connection between the feeling the work produced and some experience in your past, or did the full realization of what the work meant become clear to you only after you had lived through a similar experience yourself?

Base your reaction paper on a work that is not only interesting in its own right, something you would want to summarize and share with others, but also one that you can relate to easily, that evokes strong and specific memories from your own experience. Look for a reaction that cut deep, that actually made a difference in your actions or beliefs. Did a newsreel move you to the point of joining a protest group? Did a book affect your career choice? Did a film or short story lead to a different way of looking at someone, a greater understanding or acceptance of people you formerly rejected? Did a song embody your own inner revolution? Can you trace an actual behavioral change back to the influence of a single work?

2. *Focus on the work itself in the objective portion of your paper. Summarize, highlight a scene, or explain a theme in the work, but be faithful to the work's original tone and intention.* The work or "outside" incident gets center stage in the objective portion of your paper. Identify a work's source when you first introduce it. Include the author's name as well as the work's title in your introduction. Depending on your subject, your opening might read: "An A.B.C. documentary on physical fitness showed . . .," "An editorial in the *Chicago Daily News*, March 5, 1977, on the death penalty argued that . . .," "Katherine Mansfield's short story 'Miss Brill' presents the theme. . . ."

Summarize the material, highlight a scene, or explain a dominant idea in the work. Keep true to the author's intention. Let the work produce its own effect; let it speak for itself. Save your reaction or application for the subjective portion of your paper.

In summarizing, use your own words, but capture the work's flavor and tone by quoting key words and phrases within your own sentence structure. A skillful condensation requires a clear understanding of a work's purpose and key points. Review the "Summary Procedure" section in this chapter. It often helps to outline the material before you attempt to summarize it. Outlining a work's main ideas and supporting arguments makes it easier for you to present those ideas in proper perspective and to achieve a complementary balance of general statement and specific support detail within your condensation.

If you focus on a specific scene, clarify its relationship to the entire work after you re-create it. If you disagree with a work's attitudes or ideas, present an unbiased summary of them first, then detail your opposition in the reaction portion of your paper. Keep subjective, slanted material out of the objective half of your paper. Above all, do not misrepresent a work's original message or change an incident just to make it sound more like your parallel personal example.

3. *Keep your paper unified by using transitional statements, and*

where applicable, by following the same organizational pattern in both halves. Transitions are linking words that show the relationships between ideas. Phrases like "just as," "in the same way," "contrary to," or "on the other hand" are transitions that indicate if new material supports or opposes the material that precedes it. Use transitions to state and clarify connections between ideas for your reader; build word bridges to cross from one idea to the next.

A two-part paper relies on good transitions to keep it reading as a single unit. Two ways to achieve a unified effect in such a paper are:

A. To use a transition that clarifies the connection between the two parts.
B. To follow the same organizational pattern in both halves.

Various student example papers clearly connected their objective and subjective parts by using the following transitional statements:

"Oddly enough, a time in my life when I felt completely in tune with what the author was relating occurred when I, too, was an oblivious fourteen year old."

"This show made me think of an experience in my own life."

"In watching the movie, I developed, along with McMurphy, an extreme hatred for Nurse Ratched."

"The short story, 'Miss Brill,' by Katherine Mansfield reminded me of my grandmother and the life she and so many other elderly people live today."

"The last place I remember that people weren't treated as people but as objects in a cupboard or closet was in a convalescent home."

The second technique to increase unity is to set up an idea pattern in the objective portion of your paper, which you also follow in the subjective portion. For example, you could summarize Dostoyevsky's short story "I Leave the Prison" by focusing first on his idealization of, hunger for, and fear of the "outside" world, then on the people and friendships he will leave behind, and finally, on his parting rituals. In the subjective portion of your paper, you could then present parallel aspects of your own "leave-taking" experience following the same order.

Keep your entire paper in mind as you write the first half. Sketch out the pieces of the original and the pieces of your own experience and see what they have in common. If you focus on these aspects in the objective half and follow the same pattern in the subjective half, your paper will be that much easier to write.

4. *Keep your reactions and applications specific; use concrete examples and scenes; avoid hazy generalities.* Good writing is specific. It builds effect through concrete detail. Plan the subjective portion of your paper as carefully as you would a personal experience paper. In it, you should choose specifics over generalities, scenes over summaries.

Specific writing need not be long. You can achieve a powerful effect by piling up a series of short scenes. In "Bananafish Days," the writer describes an emotionally mauling day using this technique:

> It had been a bad day for me. My true love was seen walking down the hall right past my locker with another girl. Miss Helfrich, my Home Ec. teacher, took great, vicious pleasure in announcing that I had just put in a zipper upside-down, much to the delight of the rest of the class. Over graham crackers after school, my older brother explained, "What's a homely, retarded girl like you expect anyway?" Not grasping the magnitude of my despair, my Mother then said, "If you don't bring up your algebra grade, you'll wind up being a garbageman—go to your room and study!"

The sharper your specifics, the sharper your effect will be.

5. *Reflect both parts of your paper in your ending.* You don't have to restate all the major points of your paper in your ending. A good ending achieves a unified effect by using the wording of one part of the paper to summarize the other part. This technique indirectly focuses your reader's attention on the relationships between the two parts, enabling your ending to speak for both.

The student example paper "Sunday's Best" illustrates the effective use of this technique in its ending:

> The only difference between the old people in the rest home and the old people in "Miss Brill" is that the people in "Miss Brill" came out of their cupboards every Sunday, while the people in the rest home were like antiques that would stay in their cupboards for the rest of their lives.

If you've followed the same organizational framework in both halves of your paper, your ending on the same point in each half will also help you achieve a unified ending.

Reactions to Another's Experience: Materials to Respond to and Student Example Papers

Responding to a Friend's Experience

If a friend's experience recalls a similar situation in your own life, you have the materials for a reaction paper. The following example paper illustrates this approach.

HELPLESSNESS

Morning fog was typical for January, but today it seemed unusually depressing. I watched it swirl as I waited in an English class with three other students for our instructor, Mrs. Clark, to arrive. The girls made small talk, while Charlie and I exchanged nods. We'd only known Mrs. Clark for two weeks, but she seemed to possess a permanent enthusiasm and appeared rather young, though her skill as an instructor made it obvious she wasn't.

We saw her through the window, walking with unusual reserve and talking to another woman. She opened the door, thanking her friend, and turned to walk in. She stopped after a few feet and let the papers she cradled slide to the table. Her face was puffy and blotched red; she was crying.

"I don't know if I'm going to make it through today's small group," she sobbed. "My father's had a heart attack. They've got him in Intensive Care."

We were still as she struggled to continue.

"There was just no reason for it. He swims and plays ball; he doesn't smoke; he's not overweight; it just doesn't make any sense."

She pressed a crumpled kleenex to her swollen eyes while we remained silent, eyes to the floor. She appeared to regain control of herself as she spoke, but she didn't seem to be talking to us; she sounded alone, talking to herself. She continued to explain that she'd only come to class because the doctors wouldn't let her in her father's intensive care room, and she needed to do something to keep from going crazy.

We dragged our chairs together forming a small circle and sat down. She stared blankly at the papers in her lap and continued to dry her nose and eyes as we began work.

I knew what Mrs. Clark was going through. My own father had suffered a massive coronary about two years ago. He was alone in central California while my mother, brother, two sisters, and I were home in Seattle. The doctor had called my mother and told her it might be fatal; she should come immediately. Since he was in a town that was hundreds of miles from any airport, we decided we could get to him just as fast by car as we could waiting for planes and renting cars.

I threw whatever clothes were handy in my suitcase and checked out the oil and tires on the family car. In less than an hour, I was driving the five of us down Interstate Five in somber silence. Dad was eighteen hours away—he could die in any half second.

I knew what Mrs. Clark was going through. I knew the stunning shock, the confusion, the injustice—the helplessness—that total, consuming helplessness that leaves you nothing but to remember prayers to a God you'd long ignored.

That morning, as my instructor stood weeping, I relived that helplessness and experienced yet another. I'd wanted to comfort her, hold her, tell her I understood, but I was afraid of "making a scene" in front of the others. What would they think of me embracing the English teacher? What would the teacher think? I stood like a mannequin; did nothing, said nothing, bound by my fears of sharing a potentially embarrassing moment of social intimacy. Society had trained me well, and I kept a safe distance, arms dangling useless.

I took a quick glance at Charlie. He wore the expression of a child sorry for something he knows he's done wrong; I was sorry too.

When we gathered in our circle, I sat close to Mrs. Clark, but she was far from me, far from all of us. I remained helpless, unable to free my emotions, and wrapped my arms around myself.

—Lee Price

Questions on "Helplessness"

1. How does the writer get a double meaning from his title?
2. What scenes are re-created in the paper?
3. How does the writer link the two incidents throughout his paper?

Parallel and Thematic Approaches

The following materials show one person's reaction to a specific experience. Read through them, then see if you can identify a parallel moment from your own life. The incidents need not be identical to provide a workable reaction response.

You can also use a thematic approach to the various works. For example, compare the article "Styling in Style" to any situation where you felt old-fashioned or "out of it." The theme of insiders and outsiders is also used in "The Endless Streetcar Ride into the Night, and the Tinfoil Noose." See if Dostoyevsky's story "I Leave the Prison" evokes a memory of the end of a painful situation in your life. Maya Angelou's "Graduation" can be seen either as a "magic moment" destroyed or as a terrible moment rescued by a spontaneous act of bravery. Does either interpretation trigger memories of similar experiences in your life?

STYLING IN STYLE
A HAIR-RAISING (AND SHORTENING) EXPERIENCE[1]

LAURA PARKER

The scent hits you before you even walk in the door. Conditioners, shampoos, the smell of freshly cut hair.

Then suddenly you are plunged into a swirling world of fashion, stereo music, Boston ferns, mirrors, gorgeous women in boots and midi skirts and men in pleated slacks and well-tailored shirts unbuttoned down to here.

You're at the Rosalie Cantrell Salon.

The receptionists are beautiful. They are all beautiful—and very friendly. You are seated in a canvas studio chair, surrounded by hanging plants, copies of New York and European Vogue magazines and photographs of models with exotic haircuts.

You panic. Your mind flashes back to the times at the beauty parlor when middle-aged women with short, tightly curled permanents gave short, tightly curled permanents to other middle-aged women.

Where are the row of hairdryers? Where are the dog-eared copies of Screen World and Photoplay? Where are the platinum bouffant blonds in pink nylon uniforms?

How long has this been going on here?

It has been going on at this place for four years now. Beauty shops specializing in haircuts have been opening up all over town, and business is booming. Last year, Seattle shops reported close to $16 million in income to the Washington State Department of Revenue.

In the past five years, new shops have popped up in obscure corners of the city: Friends Hair Design in Pioneer Square, Scissors in the University District, Vibrations on west Capitol Hill.

[1]Laura Parker, "Styling in Style, A Hair-Raising (and Shortening) Experience," *The Seattle Times* (24 April 1976).

All advertise professional haircuts. All accent it with plants, carpeting, a chic atmosphere and high prices.

But right now, it's not the price that makes you nervous. You were warned that this cut could cost $15 or more. You just didn't think you would be so intimidated by all this, or feel so out of place. You with your $4 haircut and wrinkled clothes.

Your eyes start searching for the door, but it's too late. They've seen you.

A well-dressed girl with brilliant red hair comes toward you on the runway between the booths. She escorts you back past all these sexy hairdressers and shows you where to change into a strapless gown.

You don't understand the gown. You don't understand the place. It's almost like a scene out of the movie "Shampoo," you saw last year.

While the hairdressers admit they may be a little flamboyant, they strongly object to being compared with "Shampoo." One hairdresser contends the movie's wild antics have made a lot of already apprehensive people even less likely to come in.

"That movie was about Warren Beatty, not about hairdressing," another says.

At the Cantrell shop, the hairdressers regard themselves as professional artists who simply got tired of doing unnatural things to people's hair. When Rosalie Cantrell first opened her shop, she built her reputation by giving natural "wash and wear" haircuts.

Since then, she has imported three British stylists, who, with her, compose a team of specialists who travel the country teaching their techniques to other beauticians.

And although the prices are high—haircuts at Cantrell's range from $8 to $25—they justify them by saying they'd rather give a haircut once every six weeks for $20 than wash and set it every week for $10.

Apparently, the justification works, because about three fourths of the Cantrell customers accept the price and return.

But you, in your $4 hair and scuffed shoes haven't been thinking about returning. You still wish you hadn't even come in here. After a shampoo, you've been seated in a black chair in a booth adorned with more photographs.

The door is just across the aisle. There is still time to get out of here.

And then *he* comes in.

Arthur Treble, British hair stylist.

He is the man you talked to when you first came in, who disappeared during the shampoo. Now he's standing behind the chair, smiling at you into the mirror.

"Well now, young lady, what can I do for you today?" he begins.

You stammer. You don't know. You confess you've never been to a shop like this before, and you don't know what you want, but you know you don't want *anything*.

He smiles again. His "oscar" won at the world haircutting championships in Paris three years ago hangs framed in the shop. He's confident.

He keeps looking at your hair, but he hasn't touched you. And his accent makes it even worse, because you *know* he's from Europe, and you're only from Hoquiam or Centralia or Omak.

Then he explains how he'd cut the hair. He says that he'll cut it how you like, but this is how he'd do it as a *professional*.

"Well, first of all, I'd take all this off back 'ere . . . "

But his words blur together and you don't hear him. He just keeps talking and smiling into the mirror, and you keep looking at him and the shop and the plants and your shoulders sticking out of this ridiculous gown, and suddenly you agree he's right. Cut away.

He stops smiling and cuts the hair silently. Then he stands back and his assistants oohh and aahh. Sometimes he consults them. Most of the time he doesn't.

When he blows it dry, it's perfect. It's not you, you don't think, because it's *too* perfect. But now you don't feel quite so awkward and you relax and smile back at him into the mirror. You look around and grin at them, and they grin back, because now, you look just like they do.

Writing Suggestions for Laura Parker's "Styling in Style, A Hair-Raising (and Shortening) Experience"

While Laura Parker consistently uses an editorial "you" to speak directly to her newspaper audience and writes the article as if the audience were participants, her writing approach is still that of subjective personal experience. She carefully reconstructs the scene with total sensory awareness: the smell of "conditioners," "shampoos," and "freshly cut hair"; the sound of a mood-setting stereo; the atmospheric props—"Boston ferns," "mirrors," "copies of the New York and European *Vogue* magazines," "photographs of models with exotic haircuts"; and finally the "beautiful" people—"gorgeous women in boots and midi-skirts and men in pleated slacks and well-tailored shirts unbuttoned down to here."

In reacting to the scene, Laura Parker captures the feeling of being the "outsider" intruding on an "insider's" territory. She becomes the "wrinkled clothes" with "scuffed shoes" braving the world of the ultrachic; a "four dollar" small town haircut in a "fifteen dollar" big city salon. Laura's article also reflects the shock of change, old expectations confronted with a strange new world. Where were the old safe stereotypes:

the "middle-aged women with short, tightly curled permanents" giving "short, tightly curled permanents to other middle-aged women"; "the dog-eared copies of *Screen World* and *Photoplay*"; "the platinum bouffant blondes in pink nylon uniforms"? She is the initiate in an unknown ritual with gowns "you don't understand," in a place "you don't understand."

Laura's experience compares to any situation where you played the role of a "pledge" entering the sacrosanct realm of the "initiated." Did you ever find yourself the "new kid" at a school where everyone else knew each other? Were you ever at a party as someone's "date," where everyone else was a childhood friend who talked about people you didn't know, going places you'd never heard of? Were you ever the "guest" at someone else's reunion party with no one to reunite with?

Social worlds erect invisible walls. Have you ever felt on the outside of one of those walls looking in? What were the props that held up those walls? What created the atmosphere of the "insider's" world? How did the initiated dress, walk, speak, and act? What made you feel like the "outsider"? Was there a form of hazing or testing, an unspoken *rite de passage* you had to endure to gain entry? Did you want entry or did you prefer your own uncomfortable solitude to the artificial values of the crowd?

Student Example Paper Reacting to "Styling in Style"

STYLING IN STYLE NATURALLY

In Laura Parker's article entitled "Styling in Style—A Hair Raising (and Shortening) Experience," Laura nervously went to a professional beauty shop to have her hair styled. She plunged irretrievably into a swirling world of fashion. Everything was perfectly beautiful, too perfect and too beautiful for Laura's "$4 haircut, scuffed shoes and wrinkled clothes."

Laura felt out of place and found herself intimidated by the strange chic atmosphere of carpeted floors, hanging plants, European *Vogue* magazines, photographs of models with exotic haircuts, and all those beautiful people.

She wanted her hair styled, but she didn't know how she wanted it styled. She didn't know what was in style. Laura was unprepared for the flamboyant Hollywood-style treatment and the male European hairdresser that invariably reproduced his "oscar" winning haircut insisting that it was her.

Laura's feelings are not isolated. I have also felt out of place and intimidated by strange surroundings in a similar hair shortening experience.

For years I laboriously cooked my thick dark mass of kinks into perfect straightness with hot pressing irons and chemical hair straightening solutions. That was the style. But the 1960s tapped a dormant vein; black was once again beautiful, and "natural" hairstyles were springing up everywhere.

After several months of debate, inquiry, and tediously searching through the yellow pages, I reluctantly made a late afternoon appointment with a Mr. Charles at Magnificent Shears in south Seattle. A friendly male voice assisted me with directions.

I drove south on Rainier Avenue repeating the directions aloud, my eyes darting from sign to sign until Magnificent Shears winked at me. "Sure is a small shop. Well, maybe there'll only be a few people inside," I thought.

I slowly pushed the door in and squeezed down a narrow carpeted aisle lined with four large, black barber chairs on the right and four small, white studio chairs on the left. Behind each barber chair there was a large mirror, a porcelain basin, and a shelf of Afro Sheen, Afro combs, blow dryers, blow-out kits, everything possibly needed for a perfect natural.

An attractive young black male with a large, perfectly cut natural standing behind the only vacant chair inquiringly announced my entrance. I nodded in recognition. Smiling confidently, he swept the large, satin black and white bib across the chair, introduced himself as Mr. Charles, and directed me to step up and sit down.

I hesitated, wanting to turn and run out the door. But there was no place to go except straight ahead. There was hardly room to turn around.

I sat down. Mr. Charles stood behind the chair, the bib draped over his arm. He smiled into the mirror at me as he spun the chair around stopping it with his foot. I faced him momentarily looking away into the mirror at the photographs that I had only caught a spinning glimpse of. Each photograph was of a different model with a different styled Afro: long, fluffy Afros, short curly Afros, Afros parted down the middle, Afros parted on the side, and shag Afros.

"Good afternoon sister, you want your hair cut into an Afro, huh! Well you've come to the best shop in Seattle. What style of Afro would you prefer?" Mr. Charles sang uninterrupted.

"What style?" I stammered. I had thought that Afro was the style. Admitting my ignorance, I asked if he could suggest a suitable style.

He smiled gleefully, assured me that he knew the perfect style for me, and proceeded to explain the haircut snip by snip. He informed me that my hair was badly damaged from too much heat, too much coloring, and too little conditioning. "Your hair will have to be trimmed considerably, but relax, I have a fantastic style for you. You'll love it. It'll be together," he affirmed.

"Okay," I dryly squeaked as I sat perched on the edge of the large, black chair. I slowly slid back, breathed deeply, and tried to relax.

Mr. Charles reached for a pair of small, silver scissors, and I closed my eyes. Every hair style that I had ever worn flashed with each snip.

A sharp snap of the bib signaled his completion. "Finally he's finished," I thought. I anxiously peered into the mirror, but I was completely unprepared for the unveiling my eyes saw. Like Laura, I too was confronted with a perfect haircut, but not perfect for this sister. My hair was too short. It didn't even cover my head which seemed to have doubled in size. "I should never have come here," I silently scolded as I handed him twenty dollars.

Mr. Charles smiled approvingly. With difficulty I squeezed out a tight smile, thanked him, and hurriedly slipped out the door.

—Gwendolyn Jones

Questions and Exercises on "Styling in Style Naturally"

1. How does the writer use verbs to re-create sounds and effects?
2. Find examples of scenes where your view is controlled by being inside of the writer.
3. How does the writer re-create a natural tone of voice in her dialogue?
4. How does the writer pull the two incidents together even though they end differently?

THE ENDLESS STREETCAR RIDE INTO THE NIGHT, AND THE TINFOIL NOOSE[2]

JEAN SHEPHERD

Jean Shepherd (1921—   ) is a man of many talents. Besides having his own weekly radio and television show, he has acted on the Broadway stage and written articles and short stories for numerous publications. He is best known for his satires of the American scene.

---

[2]Jean Shepherd, "The Endless Streetcar Ride into the Night, and the Tinfoil Noose" from *In God We Trust, All Others Pay Cash* by Jean Shepherd, copyright © 1966 by Jean Shepherd. Reprinted by permission of Doubleday & Co.

Mewling, puking babes. That's the way we all start. Damply clinging to someone's shoulder, burping weakly, clawing our way into life. *All* of us. Then gradually, surely, we begin to divide into two streams, all marching together up that long yellow brick road of life, but on opposite sides of the street. One crowd goes on to become the Official people, peering out at us from television screens, magazine covers. They are forever appearing in newsreels, carrying attaché cases, surrounded by banks of microphones while the world waits for their decisions and statements. And the rest of us go on to become . . . just us.

They are the Prime Ministers, the Presidents, Cabinet members, Stars, dynamic molders of the Universe, while we remain forever the onlookers, the applauders of their real lives.

Forever down in the dark dungeons of our souls we ask ourselves:

"How did they get away from me? When did I make that first misstep that took me forever to the wrong side of the street, to become eternally part of the accursed, anonymous Audience?"

It seems like one minute we're all playing around back of the garage, kicking tin cans and yelling at girls, and the next instant you find yourself doomed to exist as an office boy in the Mail Room of Life, while another ex-mewling, puking babe sends down Dicta, says "No comment" to the Press, and lives a real, genuine *Life* on the screen of the world.

Countless sufferers at this hour are spending billions of dollars and endless man hours lying on analysts' couches, trying to pinpoint the exact moment that they stepped off the track and into the bushes forever.

It all hinges on one sinister reality that is rarely mentioned, no doubt due to its implacable, irreversible inevitability. These decisions cannot be changed, no matter how many brightly cheerful, buoyantly optimistic books on HOW TO ACHIEVE A RICHER, FULLER, MORE BOUNTIFUL LIFE or SEVEN MAGIC GOLDEN KEYS TO INSTANT DYNAMIC SUCCESS or THE SECRET OF HOW TO BECOME A BILLIONAIRE we read, or how many classes are attended for instruction in handshaking, back-slapping, grinning, and making After-Dinner speeches. Joseph Stalin was not a Dale Carnegie graduate. He went all the way. It is an unpleasant truth that is swallowed, if at all, like a rancid, bitter pill. A star is a star; a numberless cipher is a numberless cipher.

Even more eerie a fact is that the Great Divide is rarely a matter of talent or personality. Or even luck. Adolf Hitler had a notoriously weak handshake. His smile was, if anything, a vapid mockery. But inevitably his star zoomed higher and higher. Cinema luminaries of the first order are rarely blessed with even the modicum of Talent, and often their physical beauty leaves much to be desired. What is the difference between Us and Them, We and They, the Big Ones and the great, teeming rabble?

There are about four times in a man's life, or a woman's, too, for that matter, when unexpectedly, from out of the darkness, the blazing carbon lamp, the cosmic searchlight of Truth shines full upon them. It is how we react to those moments that forever seals our fate. One crowd simply puts on its sunglasses, lights another cigar, and heads for the nearest plush French restaurant in the jazziest section of town, sits down and orders a drink, and ignores the whole thing. While we, the Doomed, caught in the brilliant glare of illumination, see ourselves inescapably for what we are, and from that day on skulk in the weeds, hoping no one else will spot us.

Those moments happen when we are least able to fend them off. I caught the first one full in the face when I was fourteen. The fourteenth summer is a magic one for all kids. You have just slid out of the pupa stage, leaving your old baby skin behind, and have not yet become a grizzled, hardened, tax-paying beetle. At fourteen you are made of cellophane. You curl easily and everyone can see through you.

When I was fourteen, Life was flowing through me in a deep, rich torrent of Castoria. How did I know that the first rocks were just ahead, and I was about to have my keel ripped out on the reef? Sometimes you feel as though you are alone in a rented rowboat, bailing like mad in the darkness with a leaky bailing can. It is important to know that there are at least two billion other ciphers in the same boat, bailing with the same leaky can. They all think they are alone and are crossed with an evil star. They are right.

I'm fourteen years old, in my sophomore year at high school. One day Schwartz, my purported best friend, sidled up to me edgily outside of school while we were waiting on the steps to come in after lunch. He proceeded to outline his plan:

"Helen's old man won't let me take her out on a date on Saturday night unless I get a date for her girlfriend. A double date. The old coot figures, I guess, that if there are four of us there won't be no monkey business. Well, how about it? Do you want to go on a blind date with this chick? I never seen her."

Well. For years I had this principle—absolutely *no* blind dates. I was a man of perception and of taste, and life was short. But there is a time in your life when you have to stop taking and begin to give a little. For the first time the warmth of sweet Human Charity brought the roses to my cheeks. After all, Schwartz was my friend. It was little enough to do, have a blind date with some no doubt skinny, pimply girl for your best friend. I would do it for Schwartz. He would do as much for me.

"Okay. Okay, Schwartz."

Then followed the usual ribald remarks, reckless boasting, and dirty jokes about dates in general and girls in particular. It was decided that next Saturday we would go all the way. I had a morning paper route at the time, and my life savings stood at about $1.80. I was all set to blow it on one big night.

I will never forget that particular Saturday as long as I live. The air was as soft as the finest of spun silk. The scent of lilacs hung heavy. The catalpa trees rustled in the early evening breeze from off the Lake. The inner Me itched in that nameless way, that indescribable way that only the fourteen-year-old Male fully knows.

All that afternoon I had carefully gone over my wardrobe to select the proper symphony of sartorial brilliance. That night I set out wearing my magnificent electric blue sport coat, whose shoulders were so wide that they hung out over my frame like vast, drooping eaves, so wide I had difficulty going through an ordinary door head-on. The electric blue sport coat that draped voluminously almost to my knees, its wide lapels flapping soundlessly in the slightest breeze. My pleated gray flannel slacks began just below my breastbone and indeed chafed my armpits. High-belted, cascading down finally to grasp my ankles in a vise-like grip. My tie, indeed one of my most prized possessions, had been a gift from my Aunt Glenn upon the state occasion of graduation from eighth grade. It was of a beautiful silky fabric, silvery pearly colored, four inches wide at the fulcrum, and of such a length to endanger occasionally my zipper in moments of haste. Hand-painted upon it was a magnificent blood-red snail.

I had spent fully two hours carefully arranging and rearranging my great mop of wavy hair, into which I had rubbed fully a pound and a half of Greasy Kid Stuff.

Helen and Schwartz waited on the corner under the streetlight at the streetcar stop near Junie Jo's home. Her name was Junie Jo Prewitt. I won't forget it quickly, although she has, no doubt, forgotten mine. I walked down the dark street alone, past houses set back off the street, through the darkness, past privet hedges, under elm trees, through air rich and ripe with promise. Her house stood back from the street even farther than the others. It sort of crouched in the darkness, looking out at me, kneeling. Pregnant with Girldom. A real Girlfriend house.

The first faint touch of nervousness filtered through the marrow of my skullbone as I knocked on the door of the screen-enclosed porch. No answer. I knocked again, louder. Through the murky screens I could see faint lights in the house itself. Still no answer. Then I found a small doorbell button buried in the sash. I pressed. From far off in the bowels of the house I heard two chimes "Bong" politely. It sure didn't sound like our doorbell. We had a real ripper that went off like a broken buzz saw, more of a BRRRAAAAKKK than a muffled Bong. This was a rich people's doorbell.

The door opened and there stood a real, genuine, gold-plated Father: potbelly, underwear shirt, suspenders, and all.

"Well?" he asked.

For one blinding moment of embarrassment I couldn't remember her name. After all, she was a blind date. I couldn't just say:

"I'm here to pick up some girl."

He turned back into the house and hollered:"JUNIE JO! SOME KID'S HERE!"

"Heh, heh. . . ." I countered.

He led me into the living room. It was an itchy house, sticky stucco walls of a dull orange color, and all over the floor this Oriental rug with the design crawling around, making loops and swirls. I sat on an over-stuffed chair covered in stiff green mohair that scratched even through my slacks. Little twisty bridge lamps stood everywhere. I instantly began to sweat down the back of my clean white shirt. Like I said, it was a very itchy house. It had little lamps sticking out of the walls that looked like phony candles, with phony glass orange flames. The rug started moaning to itself.

I sat on the edge of the chair and tried to talk to this Father. He was a Cub fan. We struggled under water for what seemed like an hour and a half, when suddenly I heard someone coming down the stairs. First the feet; then those legs, and there she was. She was magnificent! The greatest-looking girl I ever saw in my life! I have hit the double jackpot! And on a blind date! Great Scot!

My senses actually reeled as I clutched the arm of that bilge-green chair for support. Junie Jo Prewitt made Cleopatra look like a a Girl Scout!

Five minutes later we are sitting in the streetcar, heading toward the bowling alley. I am sitting next to the most fantastic creation in the Feminine department known to Western man. There are the four of us in that long, yellow-lit streetcar. No one else was aboard; just us four. I, naturally, being a trained gentleman, sat on the aisle to protect her from candy wrappers and cigar butts and such. Directly ahead of me, also on the aisle, sat Schwartz, his arm already flung affectionately in a death grip around Helen's neck as we boomed and rattled through the night.

I casually flung my right foot up onto my left knee so that she could see my crepe-soled, perforated, wing-toed, Scotch bluchers with the two-toned laces. I started to work my famous charm on her. Casually, with my practiced offhand, cynical, cutting, sardonic humor I told her about how my Old Man had cracked the block in the Oldsmobile, how the White Sox were going to have a good year this year, how my kid brother wet his pants when he saw a snake, how I figured it was going to rain, what a great guy Schwartz was, what a good second baseman I was, how I figured I might go out for football. On and on I rolled, like

Old Man River, pausing significantly for her to pick up the conversation. Nothing.

Ahead of us Schwartz and Helen were almost indistinguishable one from the other. They giggled, bit each other's ears, whispered, clasped hands, and in general made me itch even more.

From time to time Junie Jo would bend forward stiffly from the waist and say something I could never quite catch into Helen's right ear.

I told her my great story of the time that Uncle Carl lost his false teeth down the airshaft. Still nothing. Out of the corner of my eye I could see that she had her coat collar turned up, hiding most of her face as she sat silently, looking forward past Helen Weathers into nothingness.

I told her about this old lady on my paper route who chews tobacco, and roller skates in the backyard every morning. I still couldn't get through to her. Casually I inched my right arm up over the back of the seat behind her shoulders. The acid test. She leaned forward, avoiding my arm, and stayed that way.

"Heh, heh, heh. . . ."

As nonchalantly as I could, I retrieved it, battling a giant cramp in my right shoulder blade. I sat in silence for a few seconds, sweating heavily as ahead Schwartz and Helen are going at it hot and heavy.

It was then that I became aware of someone saying something to me. It was an empty car. There was no one else but us. I glanced around, and there it was. Above us a line of car cards looked down on the empty streetcar. One was speaking directly to me, to me alone.

DO YOU OFFEND?

Do I *offend*?!

With no warning, from up near the front of the car where the motorman is steering I see this thing coming down the aisle directly toward *me*. It's coming closer and closer. I can't escape it. It's this blinding, fantastic, brilliant, screaming blue light. I am spread-eagled in it. There's a pin sticking through my thorax. I see it all now.

I am the BLIND DATE!

ME!!

I'M the one they're being nice to!

I'm suddenly getting fatter, more itchy. My new shoes are like bowling balls with laces; thick, rubber-crepe bowling balls. My great tie that Aunt Glenn gave me is two feet wide, hanging down to the floor like some crinkly tinfoil noose. My beautiful hand-painted snail is seven feet high, sitting up on my shoulder, burping. Great Scot! It is all clear to me in the searing white light of Truth. My friend Schwartz, I can see him saying to Junie Jo:

"I got this crummy fat friend who never has a date. Let's give him a break and. . . ."

I AM THE BLIND DATE!

They are being nice to *me!* She is the one who is out on a Blind Date. A Blind Date that didn't make it.

In the seat ahead, the merriment rose to a crescendo. Helen tittered; Schwartz cackled. The marble statue next to me stared gloomily out into the darkness as our streetcar rattled on. The ride went on and on.

I AM THE BLIND DATE!

I didn't say much the rest of the night. There wasn't much to be said.

Writing Suggestions for Jean Shepherd's "The Endless Streetcar Ride into the Night, and the Tinfoil Noose"

The beginning of the essay divides the world into "insiders" and "outsiders," "official people," and "the anonymous audience," "stars" versus "numberless ciphers." It then goes on to re-create the painful experience of feeling "out of it" on a first blind date.

The experience can be adapted to any time you felt unbearably awkward, ugly, embarrassed, dumb, or just plain unwanted. If you can remember such an experience, try to re-create it in the subjective portion of your essay, using the same techniques that work for Jean Shepherd. Re-create scenes in detail such as the two-hour clothes preparation scene. Laugh at yourself in retrospect. Re-create your nervousness and its effects on your conversation, your mannerisms, your coordination. Catch others' behavior and the details that stick in your mind. Just how did that doorbell sound? Do you remember the equivalent of a "JUNIE JO! SOME KID'S HERE!" line? Did you have an "arm up over the back of the seat behind her shoulders" test that failed?

Can you pinpoint your moment of intense embarrassment, of spotlighted pain—the awareness of a "Do you offend?" sign meaning you? Try to capture how your change in perspective changed the way you saw yourself. Did you suddenly feel "fatter," "more itchy"?

Contrast your experience to the one in the story. Were you the one to end up with the awkward date? How did he or she look and act? How could you detect the awkwardness or shyness that made the situation more unbearable? Or was your date forward and aggressive and you too polite or shy to show you really didn't like him or her? Can you now see the subtle rejection or cruelty practiced on the "outsider"? Any situation that has "insiders" and "outsiders" can be adapted to the subjective reaction portion of your paper whether you were a "star" or a "numberless cipher," an "official person" or one of the "accursed, anonymous audience." Whichever role you played, be aware of your adult perspective on the scene; let your humanity be reflected indirectly in your double role as adult reflector and adolescent participant.

Student Example Papers Reacting to "The Endless Streetcar Ride into the Night, and the Tinfoil Noose"

LIFE'S LITTLE PAINS

In the story "The Endless Streetcar Ride into the Night, and the Tinfoil Noose," the author, Jean Shepherd, communicates his estimation of how some squealing baby humans get to be famous, high living adults, and others go along life's road to become the average face bobbing in the crowd. The author believes there are times when the proverbial bulb is lit, and most of us realize that our route is plotted out before us. Long before we see the stars patting at drawn butter on their pancake chins, we regulars distinguish our path through a warmed up tuna casserole and a drive-in movie.

The author implies that, as children, we all advance on the journey from a common starting block. Beginning at full speed and racing toward the grand road, some of us falter: our special sprinting shoes wear down, delicate ankles twist, and we stagger. Never do we catch up with the golden figures which are disappearing into the folds of our favorite magazine. Everytime we stop to bandage an aching limb, we are hit right center in the face with the future. It's all laid out in the potholes of the trail. Some of us will stumble, while others will leap ahead to grab the shiny, blue ribbon of success accomplished.

Jean Shepherd, in his story, relates a time when on his first blind date, he was reaching out to take first prize, and how he unexpectedly ended up choking on dust from the inside of a pit on the track. He was fourteen and a top runner. He knew the entrance to easy times had a closed sign on the gate, when the firm hand of the official shook his shoulder and told him he'd might as well take another lap.

Oddly enough, a time in my life when I felt completely in tune with what the author was relating occurred when I, too, was an oblivious fourteen-year-old. I wound to the end of this inevitable evening feeling as if I had walked into the middle of a serious event wearing a set of Mickey Mouse ears and gym shorts.

The gold cup prize when I was in the ninth grade was the captain of the basketball team, Tim Berg. He was in my Algebra class struggling along with every formula. I willingly gave my helping hand for it was my hope that he would get through his x's and y's and discover me. I had more than a desire to enlighten him into the world of mathematics: I had visions of being one of the girls he would talk to in the hall before class.

Oh, you know the girls I speak of here. They were all picture perfect to me then, and all possessed the one thing I wanted more than anything in the world: straight hair. They had hair that could be sleek and smooth without tape, fourteen orange juice cans, or two pounds of Dippity-Do. I knew that the only thing that kept me from being a receiver of Tim's after class attention was my wavy, lumpy locks.

One crisp October evening, I knew that my time had come. A dance was being held at a school near my house, and Tim was going to be there. That day after school, I spent hours taming my wild follicles to fall ever so nicely around my face.

The evening was heaven. Tim asked me to dance almost every tune and then offered to walk me home. When we arrived at my front porch and I came out of my smiling stupor, I realized that the misty evening had ruined my silky hairdo. I only wanted him to kiss me good night, so I could run inside before the bird's nest twisting on my scalp reached out and woke him up also.

He was just about to give me the traditional ninth grade smack, when I saw his eyes look to something over my head. I turned to see what it was and saw my mother's eyes peeking out the kitchen window. Tim muttered something about seeing me in school Monday, and then he left immediately.

So much for my chance to break into the butter-on-the-chin crowd. I tried to convince myself that if he hadn't stopped to see my mother's accusing stare, he would never have noticed the state of my frizzled head. I can see now that everything that happened that evening was just another of the times Jean Shepherd speaks of in his story. I was discovering the differences in people along the highway, and I was learning a painful lesson in life.

—Charlene Nadeau

Questions on "Life's Little Pains"

1. Does presenting the ideas of Jean Shepherd's essay using a racetrack comparison work?
2. What details help create humor in this paper?
3. How does the writer reflect her opening in her ending?

THE LIGHT

Jean Shepherd, in his story "The Endless Streetcar Ride into the Night, and the Tinfoil Noose," begins with the sentences "Mewling, puking babes. That's the way we all start." Then he goes on to say that as time goes by, we are separated into two groups; those who seem to have all that it takes to be wonderful, and those, the rest of us, that spend time envying and worshipping the others. We wonder why we can't be like the wonderful ones, what makes the difference, and go through life trying to find the right formula, the right tricks to join the "star" group. We do this until something happens, until the light dawns, and we're made to see what we really are.

The two groups in life for me were those who had parents and knew them and those who had been adopted. There were also those who had two Black parents or two Korean parents and those, like me, who had, must have had, one of each.

I was a Korean orphan, a byproduct of the U.S. involvement in Korea. My life there could not have been very promising as children of mixed parentage are not well received. I was fortunate. I was adopted by a black family here in the States and have had the good life of most American children. I got a whole family: sisters, brothers, aunts, uncles, as well as parents. I got new clothes, plenty to eat, a chance to get an education, to get a good job, to marry, and to have a family of my own. Thoughts of Korea have not been a part of my life. I was adopted at the age of three and am completely Americanized. I have never had any desire to study Korea, or for that matter, any country in that part of the world. I've spent most of the time wishing that I had "normal" eyes like all the rest of the family, that I was just a little bit darker, and that I could write something else instead of Seoul, Korea, in blanks marked city and state for birthplace.

For the first three and one-half years of my life, I was Korean. I ate, slept, drank, walked, and talked Korean. When I first got here, every Oriental face I saw (I'm told) was a great wonder to me. But as I got older and came to feel that I was black, I wanted as little to do with the Korean part as possible. I've forgotten everything; after all, I was very young, and after all, I'm black now.

I was at the airport one day, waiting to board a plane. I was traveling by myself, and I was excited about my trip for it would end in France. It was announced that the airplane was ready for boarding. I hefted my hand luggage and moved into the line. I could see the stewardesses smiling and taking the tickets as each passenger got onto the plane. There were about twenty people in front of me; the rest were saying last minute good-byes and then taking places behind me. I was wondering who my seat partners would be. I had a window seat; I hoped it wouldn't be right on top of the wing.

Then I heard this soft singing behind me, a kind of "bum bum bitty bum bum," not humming really, but a kind of sing-song. "Korean," I thought immediately. I turned to look, and there was a young Oriental woman carrying a little girl about two years old. I smiled, and she smiled back, continuing to sing to her child.

Another woman in the line commented on the beauty of the little girl, and then asked the young woman where they were from. She answered that they were Korean and said the little girl's name; I forget it now. The other woman fussed and complimented and carried on, but I filled my eyes with this young woman and her little girl.

The woman was serene and smiling, singing gently, loving that baby. In that moment, she was the most beautiful woman I had ever seen. She was delicate and soft-spoken, with eyes just like mine, long body and short limbs—just like mine. I could have looked at her forever. Surely she was the image of my own mother.

The little girl was like a beautiful doll. She was so utterly secure there in her mother's arms, that she seemed almost arrogant. She had one arm around her mother's neck and looked out upon the world fearlessly.

The stewardess took my ticket, and I found my seat, which was not over the wing. Mother and child took seats in the same row, but on the other side of the airplane. I was embarrassed with looking at them now and gazed out the window, seeing nothing. Impossible, unanswerable thoughts grew in my head. Was my mother like that? Did she ever sing to me? Did she ever think about me? Was she alive? Did she care? On and on. I looked over again at the woman. The little girl had fallen asleep.

"It doesn't matter," she seemed to say.

My light, what dawned on me that day, was that while I was neither all Korean, nor all Black, I certainly had enough of both to be whole. When I arrived here in this country, for the first time, I, too, looked upon the world fearlessly from the arms of my new-found parents.

—Linnie Gray

Questions on "The Light"

1. Which summary of Jean Shepherd's essay did you prefer, the one in "Life's Little Pains" or the one in "The Light?" How did the summaries differ?

2. What interpretation of the "two groups" theme does the writer base her personal reaction on?

3. Which details clarify the writer's emotional reactions?

4. What does the writer achieve by focusing on the child as well as the woman?

5. What wording helps bring the paper back to the original essay at the end?

I LEAVE THE PRISON[3]

FEODOR DOSTOYEVSKY

Feodor Dostoyevsky (1821–1881) is one of the great Russian writers.

In his youth, he joined an idealistic reform group in Moscow and was imprisoned and sentenced to death as a subversive by the czar. On December 21, 1849, he and his friends were led to a square and bound to execution posts. The death sentence was read, a cross was given to each to kiss, and the symbolic sword was broken over their heads.

Suddenly a messenger on horseback interrupted the proceedings bearing the czar's message that commuted their sentences from death to imprisonment. The scene had been a cruel farce. The czar had wanted to impress a lesson on the youths.

Some of the prisoners fainted—two went insane. Dostoyevsky was sent to Siberia where he spent five years as a political prisoner. "I Leave the Prison" is the final chapter of his novel *Memoirs from the House of the Dead*, which describes the horrors of his prison experience.

. . . I had already reached the last year of my penal servitude. This last year, and especially the very end of my time in the prison, is almost as clear in my memory as the first one. But why should I talk of the details? I recall only that during that year, in spite of all my impatience to come quickly to the end of my term, I found life easier than during all the preceding years of my exile. In the first place, among the prisoners I had by now many friends and well-wishers, who had finally decided that I was a good man. Many of them were devoted to my interests and genuinely fond of me. The Pioneer was very near tears when he accompanied my companion and me out of the prison and when afterwards, although we had been released, we were kept a whole month in a government building in the town, he called on us nearly every day, simply in order to see us. There were, however, also some characters who were unfriendly to the end and who, God knows why, seemed to

[3]F. M. Dostoyevsky, "I Leave the Prison" from *Memoirs from the House of the Dead* by F. M. Dostoyevsky, translated by Jessie Coulson © Oxford University Press 1965. Reprinted by permission of the publisher.

find it a burden to exchange a word with me. There seemed to be a kind of barrier between them and me.

Towards the end I had more privileges than during all my time in prison. Some acquaintances of mine, and even some friends of my far-away schooldays, turned up among the officers serving in the town. I renewed my acquaintance with them. Through them I was able to possess more money, to write home, and even to get books. For several years I had not read a single book, and it is difficult to convey the strange and disturbing effect produced on me by the first book I read in prison. I remember that I began reading in the evening when the barracks were locked, and read all through the night, until daybreak. It was a number of a magazine. It was as though news from that other world had come through to me; my former life rose before me in all its brightness, and I strove to guess from what I read whether I had lagged far behind that world, whether much had happened in my absence, what was exciting people there now, and what questions occupied their minds. I worried every word, tried to read between the lines, and strove to find hidden meanings and allusions to the past; I searched for traces of the things that had excited men before, in my time, and how sad it was for me to recognize to what extent I was now indeed a stranger to this new life, cut off and isolated. I should have to get used to new things and learn to know a new generation. I devoured particularly eagerly an article under which I found the name of a man I once knew intimately. . . . But new names as well resounded now: new leaders had appeared, and I was greedily impatient to get to know them and fretted because I could see so few books in prospect and because it was so difficult to acquire them. Previously, indeed, under the old major, it had been dangerous to bring books into the prison. In the event of a search there would inevitably be questions: 'Where did the books come from?' 'When did you get them?' 'So you have connexions outside?' . . . And what could I have replied to such questions? So it was that, living without books, I had become wrapped up in myself, had set myself problems, tried to solve them, and sometimes tormented myself with them . . . But it is surely impossible to convey all this! . . .

I had entered the prison in winter, and therefore I was to emerge into freedom in winter, on the same day of the month as I had arrived. With what impatience I waited for the winter, with what joy, at the end of summer, I watched the leaves fade on the trees and the grass wither on the steppe. Now summer was already over, and the winds of autumn had begun to howl; now the first hesitant snowflakes began to drift down. . . . At last the winter, so long awaited, had arrived. At times my heart would begin to beat thickly and heavily with the anticipation of freedom. But strange to say the more time went by and the nearer the end came, the more patient I became. During the very last few days I was even surprised, and reproached myself: it seemed to me that I had become callous and indifferent. Many of the prisoners, meeting me in the courtyard during our leisure time, talked to me and congratulated me.

'See now, Alexander Petrovich, sir, you'll be free soon, very soon. You are leaving us poor fellows all alone.'

'And will it be soon for you too, Martynov?' I would answer.

'Me? What a hope! I've got another seven years to drag through. . . .'

And he would sigh and stand still, with an absent look, as though he were gazing into the future. It seemed to me that all of them had begun to be more friendly to me. I had visibly ceased to be one of themselves; they were already saying good-bye to me. One of the Polish gentlemen, a quiet and unassuming young man, was, like me, fond of walking in the yard in our leisure time. He thought the fresh air and exercise preserved his health and compensated for all the harm done by the stuffy nights in barracks. 'I am waiting impatiently for you to leave,' he said to me with a smile, meeting me once on his walk; 'when you leave, *I shall know* that I have exactly a year left before I get out.'

I will mention here in passing that, in consequence of our daydreams and our long divorce from it, freedom somehow seemed to us freer than real freedom, the freedom, that is, that exists in fact, in real life. The prisoners exaggerated the idea of real freedom, and that is very natural and characteristic of all prisoners. Any ragamuffin of an officer's batman was for us all but a king, all but the ideal of the free man, compared with the prisoners, because he could go about unshaved and without fetters or guards.

On the eve of my release, at twilight, I walked *for the last time* round the prison stockade. How many thousand times I had walked round it during all those years! How, behind the barracks, I used to linger in my first year, solitary, friendless, and dejected! I remember calculating then how many thousand days still lay before me. Great God, how long ago it was! Here in this corner our eagle lived out his captivity; here Petrov and I often used to meet. Even now, he had not deserted me. He came running up and, as though guessing my thoughts, walked silently at my side, like a man wondering to himself about something. Mentally I took my leave of the blackened, rough-hewn timbers of the barracks. How unfriendly had been the impression they had made on me *then*, at first! Even they must have grown older since then, but I could see no sign of it. And how much youth had gone to waste within those walls, what great powers had perished uselessly there! For the whole truth must be told: these indeed were no ordinary men. Perhaps, indeed, they were the most highly gifted and the strongest of all our people. But these powerful forces were condemned to perish uselessly, unnaturally, wrongfully, irrevocably. And whose is the blame?

That is the question, whose is the blame?

Next morning early, before the prisoners went to their work, when it was just beginning to grow light, I went round all the barracks to say good-bye to all the prisoners. Many strong, calloused hands stretched out to me in friendship. Some shook mine like comrades, but they were not many. Others understood very well that I was on the point of becoming an entirely different man from them. They knew I had friends in the town and that I should go straight from them to the *bosses* and would sit down beside those bosses as their equal. They knew this, and said good-bye to me, though in a pleasant and friendly enough way, not at all as they would do to a comrade, but as if to a gentleman. Some turned away from me and surlily refused to answer my farewell. A few even eyed me with something like hatred.

The drum beat, and everybody went off to work, but I remained behind. Sushilov that morning had been almost the first to get up and had worked anxiously and earnestly to make tea for me in time. Poor Sushilov! He cried when I gave him my old prison clothes, my shirts, my underfetters, and a little money.

'I don't want that, I don't want it!' he said, controlling his quivering lip with a great effort; 'how can I lose *you*, Alexander Petrovich? Who will be left for me here when you've gone?'

Last of all I said good-bye to Akim Akimovich.

'It will soon be your turn,' I said to him.

'I've got a long time, I've still got a very long time here,' he murmured, pressing my hand. I threw myself on his neck and we kissed.

Ten minutes after the prisoners, we too left the prison, never to return to it, I and the companion with whom I had arrived. We had to go straight to the smithy to have our fetters struck off. But there was no longer an armed guard to escort us: we went with a sergeant. It was our own prisoners who struck off our fetters in the engineering shops. I waited while my companion's fetters were removed, and then went up to the anvil. The smiths turned me round with my back to them, lifted my foot from behind, and put it on the anvil. . . .

'The rivet, the rivet, turn the rivet first of all!' commanded the foreman. 'Hold it there, like that, that's right. . . . Now strike it with the hammer. . . .'

The fetters fell away. I lifted them up . . . I wanted to hold them in my hand and look at them for the last time. It seemed amazing how that it was my legs they had been on a moment ago.

'Well, God be with you. God be with you!' said the prisoners, in gruff, abrupt, yet pleased tones.

Yes, God was with us! Freedom, a new life, resurrection from the dead . . . What a glorious moment!

Writing Suggestions for Dostoyevsky's "I Leave the Prison"

While you certainly never have experienced Siberian imprisonment, you may have experienced other extended unpleasant situations that you left with mixed emotions. Any extended period in life produces friends, ties, memories, and includes a structure you come to associate with habit and a kind of security. Leaving even a "bad" known for an unknown can be a frightening experience.

Have you ever recognized a period in your life as reaching an end point and experienced the mixture of longing for the past, fear, and excitement that such a moment can produce? Such an experience can be created by leaving the military, leaving home, finishing school, leaving a job, or ending a marriage that didn't work out. Life's prisons do not always have physical walls.

If Dostoyevsky's experience relates somehow to your own experience, scan his reactions and compare them with your own. Did you too feel there was an "outside" world that you had "lagged far behind" and lost touch with? Did you hunger for information of this "outside" world and look forward with fear and anticipation to rejoining it? Did you idealize the state of being "free," what it meant, and what you would do when you had regained it? Did you hate to leave certain people and friendships behind? What were the last hours of waiting for your moment of release like? What farewell rituals, both mental and physical, did you observe? What were people's reactions to your departure?

Few of us will ever experience having actual fetters struck from our feet so we can hold our past chains in our hands, but most of us can identify figurative "fetters" that at one time were binding. If you can identify the moment you felt your new found freedom, see if you can capture the specificity of that moment and all the subtleties of its mixed emotions.

Student Example Paper on Dostoyevsky's "I Leave the Prison"

A LEAVE-TAKING

"I Leave the Prison" is a short story by Feodor Dostoyevsky about his mixed feelings on leaving the torment of prison with its fetters and privations. Dostoyevsky experiences a sense of loss at knowing he will never again be part of that community, will never again share the other prisoners' lives on such a close level. The greatest wrench occurs when one is forced to leave good friends and good times behind—

completely entwined in a painful situation which must be ended. The friendships become the baby aborted to save the mother's life.

As I was reading, I kept remembering my own emotions and reactions on the ending of my marriage. Dostoyevsky describes his feelings as he took the last walk around the camp—the terrible waste and futility of it all, the disbelief that the time had actually passed. I remember when I left the counselor's office that unbelievably tense, lacerating day when the reality was finally acknowledged and walking into the heat of the afternoon. I kept remembering the early years, happy times, times of love, joy, and closeness, feeling a great melancholy for the loss. I also had a sensation of relief that the long months of counseling were over—the only possible ending had been started.

When the author talked about the prisoners' imaginings of freedom as being much greater than it really was, I recalled my own wistful longing for the same thing—the anticipated joy of being able to invite particular friends over, of going home to a house whose air no longer hung pregnant with tension and fury, seemed to have its own special magic—and, in fact, the glow lasted until eventually I began to take life for granted again.

I liked the detail Dostoyevsky used describing the final moments with the smithy, remembering the conversation even to the tone of voice. I can recall clearly the short, stocky psychologist crouched toward us in intensity—as if by becoming closer physically, he could more personally know our division. I can still see the dark, cool office, Ted's bitter face, and the childish art hung on the walls.

As I read the paragraph describing his taking leave of his friends, I remembered the unbelievable wrench I felt when I took leave of my husband—when through a bewildering maze of expectations and disappointments, we no longer were husband and wife. The terrible knowledge that the path must divide and that this breaking will cause great pain, yet must be accomplished—one's survival is completely dependent upon it—can be devastating, an experience that left me feeling shredded inside. I remember Ted with tears one day and curled lip and fist the next, but never a moment of understanding—and this was the greatest sadness for me. The realization that he could not begin to appreciate, or even acknowledge, the forces behind my leaving, that he could not admit it had caused me suffering, was hardest to accept.

The torment of recalling a kind, young man—naive, sweet, thoughtful, with a ready smile and affectionate hug, while living with an uncomprehending stranger who felt he had been tricked by his wife's growth from child to woman, contrasted with my need to be, to find air. I was disappointed that Dostoyevsky did not convey more sense of conflict in his essay—more emotion—a sense of being rendered. Sometimes I just wanted to throw my head back and let the agony pour out in sound.

In the final analysis, the effectiveness of a piece of writing is whether or not it works for the reader. Dostoyevsky's impressions of loss, of the euphoria of regained freedom, coupled with apprehension, recalled in me similar feelings. The intensity of my recollections testify to the success of his work.

—Sue Moran

Questions and Exercises on "A Leave-Taking"

1. How does the student reflect the order and details of Dostoyevsky's essay in her writing? How does she intensify the impact of her own situation through these comparisons?

2. Find examples of detailed descriptions that come through powerfully for you. How do the details achieve their effect?

3. Find examples of parallel constructions (repeated word patterns) in this essay. What effect is achieved by using these repeated structures?

4. How does the writer manage to both refocus on Dostoyevsky's work and blend it with her own experience in her final paragraph?

GRADUATION[4]

MAYA ANGELOU

Maya Angelou (1929–   ) is an international and diversified talent. She was a journalist in Cairo and a university lecturer in Ghana; she taught dance in Rome and Tel Aviv, and published her autobiography, *I Know Why the Caged Bird Sings*, in London.

She danced in *Porgy and Bess*, starred in Jean Genet's *The Blacks*, and produced, directed, and played one of the leads in *Cabaret for Freedom*, in collaboration with Godfrey Cambridge. Martin Luther King, Jr., requested that she act as Northern Coordinator for the Southern Christian Leadership Conference.

In addition to a book of poetry and a screenplay, she has written and produced a ten-part television series on the African traditions in American life.

The children in Stamps trembled visibly with anticipation. Some adults were excited too, but to be certain the whole young population had come down with graduation epidemic. Large classes were graduating from both the grammar school and the high school. Even those who

---

[4]Maya Angelou, "Graduation," from *I Know Why the Caged Bird Sings*, by Maya Angelou. Copyright © 1969 by Maya Angelou. Reprinted by permission of Random House, Inc. Title added.

were years removed from their own day of glorious release were anxious to help with preparations as a kind of dry run. The junior students who were moving into the vacating classes' chairs were tradition-bound to show their talents for leadership and management. They strutted through the school and around the campus exerting pressure on the lower grades. Their authority was so new that occasionally if they pressed a little too hard it had to be overlooked. After all, next term was coming, and it never hurt a sixth grader to have a play sister in the eighth grade, or a tenth-year student to be able to call a twelfth grader Bubba. So all was endured in a spirit of shared understanding. But the graduating classes themselves were the nobility. Like travelers with exotic destinations on their minds, the graduates were remarkably forgetful. They came to school without their books, or tablets or even pencils. Volunteers fell over themselves to secure replacements for the missing equipment. When accepted, the willing workers might or might not be thanked, and it was of no importance to the pregraduation rites. Even teachers were respectful of the now quiet and aging seniors, and tended to speak to them, if not as equals, as beings only slightly lower than themselves. After tests were returned and grades given, the student body, which acted like an extended family, knew who did well, who excelled, and what piteous ones had failed.

Unlike the white high school, Lafayette County Training School distinguished itself by having neither lawn, nor hedges, nor tennis court, nor climbing ivy. Its two buildings (main classrooms, the grade school and home economics) were set on a dirt hill with no fence to limit either its boundaries or those of bordering farms. There was a large expanse to the left of the school which was used alternately as a baseball diamond or a basketball court. Rusty hoops on the swaying poles represented the permanent recreational equipment, although bats and balls could be borrowed from the P. E. teacher if the borrower was qualified and if the diamond wasn't occupied.

Over this rocky area relieved by a few shady tall persimmon trees the graduating class walked. The girls often held hands and no longer bothered to speak to the lower students. There was a sadness about them, as if this old world was not their home and they were bound for higher ground. The boys, on the other hand, had become more friendly, more outgoing. A decided change from the closed attitude they projected while studying for finals. Now they seemed not ready to give up the old school, the familiar paths and classrooms. Only a small percentage would be continuing on to college—one of the South's A & M (agricultural and mechanical) schools, which trained Negro youths to be carpenters, farmers, handymen, masons, maids, cooks, and baby nurses. Their future rode heavily on their shoulders, and blinded them to the collective joy that had pervaded the lives of the boys and girls in the grammar school graduating class.

Parents who could afford it had ordered new shoes and ready-made clothes for themselves from Sears and Roebuck or Montgomery Ward. They also engaged the best seamstresses to make the floating graduating dresses and to cut down secondhand pants which would be pressed to a military slickness for the important event.

Oh, it was important, all right. Whitefolks would attend the ceremony, and two or three would speak of God and home, and the Southern way of life, and Mrs. Parsons, the principal's wife, would play the graduation march while the lower grade graduates paraded down the aisles and took their seats below the platform. The high school seniors would wait in empty classrooms to make their dramatic entrance.

In the Store I was the person of the moment. The birthday girl. The center. Bailey had graduated the year before, although to do so he had had to forfeit all pleasures to make up for his time lost in Baton Rouge.

My class was wearing butter-yellow piqué dresses, and Momma launched out on mine. She smocked the yoke into tiny crisscrossing puckers, then shirred the rest of the bodice. Her dark fingers ducked in and out of the lemony cloth as she embroidered raised daisies around the hem. Before she considered herself finished she had added a crocheted cuff on the puff sleeves, and a pointy crocheted collar.

I was going to be lovely. A walking model of all the various styles of fine hand sewing and it didn't worry me that I was only twelve years old and merely graduating from the eighth grade. Besides, many teachers in Arkansas Negro schools had only that diploma and were licensed to impart wisdom.

The days had become longer and more noticeable. The faded beige of former times had been replaced with strong and sure colors. I began to see my classmates' clothes, their skin tones, and the dust that waved off pussy willows. Clouds that lazed across the sky were objects of great concern to me. Their shiftier shapes might have held a message that in my new happiness and with a little bit of time I'd soon decipher. During that period I looked at the arch of heaven so religiously my neck kept a steady ache. I had taken to smiling more often, and my jaws hurt from the unaccustomed activity. Between the two physical sore spots, I suppose I could have been uncomfortable, but that was not the case. As a member of the winning team (the graduating class of 1940) I had outdistanced unpleasant sensations by miles. I was headed for the freedom of open fields.

Youth and social approval allied themselves with me and we trammeled memories of slights and insults. The wind of our swift passage remodeled my features. Lost tears were pounded to mud and then to dust. Years of withdrawal were brushed aside and left behind, as hanging ropes of parasitic moss.

My work alone had awarded me a top place and I was going to be one of the first called in the graduating ceremonies. On the classroom blackboard, as well as on the bulletin board in the auditorium, there were blue stars and white stars and red stars. No absences, no tardinesses, and my academic work was among the best of the year. I could say the preamble to the Constitution even faster than Bailey. We timed ourselves often: "WethepeopleoftheUnitedStates inordertoformamoreperfectunion. . . ." I had memorized the Presidents of the United States from Washington to Roosevelt in chronological as well as alphabetical order.

My hair pleased me too. Gradually the black mass had lengthened and thickened, so that it kept at last to its braided pattern, and I didn't have to yank my scalp off when I tried to comb it.

Louise and I had rehearsed the exercises until we tired out ourselves. Henry Reed was class valedictorian. He was a small, very black boy with hooded eyes, a long, broad nose and an oddly shaped head. I had admired him for years because each term he and I vied for the best grades in our class. Most often he bested me, but instead of being disappointed I was pleased that we shared top places between us. Like many Southern Black children, he lived with his grandmother, who was as strict as Momma and as kind as she knew how to be. He was courteous, respectful and soft-spoken to elders, but on the playground he chose to play the roughest games. I admired him. Anyone, I reckoned, sufficiently afraid or sufficiently dull could be polite. But to be able to operate at a top level with both adults and children was admirable.

His valedictory speech was entitled "To Be or Not to Be." The rigid tenth-grade teacher had helped him write it. He'd been working on the dramatic stresses for months.

The weeks until graduation were filled with heady activities. A group of small children were to be presented in a play about buttercups and daisies and bunny rabbits. They could be heard throughout the building practicing their hops and their little songs that sounded like silver bells. The older girls (nongraduates, of course) were assigned the task of making refreshments for the night's festivities. A tangy scent of ginger, cinnamon, nutmeg, and chocolate wafted around the home economics building as the budding cooks made samples for themselves and their teachers.

In every corner of the workshop, axes and saws split fresh timber as the woodshop boys made sets and stage scenery. Only the graduates were left out of the general bustle. We were free to sit in the library at the back of the building or look in quite detachedly, naturally, on the measures being taken for our event.

Even the minister preached on graduation the Sunday before. His subject was, "Let your light so shine that men will see your good works and praise your Father, Who is in Heaven." Although the sermon was purported to be addressed to us, he used the occasion to speak to backsliders, gamblers and general ne'er-do-wells. But since he had called our names at the beginning of the service we were mollified.

Among Negroes the tradition was to give presents to children going only from one grade to another. How much more important this was when the person was graduating at the top of the class. Uncle Willie and Momma had sent away for a Mickey Mouse watch like Bailey's. Louise gave me four embroidered handkerchiefs. (I gave her three crocheted doilies.) Mrs. Sneed, the minister's wife, made me an underskirt to wear for graduation, and nearly every customer gave me a nickel or maybe even a dime with the instruction "Keep on moving to higher ground," or some such encouragement.

Amazingly the great day finally dawned and I was out of bed before I knew it. I threw open the back door to see it more clearly, but Momma said, "Sister, come away from that door and put your robe on."

I hoped the memory of that morning would never leave me. Sunlight was itself still young, and the day had none of the insistence maturity would bring it in a few hours. In my robe and barefoot in the backyard, under cover of going to see about my new beans, I gave myself up to the gentle warmth and thanked God that no matter what evil I had done in my life He had allowed me to live to see this day. Somewhere in my fatalism I had expected to die, accidentally, and never have the chance to walk up the stairs in the auditorium and gracefully receive my hard-earned diploma. Out of God's merciful bosom I had won reprieve.

Bailey came out in his robe and gave me a box wrapped in Christmas paper. He said he had saved his money for months to pay for it. It felt like a box of chocolates, but I knew Bailey wouldn't save money to buy candy when we had all we could want under our noses.

He was as proud of the gift as I. It was a soft-leather-bound copy of a collection of poems by Edgar Allan Poe, or, as Bailey and I called him, "Eap." I turned to "Annabel Lee" and we walked up and down the garden rows, the cool dirt between our toes, reciting the beautifully sad lines.

Momma made a Sunday breakfast although it was only Friday. After we finished the blessing, I opened my eyes to find the watch on my plate. It was a dream of a day. Everything went smoothly and to my credit. I didn't have to be reminded or scolded for anything. Near evening I was too jittery to attend to chores, so Bailey volunteered to do all before his bath.

Days before, we had made a sign for the Store, and as we turned out the lights Momma hung the cardboard over the doorknob. It read clearly: CLOSED. GRADUATION.

My dress fitted perfectly and everyone said that I looked like a sunbeam in it. On the hill, going toward the school, Bailey walked behind with Uncle Willie, who muttered, "Go on, Ju." He wanted him to walk ahead with us because it embarrassed him to have to walk so slowly. Bailey said he'd let the ladies walk together, and the men would bring up the rear. We all laughed, nicely.

Little children dashed by out of the dark like fireflies. Their crepe-paper dresses and butterfly wings were not made for running and we heard more than one rip, dryly, and the regretful "uh uh" that followed.

The school blazed without gaiety. The windows seemed cold and unfriendly from the lower hill. A sense of ill-fated timing crept over me, and if Momma hadn't reached for my hand I would have drifted back to Bailey and Uncle Willie, and possibly beyond. She made a few slow jokes about my feet getting cold, and tugged me along to the now-strange building.

Around the front steps, assurance came back. There were my fellow "greats," the graduating class. Hair brushed back, legs oiled, new dresses and pressed pleats, fresh pocket handkerchiefs and little handbags, all homesewn. Oh, we were up to snuff, all right. I joined my comrades and didn't even see my family go in to find seats in the crowded auditorium.

The school band struck up a march and all classes filed in as had been rehearsed. We stood in front of our seats, as assigned, and on a signal from the choir director, we sat. No sooner had this been accomplished than the band started to play the national anthem. We rose again and sang the song, after which we recited the pledge of allegiance. We remained standing for a brief minute before the choir director and the principal signaled to us, rather desperately I thought, to take our seats. The command was so unusual that our carefully rehearsed and smooth-running machine was thrown off. For a full minute we fumbled for our chairs and bumped into each other awkwardly. Habits change or solidify under pressure, so in our state of nervous tension we had been ready to follow our usual assembly pattern: the American national anthem, then the pledge of allegiance, then the song every Black person I knew called the Negro National Anthem. All done in the same key, with the same passion and most often standing on the same foot.

Finding my seat at last, I was·overcome with a presentiment of worse things to come. Something unrehearsed, unplanned, was going to happen, and we were going to be made to look bad. I distinctly remember being explicit in the choice of pronoun. It was "we," the graduating class, the unit, that concerned me then.

The principal welcomed "parents and friends" and asked the Baptist minister to lead us in prayer. His invocation was brief and punchy, and for a second I thought we were getting back on the high road to right action. When the principal came back to the dais, however, his voice had changed. Sounds always affected me profoundly and the principal's voice was one of my favorites. During assembly it melted and lowed weakly into the audience. It had not been in my plan to listen to him, but my curiosity was piqued and I straightened up to give him my attention.

He was talking about Booker T. Washington, our "late great leader," who said we can be as close as the fingers on the hand, etc. . . . Then he said a few vague things about friendship and the friendship of kindly people to those less fortunate than themselves. With that his voice nearly faded, thin, away. Like a river diminishing to a stream and then to a trickle. But he cleared his throat and said, "Our speaker tonight, who is also our friend, came from Texarkana to deliver the commencement address, but due to the irregularity of the train schedule, he's going to, as they say, 'speak and run.'" He said that we understood and wanted the man to know that we were most grateful for the time he was able to give us and then something about how we were willing always to adjust to another's program, and without more ado— "I give you Mr. Edward Donleavy."

Not one but two white men came through the door offstage. The shorter one walked to the speaker's platform, and the tall one moved over to the center seat and sat down. But that was our principal's seat, and already occupied. The dislodged gentleman bounced around for a long breath or two before the Baptist minister gave him his chair, then with more dignity than the situation deserved, the minister walked off the stage.

Donleavy looked at the audience once (on reflection, I'm sure that he wanted only to reassure himself that we were really there), adjusted his glasses and began to read from a sheaf of papers.

He was glad "to be here and to see the work going on just as it was in the other schools."

At the first "Amen" from the audience I willed the offender to immediate death by choking on the word. But Amens and Yes, sir's began to fall around the room like rain through a ragged umbrella.

He told us of the wonderful changes we children in Stamps had in store. The Central School (naturally, the white school was Central) had already been granted improvements that would be in use in the fall. A well-known artist was coming from Little Rock to teach art to them. They were going to have the newest microscopes and chemistry equipment for their laboratory. Mr. Donleavy didn't leave us long in the dark over who made these improvements available at Central High. Nor were we to be ignored in the general betterment scheme he had in mind.

He said that he had pointed out to people at a very high level that one of the first-line football tacklers at Arkansas Agricultural and

Mechanical College had graduated from good old Lafayette County Training School. Here fewer Amen's were heard. Those few that did break through lay dully in the air with the heaviness of habit.

He went on to praise us. He went on to say how he had bragged that "one of the best basketball players at Fisk sank his first ball right here at Lafayette County Training School."

The white kids were going to have a chance to become Galileos and Madame Curies and Edisons and Gauguins, and our boys (the girls weren't even in on it) would try to be Jesse Owenses and Joe Louises.

Owens and the Brown Bomber were great heroes in our world, but what school official in the white-goddom of LIttle Rock had the right to decide that those two men must be our only heroes? Who decided that for Henry Reed to become a scientist he had to work like George Washington Carver, as a bootblack, to buy a lousy microscope? Bailey was obviously always going to be too small to be an athlete, so which concrete angel glued to what country seat had decided that if my brother wanted to become a lawyer he had to first pay penance for his skin by picking cotton and hoeing corn and studying correspondence books at night for twenty years?

The man's dead words fell like bricks around the auditorium and too many settled in my belly. Constrained by hard-learned manners I couldn't look behind me, but to my left and right the proud graduating class of 1940 had dropped their heads. Every girl in my row had found something new to do with her handkerchief. Some folded the tiny squares into love knots, some into triangles, but most were wadding them, then pressing them flat on their yellow laps.

On the dais, the ancient tragedy was being replayed. Professor Parsons sat, a sculptor's reject, rigid. His large, heavy body seemed devoid of will or willingness, and his eyes said he was no longer with us. The other teachers examined the flag (which was draped stage right) or their notes, or the windows which opened on our now-famous playing diamond.

Graduation, the hush-hush magic time of frills and gifts and congratulations and diplomas, was finished for me before my name was called. The accomplishment was nothing. The meticulous maps, drawn in three colors of ink, learning and spelling decasyllabic words, memorizing the whole of *The Rape of Lucrece*—it was for nothing. Donleavy had exposed us.

We were maids and farmers, handymen and washerwomen, and anything higher that we aspired to was farcical and presumptuous.

Then I wished that Gabriel Prosser and Nat Turner had killed all whitefolks in their beds and that Abraham Lincoln had been assassinated before the signing of the Emancipation Proclamation, and that Harriet Tubman had been killed by that blow on her head and Christopher Columbus had drowned in the *Santa Maria*.

It was awful to be Negro and have no control over my life. It was brutal to be young and already trained to sit quietly and listen to charges brought against my color with no chance of defense. We should all be dead. I thought I should like to see us all dead, one on top of the other. A pyramid of flesh with the whitefolks on the bottom, as the broad base, then the Indians with their silly tomahawks and teepees and wigwams and treaties, the Negroes with their mops and recipes and cotton sacks and spirituals sticking out of their mouths. The Dutch children should all stumble in their wooden shoes and break their necks. The French should choke to death on the Louisiana Purchase (1803) while silkworms ate all the Chinese with their stupid pigtails. As a species, we were an abomination. All of us.

Donleavy was running for election, and assured our parents that if he won we could count on having the only colored paved playing field in that part of Arkansas. Also—he never looked up to acknowledge the grunts of acceptance—also, we were bound to get some new equipment for the home economics building and the workshop.

He finished, and since there was no need to give any more than the most perfunctory thank-you's, he nodded to the men on the stage, and the tall white man who was never introduced joined him at the door. They left with the attitude that now they were off to something really important. (The graduation ceremonies at Lafayette County Training School had been a mere preliminary.)

The ugliness they left was palpable. An uninvited guest who wouldn't leave. The choir was summoned and sang a modern arrangement of "Onward, Christian Soldiers," with new words pertaining to graduates seeking their place in the world. But it didn't work. Elouise, the daughter of the Baptist minister, recited "Invictus," and I could have cried at the impertinence of "I am the master of my fate, I am the captain of my soul."

My name had lost its ring of familiarity and I had to be nudged to go and receive my diploma. All my preparations had fled. I neither marched up to the stage like a conquering Amazon, nor did I look in the audience for Bailey's nod of approval. Marguerite Johnson, I heard the name again, my honors were read, there were noises in the audience of appreciation, and I took my place on the stage as rehearsed.

I thought about colors I hated: ecru, puce, lavender, beige and black.

There was shuffling and rustling around me, then Henry Reed was giving his valedictory address, "To Be or Not to Be." Hadn't he heard the whitefolks? We couldn't *be*, so the question was a waste of time. Henry's voice came out clear and strong. I feared to look at him. Hadn't he got the message? There was no "nobler in the mind" for Negroes because the world didn't think we had minds, and they let us know it. "Outrageous fortune"? Now, that was a joke. When the ceremony was over I had to tell Henry Reed some things. That is, if I still cared. Not "rub," Henry, "erase." "Ah, there's the erase." Us.

Henry had been a good student in elocution. His voice rose on tides of promise and fell on waves of warnings. The English teacher had helped him to create a sermon winging through Hamlet's soliloquy. To be a man, a doer, a builder, a leader, or to be a tool, an unfunny joke, a crusher of funky toadstools. I marveled that Henry could go through with the speech as if we had a choice.

I had been listening and silently rebutting each sentence with my eyes closed; then there was a hush, which in an audience warns that something unplanned is happening. I looked up and saw Henry Reed, the conservative, the proper, the A student, turn his back to the audience and turn to us (the proud graduating class of 1940) and sing, nearly speaking,

> "Lift ev'ry voice and sing
> Till earth and heaven ring
> Ring with the harmonies of Liberty . . ."[5]

It was the poem written by James Weldon Johnson. It was the music composed by J. Rosamond Johnson. It was the Negro national anthem. Out of habit we were singing it.

Our mothers and fathers stood in the dark hall and joined the hymn of encouragement. A kindergarten teacher led the small children onto the stage and the buttercups and daisies and bunny rabbits marked time and tried to follow:

> "Stony the road we trod
> Bitter the chastening rod
> Felt in the days when hope, unborn, had died.
> Yet with a steady beat
> Have not our weary feet
> Come to the place for which our fathers sighed?"[6]

Every child I knew had learned that song with his ABC's and along with "Jesus Loves Me This I Know." But I personally had never heard it before. Never heard the words, despite the thousands of times I had sung them. Never thought they had anything to do with me.

----

[5]"Lift Ev'ry Voice and Sing"—words by James Weldon Johnson and music by J. Rosamond Johnson. © Copyrighted: Edward B. Marks Music Corporation. Used by permission.
[6]*Ibid.*

On the other hand, the words of Patrick Henry had made such an impression on me that I had been able to stretch myself tall and trembling and say, "I know not what course others may take, but as for me, give me liberty or give me death."

And now I heard, really for the first time:

"We have come over a way that with tears has been watered,
We have come, treading our path through the blood of the slaughtered."

While echoes of the song shivered in the air, Henry Reed bowed his head, said "Thank you," and returned to his place in the line. The tears that slipped down many faces were not wiped away in shame.

We were on top again. As always, again. We survived. The depths had been icy and dark, but now a bright sun spoke to our souls. I was no longer simply a member of the proud graduating class of 1940; I was a proud member of the wonderful, beautiful Negro race.

Oh, Black known and unknown poets, how often have your auctioned pains sustained us? Who will compute the lonely nights made less lonely by your songs, or by the empty pots made less tragic by your tales?

If we were a people much given to revealing secrets, we might raise monuments and sacrifice to the memories of our poets, but slavery cured us of that weakness. It may be enough, however, to have it said that we survive in exact relationship to the dedication of our poets (include preachers, musicians and blues singers).

Writing Suggestions for Maya Angelou's "Graduation"

Theme Analysis Questions

What message or messages come through to you in this work? "Graduation" was originally part of Maya Angelou's autobiography, *I Know Why the Caged Bird Sings*. What theme in "Graduation" is reflected in the novel's title? What does graduation mean to Maya Angelou, her mother, her teachers, her peers? How does her word choice help re-create the effect? Why does she describe the elaborate preparation in such detail?

What is the meaning of the principal's voice changing in introducing the white speaker "like a river diminishing to a stream and then to a trickle"? What other forebodings of something "off track" had Maya been sensitive to? How is Maya's exuberant mood undercut, changed, and finally destroyed by the speaker? What specifics indicate that the rest of the audience is reacting in the same way? If "graduation" marks an end of training and is the ritual of passing into the "real" world, how is the failure of the graduation ceremony ironically appropriate? How does Henry Reed's, "the conservative, the proper, the A student's," symbolic gesture of defiance at the end restore Maya's faith and self-esteem?

Application Suggestions

Have you ever had a "happy" occasion destroyed for you, or have you ever unintentionally ruined another person's "big" moment? How did it happen? What were your reactions? Have you ever felt another person looking down upon you? How did it make you feel? How did you react? Compare your situation to Maya's to account for the similarities and differences between your reaction and hers. Did you have a Henry Reed to bail you out? What painful truth did your experience provide? What themes did your experience and Maya's have in common?

Reactions to Songs: Student Example Papers

Songs of Our Past

Most of us grow up with musical accompaniment—the sounds of our youth. Sometimes a particular song and its lyrics have special meaning for us and evoke scenes from our past. If a song has strong memories for you, use it as a stimulus for your reaction paper. The following papers are examples of this theme.

MEMORIES OF BITTER TIMES

Nineteen hundred and seventy-three was the year of pulling out of Vietnam and "peace with honor." It was also the year the then relatively unknown singer-composer, Janis Ian, first recorded her song, "Dance with Me." It is a rather mild protest song about the war and the sacrifices involved, one of which was the taking of her brother's life. This song brings tears to my eyes whenever I hear it because it reminds me of my discovery of the war and what it really was.

I can remember when, in the early seventies, I first came to the realization that the war actually existed. People, especially younger people, had been so conditioned to violence on television, with shows like "Mannix" and "Hawaii Five-0," that they would watch the evening news with the same indifference. Somehow it wasn't real, just another violent television show. One night while I was watching a news clip from Vietnam that showed lifeless bodies almost in piles, it suddenly occurred to me that this scene was real. These were not Hollywood extras lying around in ketchup. They were laughing, loving people, perhaps from my hometown, who suddenly and insidiously had had their lives taken away from them. They had families who were being sent impersonal telegrams which gave condolences and thanked them for their contribution to the "American Cause."

I became very bitter, bitter toward the government for involving us in some other country's problems and bitter toward the military and its barbaric ways. I would get very emotional when I saw the news clips. Why were we doing this? What possible ends could justify our means?

This realization was probably the major reason for my involvement in politics, especially in the '72 elections. I doorbelled, distributed pamphlets on street corners, and wrote many, many letters to various congressmen. It was very hard for me to believe that these men were so powerful that they could send our troops to Vietnam no matter what the people thought. Perhaps it would be best if war could only be declared by a vote of the people. Democracy seemed a very disillusioning word: men elected to public offices on false promises.

The American military became my number one enemy. Our involvement in Vietnam was as much its fault as it was that of our politicians. The military seemed to feed on war. I began to see the Pentagon as a giant corporation whose ultimate product was to be this country's destruction, and any person who willingly supported this organization was contributing to my destruction.

My views have mellowed quite a bit since then, but "Dance with Me" brings to mind those times, those unpleasant and very bitter times, especially when Janis Ian sings these words:

> I heard of a plan
> in the President's mansion
> (high up in the sky),
> It called for a sacrifice
> And my brother paid the price.
>
> Sent him home in a bag.
> The American flag
> was draped around the box.
> The coffin lid was locked.
> The note said, "Thanks a lot."

I've never seen
in the years of my life
an intelligent sacrifice . . .[7]

—Teresa Sonneborn

Questions on "Memories of Bitter Times"

1. How does this paper build up to the effect of the song?
2. What specifics suggest that the student's reaction was more than a superficial one, that it actually led to some action on her part?
3. What two changes in the writer does the paper portray?
4. Would you have liked more information in the last paragraph or would it have taken away from the song as an ending?

"HELLO IN THERE," OLD WOMAN: REACTION TO A SONG BY JOHN PRINE

Had an apartment in the city.
Me and Loretta like livin' there.
It's been years since the kids have grown—
lives of their own, left us alone.
John and Linda live in Omaha.
Joey's somewhere on the road.
We lost Davey in the Korean War; still don't know what
for, don't matter any more.
Yet old trees just grow stronger
Rivers grow wider every day.
But old people just grow lonesome—
Just waiting for someone to say—
"Hello in there, hello."[8]

These words are from a song by John Prine about older people, senior citizens. These people are many times rejected by our society. If the husband is retired from his job, he feels that he is useless. The wife often feels the husband's uselessness. Their children have grown up and moved away. The parents don't hear from the kids, other than a

---

[7]From "Dance with Me" by Janis Ian. © 1974 Mine Music Ltd. (ASCAP)
[8]From "Hello in There" by John Prine © 1971 Cotillion Music, Inc. and Sour Grapes Music. Used by permission. All rights reserved.

birthday card or an occasional phone call on anniversaries. These calls often mean nothing to the children, but they can make an older person's day, week, or even month. All they need is someone to talk to.

Many times older people are forced to stay in their houses because of their health. Sometimes the only entertainment they have is the television and old friends who are in the same shape they are.

What they need is new faces and new people to talk to. Often they are afraid to meet new people because of crime; they are afraid of being taken advantage of.

Prine's message is for people to be nice to older folks, to take a little time to talk with them. It could make their lives less lonely.

> Me an' Loretta we don't talk much now.
> She sits and stares at the backdoor screen.
> All the news just repeats itself—like some
> forgotten dream, that we both seen.
> Some day I'll go and call up Rudy; we worked
> together at the factory.
> What'll I say if he asks what's new?
> Nothin'; What's with you? Nothin' much to do.
> Yet old trees just grow stronger.
> Rivers grow wider every day.
> But old people just grow lonesome—
> waitin' for someone to say—
> "Hello in there, hello."[9]

A few years ago, during the summer, I did some garden work for an old woman. She lived in a housing project in a high crime area. This woman was partially disabled, and she didn't see or hear well. Bad off as she seemed, she had a lot of pride in her house and yard.

Mrs. Howard was her name; her house was small, and it was overcrowded with old furniture. It smelled heavily of Lysol air freshener to hide the smell of her two cats and one dog. The dog, aptly named Brownie, was the type of animal that barked at anything and everything. It posed no threat to anyone for it cowered at the first hint of danger. Mrs. Howard was certain that Brownie could defend her against any intruder.

On the Saturdays that I would go to her house, she would be waiting in anticipation for me.

"Hello Timmy, how are you this morning?" she would ask. "Can I get you some cookies, or a soda?"

---

[9]*Ibid.*

"No thanks, Mrs. Howard, maybe later," I would reply.

She would then proceed to show me her endless supply of pictures.

"This is me and my husband in California in 1937. And this is my son when he was twelve," she informed. "He called me on the telephone not long ago; he's coming to see me soon!"

"That's nice of him," I replied.

She told me this every week when I would come to her house.

"Well, I better get goin' on the yard," I said after a length of time.

"Oh,"—a long pause—"O.K., be my guest."

I rose from the tattered couch, which the cats used for a scratching post, and went off to do the lawn work.

The old woman would sit in the dirty window, with at least one cat perched on her lap, and watch me work.

"You do a great job," she would say, "Better than I could ever do!"

After a month and a half, I began to dread going to work for her. With her son who was "coming to see her," her dead husband, and all her dead friends, I couldn't stand listening to her stories. I was glad when school came; it gave me a reason to quit working for her.

I never realized that I was about the only person she talked to all week. The old woman, whom I had no time for, died six months later, friendless.

> So if you're walking down the street sometime,
> Spot some hollow, ancient eyes.
> Please don't pass them by and stare,
> Like ya didn't care.
> Say "hello in there, hello."
> Say "hello in there, hello."[10]

—Timothy Keefe

Questions on "'Hello In There,' Old Woman"

1. What two formats are used in the reaction portions of this paper? Which format is more effective?

2. How does the writer use dialogue and details to capture the characteristics of the old woman?

---

[10]*Ibid.*

Reactions to Television Documentaries, News Coverage, or Films: Student Example Papers

Reactions to the Media

You live in a multi-media world. Chances are you have been moved more by television programs, documentaries, live news coverage, and films than by the written word.

The following example papers are based on media responses. Read them for writing techniques and topic ideas. If you can pinpoint a response to media that changed your views or caused you to become involved in action or reform, summarize, highlight, or clarify the media's message, and then reproduce the specifics and effect of your reaction.

THE SUFFERING SUFFRAGETTES

The sparse cell contained one woman. She sat on the edge of a cot—the only piece of furniture—staring at the dingy, grey walls. A shaft of light fell through the barred window casting somber shadows across her frayed flannel skirt. As she sat there, her hands folded quietly in her lap and her back very straight, she listened intently for the meal cart, and soon she heard the distant rumbling of its wheels coming closer and closer. It stopped down the hall. She slumped, and her worn, pale face relaxed for a second. Then, suddenly, she stood, rigid with fear, listening to the screaming, the choking, the vomiting of the woman in the other cell. Overcome with terror, she pushed the heavy cot across the cell door and waited silently, until she heard the cart and the clopping of the warden's heels again coming closer and closer. Abruptly, they stopped; someone tried the door. "Mrs. King, this is foolish, open this door. Open it!" Silence: the light still filtered through the bars, highlighting the sharp contours of her face. Suddenly, the glass was shattered by the nozzle of a water hose; the force of the icy water reduced her to a soggy lump, shivering on the floor. Then, they broke the door down. "Mrs. King, will you eat?" Silence. "Then, you'll be forcibly fed—again." She lay quietly, calmly on the cot. The doctor grasped the metal clamps to force her mouth open. The prongs bit painfully into her skin, but she resisted until the blood oozed down her chin. He looked at her despairingly, "We'll feed you through the nose if you keep resisting." Silence; the blood still oozed. An expressionless warden handed him the long rubber tube they usually forced down the throat, then turned to help the other wardens pin her down. The doctor bent over her, and the camera faded. . . .

This is just one scene, perhaps five minutes long, from the British series "Shoulder to Shoulder" that has kept me on the edge of my chair for the past six weeks. The Suffragettes were those brave women who fought, at the turn of the century, to get the vote for women. For fourteen years they went through hell—like the scene in the cell—before they accomplished their task. The sad thing is that they were so peaceful, so civilized, at first. They fought for their rights with letters to the prime minister and a few, quiet demonstrations. No response—except ridicule. As their demonstrations became louder and more embarrassing—they would stand in classy restaurants loudly lecturing the wealthy—the solution was to throw them into jail where they refused to eat and where they had to undergo the torture of forced feeding until the prison doctor felt that they were too ill to survive and had to be released. These women didn't go through this once; they went back again and again. (Watching the feeding turned my stomach as much as theirs.) The movement kept growing, but still the government refused to listen. Eventually, they started breaking windows, setting fire to mailboxes, and burning down buildings. It seemed like the more violent the action, the more the government listened. That's sad, very sad. In the end, it was the First World War that won them the vote. The women worked so hard—taking over civilian jobs, nursing at the front—that the vote was offered to them like a thank-you present.

But it wasn't going to end with the vote. Oh no! They believed wholeheartedly that they could change the world. "Give women the vote, and we'll get better housing, schools, government, better everything." They had yelled that for fourteen years. Now, they had the vote.

What would those women say if they knew we still had all those problems and worse. What would they say to the comfortable, cozy, middle-class women—like me, like my friends, like nearly everyone I know—who never vote, who couldn't care less?

More than anything else, this show made me feel wasted, a nothing. The Suffragettes with their strengths, their ambitions, had a purpose for living. Maybe everyone needs an ideal to fight for, something to die for, as the woman in the cell did: she threw herself under the king's horse. Death for a cause—could that give meaning to a life? I wish I knew. A void has entered my life since I watched that woman die. Could a "cause" fill it? Maybe—but, I don't have the strength or the will power to live like that, and, in comparison, I feel very weak, very useless. Were they happy? I don't think so, but they had self-respect. I thought I had self-respect, but now I'm not so sure.

I know that—although I'm worked-up at the moment—in a day or so, maybe a week, I'll have forgotten all about their suffering. I'll just sit back in my cozy chair and watch some nice, useless show like "Cannon" or "Barnaby Jones" or "Mannix" or "Hawaii Five-0." All those wonderful men fighting for us, and I won't think once of those women who really fought for me.

—Loraine Sharples

Questions on "The Suffering Suffragettes"

1. In the opening scene, how does the writer get you to identify with the woman in the cell?
2. What effect is achieved by repeating the word "silence" before giving detailed descriptions?
3. How is sound used in the descriptions?
4. What specifics does the writer include in her summary of the documentary?
5. What comparisons form the basis of the writer's reactions?

HOLY TONGUES OF FIRE

Juxtaposed in a most surreal manner, images of love and war are forever etched into my mind. I have only to close my eyes to be hypnotized by a mish-mash of technicolor memories. A brightly garbed band of acid-freaks winds its eery way through the streets of San Francisco in search of the ultimate rock concert; victorious young soldiers tromp through the rice fields on their way back to base.

The Maharishi gently fingers a rose petal as he discourses on the subject of being; a Vietnamese mother clutches her dead child and weeps to the heavens. Friends play with dogs and frisbees in a city park; national guardsmen grimly patrol a tear-gassed campus. All of these vie for space with countless other experiences, yet some images evoke such strong and complex reactions that they rise above the collection.

One picture stands out in my mind above all the others. Viewing this particular scene brings back many of the feelings of the last turbulent decade and then transcends them. *Hearts and Minds*, a documentary film about the Vietnam conflict, presents about two minutes of footage showing the death of Thich Quang Duc, a seventy-three-year-old Buddhist monk.

As the film segment begins, he sits calmly in the middle of a busy Saigon street. All the cars have stopped; their riders have become a cast of befuddled spectators. A disciple soaks the monk with several gallons of gasoline and retreats, bowing. In a dreamy span of seconds the monk sits, still in the lotus pose, while the fire ignites. The orange flames merge with his saffron robes and blacken them. In fifteen seconds, Quang Duc is a charcoal Buddha in the blaze, still holding his meditation posture. That subdued form sat long after his spirit had departed; then the charred body finally toppled onto its side. The film clip ended with the image of a collapsed heap still blazing away amidst the now horrified throng of passersby.

I could not escape a feeling of revulsion at these minutes of cinema, yet I was fascinated by the action more than shocked. Here was a man who had made the ultimate protest to the sad and evil situation he'd seen his people caught in. All of our political leaders' mumblings of "peace with honor" were reduced to absurd nonsense next to this. All dialogue was anticlimactic now, whether it was Spiro Agnew's or Abbie Hoffman's. Quang Duc's statement, uttered with every screaming corpuscle of his body, had closed the book.

A political act has seldom been so pure, and yet the monk's death held an even greater significance for me. His flames had quieted to a dead silence any skepticism I'd nurtured concerning the worth of Far Eastern philosophies. Where was that man's mind as he sat tranquilly amidst the raging fire? Where had his meditation taken him? It was a question I knew I had to answer.

—John J. Mangan

Questions on "Holy Tongues of Fire"

1. What technique does the author use in the opening paragraph of his paper? What effect does it produce?
2. How does the writer use a highlight approach to make his point?
3. What images re-create the horror of the event along with its spell of mystery?
4. Where does the author's reaction take him?

MY "ROOTS"

"Be nice to that old man that has been coming around here lately; he is your grandfather," Mom said. Since I was only four years old, he didn't impress me much; for one thing, I had never seen him before. I only remember thinking that he didn't look anything like me. He was my mom's father, with a stocky build and very dark skin. Grandfather was about eighty-five years old at this time.

A year later, an old lady came to visit us. She had long hair that hung all the way down her back. It wasn't curly hair like mine; as a matter of fact, it wasn't like any of my family's hair. She had white skin and walked all bent over. "Be nice to your grandmother, kids; she's ninety-one-years-old," said Mom.

"My God," I thought. Grandmother! How could this old white woman be my grandmother? She was my father's mother. I knew some of his sisters and brothers looked almost white, but I didn't expect his mother to look completely white! My mother then told us about her being Irish and how she came to this country from Ireland. I guess from that time on I started thinking about my roots, wondering if I could ever trace them.

Recently there was a documentary on television entitled "Roots," which showed how one man traced his ancestry. As I watched it each night, I put myself in the characters' places. My ancestors came to this country in the same way as those in "Roots."

The first night's viewing showed how the white men went to Africa, hid in the woods, and waited for the Africans to come past. They grabbed them, chained them like animals, and dragged them back to their ship.

Kunta Kinte was a young boy of thirteen. He had just finished manhood training and had to move into his own hut, according to their traditions. Thinking that his little brother might like some kind of a gift from him, he decided to make him a drum. For this project he would need a good log. Even though all the tribe had been warned against going into the woods or near tall grass, Kunta Kinte thought he would take a chance in order to get a log for his drum.

He had just found the right log, when he saw some strange men hiding in the bushes. Kunta Kinte threw the log down and ran as fast as he could, but he could not get away. The men tied him, beat him, and dragged him back to their ship where they had hundreds of Africans—men, women, and children—imprisoned.

How could these people be human? I thought, as tears rolled down my face. They must have been totally insensitive, going over to Africa and carting off human beings like they were no more than a piece of cargo simply to satisfy their own greed and lust. At that moment I felt a kind of hurt, anger, and hatred that I had never felt before. I hated all my white classmates that I had sat and had lunch with every day, friends that had once meant a lot to me. I felt as though I never wanted to see them again. How could these people be so inhuman?

The first episode of "Roots" has passed like all television programs do. The next day I went to school. I remembered the film, but I had lunch, studied, and enjoyed my white friends as much as ever. For some reason, I didn't even think of them in the same context as those people in "Roots." If I had, I would have been just as ignorant, narrow-minded, and selfish as those men who tried to destroy my "roots" hundreds of years ago.

—Louise Long

Questions on "My 'Roots'"

1. Why is it fitting for this writer to begin her paper with a specific subjective experience?
2. How might the writer have returned to the drum scene for contrast at the end of her summary?
3. What changes in emotion does the writer experience as a result of the show?
4. How does her ending reflect her philosophical position as well as her topic?

LA BOHEME

I lazily opened my eyes as the morning sun filtered through the window, warming this new summer day. Already I could hear someone rustling about the house. It was Grandma's little old house in the south side of Chicago. Typical of that area, it was small with such a microscopically minute yard that the neighbor's wall seemed to magnetically cling to hers. The sweet doughy smell of homemade noodles hovered through the air.

It was July of 1969, the last time I would see my Grandma "Fanky" ("Fanky" was a mispronunciation of her real name that stuck endearingly with us grandchildren). Since she was getting in in years, my parents had decided that all seven of us should load into our small station wagon, a haven for bickering brats, and drive back for a visit. I hadn't seen Grandma since I was a diaper-wetting toddler, and now, as a worldly sophisticate of twelve, all I knew about her was that whenever I did or said anything, I'd be told, "You're just like your grandmother. You even look like her." Of course, after hearing all that, I knew she must be special.

She was a strong, sturdy, and jolly short lady who had a calendar with Easter on the wrong day, a Bible in a funny language, and who babbled constantly to herself in a quaintly queer tongue. At twelve, I didn't know or understand much about her and just thought her to be a bit eccentric. Upon leaving for home, she pulled me aside and, with her thick accent, said stammeringly, "Never forget, Elizabeth, who your people are. Remember that you are a Bohemian from your people outside of Prague."

At that time, I just shrugged the comment off and kissed her goodbye. The word "Bohemian" conjured up images of wandering, lawless, European gypsies, or those kinky characters called beatniks in small smoke-filled cafés. I always thought I was just another average American.

These memories came to mind as I joined the millions of spectators watching "Roots," a show based on Alex Haley's search through his genealogy. Kunta Kinte, the first of the captured Africans in Haley's lineage, took heed in naming his daughter Kizzy in the proper tradition of his people, the Mandinkas. "You are Kizzy, daughter of Kunta Kinte, from the Mandinka warriors . . .," he said, raising her toward the star-studded sky while continuing to recount the story of her heritage from Gambia. He would, as he emphasized to Fiddler, pass on the ways of his people so that his daughter could stand tall and be proud of where she came from, rather than be like the American-born Blacks who had no concept of who they were in this white no-man's land.

I thought how sad it was that the story of my ancestors had not been passed on to me. At twelve, I simply let the opportunity to learn about my people slip through my hands, and now it is too late to hear that legend. A feeling of deprivation looms overhead urging me now to fill that vast vacancy society had created by squelching my relatives' bonds with their past, as society continues to do as it stamps out various heritages.

This feeling of incompleteness has led me to engulf myself in any literature dealing with this land sandwiched between Prague and the Bohemian Forest. From these sturdy and proud mountain dwellers descended, not only numerous European queens named Elizabeth, but also some very outspoken individuals. It was John Huss who, in the fifteenth century, was burned at the stake for speaking out against the corruption in the Catholic Church and for starting the Protestant movement. It was John Comenius who, in the seventeenth century, was ostracized for his views on education, which are popular today.

Great pride races through the marrow of my bones to think that I could descend from such brave individualists. But then again, I realize after breaking from the haze of daydreams, that I may not. I am left with that still unanswered question as to who my people really are. But, thanks to those few words of Grandma's, there is no doubt about it. I am La Boheme.

—Elizabeth Ann Stevens

Questions on "La Boheme"

1. What specific details characterize the grandmother?
2. What scene from "Roots" does the writer highlight for the purposes of her theme?
3. Why does the writer include the specifics of her historical research?
4. What makes the ending powerful?

FROM FAMOUS TO FORGOTTEN

While watching television one Sunday afternoon, a sports special about injuries came on. Since I'm interested in sports, I decided to watch it.

The show started by showing film clippings of different athletes getting hurt. They showed players lying in pain, football players being carried off the field on stretchers, and even a football player that died while running out for a pass.

The show also interviewed the coaches of the injured athletes. They asked questions like, "How will your team do with the loss of your great running back?" or "Who is going to replace 'Joe' now that he is out for the season?" The last part of the show included interviews with injured players. They asked questions like, "Is that leg getting into shape?" or "Who do you pick to win it all this year?" In both the interviews of the athletes and the coaches, the emphasis was on returning to win rather than on the individual players, themselves.

After watching this program, I was very irritated. At first, I couldn't figure out why. After thinking a bit, it came to me! The show said nothing about what happens to an athlete when he gets hurt and can't play ever again. What happens to the athlete that only knows how to do one thing, play a professional sport? What happens when he gets permanently injured? How does he make a living and support his family?

This show made me think of an experience in my own life. Last summer, I got a job as an orderly for a young man who was paralyzed. I was very nervous about the job. This wasn't any ordinary paralyzed man; this man had set a world record in the pole vault. He was a great athlete until one day, while he was training for the 1964 Olympic games, he had an accident. He was jumping on the trampoline and landed wrong on his neck. He was immediately paralyzed from the neck all the way down.

I had to feed him and wheel him around. As I got to know him better, I realized what pain he must have gone through and is still going through. If I spilled some food on him, he would always say that it was his fault. He never wanted to talk about himself.

His room was filled with mementoes of his athletic career. There was a huge Olympic banner from the Tokyo games plus many trophies. On the wall there were three letters: one from President John F. Kennedy, one from Jacqueline Kennedy, and one from Robert Kennedy. They congratulated him on his world record and said how sorry they were about his accident.

This great athlete has been forgotten by most people. Nobody calls on him. He is all alone except for his family and close friends. He doesn't have the chance to make any new friends.

This experience made me think about what I would do if the same thing happened to me. Would I just give up? Would I try to do something with my life?

In the television show, they didn't say anything about the great athletes that got hurt and didn't ever get to play again. I don't think the players should be forgotten just because they got hurt. After seeing the broadcast, I wondered about multi-million dollar sports organizations that value athletes when they are productive and famous, but soon forget them when they are injured and unable to play.

—Rob Staley

Questions on "From Famous to Forgotten"

1. How do the quoted interview questions show the focus of the documentary?
2. How does the writer's involvement with an actual injured athlete add to the paper's impact?
3. Which two lines characterize the athlete?
4. What effect is produced by the description of the athlete's room?

TI'S REDEMPTION

During the windup of the Vietnam war, news reporters gave the public a day-by-day accounting of the evacuation of the country.

Countless hundreds of people fought like rats to obtain any means available to leave Vietnam. Pictures flashed on the television screen showing endless lines of adults and children waiting for a way out. Soldiers fought civilians to gain access to the last airlifts. In desperation, people climbed into wheel wells and hung onto parts of the fuselage in their last attempt to make it out of the country.

The orphaned children and babies, victims of tragic and unfortunate circumstances, were afforded special airlifts out. The lifts were arranged by the orphanages and various airlines commissioned by the government.

One of the largest lifts, with approximately three hundred orphans on board, crashed shortly after takeoff. The television news gave a good accounting of this event, showing pictures of the plane and reporting how badly injured some of the orphans were.

These tragic stories seemed all too remote from the safe, secure, everyday life I was accustomed to. They were just factual accountings of something that didn't directly affect me or cause any real emotional reactions within me.

Not long after these events happened, I received a phone call from my supervisor.

"Nancy, this is Sally."

"What can I do for you, Sally?" I questioned, wondering why she would possibly be calling me on my day off.

"I have a special assignment for you, if you're willing to accept it. As you know, United Airlines is participating in a program to transport the Vietnam orphans, free of charge, to their new homes. We are looking for some responsible stewardesses to accompany the children and babies on the flights. We are assigning one stewardess to each child in order to give them special attention. This is strictly voluntary, since you won't be paid. Would you be interested?"

"I'd be happy to do it; when do I go?"

"Well, the orphans will be coming into Seattle on a flight tonight, then held here for a short time to be checked over. I suppose it will be in a few days."

I was on my way four days later to escort a child to Denver. When I arrived at the Sea-Tac Airport, I saw about twenty other stewardesses waiting to accompany a child. We all met in the boarding area and waited for instructions.

Some of the girls already had the children they were to escort; I hadn't yet received mine. Fairly soon, a jovial looking woman walked up to me with a baby in her arms. The baby was dressed in a brown parka, which was about two sizes too big, with a yellow, flannel sleep suit underneath. The woman, a social worker, informed me the baby was a girl and gave me a plastic bag containing all the baby's personal belongings: disposable diapers, special formula, medicine, diaper wipes, three baby bottles, two sleeper gowns, and a lap pad. She instructed me on medication to give the baby, but didn't mention why the baby needed it.

"The baby's name is Ti Donatti," she added.

"Ti Donatti doesn't sound like a Vietnamese name to me," I commented.

The social worker belly laughed at my bewilderment. "She's already been adopted by an Italian family, and Donatti is her new last name."

"How old is she?"

"She's about a year and a month old."

I gasped in amazement. "She only looks about four months old!"

"I know," the woman replied, "Some of these children don't look anywhere near their age compared to American children. She has quite a journey ahead of her, and she has been a very sick baby."

"I'll take very good care of her," I reassured the woman.

"I'm sure you will. Thank you very much for doing this," she said, as she placed Ti in my arms. "Have a nice flight."

I boarded the plane with the rest of the girls and their children. We all sat fairly close together. Getting situated was no easy chore; I had to make sure everything was within reach and get my seat belt fastened while still holding on to Ti.

After the plane was in the air, I took my first good look at Ti. She was still asleep. What an angelic looking baby she was, in spite of some sores around her head and ears. Her hair was thick, black, and straight; her skin was olive toned. As I tried to remove her parka, she woke up and stared at me. Her eyes were deep brown and surprisingly round. She looked like a little doll and seemed so helpless and fragile. I drew her close to my body, hoping she would sense that someone really cared.

Soon, she started to cry. Actually, it was more like a whimper. I reached in the plastic bag and drew out her bottle. She sucked on it, slowly at first, then with more enthusiasm.

During her feeding, I watched the other girls around me. One girl was struggling with a diaper; another girl was teaching one of the boy orphans, who was about six-years-old, how to pick his nose with a Kleenex. He had never seen a Kleenex before and seemed puzzled as to why he couldn't just use his finger to do the job. I giggled to myself. Sitting in front of me was a boy, about twelve-years-old, with crutches poised beside him. I was sure he was a victim of shrapnel; however, I was told by his escort that he had contracted polio at an early age.

Ti finished her bottle, and I sat her up in my lap. Soon, I noticed a rank smell and looked down. My skirt, as well as Ti, was covered with diarrhea. I was warned ahead of time to use the lap pad provided for me but had forgotten. One of the stewardesses brought me a wet rag; I cleaned myself off, then proceeded to change Ti.

As I took her little sleeper off, I noticed something attached to her ankle. It was a baggage claimlike tag attached to her with wire, and it had her medication and name written on it. I was horrified that anyone would wrap wire around her little ankle. I took it off and attached it to her coat.

Finishing the changing process, I noticed sores on her legs and the bottoms of her feet. They looked much like burn sores—and I wondered how she got them. I began to feel a love for Ti; she was such a fragile and ill baby, yet so good-natured. She smiled frequently.

During the two and one-half hour flight, I grew closer and closer to her; however, I knew I would have to give her up soon. She began to feel quite an attachment for me also. When I left her for a few minutes to go to the rest room, she fussed when someone else held her. When I took her back in my arms, she became quiet again. I was probably the closest thing to a mother she had experienced in her short life. In the orphanage, she never got any real individual attention. I found myself wanting to keep her, knowing it was impossible to do so.

The flight ended all too soon. I waited to get off the plane behind the rest of the girls so I could have a little more time with Ti. When I reached the door of the plane, I stood at the top of the stairs and gazed around me. Throngs of police cars surrounded the plane, and large vanlike vehicles waited to whisk the children away. Lined up at the bottom of the stairs were nurses and doctors—one for each child. It was an amazing and impressive sight!

The girls filed down the stairs and handed over their children, one by one. I followed. My arms closed tighter around Ti for our last few moments together, and I kissed her lightly on the forehead. When I reached the bottom of the stairs, a nurse quickly snatched little Ti out of my arms. I felt empty. God, how I hated to let her go. The nurse started walking toward the van; I turned quickly and headed for the terminal, afraid to look back over my shoulder.

My duty accomplished, I joined the other girls. One of them suggested we all go to the bar and have a drink before our flight back home. We all agreed.

I ordered a scotch and sipped on it slowly, as we shared experiences about our short-lived motherhood. We all agreed it was quite a rewarding and emotional experience.

One of the girls leaned over the table and said, "Nancy, did you know that the little baby girl you were escorting was one of the babies in that airlift crash?"

My surroundings faded as the newsreel picture of the crash and the burns on Ti's legs instantly flickered in my mind. I lifted the scotch to my lips, as uncontrolled tears found their way to my chin.

—Nancy Mercer

Questions on "Ti's Redemption"

1. How is the documentary used in this paper?

2. What details in describing the baby gain meaning at the end?
3. What scenes are re-created in telling the experience?

I'M A BARBARIAN AT HEART

McMurphy lunged at Nurse Ratched and grabbed her by the throat. She struggled to free herself from his death grip, and they fell to the floor. He grasped her tighter as she fought to get him off her breathless, convulsing body. Her face turned red from lack of oxygen, and her knuckles were white from fighting this mad man's powerful hold. Gasping for air, she began to cough and wheeze, and his grip tightened. He raised her head and pounded it repeatedly against the floor with the constant thud, thud, thud sound of her skull hitting against the tile. The other patients stood in awe while McMurphy did what they had lacked the courage to do.

In response to all the commotion in the ward, two orderlies rushed toward McMurphy to peel him away from Nurse Ratched. Their success was not immediate, but finally the nurse was freed and had regained her composure. McMurphy was dragged out by the two orderlies.

This scene is the culmination and release of all the tension and hatred one feels toward Nurse Ratched in the film version of Ken Kesey's *One Flew Over the Cuckoo's Nest*. *Cuckoo's Nest* is the story of R. P. McMurphy, who is sent from prison to a mental hospital for observation to see if he is really crazy or just a troublemaker.

The ward Mr. McMurphy was placed in had eighteen men in it: nine men were in a group therapy session, and all patients were voluntary except for four. These men came to the hospital because they were misfits in society. They looked to Nurse Ratched, their ward's nurse, for treatment, confidence, understanding, and care. They needed more than just medicine.

McMurphy arrived and things came alive. There was no more cheating at cards or whining because someone couldn't have a certain chair. If they wanted to participate, they did it right. He allowed the patients to do what they could; he made them take responsibility for their own actions.

The patients needed to feel like human beings instead of misfits. McMurphy commandeered a bus of unrestricted patients and took them fishing. They boarded a boat without permission and started out. Each passenger was given some responsibility. Cheswick piloted the boat, while McMurphy taught the others how to fish. He explained once and let them try it. He was not afraid to let them try on their own, because he was not intimidated.

McMurphy said, and did, and thought things the others were afraid to. He had playing cards with dirty pictures on them; he questioned his medication and the cigarette rationing; he told patients they were crazy, and he dreamed big.

Nurse Ratched, the antithesis of McMurphy, was emasculating, sadistic, and condescending. To the hospital administration, however, she was a strong concerned individual as well as an excellent nurse. In actuality, she made the men fear her through making them feel guilty and inferior.

She played classical music, too loudly, whether the men wanted it or not. She wouldn't let them rearrange their work schedules to see the World Series. She decided for them that they shouldn't lose their cigarettes in a card game, that their medicine was good for them, and that they liked classical music. She made a boy, already extremely insecure, feel so guilty about his normal sexual drive that, while awaiting punishment, he broke a glass and slashed his wrists.

In watching this movie, I developed, along with McMurphy, an extreme hatred for Nurse Ratched. I soon felt her belittling attitude was aimed at me too. I felt McMurphy's rage. When McMurphy was strangling her, my hands were his and I, too, was throttling a body pleading for survival. I was pounding her head again and again against the hard floor. My hands were locked tightly and my teeth were clenched—I wanted that woman dead.

When McMurphy was trying to free himself from the orderlies, who tore him from Nurse Ratched, I was shocked and outraged. How could these two men want a woman like that to live? I wanted McMurphy to break away from them and bounce the nurse against all four walls. She had reduced the men in her ward to a life without self-respect, one not worth living. I wanted her dead.

There must be a level of rage where there is no return, no calming without action. McMurphy had reached that level and acted upon his intense hatred. The level in me reached a very high point, but something clicked inside my head. I stopped thinking about the movie and realized my own highly emotional state.

I, who thought I'd been brought up in a Christian, be-kind-to-others society, wanted someone to die. I, who considered myself a loving, empathic pacifist, who considered capital punishment wrong, wished that McMurphy had choked the life out of Nurse Ratched and then kicked her a few times to make sure she was dead.

I was surprised at my own barbaric reaction. I had to laugh at myself because I was so worked up over a fictional wrong, and yet remained detached from real wrongs like Vietnam, Watergate, and our ghettos; "Don't get me involved" was my motto. As I walked out of the theatre, laughing at my foolish reaction to an actress playing a part, I still found myself remarking to my friends, "If I ever meet Nurse Ratched, I swear I'll really kill her!"

—Robin McCarty

Questions on "I'm a Barbarian at Heart"

1. How does the scene highlighted at the beginning of this paper capture the paper's key emotion?
2. What specific details does the paper use to support the contrast of McMurphy and Nurse Ratched?
3. In expressing her reaction, what line does the writer repeat for effect?
4. What insight has the writer gained because of her reaction?

Reaction to a Live Performance: Student Example Paper

THE BIRTH OF A DRUM

Sprinkles and splotches of brilliant colored hues were molded in the living mural of a thousand children waiting in the Opera House for the afternoon performance. In a back row aisle seat, I eased down, getting relaxed and comfortable. Along with the humming throngs, I searched the empty stage expectantly.

After a patient wait, the lights began to dim, causing a hush from the audience, signaling that the show was about to begin. A spotlight gazed at the side stage curtains, marking the appearance of an angular brown lady with flowing garments that represented her Indian home. Carrying an unusually shaped drum, she moved to center stage. Placing the drum at her feet, she began talking in the microphone, slowly and carefully, choosing her words so all could understand.

The Indian lady told of the little village where she was born and the seven sisters and five brothers in her family. She said, "With my father and mother, that makes fifteen of us. My mother has spent many years making babies in her womb." A bit of uneasiness spread across the young audience. "With thirteen children taking nine months each to develop, that comes to 117 months or 3,510 days my mother carried babies inside her womb," she continued. "My mother fed us from her breast for two years each. That is a total of 312 months or 9,360 days she fed us. Her body made two quarts of milk a day for each of us. That was 1,460 quarts of milk for each one of us."

I was astonished by these figures since I had nursed each of my children. I quickly computed: four children nursed nine months each or a total of thirty-six months at probably two quarts a day. I had produced 2,160 quarts of milk. This certainly wouldn't hold up to any Carnation Holstein record, but, not bad, I humbly had to admit. These facts of life impressed me so much that I missed what the woman was saying to the audience. The children were quiet, and the uneasiness they expressed earlier had disappeared. Maybe they were busy calculating too. For whatever reason, her spell was cast, and a thousand children were listening as one.

Returning my attention to the performer, I heard her explaining about the drum. It was about two feet high, made of tan wood worn lustrous from use. The drum funneled down from its stretched skin head to a small opening at the bottom.

Sinking to the stage floor, the woman pulled the drum toward her. Lifting one leg very high, she brought it down and placed her ankle around the bottom edge of the drum. Clasping the drum between her thighs, she began to pound a rhythmic beat—a very wild, saturating beat that seemed to encompass and enclose everyone in its throbbing pulse.

Then, in complete contrast, she suddenly changed the beat to a soft flutter with just her finger tips tapping the drum head. I felt as though I was straining to hear although there weren't any interfering sounds. The tempo gradually rose. Her body began to sway in unison with the beat she lay upon her drum. The intensity of the rhythm heightened as she worked the taut skin. The pulsating beat grew in strength and energy to an overwhelming cadence, striking and lashing out at all of us.

Abruptly she stopped. There was no sound or motion. We all hung there as though suspended in air. Her posture drooped, and her body draped over the drum. Every eye in the audience was intently fixed upon her.

Slowly and rhythmically she began to undulate her body and turn the drum's small end toward us. Softly, she made faint scratching sounds inside the drum and then increasingly the sound of a heart beat was heard. The heart beat grew louder and interwove with the scratching.

Suddenly I knew what had been said to the audience earlier. It all began to fall into place like the last remaining pieces of a puzzle. My eyes moistened with emotion as I realized she had been beating out conception, the following nine months of pregnancy, and finally the contractions and sensations and fatigue of birth. I knew I was right when at last she reached in the small end of the drum and gently withdrew a baby drum from its mother.

—Margilee Shelton

Questions on "The Birth of a Drum"

1. How does the writer blend observation with reaction throughout her paper?
2. Why is it more effective for the writer to give her reactions as she watches the performance than for her to first describe the entire performance and then give her reactions?
3. How does the entire paper prepare you for the ending?

Reactions to Fiction: Material to Respond to and Student Example Papers

---

Responding to Fiction

Short stories and novels not only describe incidents and emotions that may parallel your own but also present ideas or themes that can be applied to completely different situations.

Katherine Mansfield's short story "Miss Brill" presents a character study, a comment on the elderly's position in our society, and an exposure of an insensitive act. You could use any one of these themes to create a reaction paper.

MISS BRILL[11]

KATHERINE MANSFIELD

Even though Katherine Mansfield (1888–1923) produced only four slim volumes of short stories, she was considered one of the

---

[11]Katherine Mansfield, "Miss Brill." Copyright 1922 by Alfred A. Knopf, Inc., and renewed 1950 by John Middleton Murry. Reprinted from *The Short Stories of Katherine Mansfield*, by permission of the publisher.

most influential woman writers of her time for her stylistic innovations.

She was born in Wellington, New Zealand, but educated in London. After marrying the British critic, John Middleton Murray, in 1913, her ill health forced her to spend most of her time living in health resorts in France, Switzerland, and Italy. She died of tuberculosis at the age of thirty-four.

Although it was so brilliantly fine—the blue sky powdered with gold and great spots of light like white wine splashed over the Jardins Publiques—Miss Brill was glad that she had decided on her fur. The air was motionless, but when you opened your mouth there was just a faint chill, like a chill from a glass of iced water before you sip, and now and again a leaf came drifting—from nowhere, from the sky. Miss Brill put up her hand and touched her fur. Dear little thing! It was nice to feel it again. She had taken it out of its box that afternoon, shaken out the moth-powder, given it a good brush, and rubbed the life back into the dim little eyes. "What has been happening to me?" said the sad little eyes. Oh, how sweet it was to see them snap at her again from the red eiderdown! . . . But the nose, which was of some black composition, wasn't at all firm. It must have had a knock, somehow. Never mind—a little dab of black sealing-wax when the time came—when it was absolutely necessary. . . . . Little rogue! Yes, she really felt like that about it. Little rogue biting its tail just by her left ear. She could have taken it off and laid it on her lap and stroked it. She felt a tingling in her hands and arms, but that came from walking, she supposed. And when she breathed, something light and sad—no, not sad, exactly—something gentle seemed to move in her bosom.

There were a number of people out this afternoon, far more than last Sunday. And the band sounded louder and gayer. That was because the Season had begun. For although the band played all the year round on Sundays, out of season it was never the same. It was like some one playing with only the family to listen; it didn't care how it played if there weren't any strangers present. Wasn't the conductor wearing a new coat, too? She was sure it was new. He scraped with his foot and flapped his arms like a rooster about to crow, and the bandsmen sitting in the green rotunda blew out their cheeks and glared at the music. Now there came a little "flutey" bit—very pretty!—a little chain of bright drops. She was sure it would be repeated. It was; she lifted her head and smiled.

Only two people shared her "special" seat: a fine old man in a velvet coat, his hands clasped over a huge carved walking-stick, and a big old woman, sitting upright, with a roll of knitting on her embroidered apron. They did not speak. This was disappointing, for Miss Brill always looked forward to the conversation. She had become really quite expert, she thought, at listening as though she didn't listen, at sitting in other people's lives just for a minute while they talked round her.

She glanced, sideways, at the old couple. Perhaps they would go soon. Last Sunday, too, hadn't been as interesting as usual. An Englishman and his wife, he wearing a dreadful Panama hat and she button boots. And she'd gone on the whole time about how she ought to wear spectacles; she knew she needed them; but that it was no good getting any; they'd be sure to break and they'd never keep on. And he'd been so patient. He'd suggested everything—gold rims, the kind that curved round your ears, little pads inside the bridge. No, nothing would please her. "They'll always be sliding down my nose!" Miss Brill had wanted to shake her.

The old people sat on the bench, still as statues. Never mind, there was always the crowd to watch. To and fro, in front of the flower-beds and the band rotunda, the couples and groups paraded, stopped to talk, to greet, to buy a handful of flowers from the old beggar who had his tray fixed to the railings. Little children ran among them, swooping and laughing; little boys with big white silk bows under their chins, little girls, little French dolls, dressed up in velvet and lace. And sometimes a tiny staggerer came suddenly rocking into the open from under the trees, stopped, stared, as suddenly sat down "flop," until its small high-stepping mother, like a young hen, rushed scolding to its rescue. Other people sat on the benches and green chairs, but they were nearly always the same, Sunday after Sunday, and—Miss Brill had often noticed—there was something funny about nearly all of them. They were odd, silent, nearly all old, and from the way they stared they looked as though they'd just come from dark little rooms or even— even cupboards!

Behind the rotunda the slender trees with yellow leaves down drooping, and through them just a line of sea, and beyond the blue sky with gold-veined clouds.

Tum-tum-tum tiddle-um! tiddle-um! tum tiddley-um tum ta! blew the band.

Two young girls in red came by and two young soldiers in blue met them, and they laughed and paired and went off arm-in-arm. Two peasant women with funny straw hats passed, gravely, leading beautiful smoke-coloured donkeys. A cold, pale nun hurried by. A beautiful woman came along and dropped her bunch of violets, and a little boy ran after to hand them to her, and she took them and threw them away as if they'd been poisoned. Dear me! Miss Brill didn't know whether to admire that or not! And now an ermine toque and a gentleman in grey met just in front of her. He was tall, stiff, dignified, and she was wearing the ermine toque she'd bought when her hair was yellow. Now everything, her hair, her face, even her eyes, was the same colour as the shabby ermine, and her hand, in its cleaned glove, lifted to dab her lips, was a tiny yellowish paw. Oh, she was so pleased to see him—delighted! She rather thought they were going to meet that afternoon. She described where she'd been—everywhere, here, there, along by the sea. The day was so charming—didn't he agree! And wouldn't he, perhaps? . . . But he shook his head, lighted a cigarette, slowly breathed a great deep puff into her face, and, even while she was still talking and laughing, flicked the match away and walked on. The ermine toque was alone; she smiled more brightly than ever. But even the band seemed to know what she was feeling and played more softly, played tenderly, and the drum beat, "The Brute! The Brute!" over and over. What would she do? What was going to happen now? But as Miss Brill wondered, the ermine toque turned, raised her hand as though she'd seen some one else, much nicer, just over there, and pattered away. And the band changed again and played more quickly, more gaily than ever, and the old couple on Miss Brill's seat got up and marched away, and such a funny old man with long whiskers hobbled along in time to the music and was nearly knocked over by four girls walking abreast.

Oh, how fascinating it was! How she enjoyed it! How she loved sitting here, watching it all! It was like a play. It was exactly like a play. Who could believe the sky at the back wasn't painted? But it wasn't till a little brown dog trotted on solemn and then slowly trotted off, like a little "theatre" dog, a little dog that had been drugged, that Miss Brill discovered what it was that made it so exciting. They were all on the stage. They weren't only the audience, not only looking on; they were acting. Even she had a part and came every Sunday. No doubt somebody would have noticed if she hadn't been there; she was part of the performance after all. How strange she'd never thought of it like that before! And yet it explained why she made such a point of starting from home at just the same time each week—so as not to be late for the performance—and it also explained why she had quite a queer, shy feeling at telling her English pupils how she spent her Sunday afternoons. No wonder! Miss Brill nearly laughed out loud. She was on the stage. She thought of the old invalid gentleman to whom she read the newspaper four afternoons a week while he slept in the garden. She had got quite used to the frail head on the cotton pillow, the hollowed eyes, the open mouth and the high pinched nose. If he'd been dead she mightn't have noticed for weeks; she wouldn't have minded. But suddenly he knew he was having the paper read to him by an actress! "An acress!" The old head lifted; two points of light quivered in the old eyes. "An actress—are ye?" And Miss Brill smoothed the newspaper as if it were the manuscript of her part and said gently: "Yes, I have been an actress for a long time."

The band had been having a rest. Now they started again. And what they played was warm, sunny, yet there was just a faint chill—a something, what was it?—not sadness—no, not sadness—a something that made you want to sing. The tune lifted, lifted, the light shone; and it seemed to Miss Brill that in another moment all of them, all the whole company, would begin singing. The young ones, the laughing ones who were moving together, they would begin, and the men's voices, very resolute and brave, would join them. And then she too, she too, and the others on the benches—they would come in with a kind of accompaniment—something low, that scarcely rose or fell, something so beautiful—moving. . . . And Miss Brill's eyes filled with tears and she looked smiling at all the other members of the company. Yes, we understand, we understand, she thought—though what they understood she didn't know.

Just at that moment a boy and a girl came and sat down where the old couple had been. They were beautifully dressed; they were in love. The hero and heroine, of course, just arrived from his father's yacht. And still soundlessly singing, still with that trembling smile, Miss Brill prepared to listen.

"No, not now," said the girl. "Not here, I can't."

"But why? Because of that stupid old thing at the end there?" asked the boy. "Why does she come here at all—who wants her? Why doesn't she keep her silly old mug at home?"

"It's her fu-fur which is so funny," giggled the girl. "It's exactly like a fried whiting."

"Ah, be off with you!" said the boy in an angry whisper. Then: "Tell me, *ma petite chére*—"

"No, not here," said the girl. "Not *yet*."

On her way home she usually bought a slice of honeycake at the baker's. It was her Sunday treat. Sometimes there was an almond in her slice, sometimes not. It made a great difference. If there was an almond it was like carrying home a tiny present—a surprise—something that might very well not have been there. She hurried on the almond Sundays and struck the match for the kettle in quite a dashing way.

But to-day she passed the baker's by, climbing the stairs, went into the little dark room—her room like a cupboard—and sat down on the red eiderdown. She sat there for a long time. The box that the fur came out of was on the bed. She unclasped the necklet quickly; quickly, without looking, laid it inside. But when she put the lid on she thought she heard something crying.

Discussion Questions for Katherine Mansfield's "Miss Brill"

Overall themes. What themes does "Miss Brill" have in common with Maya Angelou's "Graduation"? What additional themes does "Miss

Brill" have? How do both re-create the effects of selfish insensitivity or unthinking prejudice?

Point of view. What does Katherine Mansfield achieve by telling the story from Miss Brill's point of view? How do you know you are in Miss Brill's mind?

Use of detail to suggest meaning. What indirect point is made when Miss Brill is moved by seemingly small and meaningless details like whether a song will repeat a musical sequence or whether her slice of honeycake will have an almond on it?

What are Miss Brill's feelings toward her fur? What is the "gentle" feeling that it "moves" in her?

Why does Miss Brill listen in on other people's conversations? What is the high point of Miss Brill's enjoyment in her outing? Why is her pretense of being in a play so satisfying to her? What do the young people kill for and in Miss Brill?

Use of a key image. How does her description of old people looking as though "they'd just come from dark little rooms or even—even cupboards" become significant in the story? Can you relate this image to a theme in Jean Shepherd's "The Endless Streetcar Ride Into the Night, and the Tinfoil Noose"? Why is this image referred to again at the end of the story?

Writing Suggestions Based on "Miss Brill"

Have you ever known a "Miss Brill" or witnessed a Miss Brill type of incident? How aware were the participants? What was your role in the event? Have you ever had a fantasy shattered by a cruel remark? How did you react? How did your behavior reflect your change in mood?

What comment does this story make about the role of the elderly in our society? How is society's view of the elderly coarsely reflected in the young people's remarks? Have you had firsthand experience with older people and the problems they face? How is Miss Brill's situation similar to and different from the situations you're aware of?

Example Papers Reacting to "Miss Brill"

THE CHINA CUPBOARD

The sunny August Detroit day seemed to melt away into a cold, ruthlessly gray afternoon as my family drove up to the nursing home to visit my grandmother. It had been two years since we had made the 2,000 mile trip back to Michigan to see her. As I walked into her room and really looked at the shrunken woman who was once my robust, energetic grandmother, I could see how senility had eaten away at her like a cancer. She didn't even recognize her youngest daughter, my mother. I watched her unsteadily get up and slowly trudge down the hall with me holding one arm and my mother the other. As we walked slowly through the yard, Grandma's diaper slowly fell down her legs to her feet—almost tripping her. She didn't even seem to notice it. The pain I felt at that moment wasn't a physical pain like I'd experienced playing football; it was an emotional pain, a hurt so deep that it shook my whole body and caused my throat to constrict. I turned to my mother and could see her grief as tears ran down her face.

The short story "Miss Brill" by Katherine Mansfield reminded me of my grandmother and the life she and so many other elderly people live today. Today's society, which is so geared for the young, seems to have little use for the old. Too often, people are caught up in their own life, and their parents are often forgotten or pushed aside until something tragic happens. The cupboard mentioned in this short story not only describes Miss Brill's room, but also describes her life and the life led by many older people today. Their lives are like a china cupboard. On the outside, their lives are the same day after day, definite and precise, like the sides and corners of a cupboard. But on the inside, the china cups represent all their little treasures in life—all the fond and happy memories of their past. For Miss Brill, the fur piece represented her past thrills, joys, and successes, the times she was needed and wanted, and the times in which life was worthwhile for her.

Sitting in the park and listening to the music and the people was Miss Brill's only connection with what could possibly be called a normal social life. She enjoyed going to the park and listening to other people's problems. It gave her a sense that she was still wanted, that she played a role in these people's lives. The almond in the story symbolized the only chance for a surprise in her otherwise dull, lonely life. It made her day a little bit exciting, wondering if she would get an almond in her cake or not. In order to combat the loneliness in her life, inside her china cupboard, she built a fragile world of her own. Simple things like an almond, fur piece, and trips to the park turned into big events for her.

The fragile world she created was easily broken by the insensitive statements of two kids who, unknowingly, destroyed a woman's whole world. What they said was:

"No, not now," said the girl. "Not here, I can't."
"But why? Because of that stupid old thing at the end there?" asked the boy. "Why does she come here at all—who wants her?

Why doesn't she keep her silly old mug at home?"

"It's her fu-fur which is so funny," giggled the girl.

"It's exactly like a fried whiting."

"Ah, be off with you!" said the boy in an angry whisper.

Then: "Tell me, *ma petit cherie——*"

"Not here," said the girl. "Not yet."

Within a few minutes, in just a few words, Miss Brill's china cupboard world crumbled. The loneliness, which she had fought for so long, came back all at once, and she became like all those other lonely old people in the park just sitting there letting the world pass them by.

My grandmother's china cupboard world began in her early sixties shortly after my grandfather died. In the years that followed, she began to draw into herself more and more as she created her own inner world. By 1968, she was senile and came to live with us until 1973 when, after the death of my brother, she became too much for the family to handle. Finally, after a year of prayer, heartache, and soul searching, my mother's brothers and sisters decided it was best for Grandma and everyone if she would live in a nursing home. There her diabetes, high blood pressure, and senility could be better controlled. With the last thread of a normal life cut away from her, plus a series of mini-strokes as a result of arteriosclerosis, Grandma withdrew to a world inside of herself—forgetting the names and faces of even her own children.

As we ended our visit a year ago, I remember the feeling I had. I had seen a grandmother who once was smart, witty, and generous to her children and grandchildren, sitting motionless and speechless before me—like those old people Miss Brill described in the park. My heart sank for them all.

—Mark Mauren

Questions on "The China Cupboard"

1. What incident creates the greatest impact in the opening description?
2. How does the writer incorporate the "china cupboard" image into his presentation of theme?
3. What scene does the writer allude to in ending his paper? How does it work?

SUNDAY'S BEST

In "Miss Brill," Katherine Mansfield points out some of the things old people enjoy and the cruel and indifferent way they are often treated by younger people.

Miss Brill found great pleasure in her Sundays. The way she prepared for them, the pastimes she engaged in, seem trivial to most nonelderly people. Who, but an older person, would find insurmountable joy in putting on a fox fur, in spending an afternoon second-guessing a band, or in having an almond in a slice of honeycake? Only to a lonely, older person are these events of any significance.

Miss Brill noticed something strange about the people in the park. "They were odd, silent, nearly all old, and from the way they stared they looked as though they'd just come from dark little rooms or even— even cupboards!" What Miss Brill didn't realize, until the boy shooed her off the bench, was that she was just like all the other people in the park; she had also just come from a cupboard.

Miss Brill and her cohorts came out of their cupboards each Sunday and went through the ritual of going to the park, just as many people bring out their special dishes for Sunday dinner or pull out their Sunday clothes for church. A lot of people treat the elderly as the boy did, not as a person, but as an object.

The last place I remember that people weren't treated as people, but as objects in a cupboard or closet, was in a convalescent home. I have only been in a convalescent home once in my life. My mom took me there to visit my great-grandmother. I was about ten-years-old and eager to see her, until we walked in the front door. A strange smell met us as the door swung open. It wasn't the same smell that is in hospitals or doctors' offices, but it was somewhat similar.

A large, empty, sterile looking waiting room greeted us. There were a few grey people sitting in the chairs along the walls. Muffled gibberish from a television set drifted out from the nearby "recreation area." We asked a starched receptionist in a stiff white uniform the way to grandma's room. An aide led us down a spic-and-span corridor and into her room. All the walls were white in this place. I guessed that this was so that they could spot and do away with any germs that escaped.

Grandma didn't look well, but we tried to be pleasant. It was hard, especially when she insisted on calling me some name I'd never heard of.

After the least amount of time that could be considered proper, we left. We walked down the white-washed hall and through the waiting room. It was strange to me that a place painted like that one could be so gloomy.

Something was different about the waiting room this time. It was almost full with small, withered people of the past. A couple of ladies were fighting over a small item, like a couple of four-year-olds. As Mom and I walked by, everyone turned and looked at us, each one wondering when his visitors would walk through the door. Mom and I knew, that unfortunately for most of those people, that special visitor would never come.

The only difference between the old people in the rest home and the old people in "Miss Brill" is that the people in "Miss Brill" came out of their cupboards every Sunday, while the people in the rest home were like antiques that would stay in their cupboards for the rest of their lives.

—Cathy Russell

Questions on "Sunday's Best"

1. What ideas are reflected in this paper's title?
2. What techniques does this paper use to effectively summarize and condense the ideas in the original story?
3. Which details in the description of the waiting room convey the mood evoked by the scene?
4. How does the ending reflect both parts of the paper?

Further Paper Possibilities and Student Example Papers Based on Fiction

You don't have to limit yourself to the stories and suggested assignments in this book. Any work you've read that presents a theme you can respond to or see in your own experience will do. The following papers present reactions to works of fiction that their authors were inspired to apply to their own lives.

BANANAFISH DAYS

Love, hate, fear, and anger are all regular emotions, exciting maybe, but regular. When I was fourteen, I discovered an all new emotion that has actually been around since the beginning of time, but I never knew its name. You throw the aforementioned feelings into a blender, osterize the hell out of them, and you end up with this new one—bananafish.

It had been a bad day for me. My true love was seen walking down the hall right past my locker with another girl. Miss Helfrich, my Home Ec. teacher, took great, vicious pleasure in announcing that I had just put in a zipper upside-down, much to the delight of the rest of the class. Over graham crackers after school my older brother explained, "What's a homely, retarded girl like you expect anyway?" Not grasping the magnitude of my despair, my mother then said, "If you don't bring up your algebra grade, you'll wind up being a garbageman—go to your room and study." I felt emotionally mauled by the end of the day. Reading in bed that night, I found a story that made me feel emancipated: there was another tortured soul. Better yet, there was a name for that feeling—bananafish.

"A Perfect Day for Bananafish" is a short story by J. D. Salinger, published in 1948. Seymour Glass had just come home from World War II (Germany) to his rich wife Muriel, Muriel's mother, and the affluent, snobby New York society. Muriel and Seymour took a vacation at a hotel and beach in Florida. Seymour drove. Muriel's mother phoned her long distance. The ensuing conversation told a lot about them. Muriel, lacquering her nails, reading excerpts from "Sex Is Fun—Or Hell," moving a button on her Saks blouse, tweezing out hairs in a mole, and smoking a cigarette, explained that yes, Seymour had driven down and much to her amazement had done well. Yes, he kept close to the white line. No, he hadn't tried any of that funny business with the trees. Muriel's mother told her that Muriel's father had told Dr. Sivetski everything—what Seymour did to the windows, that business with the trees, the horrible things he'd said to granny regarding her plans for dying, and what he'd done to the pictures from Bermuda. "The psychiatrist said Seymour is liable to lose complete control of himself." She added how sad it was, and how did her new blue coat fit? She emphasized how worried she was about Seymour's well-being, and how was the length on that ballerina dress? Muriel reassured her that everything was fine, but the ballerina dress was too long. She added that there was a psychiatrist in the hotel that was supposed to be good, and that the blue coat, after removing the shoulder pads, was just fine. Mom re-emphasized how sad it was, and asked what the latest fashions were like in Florida this year.

Seymour, meanwhile, was on the beach having a discussion with Sybil, a four-year-old girl. He told Sybil how well he liked her blue bathing suit, replied to her query about his wife—"She's probably in the room making dolls for the poor children"—and told her that he let Sharon sit by him at the piano because she wasn't mean to the little dogs in the lobby, even if she was only three. Sybil told Seymour that her bathing suit was yellow and demanded that he push Sharon off the piano bench next time she sat there. She inquired whether he'd read *Little Black Sambo* and how he felt about green olives and wax. Seymour responded that yes, she was quite correct—her bathing suit really was yellow, he'd just finished *Little Black Sambo* and never went anywhere without a pocketful of olives and wax. He suggested that they go bananafishing, as it was a perfect day for them. He explained that these fish led a peculiar and tragic life—they swim into a hole where there are bananas, they eat too many, and unable to swim back out, they die. He further explained that for this reason, the fish were rarely seen. Seymour and Sybil saw one that day.

Sybil then left. Seymour went back to the hotel, rode up the elevator, asked a well-dressed woman why she was staring at his feet, got to his room, looked at his sleeping wife, and shot himself through the head.

So, to have a bananafish day, you must feel Seymour's hopelessness, his knowing that there's only one way to fix things, his realization that he's unacceptable and can't conform.

I'll always remember all my bananafish days, but one stands out as the epitome of what I'm trying to say. It was a rainy, grey day (these type days usually are). I sat down across the large mahogany desk from Miss Johnson, the director of the school of nursing, for my first evaluation of my performance as a student nurse. "Now dear, we have all decided that you are quite immature as yet. You are sadly lacking judgment, organization, imagination, and the ability to apply your knowledge. We're giving you a 'C−' in performance for now and will let you stay. We'll be watching you." My stomach in my throat, I felt dizzy, utter despair. I knew I'd been trying my best. How could I do better than my best? I knew I'd end up being the disgrace of the family. My mother's threats came back—"You'll end up being a garbageman." I slunk out of Miss Johnson's office muttering, "Bananafish." "What did you say?" "Oh nothing," I said.

That night I read this story for about the twelfth time. Once again I knew I was a Seymour. The Muriels and Muriel's mothers of my life were getting me, but I wasn't going to let them defeat me like Seymour did. Seymour gives me renewed strength every time I have a bananafish day.

—Nancy A. Nichols

Questions on "Bananafish Days"

1. How does the writer first define and then illustrate her key term?

2. What details are used to summarize the original story? What framework holds her details together?

3. Is the writer's insertion of the story summary between two personal experiences effective?

4. How does her ending draw together the different parts of the paper?

A SLAP ON THE BACK AND A SMILE

Kurt Vonnegut, Jr.'s story, "Adam," opens with a normal, day-to-day event. Heinz Knechtmann is waiting in the maternity ward for news of his first born. Waiting with him is a big man, Mr. Sousa, who receives news that his wife had a girl, their seventh. He storms out of the room wondering why everyone else can get a son but him.

Mr. Knechtmann's parents, brothers, and sisters were killed in a German concentration camp. Heinz and his wife survived the ordeal, and to see life begin anew after all that death could only be a miracle.

The doctor enters the waiting room and informs Mr. Knechtmann it's a boy. The doctor has been methodically delivering babies for thirty-six hours and confuses Mrs. Knechtmann's condition with someone else's. Heinz finally straightens him out.

Heinz then goes to see his new son. The woman in the nursery looks only at his name on a card, not at his smiling, radiant face. She can't share his joy, as she has been through this scene thousands of times.

Having no relatives to share his happiness, he leaves the hospital to seek companionship in a tavern across the street. In it are just the bartender and Mr. Sousa. Happily he buys them both a beer. They tell him that a baby is a minor event. "Wait'll you've racked up seven, then you come back and tell me it's a miracle," says Mr. Sousa. The subject changes quickly to baseball. Heinz isn't a fan, so he leaves.

He then goes to the train station to catch a late shuttle home and meets a coworker there. Heinz tells him of his new son and of the miracle of a new life. His coworker pretends to be interested and happy for Heinz, but it's all a front. Heinz can see that he's far more interested in the girl he's with.

Throughout the story, Heinz has tried to communicate his joy, that having a baby is the epitome of wonder; he is greeted with anything from apathy to hostility. Heinz realizes that too many people are just too busy; another baby born is just another mouth to feed.

When I first started to read "Adam," my thoughts were "Oh God, another happy baby story." I am very down on having babies because I hold the opinion that no one in his right mind would want one. They scream, cry, and mess up thousands of diapers. On top of that, I believe that maybe one in ten parents knows beans about what he or she is actually getting into. But then I realized the baby theme was just a theme, and that many situations and events could be applied to the same story. I began to sympathize with Heinz Knechtmann.

I remember pitching my first no-hitter in Little League. I was quietly proud on the outside, but inside, I could hardly contain it. My parents were thrilled, but then parents are always thrilled. My friends and peers who weren't on the team couldn't have cared less. Their lives weren't touched by it.

Another incident was when I bought my first car. I purchased it from a used car dealer after months of careful shopping. I felt just like a real person, signing a credit application, a title form, and all the other legal rigamarole that comes with being an owner. Finally, I brought it home. I had to physically drag my mother outside to see it. All she said was, "It looks very nice." My friends said the same thing, adding they hoped it would hold up. It was an effort to find someone to share that December twenty-fifth feeling with me. I finally impressed my fourteen-year-old sister.

This generally uncaring attitude toward accomplishment can truly hurt a person. We all need that slap on the back, that smile, and that magic phrase "Nice job" once in awhile, or we begin to feel unwanted and insignificant.

—Alan Kaufer

Questions on "A Slap on the Back and a Smile"

1. Which scenes does the writer include in his summary of the original story?

2. How does the writer clarify his transition from "birth of a baby" to the success incidents?

3. What effect do his specific personal examples create?

4. What insights are produced by the writer's reaction?

Chapter Three

Analytical Writing: Focusing Outside the Self

> **Analysis** Breaking a whole into its *parts*; exploring the relationships of those parts to the whole.

When you analyze, you divide a *whole* into its parts and investigate each part's relationship to the whole. Examining the parts clarifies the whole: its make-up, purpose, and function. This process is like taking a clock apart to see how it works. If you correctly analyze the parts and their relationship to each other, you can reassemble the clock successfully. If your analysis is off, you have a jumble of uncoordinated parts—and are out one clock. The process remains the same whether you analyze a chemical substance, a mathematical equation, a machine, or a concept. In analytical writing, you apply the process to ideas.

A complex idea contains component parts. Each part relates to and helps express a total meaning larger than its own meaning. This larger meaning—which you could label as thesis, theme, concept, controlling idea, or philosophy—is what you're defining, proving, or clarifying when you write analytically. If your analysis works, you account for all the parts and fit them into the whole.

Closer to Objective than Subjective Writing

Analytical writing uses subjective opinions, interpretations, or evaluations, but it presents them objectively by emphasizing the ideas rather than the person who has the ideas. This focus on ideas makes analytical writing more objective than subjective.

Writing analytically is like operating on an idea. First you isolate and identify parts, then you dissect and examine them. If you perform your thought surgery successfully, you focus so totally on findings and results that your reader is hardly aware that you are operating behind the process.

A good analysis provides the same satisfaction for the writer as a successful experiment produces for a chemist. Both have discovered what a thing is or how it works; both have created order and turned unknowns into knowns.

Relationship of Analytical Writing to Personal Experience Writing

Analytical writing reverses the approach used in personal experience writing, since its purpose is to "tell" rather than "show," to interpret rather than re-create. In personal experience writing, you avoided labeling the effect you were describing and re-created it instead, letting your reader find his own label. In analytical writing, your purpose is to produce, examine, and clarify labels. You interpret and guide, leading your reader from main idea through supporting details to the conclusion you want him or her to reach.

Analytical writing differs from personal experience writing in focus and format. While personal experience writing focuses inside the self, analytical writing focuses outside the self. Writing an analysis paper is like writing a personal experience paper backwards. In personal experience writing, you produce parts that build to an effect. In analytical writing, you start by labeling and defining an already conceived conclusion or effect and then trace that effect back through the parts that produced it.

A good analytical paper not only "tells" but teaches. It takes a reader through an idea: defining, explaining, and clarifying connections, building the pieces back into an understandable whole. By making the thinking process visible, analysis makes complex ideas easier to follow, to comprehend, and to enjoy.

Starting with a Thesis

> **Thesis**   A paper's position statement; the central idea or framing concept that controls a paper.

All forms of analytical writing rely on a controlling thesis statement. The word "thesis" comes from the Greek verb "to place," and a thesis statement does just that: it "places" your position on a topic, and it clarifies the controlling idea behind that stance.

In analysis, you start with the whole, which you then break into parts and investigate. Your statement announces the whole idea you will analyze and signals the major support points you will explore. A clear analysis requires a clear thesis position. To obtain this clarity, you need not mechanically state your thesis in your paper's opening line, but you do need to have a thesis before you begin to write, and this thesis should come through clearly to your reader after reading your paper.

Your thesis should be narrow enough so that you can thoroughly support it in the length of your paper, and yet commanding enough to deserve your paper's central attention. Sometimes it helps to think of your thesis as the answer to some guiding question that prompted your analysis. For example, if you were exploring the question, "What are the problems facing the elderly in our society, and what can be done to solve them?" your answers would fall into two parts: identification of problems and identification of solutions.

Identify Key Support Areas to Create a Writing Framework

After listing a number of specific problems the elderly contend with, such as low income, rising cost of living, poor health, isolation, and low self-image, your next step would be to identify the key areas you could group these problems under. The student paper on this topic that follows, for example, groups the problems under three categories: economic, physical, and emotional. Possible solutions for each problem area are grouped under the categories: increased independence, recreational outlets, and companionship. After identifying these key support areas, the writer then uses them to create the basic framework for her paper.

Develop Each Framework Area in Elaborating on Your Thesis

After stating your main idea (thesis) and its key support points in an opening paragraph, use succeeding paragraphs to develop and substantiate each point.

The following student example paper illustrates this approach. It states its thesis and support area in its opening paragraph, then uses each of its developing paragraphs to elaborate on each area. The solutions suggested in the last half speak to each of the problems presented in the opening half. The conclusion re-emphasizes and resolves the opening thesis statement.

Example Analytical Paper

ON AGING AND INVOLVEMENT

Thesis: Identification of three problem areas

Elderly people in the United States are faced by a number of economic, physical, and emotional problems. Old age must be understood and reckoned with sympathetically by all ages in order to change these problems.

2   The economic problem is, perhaps, the greatest of the three. Retirement brings about a lowering of income and decreasing involvement with the world around the elderly. The retirement age is sixty-five; in all truth, it is a way of saying "You're all washed up." A lot of these

Elaboration of problem no. 1

people are willing and physically able to work after sixty-five; however, the majority of employers are unwilling to hire them. The aged usually depend on a fixed income such as Social Security and pensions—hardly enough to keep up with the continual rise in the cost of living. With such a meager amount of income, it becomes increasingly difficult for elderly persons to eat properly and afford their everyday costs: medications, clothing, housing, utilities, transportation, and the like.

3   Physical problems add to their frustrations. As is natural, a decrease in health comes about through changes in the body structure

Elaboration of problem no. 2

caused by aging. The bodily functions slow down, making the elderly more aware that they cannot move about as easily as they did when they were younger. Many times, they have trouble remembering things, and their sight worsens. Retirement often brings on many of these physical ailments because of a lack of both mental and physical activity.

4   Emotionally, too, many problems exist. America puts so much emphasis on the youth culture that the elderly feel pushed into the

Elaboration of problem no. 3

background. Advertisements about Polident can't possibly compare with Ultra Bright's "sex appeal" ads. Also, a less active life leads to emotional problems; the elderly person has plenty of time on his hands to sit around and brood or vegetate. Loss of friends from death also puts great emotional stress on the elderly. With their old friends gone, they begin to wonder why they should exist.

Transition to possible solutions Identification of 3 possible solutions

5   Clearly, all three problems interact with each other; therefore, all three need to be considered when trying to change the elderly person's life for the better. Society can help these problems by giving the elderly increased independence, recreational outlets, and companionship.

Elaboration of solution no. 1

6   The feeling of independence could be brought about by special housing, which would allow them to have a place of their own to care for and keep up. Encouraging them to do as many things as they can on their own, instead of automatically assuming they cannot do them, would bring about more independence.

Elaboration of solution no. 2

7   Recreation is also necessary in order to keep the elderly occupied and mentally alert. There is a great need for activity centers in which the elderly can paint, exchange crafts and ideas, play games, and take education courses. The satisfaction, morale, and self-esteem are higher among the elderly who remain more active.

Elaboration of solution no. 3

8   Companionship is a definite necessity. Interaction with the younger generation, as well as with people their own age, could bring new vitality to the aged. Through more interaction of this sort, elderly people gain the companionship they need, while society as a whole benefits from the valuable experience and knowledge they have to offer.

Conclusion

9   In short, it may not always be possible for us to drastically change the physical or economic facts of the lives of the elderly, but we can try. An understanding attitude can greatly add to their happiness. More and more people are becoming part of the older generation. It's important to get together in joint efforts to improve the lives of the aged— after all, we will all be there someday.

—Nancy Mercer

Keep a Clear Idea Focus

To focus is to direct your reader's attention to your key point or idea. The previous paper, "Aging and Involvement," maintains a clear idea focus. Its first paragraph states the main controlling idea for the entire paper, and each paragraph that follows centers on a key supporting area.

The example paper that follows, however, lacks a clear opening thesis statement and mixes the focus within its paragraphs by skipping from idea to idea rather than clarifying one point at a time. The paper contains enough ideas for a good analysis, but it needs to be reorganized and rewritten.

As an exercise in focus, try reworking the paper, clarifying its thesis, identifying support areas, and providing clear topic or idea sentences for each paragraph. Use the questions and exercises that follow it for further help and ideas.

Example of a Paper with Faulty Focus

AGING UMPIRES

1   Umpires are a rare breed: they are usually retired or it's a second job. Today, more than ever, coaches are yelling and appealing umpires' calls. I believe umpires can control the outcome of a baseball game.

2   About five years ago, umpiring was reserved for ex-baseball players, whose careers were ended but still wanted to stay with the game. Later, umpiring became a second job. Today, every Tom, Dick, and Harry thinks he can umpire. One of the major areas affected by bad calls is the outcome of a game. A team could have the bases loaded with two outs, and the umpire calls strike three on a ball in the dirt. All the bitching in the world won't help the outcome of the game. The player's individual performance is altered because of a miscue by the umpire. Also, a player's mental game is thrown off as a result of a bad call. Umpires can change the momentum of a team and take the bat right out of your hands with one bad call.

3   Many physical and mental reasons lie behind bad calls. An umpire could remember your face from a previous encounter where he threw you out of the game for arguing. Or, an umpire could be half asleep and miss the play altogether. The position of an umpire can greatly affect the view of a close play. Also, the umpire may get screened out by one of the fielders and fail to get an accurate view of the play. Bad calls happen in so many situations. The two extra players dressed in blue probably could use more training. This would enable the umpires to know what to do in every situation. Once a year umpires meet to go over new rules, review and update old ones, and renew old acquaintances. An umpire is under a lot of pressure for every call he makes. If it's a bad call, the home team will razz the ump. One player might say, "Shake your head ump, I think your eyes are stuck." Favoritism is another reason for bad calls. The umpires usually give the home team all the breaks.

4   A possible solution to these umpires' minor faults is to require them to receive adequate training and to keep up to date on rule changes. Every year, they should take a test before each season starts to review procedures and rules. Umpires must remain objective in order to make good calls. Also umpires should learn to stay cool and set a good example for the ballplayers. Each player should be courteous to all umpires and respect their calls.

5   In order to overcome bad umpiring, unity between players and umpires is needed. Players must respect the umpires' decisions, and umpires should be unbiased and make alert calls.

Questions and Exercises for Reworking "Aging Umpires"

Paragraph 1. What two interpretations could apply to "a rare breed"? Why is the term misleading? What actual problems are implied but not openly stated in the second half of the sentence? How does the second sentence shift focus? How might the last sentence be included as the concluding part of a thesis statement? What should the first part of the thesis clarify? How might the paper's title be worked into the thesis?

Paragraph 2. Why is the opening sentence too limited? What additional information does the second sentence need? Which line shifts this paragraph's focus? What material could be placed in a separate paragraph? Write a topic or controlling idea sentence for that paragraph.

Paragraph 3. This paragraph starts with a good controlling idea. How do the examples that follow it, however, come in a reverse order? What material in this paragraph would you relocate and develop in a separate paragraph? How do the last five sentences return to the paragraph's original focus?

Paragraph 4. Expand this opening sentence to include both of the main points covered in the paragraph. What information from paragraph three should be relocated in this paragraph? How does the last sentence switch focus? Where might this information be placed or should it be eliminated?

Paragraph 5. How does this paragraph switch to a new idea rather than summarize what has been presented? Rewrite an ending that emphasizes the paper's key ideas.

Type of writing   Analytical
Approach   Objective
Purpose   To focus on your own or another's idea, opinion, problem, or area of interest and to analyze it following a thesis framework

---

Possible Analytical Assignment Options

> Option no. 1   *Analysis of Your Own Opinion or Idea*
> Option no. 2   *Analysis of Another's Opinion or Idea*
> Option no. 3   *Analysis of a Problem*
> Option no. 4   *Analysis Explaining a Topic of Interest*

Before you try any of these assignments, first find, narrow, define, and articulate a possible thesis or central focusing idea. You will use that thesis to predict, restrict, unify, and control every statement in your paper.

Topic Ideas

Finding a Topic

Keep your topic limited and your focus specific. Scan a recent newspaper and note your reaction to subjects it presents. Look for topics that intrigue, excite, enrage, frustrate, or terrify you. What is your personal position on marriage, children, sex, violence, crime, education, male-female relationships, lack of jobs, our campaign-election process, automobiles, television programming, or advertising? How do you feel about politics in sports or failing school levies? What problems does a person face when re-entering school after an extended time away? Evaluate a potential topic, according to the three "i's":

Three "i" Criteria for Topic Choice
1. **interest**
2. **involvement**
3. **information**

---

1. *Interest.* The topic interests you; you've already read and thought about it; using your own reasons rather than someone else's, you could argue for or against it.

2. *Involvement.* You have some personal stake or firsthand involvement in the topic. The outcome of the problem would make a difference for you: your child's school is being closed for lack of funds; you are facing a depressed job market and need a job; your house has been burglarized repeatedly; television influences your children more than you do; you want to conserve gas but think small cars are unsafe and overpriced; you want to leave home, but can't afford both an apartment and college tuition. Pick a topic that looks into the causes of your problem and seeks an objective answer, one that counts personally.

3. *Information.* Since this is not a lengthy research project, you need to write about something you either already have information on or know where you can readily obtain such information. For example, you wouldn't have time to explore all our ecological problems in this paper, but you could focus on one particular problem such as water conservation in your state. Bite off small areas that you can digest thoroughly before you write.

Select a topic you find challenging, offbeat, or unusual. Don't write the umpteenth paper on capital punishment, abortion, prison reform, legalization of marijuana, or environmental pollution, unless the topic really moves you. Try approaching a topic from a new angle or investigate the unpopular side of an issue. Expand your thinking. Challenge yourself to clarify a muddy issue in your mind.

Whatever you choose, focus on the idea rather than on yourself. If your argument rests on emotion, analyze the emotion: what produced it; how reliable is it; what could change it. Analysis should clarify your position. If analyzing your thoughts exposes some fuzzy thoughts or shaky supports, recognize them as such. Feel free to go back, rethink the issue, and rewrite your thesis, firm up your support, and try for a sounder conclusion. Crystallize your arguments, pinpoint the origins, and weigh their credibilities.

How to Narrow a Topic

Say you were interested in writing about the effects of sexual stereotyping in our society. To narrow your topic, you could:

1. *Explore a specific area.* Investigate sexual stereotyping in jobs, education, child-rearing, marriage expectations, or different cultures.
2. *Explore a specific format.* Investigate sexual stereotyping in ad-

vertisements, children's literature, fairy tales, myths, cartoons, films, women's magazines, men's magazines, or literature from a particular time period.

3. *Explore its effect on a particular audience.* How does sexual stereotyping affect younger children, teenagers, single people, married people, or older people?

4. *Explore a specific case.* Document a known case of discrimination in one business area. Investigate a college's course catalogue for stereotyping. Trace sexual stereotypes as they appear in one Sunday's comics. Analyze sexual stereotypes as they appear in a film, book, play, magazine article, or newspaper editorial.

These techniques can be used to narrow any general area down to a more manageable writing topic.

Check Lists

> ### Check List for Analytical Writing
>
> 1. *Work from a thesis statement that provides a writing framework.*
> 2. *Define key terms.*
> 3. *Keep an idea focus.*
> 4. *Use an inverted pyramid structure: start the paper with your main controlling idea; start each paragraph with a key supporting idea.*
>
> (Note: As long as you have a controlling thesis firmly behind your writing, an optional structure would be to build to this thesis presenting it at the end. Using this approach, you will still start paragraphs with their key support points.)
>
> 5. *Include as many concrete details and specific support examples as possible; credit the source of your examples.*
> 6. *Explain the significance of your examples.*
> 7. *Work quotations and examples into your own sentence structure.*

```
8.  Check for clear transitions.
9.  End by re-emphasizing your thesis.
10. Cut wordiness.
11. Use parallel construction.
12. Check your mechanics.
```

Expanded Check List for Analytical Writing

The strength of your analysis depends upon the ideas you start with, your clarity in presenting those ideas, and your thoroughness in supporting them. The following check list will help you understand and use an analytical approach successfully. Its points adapt to most situations where analysis is required.

1. *Work from a thesis statement that provides a writing framework.*

Analytical writing is like assembling a jigsaw puzzle. It is easier to put the puzzle together if you keep the picture in mind as you place each piece. In analytical writing, your thesis (that is, your major concept, controlling idea, main point, or position statement) forms the equivalent of the puzzle picture. You give this concept to your readers first and then reconstruct it by reassembling its supporting parts.

Read the thesis paragraphs in the example papers in this chapter and note how they not only state the writer's position but also how they provide a framework for the papers to follow. For example, the thesis question of the student paper "Boob-tube Blues" reads:

> Although television has contributed greatly to our education and entertainment, is it worth the price we're paying in shrunken verbal skills, the creation of false realities, an increase in violence, and weakened family relationships?

The paper then goes on to explore the role of television in each of the areas mentioned in this framework opening.

You can create an opening framework sentence by stating your general theme or idea and then listing the major subparts that support it. An example of a framework opening could be:

In (name of material discussed), (name of author) explores the concept of (state your idea thesis) through his use of _____, _____, and _____ (list your major subparts).

Your paper will then follow the order of your subpart list: that is, the first paragraph after your thesis opening will present the first supporting point on your list; the second paragraph (or section, if the parts are longer) will present the next supporting point and so forth. You should be able to read the first lines of each paragraph in a well-organized analytical paper and come away with its main ideas.

2. *Define key terms.*

Check your thesis for any abstract terms that need defining. For example, both the student paper on "The Medical Value of the Human Aura" and the one on cryonics, which follows it, deal with specialized terms that need to be defined for the reader. Both papers follow their thesis statement with a clear definition of the term involved.

The paper on the human aura states:

> "Aura" comes from the Greek "avra," which means breeze. The aura, or energy field, is a light cast of the body energies. In effect, the aura is a reflection of the energies of the life processes. Basically, the human aura is described by the trained observer as an egg-shaped shell surrounding the body within which a particular intricate rainbow swirls and flows.

The paper on cryonics provides the following definition:

> Cryonics is a process of freezing a dead body in a tank of liquid nitrogen in order to preserve it and one day bring it back to life.

3. *Keep an idea focus.*

Don't call attention to the writing process or announce what you are going to write about. State your idea and begin with it. Focus on the material that you are presenting rather than on yourself. Instead of saying, I see _____ and _____ in this article, say _____ and _____ are in this article because. . . . Put your idea first where it will receive the emphasis. Since a reader knows that you are writing the paper, you don't have to continually start ideas with "I think" or "in my opinion" to qualify them as your own.

4. *Use an inverted pyramid structure as shown on pages 166 and 167: start the paper with your main controlling idea; start each paragraph with a key supporting idea.*

The pyramid order of presentation moves from large to small, from abstraction to supporting detail. Take your largest idea as your controlling thesis and start your paper with it. Begin each paragraph with a major supporting idea, and then give the examples that back it up.

Clarify how each example relates to the idea. Limit the paragraph and its examples to the idea presented in the first sentence. If it gets more complicated, either split the material into more paragraphs or rewrite your paragraph opening to include all its points.

For example, paragraph 4 in "Aging Umpires" starts with the sentence, "A possible solution to umpires' minor faults is to require them to receive adequate training and to keep up to date on rule changes." While this sentence focuses on the need for training, it fails to include the need for "objectivity," which the paragraph also explores. A more effective opening would include both ideas and might read: "Umpires need both training and objectivity to perform their job well."

If you select the optional structure of building to your thesis, keep your thesis firmly in mind as you present your support details. This approach can be especially useful in presenting an argument or opinion to a potentially hostile audience. Point by point build to your position so, hopefully, you've convinced your audience at the same time as you take your stance.

5. *Include as many concrete details and specific support examples as possible.*

Back up every assertion with an example, if possible. Notice how Paul Chadwick, in his essay "On Involvement," builds his case, point by point, example after example. Notice how concrete and detailed even small examples are in his paper. He clarifies "mind boggling" reports of people's insensitivity, for example, through specific descriptions like:

> Scores of people look on as a girl is stabbed dozens of times, finally to death. On a frozen Wyoming highway in a stalled car, a man with a bullet in his brain and a pistol in his hand is found clutching a note explaining that his day-long efforts to flag down cars went unheeded, and that he could no longer stand the cold.

He backs up his point on "dilution of responsibility when others are present," first by the specific comparison to one's hesitating to help "an ailing man on a secluded mountain trail," and then through two extended examples, one from an incident in Herman Melville's life, the other from a scene in the film *Midnight Cowboy*. Every point in the paper has one or more examples. Try for similar backup in your own writing. Remember that your argument is only as convincing as the support you include.

Credit the source of your examples the first time you use them in the body of your paper with phrases like "according to _____" or "_____ states in _____." If all examples are from one

Inverted Pyramid Structure for Presenting Ideas

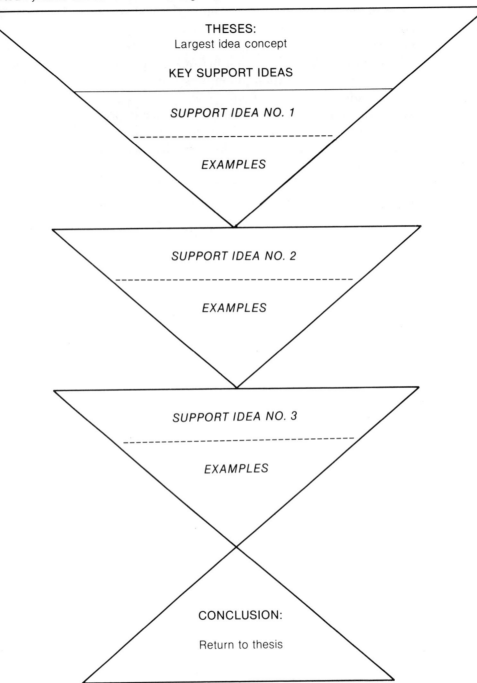

Example of Pyramid Structure Applied to a Specific Thesis

THESIS:

Elderly people in our society must deal with increased economic, physical, and emotional problems.

KEY SUPPORT IDEAS

SUPPORT IDEA NO. 1: The economic problem is the most severe.

EXAMPLES: Fixed income, unemployable, effects of inflation.

SUPPORT IDEA NO. 2: Physical problems increase.

EXAMPLES: Bodily functions slow down. Problems with seeing, hearing, and remembering. Activity increases the problems.

SUPPORT IDEA NO. 3: Emotional problems accompany the other problems.

EXAMPLES: Loneliness, loss of friends, boredom, and feeling of uselessness.

CONCLUSION:

Our society needs to devote more time and resources to combating the increased problems our elderly face.

source, you can follow quotations with page or paragraph references in parentheses right after you present them.

6. *Explain the significance of your examples.*

Clarify what your examples mean and how they support the point you are making. Don't assume that they speak for themselves. Explain material at the same time you present it.

In his essay "On Involvement," Paul Chadwick explains how increased populations in urban centers, at times, produce a feeling of "dilution of responsibility." He then uses an example from the film *Midnight Cowboy* to support his point, explaining the significance of the scene as he presents it:

> A short but potent scene in the film *Midnight Cowboy* illuminates the same gloomy truth. The naïve country-raised hero strolls down a New York sidewalk and nearly steps on a well-dressed man stretched out on the sidewalk. Shocked, he halts, but seeing the streams of city people neatly sidestepping the prostrate form, he resumes walking with at first jerky, uncertain steps, which become increasingly smoother as he leaves troubling doubt and bewilderment behind him.

7. *Work quotations and examples into your own sentence structure.*

By working examples into your own sentence structure, you can condense your material at the same time as you focus it on the idea it supports. Try presenting a series of different examples that support a single point, rather than giving each example in its entirety.

The paper "Boob-Tube Blues" combines a series of examples to support its contention that television distorts the real world:

> Children can also learn a false reality from television. They may believe absurd situations to be true. A kid may think that he has to be like the "six-million dollar man" to survive in the world. Television to often resorts to stereotypes, also. Mrs. Cunningham represents an average housewife; "Charlie's Angels" portray women who seem to win because of their good looks; and all school principals are rotten according to "Welcome Back, Kotter."

Use an entire quotation of some length only if all parts are needed, if the style is particularly noteworthy, or if you want to refer to the exact order and wording of the original. If you do include an entire quotation, also include a complete analysis of its significance. You want your paper to clarify material for your reader, not simply to present it.

8. *Check for clear transitions.*

Transitions provide the glue that hold your ideas together. They cement parts to each other by showing how one relates to the other and finally reconnect all parts to the whole. Use transitional words to clarify connections for your reader. Use key words from your framework sentence to indicate relationships. Repeat significant words from preceding paragraphs to tie material together. To show you are adding similar ideas use words like "just as," "also," "in the same way," "in addition to," or "similarly." To indicate a contrasting or opposing point use "on the other hand," "however," "in contrast to," or "in opposition to." Signal the close of your paper with words like "finally," "in summary," "therefore," or "in conclusion."

Look over the transitions in the example papers in this chapter for effective ways to link material together.

9. *End by re-emphasizing your thesis.*

A good ending returns your reader's attention to your main idea and pulls the parts back to the whole. You can summarize or reinforce your main argument, but don't bring in new ideas at this point. At the beginning of your paper, you stated a position you were going to prove and present. At the end of your paper, your position should be well substantiated. Let your ending reflect the completed, finished status of your thesis.

10. *Cut wordiness.*

When the content of your paper is complete, go back and tighten up your wording. Combine and shorten sentences, replace phrases with single words, eliminate needless repetition. The style exercises following this check list will help you cut deadwood and retain the active voice.

11. *Use parallel construction.*

Parallel construction Presenting ideas in the same sentence structure, repeating the same connecting words, parts of speech, and word endings.

Parallel construction uses the same word pattern to present different ideas. You are probably most familiar with it in famous quotations like Lincoln's ". . . of the people, by the people, and for the people . . ." or Patrick Henry's "Give me liberty, or give me death."

Use parallel construction whenever you're using lists or emphasizing equally weighted points around expressions like "not only . . . but also," "either . . . or," "both . . . and," and "__ as well as __." You can also create a unified effect by introducing larger parts of your paper repeating the same word patterns. For more examples and ideas using parallelism, go over the style exercises at the end of this check list.

12. *Check your mechanics.*

Don't let poor mechanics take your reader's attention from your ideas. Double check your spelling (including where to hyphenate words you split at the ends of lines) and your punctuation. Check sentences for clarity and completeness. Be consistent in your use of pronouns (don't switch from "I" to "you" to "we"), of tense (don't switch from past to present), and of tone (don't switch from formal to informal.) Clarify what all your "this's" and "its" refer to. Put apostrophes in possessives (for example, Tom's opinion) but not in plurals (that is, two Toms). Check for tricky pronoun agreement pairs:

everybody	—her, his
everyone	—her, his
the company's	—its
the town's	—its
the public's	—its
the students'	—theirs
the voters'	—theirs

Perfecting your mechanics is like washing a dirty car before you try to sell it. Potential buyers, like potential readers, can be put off by appearances.

Style Exercises

Style Exercises for Analytical Writing

Pruning Deadwood

> **Deadwood**   Unnecessary words that take up space but add no meaning.

Just as pruning a tree improves its vitality, likewise cutting unnecessary words strengthens your writing.

Look for the following problem words and phrases:

1. *Too many "of's."* Little words can clutter up your writing as easily as big words. "Of" is a notorious "of" fender. You can get by with one "of," but an informal rule might be:

> With two "of's," start checking.
> With three "of's," start chopping.

Try substituting possessives for "of's." Replace "tail of the dog" with "the dog's tail."

2. *"That, which, and who" phrases.* Replace "faucets that drip" with "dripping faucets."

3. *"There is," "there are" openings.* Start your sentence with the subject that immediately follows "There is" and you will automatically say more, sooner. Replace "There are many problems in today's education . . ." with "Problems in today's education include. . . ."

4. *"–tion" words.* Sentences loaded with "–tion" nouns like institu*tion*, condi*tion*, realiza*tion*, constitu*tion*, idealiza*tion* tend to get bogged down. Replace "Educa*tion* is an institu*tion* that leads to the realiza*tion* of our dreams," with "We educate to achieve our dreams." Whenever possible, shun "–tion."

Further Deadwood to Chop

Create a horrible example combining phrases from the following list with other wordy expressions you know. Then cut your example down to its basic message.

Deadwood List

In the book it states that . . .	Along the lines of . . .
According to the fact that . . .	In the very near future . . .
The reason why you do that is because . . .	Before I ever started with . . .
At the present time . . .	I believe my statement will show . . .
For the purpose of . . .	During the course of . . .
During the time that . . .	In regard to your remark . . .

In a precise manner . . .	In the event that . . .
Come in contact with . . .	In the month of May . . .
In the event that . . .	It involves a great deal of . . .
	Due to the fact that . . .

Horrible example:

In regard to your remark that the institution of education in this day and age involves a great deal of money, it is a statement that I'm not in a position to refute at the present time.

Condensed version:

You're right. Education costs a lot.

Variation of the Deadwood Exercise

Create "deadwood" versions of simple folksayings, and see if others can guess the original.

Horrible example:

It is a fact that you should hypothetically survey your immediate surroundings before you take it upon yourself to turn yourself into a projectile.

Translation:

Look before you leap.

Expand the following (with apologies to Ben Franklin):

A fool and his money are soon parted.
A penny saved is a penny earned.
Waste not; want not.
The early bird catches the worm.
Fish and visitors smell in three days.

Use the Active Voice

> **Active voice**   Starting sentences with subjects that perform the action indicated.
> **Passive voice**   Starting sentences with subjects that receive action or are acted upon.

In the *active voice*, your subject *does* the action in your sentence; in the *passive voice*, your subject *receives* it.

> *Active:* "I shut the door." ("I" *does* the action)
> *Passive:* "The door was shut by me." ("The door" is *receiving* the action).

Advantages of Active Voice

1. Shorter (In the example, six words are replaced by four)
2. More forceful (It's more direct)
3. Places emphasis on verbs ("Shut" is more powerful than the diluted "was shut.")
4. Assigns responsibility (You know who did it!)

Scan your papers for weak passives and replace them with active voice. Start sentences with "doers" whenever possible.

Active versus Passive Voice Exercises

Exercise no. 1: Underline all the passive verbs in the following paragraph and rewrite them using active voice. Feel free to reword or add information to supply missing *doers*, but try to retain all information present in the paragraph.

> A student was seen driving into the school parking lot at an unreasonable speed. The check-in kiosk was passed without stopping, even through a permit sticker was lacking from the car's window. Other cars were passed by the erratic driver until a tree was crashed into by the student speeder. The scene was rushed to by curious onlookers. The student was pulled out of his smashed car by two campus guards, and he was found to be shaken but unhurt. It was explained to the guards by the student that an exam had to be taken by him, and he was hurrying to it. The student was informed that now he was not only late, but also under arrest.

Exercise no. 2: Construct a paragraph from raw information given below. Use *only* active verbs throughout your paragraph.

> Jerry Jessup, student at M.W.U.
> Straight out of high school.

Bridge games instead of class.
Good weather, skip class.
Long lunches, conversations, little studying.
Television at night.
Rock concerts on weekends.
End of quarter, probation.
End of year, out.

Using Parallel Construction

Parallel construction deliberately repeats word patterns for emphasis, for clarity, and for effect.

Exercise no. 1: Underline and discuss all the examples of parallel construction in "Kennedy's Inaugural Address":

INAUGURAL ADDRESS[1]

JOHN F. KENNEDY

My Fellow Citizens:

1   We observe today not a victory of party but a celebration of freedom—symbolizing an end as well as a beginning—signifying renewal as well as change. For I have sworn before you and Almighty God the same solemn oath our forebears prescribed nearly a century and three quarters ago.

2   The world is very different now. For man holds in his mortal hands the power to abolish all form of human poverty and to abolish all form of human life. And, yet, the same revolutionary beliefs for which our forebears fought are still at issue around the globe—the belief that the rights of man come not from the generosity of the state but from the hand of God.

3   We dare not forget today that we are the heirs of that first revolution. Let the word go forth from this time and place, to friend and foe alike, that the torch has been passed to a new generation of Americans—born in this century, tempered by war, disciplined by a cold and bitter peace, proud of our ancient heritage—and unwilling to witness or permit the slow undoing of those human rights to which this nation has always been committed, and to which we are committed today.

---

[1]John F. Kennedy, "Inaugural Address." Delivered at the United States Capitol, Washington D.C., 30 January 1961.

4   Let every nation know, whether it wish us well or ill, that we shall pay any price, bear any burden, meet any hardship, support any friend or oppose any foe in order to assure the survival and success of liberty.

5   This much we pledge—and more.

6   To those old Allies whose cultural and spiritual origins we share, we pledge the loyalty of faithful friends. United, there is little we cannot do in a host of new co-operative ventures. Divided, there is little we can do—for we dare not meet a powerful challenge at odds and split asunder.

7   To those new states whom we now welcome to the ranks of the free, we pledge our word that one form of colonial control shall not have passed merely to be replaced by a far more iron tyranny. We shall not always expect to find them supporting our every view. But we shall always hope to find them strongly supporting their own freedom—and to remember that, in the past, those who foolishly sought to find power by riding on the tiger's back inevitably ended up inside.

8   To those peoples in the huts and villages of half the globe struggling to break the bonds of mass misery, we pledge our best efforts to help them help themselves, for whatever period is required—not because the Communists are doing it, not because we seek their votes, but because it is right. If the free society cannot help the many who are poor, it can never save the few who are rich.

9   To our sister republics south of our border, we offer a special pledge—to convert our good words into good deeds—in a new alliance for progress—to assist free men and free Governments in casting off the chains of poverty. But this peaceful revolution of hope cannot become the prey of hostile powers. Let all our neighbors know that we shall join with them to oppose aggression or subversion anywhere in the Americas. And let every other power know that this Hemisphere intends to remain the master of its own house.

10   To that world assembly of sovereign states, the United Nations, our last best hope in an age where the instruments of war have far outpaced the instruments of peace, we renew our pledge of support—to prevent its becoming merely a forum for invective—to strengthen its shield of the new and the weak—and to enlarge the area to which its writ may run.

11   Finally, to those nations who would make themselves our adversary, we offer not a pledge but a request: that both sides begin anew the quest for peace, before the dark powers of destruction unleashed by science engulf all humanity in planned or accidental self-destruction.

12   We dare not tempt them with weakness. For only when our arms are sufficient beyond doubt can we be certain beyond doubt that they will never be employed.

13   But neither can two great and powerful groups of nations take

comfort from their present course—both sides overburdened by the cost of modern weapons, both rightly alarmed by the steady spread of the deadly atom, yet both racing to alter that uncertain balance of terror that stays the hand of mankind's final war.

14   So let us begin anew—remembering on both sides that civility is not a sign of weakness and sincerity is always subject to proof. Let us never negotiate out of fear. But let us never fear to negotiate.

15   Let both sides explore what problems unite us instead of belaboring the problems that divide us.

16   Let both sides, for the first time, formulate serious and precise proposals for the inspection and control of arms—and bring the absolute power to destroy other nations under the absolute control of all nations.

17   Let both sides join to invoke the wonders of science instead of its terrors. Together let us explore the stars, conquer the deserts, eradicate disease, tap the ocean depths and encourage the arts and commerce.

18   Let both sides unite to heed in all corners of the earth the command of Isaiah— to "undo the heavy burdens . . . (and) let the oppressed go free."

19   And if a beachhead of co-operation can be made in the jungles of suspicion, let both sides join in the next task: creating not a new balance of power, but a new world of law, where the strong are just and the weak secure and the peace preserved forever.

20   All this will not be finished in the first 100 days. Nor will it be finished in the first 1,000 days, nor in the life of this Administration, nor even perhaps in our lifetime on this planet. But let us begin.

21   In your hands, my fellow citizens, more than in mine, will rest the final success or failure of our course. Since this country was founded, each generation has been summoned to give testimony to its national loyalty. The graves of young Americans who answered that call encircle the globe.

22   Now the trumpet summons us again—not as a call to bear arms, though arms we need—not as a call to battle, though embattled we are—but a call to bear the burden of a long twilight struggle, year in and year out, "rejoicing in hope, patient in tribulation"—a struggle against the common enemies of man: tyranny, poverty, disease and war itself.

23   Can we forge against these enemies a grand and global alliance, north and south, east and west, that can assure a more fruitful life for all mankind? Will you join in that historic effort?

24   In the long history of the world, only a few generations have been granted the role of defending freedom in its hour of maximum danger. I do not shrink from this responsibility—I welcome it. I do not believe that any of us would exchange places with any other people or any other

generation. The energy, the faith and the devotion which we bring to this endeavor will light our country and all who serve it—and the glow from that fire can truly light the world.

25   And so, my fellow Americans: Ask not what your country will do for you—ask what you can do for your country.

26   My fellow citizens of the world: Ask not what America will do for you, but what together we can do for the freedom of man.

27   Finally, whether you are citizens of America or of the world, ask of us the same high standards of strength and sacrifice that we shall ask of you. With a good conscience our only sure reward, with history the final judge of our deeds, let us go forth to lead the land we love, asking His blessing and His help, but knowing that here on earth God's work must truly be our own.

Exercise no. 2: Examples of parallel construction from the first paragraph in Kennedy's speech are:

not a _____ of _____
but a _____ of _____
symbolizing an _____ as well as a _____
signifying _____ as well as _____

Use these word patterns to present a different topic or use the word patterns in another paragraph in the speech to present a new message. What effect does the parallelism achieve?

What examples of larger parallelism unite the various sections of Kennedy's speech?

Option No. 1–Analysis of Your Own Opinion or Idea: Student Example Papers

---

Student Example Papers for Option No. 1

First read each essay for its impact and ideas; then reread it scanning the marginal notes that highlight its organizational structure: thesis and support parts. Scan the question and comments that follow each essay for further ideas on content and writing techniques.

ON INVOLVEMENT

Background
materials

Statement of
problem

Use of concrete
examples

Statement of
people's reaction
to the problem

Transition

Writer's actual
thesis

General
statement of
supporting areas

Transition

Background for
1st supporting
idea

Specific support
examples

Statement of 1st
supporting idea

Use of concrete
specifics

Transition

1   Much, maybe too much, has been said about the dehumanizing effects of cities and other much-prevalent facets of modern life. Over the news wires come an incessant electronic stream of mind-boggling reports concerning incidents where people have sat idly by to see their neighbor maimed or killed, when the slightest action would have saved him. Each one seems more incomprehensible than the last. Scores of people look on as a girl is stabbed dozens of times, finally to death. On a frozen Wyoming highway in a stalled car, a man with a bullet in his brain and a pistol in his hand is found clutching a note explaining that his day-long efforts to flag down cars went unheeded, and that he could no longer stand the cold. With each new absurdity, we grimly shake our heads, marveling at people's seemingly limitless capacity for insensitivity, and think of the heartless, faceless passersby with utter contempt.

2   Perhaps this contempt isn't really justified, though. Possibly these people are simply behaving in a rational, predictable manner, not evil but the result of a multiplicity of circumstances and forces we can identify and understand. From things I've read and heard, as well as from personal experience, I've been forced to recognize some of these forces as powerful and often inescapable. It seems that people are pushed into behaving as they do by sociological forces and their own psychological nature.

3   Oddly, one factor would seem to be tied to the thing that makes us *want* to help the man in the jam. Its names are many: conscience, compassion, the Golden Rule, the super-ego. The psychologists tell us we build this shaky mental structure with countless scraps of approval and disapproval, first by our parents ("Stop teasing the cat, Billy!") and later by the other people who rub and bruise elbows with us. The small child, not yet graced with the imprint of society, is remarkably savage; in the bombed-out ruins of Berlin, it was the very young who survived, by sheer dint of ruthlessness. The older children's handicap of scruples outweighed their advantage of age. The paradoxical thing is that while it is this desire for approval that leads to compassion, so is it that same desire that can hold back the helping hand. Call it some sort of sheep instinct if that sounds right, but in that uncertain moment of sudden violence, if everyone else is holding back from pitching in to help, it could be that there's a good reason not to do so. Perhaps they all know something that we don't; he's a drunk, not the victim of a coronary occlusion—it is wrong to help. Even if the situation is thought through and it is realized that everybody thinks the same thing about everybody else, in that brief, confused time in which a decision has to be made, it can make the difference.

4   Having other people around, as is increasingly the case as popu-

Statement of 2nd supporting idea

Specific examples

Extended example from the past

Extended example from the present

Transition

Statement of 3rd supporting idea

Expanded public example

Expanded private example

lations swell and cities sprawl, has another effect. There is a strange dilution of responsibility when others are present. Should we find an ailing man on a secluded mountain trail, we wouldn't think that someone else will or should take responsibility; with others around, we feel (perhaps rightly—who's to say?) they have just as much responsibility as we do. As that commodity is spread thinner, it is felt less by each individual. This process can become custom, strengthening its effect beyond the initial rationalization. As a young man, Herman Melville, not yet acclimated to this way of thinking, came upon a young woman and her child who were literally starving to death in a London alley. He was horrified, not only by the sordid fact itself, but also with the indifference he met when he tried to get people to do something about it. He finally managed to bring the authorities back to the alley, only to find that the pair had died. A short but potent scene in the film *Midnight Cowboy* illuminates the same gloomy truth. The naive country-raised hero strolls down a New York sidewalk and nearly steps on a well-dressed man stretched out on the sidewalk. Shocked, he halts, but seeing the streams of city people neatly sidestepping the prostrate form, he resumes walking with at first jerky, uncertain steps that become increasingly smooth as he leaves troubling doubt and bewilderment behind him.

5   Another doubt that edges into the potential hero's mind is the "probability" that something has already been done and that personal action might be unnecessary or ineffectual. Surely a good many of the Queens, N. Y., residents who quietly watched from apartment windows as Kitty Genovese was slowly, laboriously stabbed to death felt that somebody had certainly called the police. Unfortunately for Kitty, *everybody* assumed that—at least nobody called. As for myself, just recently I was enroute to Bainbridge Island when the ferryboat's public address system rumbled out a plea for a doctor or anyone with first aid experience to come to the second mate's office. That week I had just finished the second session of a first aid course and knew nothing beyond cardio-pulmonary resuscitation, which nevertheless could save a life. The rationalizations came thick and fast. Surely, with a packed boat as it was, there'd have to be a doctor or some aid-wise hiker type to attend to the victim's ailments. With my limited knowledge, I doubted whether I'd be at all effective anyway. Also, even if CPR could have made a difference, I knew that Seattle was, according to statistics (and to Morley Safer on "60 Minutes"), the safest city in the country to have a heart attack in, as one person in every five knows how to administer CPR. And even if the sheer weight of statistics and probability didn't deliver a CPR practitioner, I knew my sister, who had been taking the course along with me, was on board and would certainly offer her assistance (she did, I later found out). It turned out that some poor soul had snapped an arm bone on the car deck and was

promptly seen by a pack of alert MDs, but I wonder how many other potential bandage jockeys shared my mental machinations.

6   Not to be discounted is the consideration of personal risk. *Time* has quoted Norman Mailer as stating something to the effect that the state of today's cities has caused the word paranoia to be semantically equivalent to common sense. People cannot be expected to be totally selfless, and concern for "number one" is an acceptable partial excuse for inaction. Even when there is no physical danger present, in the absence of effective "Good Samaritan" laws (which is the case in Washington, I'm told), the mishandling of first aid or a rescue can tailor-make a lawsuit. Similarly, although on a less urgent level, is the decision whether or not to pick up a hitchhiker. The paranoia-induced stories are numerous and often close to home. My sister tells me of the bloody, battered man stumbling along the shoulder of a lonely stretch of highway who explained when she stopped that a couple of hitchhikers had beaten him and taken his car. The threat of personal risk is another weighty consideration that drags on the helping hand.

7   One of the stranger inhibitors concerns one's embarrassment for the victim in need of assistance. A friend tells me of how a stroke victim was ignored by people who explained that they refrained from coming to his assistance out of concern for his pride. Collapse is an embarrassing position to be in, and by not acknowledging it—letting the fallen person get up on his own—perhaps some feelings are spared. It seems silly on the surface, but again, such decisions are made in a state of stress and confusion, and there is a sort of jumbled priority logic about the notion.

8   Finally, one phenomenon certainly more widespread today than it has been in the past is the frightful brevity of exposure in situations where life-saving help is needed. Often such situations are the results of accidents involving a great, sudden force, as is usually present when people are on the move. Our glass-and-metal shells whisk us too quickly beyond the zone of injury and decision-making. We get a brief flash of somebody who *perhaps* needs help, but so soon are we beyond it that it is easy to leave it to the people who are still back there. We don't really trust the input we got while back there because of its abruptness; perhaps, we think, no help was needed at all. I recall one

time when I was rocketing down a steep hill on my bike as a child when the book tied to the handlebars began to come loose. I fumbled with it, and when I looked back up, I found I was drifting off the abrupt edge of the asphalt. Losing control, I executed a spectacular flip which twisted the front of my bike around unnaturally like a man with a broken neck, shredded my jeans, and rasped off enough skin to make a small lamp shade. As I lay in the dirt and rocks and weeds, paralyzed with shock and pain, I watched with outraged amazement as car after car jauntily sped by, my agony unnoticed. Eventually I gathered together all my loose parts and painfully limped home. It wasn't until several years later that I understood how easy it was not to stop.

Transition

Self as passerby

Extended example

9 The time I learned that, my sister, grandfather, and I were returning home through nighttime Seattle. A traffic signal cued my sister to yank the parking brake, the beginning of the ritual drivers of cars with clutches must go through to start an incline. As I looked to my left, I caught a jolting glimpse of a young, nicely attired man sprawled face down on the uneven rubble of the torn-up street. Not ten feet away, silhouetted by the eerie, dirty-pink glow of a mercury streetlamp, stood two young women who were paying absolutely no attention to him. "There's a guy lying in the street over there!" I cried as we jerkily passed under a green light. I described further what I had seen, not suggesting outright that we should do something, but implying it. My sister said she thought an aid car was across the street. My grandfather recited a limerick about how a man who can still get up off the floor hasn't had too much to drink. By that time we had put some distance between ourselves and the scene, and as if it were some sort of radiant energy emanating from that point, the feeling of obligation steadily faded away.

Specific responses

Statement of conclusion

Summary of supporting ideas

Restatement of thesis

10 All these factors are unfortunate, particularly for the victims, although there is also the price in self-respect that the nonhelper pays when he passes by. However, the factors are understandable, and it is easy to see how they can account for what at first might seem like unfathomable callousness. The psychological factors of the need for approval, the sociological factors of large numbers of people and the subsequent dilution of responsibility, the assumption of the lack of necessity for personal action, the consideration for personal interest, that strange backfiring of compassion where an inordinate premium is placed on pride, and the speed with which we pass through crisis situations all conspire to withhold aid from the individuals who desperately need it. The problem isn't that people are inhumanely heartless; it is that they are all too human.

—Paul Chadwick

Questions and Comments on "On Involvement"

1. In what way is the writer's position an unusual or unexpected approach to his topic? How does his concrete portrayal of the problem in paragraph 1 add to the surprise effect of his actual thesis stated in paragraph 2?

2. What transitional techniques does the writer use in presenting

each new idea? Which words provide the transitional effect in each case? Which transitions are most effective?

3. Notice the concrete examples substantiating every idea presented. Which ones influenced you most?

4. What indirect comment does the writer make by supporting his "dilution of responsibility" point (in paragraph 4) first with an extended example from the past and then with an extended example from the present?

5. What effect does he achieve by following his public example of failure to respond with a private example (in paragraph 5)? Why is this order the best one for his purposes?

6. How does he make a similar point by using examples first with self as victim (in paragraph 8) and finally with self as one of the "passersby" (in paragraph 9)? How do the specific responses of others reinforce his point?

7. How does the ending tie the parts of the paper together? What organizational pattern is repeated in the long summary sentence? What does the final sentence accomplish?

A DIVINE PLAN

Personal reaction

1   I've been reading in Yogananda's *Autobiography of a Yogi* and Maharishi Mahesh Yogi's translation of the *Bhagavad-Gita*, and in both, there is a lot of reference to the Divine Plan. My first reaction to mentions of a divine or cosmic plan is always to feel a little huffy, resentful, reluctant to even consider the possibility. You mean to say that with all the agonizing I do over simple decisions—hoping I'm making the right one, praying I'll not wish I'd chosen another, closing my eyes for the leap—it's all been planned anyway? And all this time, I thought I had some say in how my life happens. Boy, see if I ever lift a finger again.

2   But Maharishi says that "the nature of life is to evolve," and I understand that I can't just sit and expect to do much growing that way. Evolution—not only my own but of the universe—is dependent upon my performing actions in the outside world, participating in "karma"— the universal law of cause and effect. He also says that "the wise" (the enlightened of men) "are tools in the hands of the Divine; they innocently carry out the divine plan." Well, I wouldn't label myself as enlightened or anywhere near, but hopefully on the road, and a possible proof of a cosmic plan is my new awareness of my part in the complicated chain of events. How strange the way all the little happenings

Thesis

during the day add up to my being in a certain place at a certain time to perform a certain action. Sometimes it is only to be a witness to someone else's action, which causes me to act in a resulting way some time later. But there have been instances when it would have been drastic for other people had I not coincidentally been somewhere at the exact moment to grab an elbow or catch a door before it slammed on a foot.

Major examples

3   A couple of weeks ago I was in Seattle, running for the monorail, and I stopped to grab the shoulders of a blind boy who had just run into a light post and was getting ready to fall into a planter. I ended up taking him all over the city—helped him do his grocery shopping—and he bought me coffee in a little cafe. It was kind of a bizarre experience, really, and I'm glad I was there so it could happen.

Example no. 1

4   Last summer I think I saved a life. That's actually when I first started wondering about this divine plan thing. It was a really early morning, and I'd been riding my bike all over for a couple of hours, getting off when something caught my interest and following whatever road looked good. I'd even stopped to draw the geese at the lake, just fooling around, taking my time. I was pushing my bike up a steep hill with a handful of flowers when I looked up to see a little kid just standing in the far lane and wearing nothing but his pajama bottoms. He was shivering like crazy and looked like he'd done a lot of crying. I thought, "Oh boy, the good deed-doer's dream—a little lost kid." Then I yelled, "Quick! Run over here! There's a car coming!" The kid startled into a little patter towards me, and the car shot into view over the crest of the hill and on down behind us. If all the fooling around I'd done that morning hadn't added up to my being there to call him across the road, that kid would have been hit and probably killed. And even if, for some reason, neither I nor the car was there when he was, he was lost and on the verge of hypothermia. As it was, it took me a good half hour—with him stuck on my hip and his feet in the flaps of my sweaty overalls and my arms around his shoulders—to even find someone who was up at that hour and could give him a warm house to wait in until the police got hold of his mother. It really made me ponder.

Example no. 2

Minor examples

5   Of course, it's not always that dramatic. Most times, it's just tiny—like passing people you'll never see again but sharing a smile, wondering how it affected the rest of their day and knowing yours was better for it. So many times my days full of actions seem mundane and worthless; I don't get to see the reasons for my acting. My own benefits are too long-range for me to catch. But when the results are direct—wow! It's like a slap in the face.

6   Like one night I was in Seattle visiting friends and lingered talking so long at the door that I tore out of the monorail just in time to miss the 9:45 bus and was stuck with two hours until the next (and last) one

came through. I didn't have any more money—only bus tickets—so the monorail lady let me ride on credit back to the center to wait where

it was warm with no bums. First I ran back to my friends' house to get change for bus tickets, but they were in bed, and I had to ask around in a "Dick's" until somebody could do the exchange. Back at the Center House, I moped furiously around trying to figure out why it was happening, and I couldn't. So much time going to waste and I couldn't do a damn thing about it. No book to read and no pen or paper to write a mad letter with. Then the guard started up a conversation with me, and we talked about the most unlikely things: reincarnation, talking to plants, and—briefly—transcendental meditation. When it was finally time for me to leave, he asked me if I would bring him some literature on TM, and it was like the old light bulb in my head—so that's why I missed my bus!

One more example: I've been thinking for a long time about being a student counselor, but can't quite make up my mind. A couple of months ago I was walking out to the parking lot with a friend who suddenly knocked himself on the head and ran off to get something he'd

forgotten, and while I was waiting, a woman came up and asked if I would answer some questions about counselors. She was taking the schooling to become one and was doing a survey to find out what people thought of them. Well, we ended up talking for almost thirty minutes (much to my friend's impatience), during which she straightened out a lot of questions in my head about being a counselor, and I gave her back some views she hadn't gotten yet. It was a mutually beneficial encounter. Who decided my friend should forget his book and I should be left standing, ripe for the knowledge this woman had to offer?

I don't know. Maybe the divine plan is only that we all be used to help each other in our evolutions. Should that be the case, I am excited

and thrilled as my unconscious part in the drama becomes more and more obvious to me. How many ripples will the little stone of this paper make in the pond? There's no way I can ever know. "Unfathomable is the course of action"—*The Bhagavad-Gita*, chapter IV:17.

—Jill Harris

Questions and Comments on "A Divine Plan"

1. How does the writer incorporate her own uncertainty into her thesis? What effect does this have on the paper's tone and purpose?

2. What effect is achieved by presenting both major and minor examples? Which examples are most convincing or effectively presented and why?

3. How does her conclusion fit her thesis?

A TWENTY-FIVE CENT TOUR

Thesis

1   I'm house-sitting for my parents again. They're in Colorado. Being used to the noise, disorganization, and general confusion at my house on Capitol Hill (a kid sitting on our front steps one day asked me, "Is this some kind of sorority house or what?"), the quiet of Normandy Park is a welcome change. In my words at age fifteen, "It makes me all pensive and everything." One depressing evening, I thought about why I didn't have a date (I brush my teeth), which made me wonder why I shouldn't go to the store for some chocolate chip cookies (my anti-depressant), which made me wonder, "If I hanged myself who would care?" Which made me wonder what makes people care. Is it learned or inborn? I came up with an answer for myself by taking a tour of this house where I grew up.

Example no. 1

2   The kitchen. Over there at the stove was where many of my first culinary disasters took place: granulated fudge, blackened biscuits, fallen cakes suitable only for discus throwing, salty cookies, sugary spaghetti, and charred chicken. Also it was where my mother once told me, "We love you. If anything ever happens to you that you can't handle by yourself, please come to us." Sitting at the kitchen table, I recalled the time Margie Weeks and I sat and took a couple of swigs of each bottle in my parents' liquor cabinet—the folks weren't home. The result was obvious—two drunk and very ill young ladies. That same table is where, on my older brother's wedding night, we sat, talked, and cried about love and permanent relationships.

Example no. 2

3   The dining room. There was where I had to sit and eat lima beans with the timer in the kitchen going. "If you aren't finished in ten minutes—no dessert," my mother threatened. (Oh, the pressure.) It was also the setting for many a discussion about what I had learned that day, where I was headed, who I was, why I was . . . they kept bugging me.

Example no. 3

4   The living room . . . sometimes the dying room. In this room, the grand jury—that man and woman in those two orange chairs—handed down many a decision. One memorable day, they announced that I was "on restrictions" for one month. I had gone to school, decided to skip, gotten hit by a Volkswagen during the escape, was seen getting hit, and had skipped anyway. This had necessitated the principal of my school calling my mother and explaining, "Mrs. Nichols, your daughter was hit by a car this morning and hasn't been seen since," which further necessitated the notification of the police, firemen, and every hospital in the city. A "bananafish day." The front door is adjacent to this room. My older brother walked through this door when he left for the navy. My mother and I stood in it for a long time after he left. When had he quit being a creep and turned into someone I loved? At six

years old, he said, "Don't you talk like that to her—she's my sister," to the neighborhood bully. At sixteen years old, he said, "Dad, she shouldn't go out with him—he has a bad reputation." I guess he never was a creep.

Example no. 4

5   My bedroom. Once I went out on a date and arrived home very late. I sneaked in the house successfully only to discover that I had left my collection of 325 marbles spread out on my bed. Picking up each individual marble and trying to soundlessly replace it in the coffee can took fourteen hours and twenty-seven minutes. The following morning my mother commented on playing marbles at four in the morning. She said no more. From then on, I killed myself to get home on time. This room also contains the bed I threw myself on and cried for half an hour because my dad said, "That boy is bad, and I don't want you to see him anymore." After I was done crying, he walked into my room, put his arms around me, and said nothing except, "Please understand."

Example no. 5

6   The patio. To this day I recall working for hours trying to make that clothes line jump rope swish under my feet without my stepping on it: all the girls at school could do it. This scene included one of my better remembered temper tantrums—wadding the rope up in my hands, throwing it onto the ground, and stomping on it as hard as I could, hoping to hurt it. Then there was June 4, 1968. I stood on that same spot with my graduation gown on. My mother cried, "You're just too young, and you haven't learned enough yet. What have we had time to teach you?"

Conclusion

7   At what stage in one's life does one learn to care about someone else? Caring comes in degrees, I believe, and the only way one can tell how one is doing is to compare oneself to the rest of the world. "What have we had time to teach you?" Well, I think a high degree of caring is a very valuable gift. I've had the privilege of seeing it in action since I was first able to look.

—Nancy Nichols

Questions and Comments on "A Twenty-five Cent Tour"

1. How does the writer blend her thesis idea with the physical presence of her parent's house in her opening paragraph?

2. The organization of this paper is original and unusual. Does it work? How does the writer continue to blend location with abstract idea in each of her supporting paragraphs? Which lines tie each paragraph back to the thesis?

3. What secondary theme is presented in her graduation example. How is this theme blended with her main thesis in the concluding paragraph?

Option No. 2–Analysis of Another's Opinion or Idea: Student Example Paper

How to Go About Analyzing Another's Opinion or Idea

Find an essay, newspaper editorial, or magazine article, and analyze its arguments as well as your own position on the topic. You will need, in a sense, a dual thesis that combines the source's main idea with a statement of your own. Keep this double purpose in mind as you formulate your thesis to make sure that it includes and clarifies both positions.

You can analyze a work from many different angles. For example, you might analyze what techniques a work uses to produce its effect and assess the validity of those techniques, or you might disagree with a work's final position and counter its arguments with opposing points as you analyze them. Try to keep a consistently objective approach. Focus on an article's arguments and how it presents them, dispassionately and fairly. Remember that your purpose in analysis is to clarify and explain, not to launch an emotional attack.

An Article to React to Plus Student Example Paper

Mike Royko in his article "Death Penalty, Pro or Con?" presents an argument for capital punishment, while Carol Wright disagrees with him and analyzes the weaknesses in each of his points. Analyze the same article, or Carol Wright's reaction to it, or use your own article. Let your interest select your material, and your combination thesis become your guide.

DEATH PENALTY, PRO OR CON? WRITER MADE DECISION IN 1962[2]

MIKE ROYKO

1   CHICAGO—The United States Supreme Court will rule on a key capital-punishment case in the summer, and this could lead to a rever-

---

[2]Mike Royko, "Death Penalty, Pro or Con? Writer Made Decision in 1962," *The Chicago Daily News* (23 April 1975).

sal of the court's ban on the death penalty. So once again the public debate is on.

2   But regardless of what the court does, or anyone says, my mind is made up on this subject.

3   I used to waver. For many years I jumped from one position to another.

4   As a kid, I felt that the death penalty was deserved by anyone who stole my bike or ran over my dog.

5   Later, as a young reporter, I covered an execution, got sick to my stomach, and thought it should be banned.

6   But as a police reporter, I talked to the families of ordinary people who had been murdered in robberies, sadistic sex crimes, or just for the hell of it, and thought that maybe the electric chair wasn't such a bad piece of furniture after all.

7   I listened to all the arguments, pro and con, read court decisions, tried to digest the statistics of criminologists and sociologists, and became completely confused.

8   Then in 1962, my mind was made up. I reached a position, and I haven't wavered from it since.

9   A well-known mass-murderer had been caught and brought to trial that year.

10   As the testimony came out, I found myself filled with loathing for the man, hoping he would be convicted and executed. In fact, I was all for doing it slowly so he would suffer.

11   Then I searched my soul. What good could possibly result from killing him? Would it bring his victims back?

12   The answer was, no, it wouldn't bring them back.

13   But it would make the survivors of his victims feel better.

14   So I searched my soul further. Would it not serve society just as well to lock him up for the rest of his life? Wouldn't that isolation be a terrible punishment?

15   Sure it would be a terrible punishment. But as long as we were going to punish him, why not go all out and let him have the ultimate in punishments?

16   In another corner of my soul I encountered the question: Would his execution deter others from committing murders?

17   Maybe. Or maybe not. If it deterred others, great. And if it didn't deter others, we would still be rid of a loathsome creature. So how could we lose?

18   From another soul-cranny came the question: Didn't I revere human life?

19   Sure I did. But that killer obviously didn't, so let him be punished by his own cold standards.

20 My conscience kept twitching. Wasn't this punishment cruel and unusual, since others had committed the same kind of acts but had gone unpunished?

21 Possibly, and that argument is why the death penalty is now banned. Many killers were convicted, but few were executed, which made their punishment cruel and unusual. But I figured the solution wasn't to let this particular louse off the hook, but rather to execute the others too. Then it wouldn't be all that unusual.

22 Just about the time I finished frisking the last nook and cranny of my soul, the verdict came in.

23 Guilty as charged. The penalty was to be death.

24 Oh, there were some technical objections as to the way be had been arrested, but they were overcome. And there was no doubt as to his guilt.

25 So he was given his last meal, walked to a small room, and his life was extinguished.

26 Just like that. One moment he was living, breathing, probably terrified. Maybe he was thinking about his plump wife and sweet-looking little son, only six years old. The next moment, he was dead forever.

27 That's when my harsh feelings about him were put to the test. I waited for my stomach to feel sick.

28 Nothing happened. I felt pretty good. As I recall, I went out and ate a pizza.

29 Since then, I've been in favor of capital punishment. Not for every murder case, of course. But for those cold-blooded, remorseless, sadistic people, who kill for profit, pleasure, for the hell of it, for those who are not blinded by insanity or some overwhelming passion, but have a choice and choose to kill.

30 Had it been up to me, Richard Speck would be gone. So would Charles Manson and most of his playmates. So would the guy who robbed the aged grocer and blew him apart with a shotgun as a cruel afterthought.

31 So would the punk who did the same thing to the night counterman in a diner. Or to the docile cabby. So would any hired killer from the Syndicate. So would the planners and doers of the Jablonski case. I'd have the electric chair going off like a pinball machine.

32 I can't help feeling that way now, because that's how I felt in 1962 when a former S.S. officer named Adolf Eichmann was executed for murder.

33 If I believed that the killer of a grocer, a cabby, some Phillipine nurses should be spared, then I'd have to be consistent and say the same in Eichmann's behalf.

34 I'll never be that soft in the heart. Or in the head.

Questions and Exercises on "Death Penalty, Pro or Con? Writer Made Decision in 1962"

1. What is the tone of the article? How is it achieved?

2. What changes did the writer go through in making his decision? Which examples back up each change?

3. List each of the writer's arguments and his supporting material for each. How valid or convincing is each argument?

4. Why does the writer not identify the mass-murderer in question until the end of his article?

5. How objective or subjective are the writer's arguments? What is the article appealing to?

Student Example Paper

DEATH PENALTY, PRO OR CON? WRITER DISAGREES WITH FAVORITE COLUMNIST

Writer states criteria for judging journalists

1 A really good columnist serves as a guide through the confusion of news that confronts us each day. He puts current events into perspective, raises issues that may have passed unnoticed, and doesn't hesitate to lay his opinion on the line regarding controversial issues. Mike Royko, syndicated columnist for the *Chicago Daily News*, is a superb example of this type of journalist. For years he has commented with pungency and wit on the state of American politics, particularly as practiced in Chicago, the city he loves and hates. During the three years I lived in that incredible city, Royko's lively columns gave me insight into the Chicago way of life, something quite apart from anything I had previously experienced.

Writer's thesis statement

2 However, a recent column of Royko's, "Death Penalty, Pro or Con? Writer Made Decision in 1962," is not up to his usual responsible standards. Because capital punishment is such a controversial issue, and because the Supreme Court will rule on it again in the near future, it deserves clear, objective analysis. Royko, this time, doesn't come through. He clouds the issue more than he clarifies it.

3 In what seems to be an internalized review of his thoughts as he considered the question, he tells his readers how as a young reporter exposed to both sides of the issue, he wavered, but in 1962 he reached a final decision, and he says he has not wavered since. Unfortunately, his decision was made in emotional reaction to horrifying details of the crimes committed by a mass murderer who was then on

Thesis of work being analyzed

trial. The details were so ugly, so grim, that no sensitive person could, in that climate, reflect rationally on what it all meant. The criminal? Adolf

Eichmann. And Royko, gripped by the painful emotion of that time, came to the conclusion that since Eichmann could only deserve death—preferably slow death—society ought to be consistent and sentence to death all "who kill for profit, pleasure, for the hell of it," punishing them by their own "cold standards."

4   Royko reached his position in an understandable manner. Who could have heard without anguish the testimony in that courtroom? But Royko's thinking did not go far enough or deep enough. Eichmann, captured, tried, found guilty, sentenced, and put to death by the Israelis, served as a symbol of retribution for all the Jews who died in Nazi concentration camps. Because there was such an overwhelming, compulsive need for Israel to symbolically state with Eichmann's execution that the Jewish people would never again be victimized, the sequence was almost inevitable. However, Eichmann, the S.S. officer, does not equate with a murderer captured and tried in American courts, nor does this country's need to deal with that criminal in a way that punishes him and protects society from him equate with Israel's need to make a symbol of Eichmann.

5   Royko's thoughts while mulling over this issue are fragmentary, their implications not fully realized. For instance, if we took seriously Royko's suggestion that murderers be punished by their own standards, and assumed that it were possible to do so, then following his rule of consistency, we would apply this manner of dealing out punishment to all criminals—and reach absurd extremes. As an example of this kind of justice, let us say a drunken driver has been tried and found guilty. The judge could then sentence him to "x" number of hours driving on a freeway filled with other drunken drivers. A convicted pusher could be sentenced to a lifetime of addiction. The corrupt politician—well, let's sentence him to a lifetime in Chicago. The possibilities are intriguing, but practicable? No, I'm afraid not.

6   Royko says that a murder victim's survivors would feel better if the killer was executed. Perhaps, but a more constructive way to help the survivors would be to compensate them. Such a system is currently practiced in Great Britain, and it reflects a positive, rather than negative, way to aid those whose lives have been grievously affected by violent crime.

7   In an offhand way, Royko considered the possibility that the death penalty may serve as a deterrent. As the well-informed journalist that he is, I'm sure that he knows that that argument is not defensible. It has not been resolved that capital punishment is a deterrent.

8   To Royko's credit, he does not bring in the most noxious argument of those who favor bringing back the hangman, the money it costs to keep a criminal in prison. Those who equate human life with dollars and cents cannot be reached.

9   However, Royko can be reached, and I hope he will be nudged

Refutation of point no. 1

Refutation of point no. 2

Specific supporting examples

Refutation point no. 3

Specific example

Refutation of point no. 4

Refutation of extra point

into re-examining his 1962 decision in more depth. Capital punishment is a far more complex question than he leads his readers to believe. In a country that has been slowly and falteringly lurching toward a more compassionate humanity, the resumption of this barbaric custom would, in my opinion, have adverse and ugly consequences.

Statement of writer's position

10   I believe there are factual reasons why capital punishment should not be brought back, the most potent being that the death penalty was never dispensed justly in the past, and it can never be in the future. Discrimination against the poor, the friendless, the ignorant, and most of all against minorities removes capital punishment from the area of justice administered dispassionately and puts it in a jungle of untamed fear and prejudice.

Supporting point no. 1

11   Dealing with the question on a subjective level, as Royko does, I strongly believe that the value of all life is diminished when one life is considered expendable. The ritual taking of life, directly or indirectly, can only result in less regard for life and, in a curious way, Royko's column illustrates this. As his opinion solidifies, his voice becomes more harsh and strident, his humanity less obvious, to the extent of having the "electric chair going off like a pinball machine." To claim to revere life, as Royko does, and then to make a statement like that is hypocrisy.

Supporting point no. 2

12   Royko ended his column by implying that to feel otherwise would be soft in the head, but I believe that with *hard-headed* reappraisal on his part, we could look forward to another of his brisk readable columns entitled, "Death Penalty, Pro or Con? Writer Changed Mind in _____."

Conclusion

—Carol Wright

Questions on "Death Penalty, Pro or Con? Writer Disagrees with Favorite Columnist"

1. What are the writer's criteria for a good columnist? What experience does she have with Royko's writing? Why does she present this material first?

2. What is the writer's thesis? How does it relate to the criteria in paragraph 1?

3. Why does the writer mistrust the basis of Royko's reaction? Does she indicate any similar basis for some of her own reactions? If so, where?

4. What is Royko's position? How does the writer account for it?

5. The writer refutes five arguments for capital punishment: four presented by Royko and one added by herself. Which refutations are most effective? How are the refutations linked to Royko's article in their presentations? Which ones are supported best? Could any use more support? If so, what support might be added? Which refutations are most objective? Most subjective?

Does their objectivity or subjectivity influence their effectiveness? Their credibility?

6. Find examples of effective transitions in the paper. Why are they effective? What other organizational techniques hold the paper together?

7. Where does the writer switch from refuting Royko's position to supporting her own? How does she smoothly accomplish this change?

8. Which of her support points comes through most powerfully and why? How does the writer use Royko's own words to support her point? Why is this effective?

9. How does the conclusion play on the wording and ending of the article to achieve a finished effect?

Option No. 3–Analysis of Problems: Student Example Papers

Focusing on Problems to Analyze

Specific problems can provide good analysis topics since they often have easily definable structural parts such as causes, areas affected, and possible solutions. Narrow your topic by focusing on only one of these areas or combine areas for a more thorough coverage. The following student papers illustrate problem analysis of varying degrees of complexity.

Student Example Papers Analyzing Problems

ON RESPECT

Thesis question

1   Why is it today that in little league, jr. high, and high school, whether it's during soccer, football, baseball, or basketball games, unsportsmanlike conduct toward the referee is rising? To answer this

Supporting areas

question, it is necessary to look closely at how the examples of professional players, coaches, media, and parents affect young people.

2   Today's newspaper coverage of sports events often shows blown-up pictures of players or coaches furiously storming at the ref-

Picture example of a coach

eree after a close call. A good example appeared on November 3, 1976, in the sports section of the *Seattle Times*. An 8″ by 5″ picture portrayed Butch van Breda Kolff, coach of the New Orleans Jazz, standing in front of the referee, arms spread out in front of him in a frantic gesture, eyes blazing in rage, and face wrinkled in fury. In the picture, the referee stands calmly in front of Kolff, firmly pointing a warning finger at him. From pictures like this, children pick up the message that it's O.K. and even "cool" to storm at the referee when he makes a call they don't like.

Indirect newspaper example

3 Newspaper pictures are not the only way that these incidents are publicized. Often, newspaper articles do the same thing, either indirectly or directly. An example of writing that indirectly puts down a referee's authority appeared in an article from the *Seattle Times*. The headline read, "Hawks Survive Flag Day at Tampa Bay." The article explains the highlights of the Seahawk game and contains only one sentence stating the number of fouls called (35). The readers must draw their own conclusions about how good a job the referee did. A

Direct newspaper example

good example of an article that directly refutes a referee's authority appeared in the *Bellevue American* on November 4, 1976. The headline read, "No respect for N.F.L. flags." In the article, an offensive lineman complained about the rising number of flags thrown for offensive holding so far this year. This open or indirect dispute of the referee's authority, whether the official is right or wrong, does more harm than good. Because children look up to and imitate the professionals, care should be taken by them—and the newspaper for the examples they set.

Radio and television examples

Effect of commentators and instant replay

4 Newspapers shouldn't receive the full responsibility for this situation. Children get the same kind of bad examples from watching games on television or listening to the radio broadcast of the games. Overexcited commentators often make biased or harsh comments about the officials during a game. Children pick this up and often assume all referees are bad. Instant replay during a game can subtly question the authority of the referee depending on how the replay is handled. During a game, close calls are often replayed so the audience can get a second look at the penalties. Unfortunately, the credibility of the officials seems to be on the line in this approach. Often, the viewer only remembers the one or two "bad" calls made during a game. The children walk away with more evidence to support their stereotype that all referees are the bad guys making bad calls.

Examples set by parents

5 Finally, the parents who are supposed to set a good example for their children are often the worst in terms of respect for the referee's authority. A good example of this behavior can be seen at any little league game. The parents are often the ones umping the game from the stands, yelling comments like, "It's too bad the kids have to lose the game because of the umps," "He must be getting paid by the other team," "This has to be the worst job of umping I've ever seen," and

"Ref, get your head out of your ass." The players pick their comments up, and they can be heard on the field and after the game. This is a shame because it shows many parents value winning at any cost more than seeing that their kids play their best and have fun learning the game. Too often parents treat their children as ego extensions—pushing their youngsters into and through competitive sports because they either excelled at that particular game or wish they had. This attitude poisons the kids' sense of fair play.

Examples of players

6   The example set by the media, professional players, coaches, and most of all the parents has been one of growing disrespect for the authority of the referee who, after all, is only human and trying to do his best. In my own personal experiences, I have seen players throw their bodies to the ground to protest a call, hoping to gain the spectators' sympathy. I have seen players pick up the nearest object and throw it at the referee. I have seen players stamping after a referee yelling obscenities, "cheap shots" all the way. This doesn't happen all the time but enough to make me wonder if the main idea behind sports has been forgotten. Healthy competitions have become shouting matches.

7   This rising disrespect for the authority of the referee damages our younger players. This fact comes across in an article written by Denny Warnick, a sports editor. He said, "I can't help wonder . . . how many more fine young men are missing their chance to develop into outstanding ballplayers because their parents encourage them to spend time umping rather than working harder to play the game as it should

Summary conclusion

be played." Clearly, the rising disrespect for the referee's authority on the professional level, the presentation of that disrespect by the media, and, most importantly, the poor attitudes of the parents at games, correspond directly to the rising disrespect toward a referee's authority in the younger generation of today.

—Mark Mauren

Questions and Exercises on "On Respect"

1. How does the writer combine support areas in presenting examples? Can you rephrase the support area list so it follows the order of the paper's examples?

2. Which points are most convincing and have the most specific examples?

3. Rewrite the opening of paragraph 6 so it clarifies the main focus of the paragraph.

4. Find an example of parallel construction in paragraph 7.

ON CHILD ABUSE

> There was an old woman
> who lived in a shoe.
> She had so many children,
> she didn't know what to do.
> She gave them some broth,
> without any bread,
> and whipped them all soundly,
> and put them to bed.

Introductory examples

1   Nearly all little children have, at some time, heard this popular nursery rhyme, and not many youngsters go through their early years without a spanking. However, what parent would burn an infant's flesh, immerse a baby in a tub of scalding water, or continually break a child's bones? These all too familiar examples of child abuse appear in the growing body of literature, as evidence of what is known as "The Battered-Child Syndrome," or "Child Abuse."

Definition of key term

Result of abuse

2   Child abuse is a clinical illness. It is a condition in children who have received serious physical abuse and is a frequent cause of permanent injury or death. These injuries are usually inflicted by the parents. As a result, more than 10,000 children die from abuse each year; others are paralyzed, physically deformed, or mentally retarded for life. Estimates show that two children a day die from beatings, and child abuse causes more death among children than do auto accidents, leukemia, cystic fibrosis, and muscular dystrophy.

Types of abuse

3   One of the most horrid facts the American Humane Society learned about the battering parents of these children is that the parents beat, burn, drown, stab, and suffocate their children with weapons ranging from baseball bats to plastic wrap.

Examples

4   Examples of the brutality are not hard to find. For instance, a severely beaten two-year-old boy died in Patterson General Hospital, New Jersey, after the boy's father, according to the police, made the boy, bleeding from head and body, walk to the hospital. The boy died eleven minutes after he arrived. In another case, a mother became indignant because her two-and-one-half-year-old daughter wouldn't respond readily enough to toilet training. The mother gave the child an enema with near scalding water. Further, a mother of a twenty-nine-month-old boy claimed the baby was a "behavior problem." She beat him with a stick and screwdriver handle, dropped him on the floor, beat his head on a wall, and threw him against it. She even choked him to force his mouth open to eat. Then, one morning she found the child dead in his bed. The mother pleaded guilty to murder.

Consequences

5   From things I've read and heard, and from my own personal experience as a babysitter for a woman who insisted her little girl was

naughty and deserved to be beaten with a piece of driftwood until she bled, I conclude that the consequences of lasting pain, and lifelong memories, stay with the child for life.

Role of child protection agencies

6   These cases, like many, are reported first to the police, and then referred to a local child protection agency. Child protection agencies act as a service for the burdened family. The service itself does not try to change deep personality problems of the parent that are so often the case. Instead, with the help of a social worker, the parent is expected to change the current condition of child neglect. Many parents are able to change so the children may remain at the home under improved circumstances. However, often abused children are removed from the home and put in foster care when the parents are unable to cooperate.

People afraid to get involved

7   One hindrance to stopping child abuse is the unwillingness of friends, neighbors, and relatives of the battered child to report such goings on. From my point of view, standing as a witness to child abuse, nobody wants to be the first to point the finger. Later I discovered all the friends and neighbors of the family I had my experience with knew the child was being "severely punished," but no one was willing to get involved.

Reasons for lack of involvement

8   It is often believed that aggression by parents is basically for good ends, and that the child victim must have done something to deserve such treatment. Perhaps this contempt seems rational, but more often than not, the circumstances and forces that would limit such child abuse are kept quiet. The reasons for such silence in reporting victims of child abuse are plain and clear. Nobody wants to tattle on their neighbors; nobody wants to recognize the bruises and burns on their daughter's best friend's arms; nobody wants to come to grips with reality.

Conclusion

9   All these factors, as well as yet to be discovered factors, are unfortunate, particularly for the helpless child. However, the conditions are not rare: child abuse does not happen to just "the other guy." In each case, child abuse remains a problem. Whether it is a problem of personal anguish and frustration, or whether it is a society-caused conflict, child abuse should be recognized and treated as a number one *crippling* disease.

—Claudia Milligan

Questions and Exercises on "On Child Abuse"

1.   How effective is the paper's opening with a familiar nursery rhyme?

2.   What is the paper's thesis? How might this thesis be stated more clearly in the paper's opening paragraphs?

3. Find sections in this paper you would reposition to achieve a tighter organization.

4. How might paragraphs 7 and 8 be combined under a single controlling idea?

BOOB-TUBE BLUES

Thesis and supporting areas

1   Television is a marvelous invention, but it has created problems that people may not realize, mainly because the tube has brainwashed them into believing these troubles are normal. Although television has contributed greatly to our education and entertainment, is it worth the price we're paying in shrunken verbal skills, the creation of false realities, an increase in violence, and weakened family relationships? If this tool were used correctly, it could have greater social value, but television is so geared to serving commercial purposes that the viewer is losing out.

Positive value no. 1—expanding horizons

2   Television can be a wonderful device. It has stretched our horizons so that we have experienced things that people fifty years ago never had a chance of seeing. People are now aware of the ravages of war and famine. We have witnessed men walking on the moon and exploring ocean depths. We have been informed of world events as they are still happening and can have our choice of sports events, often seeing and hearing more than the fan who is attending the game. It can reinforce values, support ideologies, and challenge us to improve a situation. Television has helped us to fight human obsolescence by multiplying the amount of information we receive in our life time.

Positive value no. 2—educational

Negative effect no. 1—decline in reading

3   Television has a great educational value. A child no longer has to read to be able to acquire knowledge but can begin to learn earlier in life. By the time children enter first grade, they have spent more time learning than a student working on a B.A. degree.[1] Rather than cramming a mind with facts, a teacher must now put this knowledge in order. But children are doing more listening and less reading. They no longer see as much of the English language. From 1966 to 1973, the number of S.A.T. verbal scores over 600 shrank from 178,000 to 134,000. The number of scores over 700 went from 32,800 to 16,200, a reduction of over 50 percent.[2] Children no longer can use the English language as well.

Negative effect no. 2—teaches bad speaking habits

4   Television can also teach bad speaking habits. One grade-school teacher I know says she's going to hit the next pupil that says "aaaeee" like the Fonz. Kids who idolize Barbarino and gang on "Welcome back, Kotter" start imitating them, and soon they're all talking the same way. I

---

[1]Jeffrey Schrank, "Boob Tube or Bright Light?" *Senior Scholastic* (April 10, 1975), p. 9.

[2]Ibid., p. 8.

know one very bright boy who talks like this to be "cool." Networks should realize this and attempt to correct the situation. Often children don't realize what's incorrect, and they start picking up bad habits.

Negative effect no. 3—shows a false reality

5   Children can also learn a false reality from television. They may believe absurd situations to be true. A boy may think that he has to be like the "six-million dollar man" to survive in the world. Television too often resorts to stereotypes, also. Mrs. Cunningham represents an average housewife; "Charlie's Angels" portray women who seem to win because of their good looks; and all school principals are rotten according to "Welcome back, Kotter." In this way, television can teach wrong attitudes toward others.

Negative effect no. 4—teaches techniques of violence

6   Is television responsible for an increasing amount of violence in the community? Studies made have not been able to prove that children become violent from watching television, but surely kids could learn the techniques of violence. Television serves us an average of 7.29 killings per hour.[3] By age fourteen, a child has usually watched 18,000 murders, and it isn't just the "bad guy" performing these acts.[4] A majority of television's superheroes use violence to battle injustice. They use immoral means to eliminate immoral people because this seems to be the fastest solution. They provide a bad model for impressionable minds. Children could copy all sorts of immoral acts from television shows.

Programming is commercial

7   Unfortunately, television programming is commercial in intent. The object is to see what can hold viewers to the screen the best and then to sell these audiences to the highest bidder. The quality and content of a show is irrelevant. The average person has been bombarded by 350,000 commercials by the age of eighteen.[5] These ads present both real and created needs, and it has become hard to distinguish between them.

Creates artificial needs

We NEED to be well fed, beautiful, pain-free, powerful, happy, and care free. One phenomenon in my own home that relates to this is a sort of lethargy in my two teenage sisters. At times, they are almost lost without the tube in front of them to entertain and motivate them.

Creates lethargy

They don't know what to do when deprived of it. Many people have become confused. They must separate themselves from the pressures of television to discover what their real needs are.

Effect on programs

8   Because television serves commercial, not social purposes, even worthy programs have been affected. News programs are a good example. Only events with dramatic value are covered, and issues that are important but lacking excitement are often squeezed out. It is difficult to figure out the importance of an event judging from the coverage given. Networks think documentaries are fine, as long as the pro-

---

[3]Ibid., p. 9.
[4]Ibid.
[5]Ibid., p. 10.

ducers don't try to get them on during prime time when competition is highest. Thus networks have little concern for the quality of their programming.

Entertainment value

9   Certainly television is entertaining. It often provides companionship. Sweden's suicide rate declined noticeably when radio stations began broadcasting around the clock. Television acts in a similar manner. It can provide diversion from reality. It relieves pressure by helping people to laugh at themselves and their problems. More and more, Americans are reaching for heavy doses of this laugh medicine.

Dependence on television

10   Is this dependence healthy? In one study, people were paid not to watch television for one year. Results were good at first. Families became reacquainted. But soon tension arose and fights broke out, even to the point of wife-beating and child abuse. By the end of five months, everyone returned to watching television and harmony again prevailed.[6] Has television become addictive?

Adds to generation gap

11   Still, television is partly to blame for the widening of the generation gap. *Time* quotes Alexander Haley as saying, "T.V. has contributed to killing off the old form of entertainment where the family sat around listening to older people. T.V. has alienated youth from its elders. . . ."[7] Many families have been split into viewing groups. Family activities are often planned around the television schedules. At least 50 percent of one group of people interviewed altered their eating and sleeping habits to conform to television programming.[8] Television is often used as an electronic babysitter when parents don't want to take care of their children. Thus it seems to have separated people and interfered with social interaction, even within families.

Summary conclusion

12   Too often people don't realize the power that television exerts over them. It is an educational tool, yes, but it uses this fact as a subterfuge to manipulate them. It offers many good documentaries, fine dramas, news reports, and educational programs, but many other shows provide viewers with undesirable ideas. Television reduces our acquaintance with the English language and with other people. It offers escapism that can be bad as well as good. Television has been a boon and a bane to mankind.

—Heather Barr

Questions on "Boob-Tube Blues"

1. What effect does the writer gain by presenting the positive values of television first?

---

[6]Ibid., p. 8.

[7]William Marmon, "Haley's RX: Talk, Write, Reunite," *Time* (February 14, 1977), p. 72.

[8]Schrank, p. 8.

2. Which statement or statements function as framework sentences for this paper?

3. Should paragraph 3 have been divided into two paragraphs or its opening idea expanded?

4. Which paragraphs have the most effective support material?

5. Why did this paper need to be footnoted?

6. Should paragraph 9 be placed closer to the beginning of the paper?

7. How effective is the conclusion?

PRO FOOTBALL AND AMERICAN SOCIETY

Tone-setting quotation

I don't realize how brutal the game is until the off-season, when I go out to banquets and watch movies of our games. Then I see guys turned upsidedown and backwards, and hit from all angles, and I flinch. I'm amazed by how violent the game is, and I wonder about playing it myself.

—Jerry Kramer, All-Pro Guard,
Green Bay Packers, 1967
Instant Replay

Background information

1   Violence and impersonal abandon toward winning have become a trademark of professional football, such a trademark that many have questioned its effect on our society. They maintain it is unhealthy for normally humane, moral men to spend their weekends urging two opposing teams of men to tear each other apart. Former quarterback Joe Kapp defined this Sunday spectacle in these terms: "It's the lions and the Christians." But can pro football be fingered as the cause of the general attraction to violence in our society or is it merely a symptom?

Thesis

Professional football, with its emphasis on violence, on winning, and on sacrificing one's individuality for "the team," reflects American values more than it influences them.

Violence is unique to football

2   The violence that is perhaps the most outstanding feature of football is unique to the game. No other sport so openly emphasizes the all-out physical destruction of one's opponent. For example, Ray Jacobs, a defensive tackle in the American Football League a few years ago, was famous for putting as much of his 285 pounds of momentum as he could behind a forearm slam to the head. One player, during a game in which he was playing against Jacobs' team, recalled his teammate coming back to the huddle with his helmet

Specific supporting example

screwed halfway around on his head so he was peeping out one of the earholes.

3   "I didn't know Jacobs was in the game," said the first player, watching his friend tug at the helmet.

Option No. 3—Analysis of Problems: Student Example Papers

4   "Yeah, he just came in," his teammate replied.

Effect of violence

5   This violence leads to a strange sort of dehumanization. Deacon Jones, a former defensive end for the Los Angeles Rams, said, "We're like a bunch of animals kicking and clawing and scratching at each other." But Paul Zimmerman said in his book, *The Thinking Man's Guide to Pro Football*, "These men aren't sadists. It's just that intimidation is part of their game."

Coach's expectations

6   They may not be inhuman sadists, but they are often expected to act as such, not only by the general public, but by their coaches as well. In his book *Instant Replay*, Jerry Kramer gives an example of this attitude. "The grass drills are exquisite torture. You run in place, lifting your knees as high as you can, for ten, twenty, sometimes thirty sec-

Specific example

onds. When Coach Lombardi yells, "Down," you throw yourself down on your face, your stomach smacking the ground, and when he yells "up," you get up quick and start running in place again. . . . when Vince Lombardi is in a good mood, he gives us only three or five minutes of them. If he's upset, he'll keep going till someone's lying on the

Result

ground and can't get up. . . ." Kramer says the only way to survive is to "black it all out of your mind and function as an automaton."

Pressure to win

7   Added to this inhuman violence is the constant pressure to win. Football recognizes only winners; a title of "greatest" attached to any player or team is equated with "winningest." Losers are soon forgotten in a game where "winning isn't everything, it's the only thing," a motto of the late, great Vince Lombardi, a most successful and, of course, winning coach.

American society values these characteristics

8   Is this violent, dehumanizing game with its warped standards of success a detriment to our society? Perhaps, it should be pointed out that these are the exact characteristics found in American society, and they have been a part of the American way of life a lot longer than pro football has been around. Were not the earliest settlers, the forefathers of our country, guilty of ruthlessly slaughtering both man and animal?

Specific examples

Hasn't America always glorified its winners: Abe Lincoln splitting the most rails, the "Flying Ace" getting the most kills, the *first* men landing on the moon? Pro football is more a symptom of American society, an effect rather than a cause.

Football as a mirror of ourselves

9   Pro football simply concentrates the desires and goals of the society that created it. It may exaggerate those values, like a sort of obscene burlesque, but it nonetheless does serve as a mirror of our true selves. We are all violent and at times dehumanizing, and we all want to win.

Football as a safety valve

10   If football has any useful purpose, perhaps it is as a safety valve. If Joe Average can blow off some of those pent-up aggressions by watching Larry Csonka collide with "Mean" Joe Greene, perhaps it is

best. The American public's infatuation with pro football may be in the best interest of both parties.

—Ken Cofield

Questions and Exercises on "Pro Football and American Society"

1. How does the opening quotation set the tone for the essay?
2. How do direct quotations continue to add to the interest of the paper?
3. The paper's thesis states that professional football puts its emphasis "on violence, on winning, and on sacrificing one's individuality for 'the team.'" Which of these areas receives least development in the body of the paper? What examples might be presented to support it?
4. Do you agree with the paper's concluding statements in paragraphs 8 and 9? Does paragraph 8 provide enough support material to convince you?

ON SPECIALIZATION

Thesis

1   The specialization necessary for survival in modern life has created an atmosphere, unhealthy, not only for each of us, but for society as a whole. While necessary in the areas of science and technology, when specialization is extended to people, it alienates and impoverishes.

Benefits of specialization

2   The benefits provided by specialization are enormous. We have better schools, health care facilities, medicine, transportation, and marketing than ever before. Unfortunately, the side effects of these benefits can be a separation from others and a limited exposure to the variety and reality that is around us.

Specific examples

3   We have hospitals in which to be born, preschools in which to spend ages two-and-a-half to six, and schools in which to acquire the specialization that will assure our separation throughout life. We have nursing homes in which to spend our unproductive years, hospices in which to die, and finally, funeral homes in which to be dead. Protected as we are from the unpleasant realities of life, secure in the little niches we have worked so hard to achieve, we find ourselves separate, both from others, and from the growth that is possible in new experience.

Result

Advertising exploits fears

4   Advertising, that specialized arm of marketing, reflects our alienation and impoverishment. Most ad campaigns today exploit our fear of being alone and our impoverished self-esteem. Billboards flash, "People's—the bank with you in the name," a sultry voice sings, "Albertsons'—we care about you—," and even the pencil I'm using is imprinted with, "Be someone special—go Navy."

Specific examples

Option No. 3—Analysis of Problems: Student Example Papers

Advertising makes situation worse

5   Advertising, motivated solely by profits, has apparently diagnosed our illnesses accurately, and in treating us as objects to be exploited, becomes part of the problem. Advertising, which can't make good its promises of personalized caring and providing us with a sense of uniqueness and importance, panders to our symptoms while contributing to our disease.

Specialized medicine

Problems

6   In spite of the many advantages of specialized medicine, there has been a recent trend in medicine back to family practice. This trend is a direct reaction to the problems caused by specialization. In concentrating separately on the knee, eyeball, or liver, the relationship between the emotional and physical state was lost. Many now see the need for doctors to treat the patient as a whole person, rather than as a collection of isolated and specialized functions.

Conclusion

7   Most of the areas of specialization mentioned are useful and helpful functions, and as population, knowledge, and technology increase, still more specialization is inevitable and often desirable. The problems resulting from specialization occur when we allow it to color our perspective of ourselves and others. In doing so, we place ourselves and others in limiting compartments, thereby separating ourselves from others and from new experiences.

Return to thesis

—Jeanne Wartes

Questions and Exercises on "On Specialization"

1. Eliminate some "of's" in sentences in this paper.

2. The paper starts with a series of specific examples and then elaborates on examples in advertising and medicine. How might the paragraphs introducing the extended examples have stronger transitions?

3. Does the last sentence sound too much like the end of paragraph 3? How might it be reworded? Does the "new experience" point need more specific support in the body of the paper? Where might such support be introduced?

MANKIND PROGRESSES

Lake Washington in the past

1   Driving in from Bellevue to Juanita on one of the few lovely days that we were privileged to enjoy last winter, I received a shock. Lake Washington had disappeared! Thinking back to the many days that I took the lake road through Kirkland, instead of the 405 freeway, I felt sick. The lake, shining like a huge diamond, gleaming in iridescent beauty under the sunshine, always acted on me like a tranquilizer. On days when utter depression or irritation seemed to grate on my nerves

like sandpaper, just being able to look at the dark, rippling mirror of water was as soothing music to me. On other days, the choppy churning wavelets seemed to pull me into a happy, hopeful frame of mind. On still other days, the sailing fleet would be having a race. Those white triangles dotting the lake like sheets flying in the wind were a glorious sight. On any one of these days, by the time my car was winding its way up the hill toward Juanita, my spirits would be soaring, and I would find myself singing the rest of the way home. But now the lake is gone, just as it is no longer there on the west side, from Kenmore down to Lake Forest Park. Of course, the rest of the lake from Lake Forest Park down through Seattle hadn't been visible for years, but up until last winter, that one stretch for about three miles north of Lake Forest Park made driving a joy because a wide view of Lake Washington was possible to see. Today the whole area is just another concrete jungle.

2   Fifteen years ago, after traveling for 3,000 miles and taking three weeks to see every inch of it, our family, looking and feeling like dust-covered, travel-worn gypsies, wandered into the city of Bellevue and had to find our way around the beautiful lake surrounded by miles of tall evergreens to Seattle. Coming around by way of Kirkland meant traveling a two-lane country road to Juanita and then following a lovely road winding its way in snakelike fashion through several miles of woods and coming out in Kenmore where once again we met the lake in all of its glory. The lake like a faithful guide showed us the way into Seattle. What a wonderful way to enter our new home. Six weary "gypsies" felt the soothing joy of this flowing jewel that lay pointing our path for us. Upon arriving in Lake City, which did not resemble a city since it was mostly filled with tall evergreens, shops, and small businesses sprinkled here and there, we found an apartment motel and happily tumbled into our first home away from home.

3   Eight years ago this coming January, we once again were moving into Washington. For five years, we had lived in Texas, but we discovered our roots were in Seattle. Once again, six tired nomads landed in Bellevue after driving 2,000 miles through a desert and the mountains covered with snow, and then missing death by a miracle, when three cars met head-on and instantly killed everyone in them. One minute we were in the path of these cars and the next minute they had shuddered to a stop and lay in a silent heap in the middle of the highway, and we were fleeing down the road in silent shock. In a single instant, we were able to swerve and miss an appointment with death. We went back and learned the gruesome details. Thus once again driving along the two-lane country road through Kirkland, the lovely pine trees gave us a secure feeling, and the lake welcomed us like an old friend. There it was shimmering and sparkling like a lovely diamond. Once again, peace spread through us, and we quietly drove by, savoring its beauty. Once again we followed it into Lake City, which by now had

Specific memories

Lake Washington today

Fifteen years ago

Beauty of the area

Eight years ago

Some change evident

Option No. 3—Analysis of Problems: Student Example Papers

become a "real city." Gone were the tall evergreens. They had been replaced by tall two- and three-story buildings and cement sidewalks. Lake City had become a "concreteopolis."

One year ago

4   One year ago, driving by way of Kirkland in lieu of the freeway, instead of a quiet enjoyable ride through the quaint lakeside town, I found bitter disappointment. The lake was not there! The lake is there, of course, but it is hidden behind three-story apartment houses, condominiums, and businesses of all kinds. Two small sections portioned off as parks and marinas are a concession to the public. Traffic is heavy coming through there sometimes, and the feeling of being hemmed in by buildings and concrete overwhelms you. To be caught in a slow traffic jam causes irritation to mount in a person; impatience grates on a person's nerves. There isn't a good reason any longer to avoid the freeway and take the "scenic route." There isn't any scenery. On the west side of the lake from Kenmore to Lake City, business is thriving. Business is doing so well that it has taken over every inch of ground for about three miles, and the lake can only be seen in bits and pieces.

Drastic change evident

5   We, the people, are continually complaining that urban sprawl is taking over. City planners constantly tell us, by way of the local newspaper, that Kirkland is not going to "die," that all buildings must be a reasonable distance from the lake shore, and that Kirkland will not become another mortar and concrete blob. I have news for the city planners—it already has!

The present

6   Progress and prosperity do not have to mean destruction of nature. Both can be equal partners for the benefit of mankind. Careful planning and wise decision-making should be the solution. The public interest should come before everything else. People need warm living nature all around them to offset the cold rigid man-made creations. Lakes, mountains, and trees in their natural state help to quiet jangling nerves and to soothe harried people. Nature takes people away from everyday problems and washes them with tranquility.

Thesis

7   There was no reason to build on the lakeshores; the city could have been built around the lake but away from the shore—about 500 feet away! Now only those rich enough to buy homes on the lakeshore or those lucky enough to work in one of the buildings or those both rich and fortunate enough to own a boat, can enjoy the lake. I feel sick!

Mistakes made

8   There is one healing thought that consoles me. Nature will, if given the slightest chance, take over and completely obliterate whatever monstrosities man has used to scar it. Nature is still the strongest force in the creation of the universe. In the meantime, we, the people, are paying a high cost for injuring and trying to destroy nature. We are doing without nature!

Conclusion

—Gina Ganz

1. How does the writer blend her own past with the history of Lake Washington?

2. What single sentence best sums up the present condition of the area surrounding the lake?

3. Does the auto accident detract from the paper's focus? What transition attempts to turn the incident back to the lake?

4. Why does the writer hold her thesis until mid-way through her paper?

5. Find examples where the writer gains a feeling of intimacy by personifying the lake.

6. Are the subjective reactions in this paper needed for its effect or might some be eliminated or toned down?

Analysis to Present Information on a Topic of Interest: Student Example Papers

---

The following example papers don't deal with problem areas but simply clarify a topic of interest by analyzing its parts.

Student Example Papers on Clarifying a Topic of Interest

THE MEDICAL VALUE OF THE HUMAN AURA

Thesis

1   In our society today, significant research on the human aura is being conducted by people concerned with an "expanded awareness" of one's potential abilities. Presently, the human aura can only be seen by a small number of psychic or clairvoyant people; however, current research has revealed the existence of the aura through scientific and empirical findings. This research indicates increasing possibilities for physicians or technicians to diagnose ailments of a physical, mental, or spiritual nature through the observation and study of the human aura.

Definition of term

2   Aura comes from the Greek "avra," which means breeze. The aura, or energy field, is a light cast of the body's energies. In effect, the

aura is a reflection of the energies of the life processes. Basically, the human aura is described by the trained observer as an egg-shaped shell surrounding the body within which a particular intricate rainbow swirls and flows. Both psychics and researchers of paranormal abilities believe these colors emanating from the aura can be used to interpret or diagnose an individual's general health.

3   One particular psychic with the ability to see the aura is Dr. Lobsang Rampa, a Tibetan lama and author of the book *The Third Eye*. In this book, Rampa states that "people have auras, colored outlines which surround the body, and by observing the intensity of those colors, those experienced in the art can deduce a person's health, integrity, and general state of evolution." According to Rampa, every aura is composed of many colors and many striations of colors, and it is the colors that are important. Rampa believes that the colors and striations must match each other before two people can be compatible. In other words, if a particular color in a room irritates someone, then this color clashes with his own aura. Good deeds—helping others—makes one see the world through "rose tinted glasses." A good deed brightens one's outlook by brightening one's auric colors. Lobsang Rampa is a trained observer of the aura. He believes the biggest difficulty in seeing the aura is that most people do not believe that they can see it or do not know what they are seeing.

Dr. Rampa's explanation of the aura

4   Dr. Rampa visualizes a thing like an instant-photograph camera, which would take a photograph of the aura of a person so that anyone could see the colors. If one looks at an aura and sees the color of a disease, then, given suitable apparatus, the disease could be cured before it got hold by applying the necessary contra-colors to change the degraded color of the illness. By sympathetic reaction, the person would be cured from the aura's effect on the physical body. Dr. Rampa is gifted not only with the ability to see the human aura but with the ability to understand its significance in emotional, physical, and spiritual well-being.

Use of the aura to control disease

5   The role of the human aura begins to unravel as the psychics and researchers reveal their individual and clinical findings. An area of research that holds considerable promise is Kirlian Photography, in which a visible aura shows up around any living object in the photograph. Stanley Kripner and Daniel Rubin have edited *The Kirlian Aura*, a collection of papers that cover this unusual topic. Kirlian photographers insist the nimbus or aura present in their pictures emanates directly, like a force field, from the object photographed, and not from external electricity or calculated trickery in the photographic process.

Photographing the aura

6   The Russian biologists Semyon Kirlian and his wife Valentina electrophotographed a healthy plant leaf that showed the distinct outline of a vibrant aura. However, a cut leaf emanated a dull aura, indicating a weak life source. Similarly, in a human, the vibrant aura signifies good

Photographs of plant auras

health, and the dull aura indicates poor health. When photographing the aura of a psychic healer's finger, a considerably different image is produced from someone who is not a healer. In addition, a radically different flare pattern occurs in the photograph of this same psychic healer's finger during a healing. From these observations and other experiments, the Kirlians noted that when a person is in poor mental and/or physical health, the photographs taken of that person reflect changes in aura: in dimension, in color, in regularity. What is perhaps most important is that the Kirlian process makes possible a direct physical measurement of holistic types of change in the body, such as emotional states and general changes in body energy which may precede the occurrence of disease. Presumably, we in the West believe our senses only insofar as their impressions are verified by human machines, and Kirlian photography supports the plausibility of the aura's existence in the Western technological manner.

7   The late American clairvoyant, Edgar Cayce, produced many readings regarding individuals' health problems. In a booklet by Edgar Cayce and Thomas Sugrue, emphasizing the implications of what it means to see the aura, Cayce states: "I do not ever think of people except in connection with their auras; I see them (the auras) change in my friends and loved ones as time goes by—sickness, dejection, love, fulfillment—these are all reflected in the aura, and for me, the aura is the weather vane of the soul." Perhaps with modern technology and an interest in a higher consciousness, more people can learn to see the aura and begin to explore its possible significances in emotional, physical, and spiritual well-being. This interest in a higher consciousness could very well become a new goal for the research in psychic or paranormal abilities, the medicine of tomorrow.

8   Presently available information, and information yet to come from study and research on the benefits of observing the human aura in the field of medicine, will provide us with an important opening toward a full understanding of the enormously complex entity called the human body and its relation to the cosmic environment.

—Gregory Brown

Plants compared to humans *(margin note)*

Supporting quotations *(margin note)*

Conclusion *(margin note)*

Questions and Exercises on "The Medical Value of the Human Aura"

1. What does the writer achieve by devoting a paragraph to defining his key term?

2. Why does the writer retain an objective almost scientific approach to his topic?

3. Cite effective uses of comparisons in the paper.

ONE MORE LIFE TO LIVE

1   In the December 1971 issue of *Natural History,* the article called "Immortality and the Freezing of Human Bodies, the Case For" by John P. Wiley, Jr. discusses the subject of cryonics. Cryonics is a process of freezing a dead body in a tank of liquid nitrogen in order to preserve it and one day bring it back to life. This process was started in 1967, and as of today, no attempt has been made to bring the thirteen humans back to life.

2   Wiley explains the process of freezing involved in cryonics. He feels that "If they [people] allow their bodies to be buried or cremated then, in fact, there will be no chance whatever for revival and immortality. If frozen instead, at least there is some possibility that one day the bodies can be brought back to life and nothing is lost if the bodies are put in the deep freeze." After reading the article, I feel that Wiley does not take all the problems involved in the process into full consideration. Such problems as how to bring a person back to life, how to cure a person of death, and how to thaw out a person without damages, increase the odds against cryonics working. No human beings have been brought back to life nor is proof of its being performed on complex organisms available. Expenditures of $8,500.00 plus $1,000.00 a year to keep a body frozen are high prices. Cryonics gives false hopes, takes peoples' money, and shows little action.

3   Freezing might preserve dead bodies, but scientists, and Wiley, himself, have admitted that "freezing in itself damages the body." Inside a cell, the expansion of water as it freezes can rupture the cell's membranes; between cells, it can crush them. "Freezing of any water can leave a residue of various salts in lethal concentrations." Wiley writes, "It appears possible that some of the physical effects of freezing can be obviated by freezing under such high pressure that the water cannot expand as it turns to ice." This might be so, but salt residue would still be a problem. Other problems yet to be solved include temperature shock, the freezing and thawing process, damage to cells during the time the body is left unfrozen, and ice crystallization in the cells.

4   Wiley states, "So far, biologists have been able to freeze human blood and sperm. Both have been thawed and successfully put to use." Frozen mouse embryos were also thawed successfully, and a cat's brain which showed "nearly normal" activity, and Arctic beetles have survived freezing. While banking spermatozoa for the animal-breeding industry has made good profit, still, 30 to 50 percent of the cells do not survive and these are only one-celled structures. We are far more complicated than just one cell. If 30 to 50 percent of one-cell-type structures do not survive, how can the billions of cells in humans survive?

5   Wiley assumes nothing would be lost if a body was put in "deep freeze," but the subject is far more complex than Wiley's article indicates. Although being brought back to life may be attractive to some people and some scientists, many questions are left unanswered. No animal or human has been brought back to life yet. Other problems would occur if one could be brought back to life. How would that person return? Old? What would happen if one woke up twenty years later? Would family and friends still be here? Would one be put back in the "deep freeze" after another death? A "there is nothing to lose" attitude is not enough to justify the high expenses of cryonics with its false hopes and lack of proof.

6   The money people could spend on cryonics could go for research on diseases so people might live longer, healthier lives. It is hard to say what the future may hold, but cryonics appears to be only a hope with thus far little evidence to back it up.

—Ann Lehoczky

Complexity of the task

Problems to contemplate

Conclusion

Questions on "One More Life to Live"

1. Would it have been better for the writer to indicate her position sooner in a dual purpose thesis statement?

2. What are the student writer's key arguments against cryonics? How convincing are they?

NEW JAZZ

Thesis

New jazz styles

1   "Music is a world within itself," says Stevie Wonder in a song on his latest album. Jazz is certainly a main part of this world and through new innovations and more exposure is now more popular than ever before. Such prominent musicians as George Benson, Grover Washington, Jr., Herbie Hancock, and Miles Davis have commercialized their music so that it appeals to more people, not just jazz fans alone. The "New Jazz" as some people call it today, can touch on other types of music as well.

George Benson

Jazz and rock

2   Some of guitarist Benson's latest cuts have the steady, melodic rhythms of rock and roll that are easy for anyone to follow. This style along with his "Nat King Cole-" like singing voice have brought about his surge in superstardom. His singing in the modern version of the song, "Masquerade," is what helped his album, "Breezin'," sell over two million copies. With this album, he successfully bridged the rock and jazz gap.

Grover Washington

3   Grover Washington, though not as popular as Benson, has also flirted with success. The emotion and vitality of his saxophone playing,

Jazz and soul

his quiet but dominant personality, and the success of his album, "Mr. Magic," have made him a considerable force in popular music. His style is closely related to soul music with his saxophone substituting for vocals.

Herbie Hancock

4   Herbie Hancock has been a fixture in jazz longer than either of the previous two. He was a prominent member of Miles Davis's quintets in the early sixties. Hancock went about a more abrupt change in his music. When playing with Davis, he had always been a backup member with the band. His classical music background was evident in his piano solos, but his solos were short and not nearly as complex as they are now.

Change in style

5   Hancock separated from Davis's band in 1968 and formed his own group. For the next two years he experimented with different sounds. He switched from·playing a regular piano to an electric piano and began to use the moog synthesizer. The synthesizer is an electronic device that can put out any sound from an orchestral background to the whining, crying sound of a baby. In 1973, he came out with an album entitled, "Headhunters," that combined his complex piano style with the steady, thumping rhythms of an African jungle.

Miles Davis

Experiment with electronic sound

6   Trumpeter Miles Davis paved the way for many "New Jazz" musicians. Davis's roots go back to playing with Charlie Parker in the mid-forties, when he was a teenager. In 1970, Davis put out an album that revolted against traditional jazz. "Bitches' Brew" was the first album to experiment with electronic sounds. The album was highly successful and opened the door for different sounds in music.

Newer style is more complex

7   Davis had always been a conventional jazz player. Over the years, he had played mostly blues and be-bop tunes with no electric instruments. Comparing "Bitches' Brew" to one of his older albums would be like comparing an old Sylvania black and white television to a Sony Color Trinitron. Both are televisions, but the Sony Trinitron is newer, more complex, and more refined.

Writer's own interest change

8   I can associate the rise in popularity of jazz with my own growth in interest. When I was a senior in high school in 1972, I began to associate with a few friends who were avid fans of jazz. When first listening to this music, I hated the sound of it, preferring the raunchy, foot-stompin' music of rock and roll. But after a few months of hanging around these guys and listening to all their positive compliments about jazz, I began believing them. This music certainly deserved some listening to. I listened to it with intent more and more. It's phenomenal how certain saxophone players can take off on their own during a song but never lose the beat.

Some new styles don't sell

9   "New Jazz" is a wave that has hit music and continues to grow each year. Only certain jazz musicians have been able to successfully adapt their styles to it. Musicians like trumpeter Freddie Hubbard, saxophonist Hank Crawford, and vibraharpist Roy Ayers have been

successful in the past, but when they tried to adapt to a newer, different style have had trouble selling their records and thus have run into financial difficulties.

Conclusion

10   It is a constant struggle to rise to the top, and George Benson has risen there the same way he sings and plays his guitar—effortlessly. But jazz is open for new concepts and different styles, and if someone comes up with the combination that will appeal to the public, then he'll rise to the top. It is this competition for newer sounds which has made "New Jazz" a success.

—John Pregent

Questions and Exercises on "New Jazz"

1. How does the writer combine personalities with style in his presentation?

2. Find effective examples of defining a particular musical style. What writing techniques are employed?

3. Does the writer's personal example work in the paper?

4. How does the paper's conclusion reflect back on its thesis?

Chapter 4

Expanded Analysis: Contrast and Comparison Writing

Relationship to Analytical Writing

Contrast and comparison writing applies analysis to an extended base. Instead of limiting analysis to the themes of one essay, the characteristics of one object, or the points of one argument, it mixes and matches the pieces of various works under one controlling idea or framework.

In contrast and comparison writing, the individual units can be any pair of things you wish to compare: objects, people, places, activities, stories, or ideas. Begin exploring topics by first defining what they have in common and pairing like with like, trait with trait, point with point, idea with idea, style with style. Potential topics must have some points of similarity in order for their differences to be of interest or significance.

Advantages of Contrast and Comparison Writing

You may have felt that you knew a friend well until you tried to mix that person with a different set of friends, or you may have felt that you understood your country well until you traveled and saw it reflected from a foreigner's point of view. Both of these situations would have increased your understanding because you viewed them from a new perspective. This method, which your new perspective enabled you to employ, is contrast and comparison. By enlarging your viewpoint, contrast and comparison enables you to see more.

When you write a longer paper, contrast and comparison provides a useful format choice, since doubling the material you have to work with makes it easier for you to create papers of increased scope and complexity. Contrast and comparison writing helps create its own content; it automatically gives you something to look for and to do. It's often easier to see how one work or idea compares and contrasts with another than to study either in isolation. Determining the similarities and differences between two things usually clarifies and dramatizes the basic qualities of each.

Type of writing   Contrast and comparison
Approach   Objective
Purpose   To analyze the ideas or traits of two or more things using comparisons and contrasts to clarify your points and observations.

Topic Ideas and Possible Organizational Formats

Possible Writing Topics

Contrast and comparison writing provides almost limitless possibilities for topics. You can take one work and contrast and compare two characters, two incidents, two points of view, two images, or two themes within it, or you can do the same in two works by the same author.

You can contrast and compare two arguments, lifestyles, or philosophies; two people (relatives, teachers, friends, actors, singers, sports figures, authors); two objects (cars, radios, stereo sets, houses); two art objects (paintings, sculptures, pottery); two stories, essays, songs, or poems.

Finally you can mix media, comparing movies with books, books with plays, plays with movies—any combination that's available and interesting to you. Many modern novels such as Ken Kesey's *One Flew Over the Cuckoo's Nest* now have both a play and movie version. John Steinbeck's *Of Mice and Men* is not only a novel, a movie, and a play, but recently has been made into a modern opera! You can use different media renditions of the same work or contrast and compare the same theme in two different works in two different media. The combinations are as open as your imagination.

Start with Idea Lists

Make your planning easier and more visible by starting with idea lists. An idea list roughly sketches out the main ideas in your topic and includes possible supporting detail. You can make idea lists in any order or form since they are only your rough working sheets.

Effective comparison and contrast writing, like all analytical writing, depends on the ideas it presents, the clarity of its presentation, and the thoroughness of its supporting detail. The more thorough and detailed you make your idea lists, the more material you have for potential support. The more time you spend thinking through which details support which idea patterns and how they contrast and compare with each other, the clearer you can make your final organization.

Sample Idea List

If you decided to compare and contrast the relative advantages and disadvantages of a small car versus a large car, for example, you first might narrow your topic to two specific cars, say a Volkswagen as opposed to a Cadillac.

Your next step would be to list items to compare and contrast in each such as:

original price	power
mileage	speed
type of gas used	size
styling—exterior and	image
interior	accident statistics
comfort	engine placement
safety factors	foreign versus domestic
maintenance—cost and	product
availability	resale value
maneuverability	
options available	

Now look for larger controlling areas to group items under. Consider areas such as:

Cost	Performance	Image	Safety
original price	maneuver- ability	social status	specific features
gas used	power	options available	accident statistics
maintenance	speed	styling— exterior and interior	engine placement
resale value	mileage	foreign versus domestic pro- duct	
		size	

Finally, form a thesis statement that includes the names of the cars compared, the controlling areas governing the comparison, and the reason for making the comparison.

Sample Thesis

The advantages and disadvantages of owning a Volkswagen instead of a Cadillac are determined by cost, performance, image, and safety factors.

Now you are ready to choose an organizational format.

Three Possible Organizational Formats

Three possible organizational choices are:
1. *The Unit by Unit Approach*
2. *The Point by Point Approach*
3. *The Similarities and Differences Approach*

The Unit by Unit Approach

The unit by unit approach presents material in large blocks or units. First you trace traits or ideas through one entire work, then you trace them through the second work following the same order of presentation.

Advantages and Disadvantages of the Unit by Unit Approach

Using the unit approach, you thoroughly present a detailed analysis of the first item and then refer to your first analysis as you contrast and compare in the second half. This approach simplifies the amount of material you have to deal with at one time and avoids the ping-pong effect of rapidly skipping back and forth.

However, your readers must retain all the information from the first part as they read your second part, and the material cannot be combined as thoroughly or contrasted and compared with the same immediacy as it would if you had presented both works as you went along.

Example of a Unit by Unit Outline: Volkswagen versus Cadillac

Thesis: The advantages and disadvantages of owning a Volkswagen instead of a Cadillac are determined by cost, performance, image, and safety factors.

I. Volkswagen
   A. Cost
      1. Original price
      2. Gas used
      3. Maintenance
      4. Resale value
   B. Performance
      1. Maneuverability
      2. Power
      3. Speed
      4. Mileage
   C. Image
      1. Social status
      2. Options available
      3. Styling
         a. Exterior
         b. Interior
      4. Foreign versus domestic product
      5. Size
   D. Safety
      1. Specific features
      2. Accident statistics
      3. Engine placement

II. Cadillac
   A. Cost
      A. Original price
      2. Gas used
      3. Maintenance
      4. Resale value
   B. Performance
      1. Maneuverability
      2. Power
      3. Speed
      4. Mileage
   C. Image
      1. Social status
      2. Options available
      3. Styling
         a. Exterior
         b. Interior
      4. Foreign versus domestic product
      5. Size
   D. Safety
      1. Specific features
      2. Accident statistics
      3. Engine placement

2. The Point by Point Approach

The point by point approach presents both items at once, contrasting and comparing them under points they have in common.

Advantages and Disadvantages of the Point by Point Approach

Using the point by point approach, you focus on both items as you go, and your contrast and comparison can come through more immediately.

    Be careful, however, to avoid the ping-pong effect caused by switching from one item to the next every other sentence. Focus on one work and give adequate supporting detail for the point you're making or interweave both works as you go, letting the idea control the order and amount of material presented from each.

Example of a Point by Point Outline: Volkswagen versus Cadillac

Thesis: The advantages and disadvantages of owning a Volkswagen instead of a Cadillac are determined by cost, performance, image, and safety factors.

I. Cost
   A. Volkswagen
      1. Original price
      2. Gas used
      3. Maintenance
      4. Resale value
   B. Cadillac
      1. Original price
      2. Gas used
      3. Maintenance
      4. Resale value
II. Performance
   A. Volkswagen
      1. Maneuverability
      2. Power
      3. Speed
      4. Mileage
   B. Cadillac
      1. Maneuverability
      2. Power
      3. Speed
      4. Mileage
III. Image
   A. Volkswagen
      1. Social status
      2. Options available
      3. Styling
         a. Exterior
         b. Interior
      4. Foreign versus domestic product
      5. Size
   B. Cadillac
      1. Social status
      2. Options available
      3. Styling

            a. Exterior
            b. Interior
        4. Foreign versus domestic product
        5. Size
    IV. Safety
        A. Volkswagen
            1. Specific features
            2. Accident statistics
            3. Engine placement
        B. Cadillac
            1. Specific features
            2. Accident statistics
            3. Engine placement

3. The Similarities and Differences Approach

The similarities and differences approach, a variant of the point by point approach, organizes by similarities and differences rather than by the controlling ideas.

Advantages and Disadvantages of the Similarities and Differences Approach

Use the similarities and differences approach when the point of your argument or essay relies more on similarities and differences than on ideas alone. You can vary this form further depending on whether you give all similarities first and then switch to differences or whether you alternate similarities and differences as you go. Choose the approach that best complements your purpose. For example, if you are showing the superiorities of one car over another, you might end by stressing differences that act to your advantage or you might alternate similarities and differences to show the advantages of your car in each category.

The similarities and differences approach is less flexible than the point by point approach since it limits you to presenting only one side of an argument at a time, whereas the point by point approach allows you to interweave and combine arguments when it fits the point.

To apply the similarities and differences approach to the "Volkswagen versus Cadillac" topic, you might have to develop some new categories for comparison and to rework your thesis statement to reflect your new approach.

Examples of Similarities and Differences Approach Outlines

Organization Emphasizing Similarities First, then Differences:
Volkswagen versus Cadillac

Thesis: While Volkswagens and Cadillacs are both well-known cars with readily available service and parts and each has a distinct image that appeals to a particular clientele, they differ greatly in cost, performance, style, and safety.

I.	First similarity:	well-known, popular cars
II.	Second similarity:	readily available service and parts
III.	Third similarity:	set image
IV.	Fourth similarity:	set clientele
V.	First difference:	cost
VI.	Second difference:	performance
VII.	Third difference:	style
VIII.	Fourth difference:	safety

Organization by Alternating Similarities and Differences:
Volkswagen versus Cadillac

Thesis: While Volkswagens and Cadillacs are both well-known cars with readily available service and parts and each has a distinct image that appeals to a particular clientele, they differ greatly in appeal, cost, style, and performance.

I.	First similarity:	well-known, popular cars
II.	First difference:	appeals to different clientele
III.	Second similarity:	readily available service and parts
IV.	Second difference:	cost of service and parts
V.	Third similarity:	set images
VI.	Third difference:	different styles
VII.	Fourth similarity:	performance conscious
VIII.	Fourth difference:	types of performance

Suggested Group Exercises for Contrast and Comparison Writing

1. Form small groups, and, working under a set time limit, see which group can produce the most thorough list of comparison and contrast points on two items such as : sports, television programs, jobs, personalities, and characters.

2. Try producing and switching a unit by unit outline to a point by point outline on a given topic.

3. Try switching the approach in an example paper in this chapter from one format to another. Discuss which approach seems to be the most effective for the material; support your stance.

Check Lists

> ### CHECK LIST FOR COMPARISON AND CONTRAST WRITING
>
> 1. *Begin with idea lists.*
> 2. *Select a topic; choose an approach; make an outline.*
> 3. *Follow analysis procedure; keep your tone objective.*
> 4. *Employ double-duty transitions when needed; in unit comparisons, follow the same order in presenting the second half.*
> 5. *Check for focus and smoothness.*
> 6. *Condense and combine support material; cut unproductive repetition; use productive repetition for emphasis and effect.*
> 7. *Use parallel construction in presenting comparable ideas.*
> 8. *Check for balance between items compared.*
> 9. *Check your pronouns for clear referents.*
> 10. *Include both items compared in your opening and your ending.*

Expanded Check List for Comparison and Contrast Writing

1. *Begin with idea lists.* Effective contrast and comparison papers combine thorough support with tight organization; idea lists provide a good starting point for achieving this combination. First list all your ideas on each work separately. Then check these lists for similarities and differences that suggest a thesis idea. Next look for ways of grouping your support material to provide your paper's organizational framework.

2. *Select a topic; choose an approach; make an outline.* After selecting your topic, see which organizational approach best complements your material. Scan the advantages and disadvantages and the examples of each approach at the beginning of this chapter. Once you've settled on an approach, make an outline. Maintain parallel construction in all

parts of your outline, and be sure that if you break a large point into subpoints, that you have at least a B for each A or a 2 for each 1, since logically you can't break something into just one part.

3. *Follow analysis procedures; keep your tone objective.* (Review the analysis procedure and check lists in chapter 3.)

Try to remain objective in tone. Avoid preaching in your paper; clarify the points you are presenting through details and facts. For example, if a television documentary on hunting annoyed you with its one-sided or slanted coverage, don't deliver an emotional tirade against the program. Instead, analyze what techniques the program used to slant its presentation or achieve a one-sided effect. Then, if you wish, make a point by point rebuttal to each of the techniques.

4. *Employ double-duty transitions when needed. In unit comparisons, follow the same order in presenting the second half.* A double-duty transition not only shows links within a work but also shows how that work relates to the work you're comparing it to. If you use a unit approach, use transitions in presenting your second work which perform this double duty function. Look over the example papers using the unit approach for ideas on how to write transitions that perform more than one function without getting bogged down by length.

Another way to connect material is to follow the same order in presenting both parts. Unit comparisons are clearer if you make an outline and follow it to keep your order pattern clear.

5. *Check for focus and smoothness.* Make sure that each paragraph has only one main focus, which is clearly presented in the opening sentences. Also make sure your material reads smoothly. When using a point by point format, blend items compared by focusing on the point they have in common; avoid jerking your reader from one item to the next.

6. *Condense and combine support material; cut unproductive repetition; use repetition for emphasis and effect.* Since contrast and comparison writing covers more material than analysis of a single work, you need to effectively condense and combine example material to keep your length within reasonable bounds. The easiest technique for condensing material is to phrase examples in your own words and to combine them under a single focal point.

The paper comparing the film *Midnight Cowboy* to the novel *Of Mice and Men* illustrates the interdependence between characters through a series of condensed examples:

> Rico Rizzo's relationship with Joe in *Midnight Cowboy* parallels George's relationship with Lennie in *Of Mice and Men*. Joe Buck is

dependent upon Rico, as Lennie is dependent upon George, but this dependence is a need for Rico's and George's mental guidance rather than a physical dependence. George looked after Lennie when Curly bullied him, and Rico gave Joe Buck the "lowdown" on getting along in New York City. Still, the dependent characters made up for what was lacking in their partners: Lennie with his bigness was like a dog that could be sicced on someone like Curly, whom George disliked; Joe Buck with his good health became nurse to Rico when Rico began suffering from tuberculosis. In each case the buddies stuck together until the death of one partner because each met the other's needs.

Repeat only to achieve effective parallelism, to add new material, or to support a new point. If you're adding nothing new to the material you're repeating, either eliminate it or amplify your first presentation of it to include all relevant points.

Check for the following types of *unproductive* repetition in your paper:

A. You've used the same word repeatedly in the same sentence or in adjoining sentences, when you could combine or condense and use the word only once.

Example: Mary was proud. She was proud of her garden and took a lot of pride in her appearance. Her pride made her conceited.

Improved: Mary's pride in her garden and her appearance made her conceited.

B. You've used two words where one will do.

Example: Mary was conceited and stuck-up, and she appeared snobbish and stand-offish.

Improved: Mary's conceit made her appear stand-offish.

C. You've repeated the same information in different paragraphs in your paper without adding anything new to it or changing its focus.

Examples: The following two paragraphs repeat many of the same examples to make essentially the same points. The second paragraph should be eliminated.

Besides a lack of confidence in himself, Rosen had poor insight into himself and others. When Davidov asked him why Axel died, he said, "Broke what breaks." He didn't understand that Axel had lost his pride. Once pride is lost, there is nothing to live for. When he saw Axel's store, he tactlessly cut him down, saying, "Kiddo this is a mistake. This place is a grave. Here they will bury you if you don't get out quick!" Rosen didn't realize that the store was their identity, a way to build their pride up again.

Rosen also didn't understand that when someone loses his pride, he has nothing to live for. When Axel died, Davidov asked, "How did he die? Say in one word." Rosen answered, "From what he died? —he died, that's all. Broke in him something. That's how." Rosen wouldn't face the fact that Axel had lost his pride. His pride had been broken. Davidov pressed again, "Broke what?" Rosen wouldn't face the truth and said, "Broke what breaks." Rosen had failed to see how important pride is, and that Axel had lost his and had nothing to live for.

Productive repetition

A *productive* form of repetition appears in the following situations:

A. You may repeat words or word patterns deliberately to obtain parallel construction.

Example: She was proud; she was vicious; and she was destructive.

B. You may repeat a point and add new information to form a transitional sentence.

Example: In her essay "Twenty Years Between," Diane Brown compares two outstanding teachers. She uses her summary statement about the first teacher to open her portrayal of the second:

Today I am grateful to an extraordinary woman for a wonderful legacy. Because of my brief but rewarding association with this remarkable woman, I feel qualified to recognize a second educator who shares the same love and gift for expression.

C. You may repeat the same example, but use it to illustrate two different points.

For example a car's styling might be discussed in a paper's section on practicality as well as its section on social image.

D. You might repeat your opening points in your summary ending. Good endings repeat, but with a difference. A good ending does not just repeat a beginning; it clarifies what has been proven about the material presented.

> *Example:* Compare the opening of Becky Payne's paper "Work, Work, Work" to its closing. Using similar material, the opening clarifies the topic and key support area, while the ending states the writer's concluding position.

Opening
> The menial labor of sorting tomatoes on a harvester and the responsibility of supervising children at a playground appear to be very different. Differences in several aspects, environment, work, and pay are plain. However, similarities in other aspects, boredom and satisfaction, also exist.

Ending
> The labor of sorting tomatoes and the work of running a playground have different advantages and disadvantages, but they are both growing experiences, preparing the employee to leave the world of summer jobs and enter the adult job market.

7. *Use parallel construction in presenting comparable ideas.* Parallel construction can emphasize similar points by presenting them in similar forms. When condensing and combining examples, try presenting them in parallel lists. Utilize parallel formats in contrasting or comparing two points. Experiment with parallel beginnings in unit comparisons to call attention to ideas that are similar in each half.

8. *Check your balance between items compared.* In contrasting and comparing two works, devote adequate attention to each. You won't always have equal discussions under each point since not all points may be present to the same degree; however, if you discuss a point in length in the first work, at least mention it in the second, even if it's only to note its absence and the significance of that absence. A good outline should keep you balanced in your coverage of both works. If you use the unit approach, give equal coverage to the second half. Be careful you don't skimp as you become more fatigued and eager to finish.

9. *Check your pronouns for clear referents.* An unqualified "this" is the chief pronoun offender that creates confusion in analytical writing. Qualify your "this's" whenever possible by following them with specific nouns that identify their referent. For example, instead of writing "This shows that . . .," write "this (choose a specific noun that identifies your "this" such as: problem, incident, conflict, example, episode, scene)

shows that. . . ." Remember that "this" is a singular pronoun and cannot refer to multiple examples. Nor can you explain a series of problems and then say, "This is what I mean"; say instead, "These problems show what I mean." If you have more than one person in a sentence, make sure that your "he's" and "she's" are clear. Repeat names where necessary to avoid confusion.

10. *Include both items in your opening and your ending.* To create the appropriate focus, mention both items or works as you present your opening points. Make your ending support your entire paper by returning to both items in your closing remarks. You might also try including key framework words from your opening thesis in presenting your closing summary.

For example, Diana Brown's paper "Twenty Years Between" utilizes an effective ending that relates both subjects back to key framework ideas:

> In similar and brief encounters, two women, one old and suffering, the other young and vibrant, opened doors I thought would remain closed forever. Through Aunt Viola's patience, I grasped the mechanical aspects of writing, and through Susan's determination, I gained the courage to use words to their fullest advantage. Together, they influenced my attitude toward written communication, and because of them, I gained insight into myself and my abilities.

Student Example Papers

Example Paper Comparing Two Things

THE POOR MAN'S COW

Thesis question

1   To drink cow's milk or to drink goat's milk, that is the question.

2   "Children of the harvest, join the celebration. Ahhh, milk beautiful milk!!!" Every once in a while you hear the sexy, enthusiastic voice of

Cow's image

Cat Stevens sing this pleasing tune. Almost instantaneously, cold, white milk is flowing through your mind (actually, all I see is Cat Stevens), and you hear the faint moo of a homey Holstein cow in the background. Beyond the cow, however, there is another obliging animal. It is the goat.

Goat's image

3   Unlike the cow, the goat is unfortunately associated with the tin can. This fallacy has given the goat the unjust appearance of a nonchalant garbage grinder. There is no record in history of a goat having eaten a tin can. They have, however, been noted for occasionally devouring a label. In reality, the goat has a dainty, fastidious appetite.

Goat's milk gaining in popularity

4   The Poor Man's Cow is a label that the rich gave the goat many years ago. Like brown bread, goat's milk was considered a humble and uncultivated item. Today, brown bread is in style, and the popularity of goat's milk is on the rise.

Cost and nutrition

5   It is not only an issue of money, it is a matter of nutrition. The old faithful quart of cow's milk is a down-to-earth buy at forty cents, whereas, one quart of creamy raw goat's milk is a delicacy at ninety cents. The real treasure of goat's milk lies beyond dollars and cents.

6   The following description of goat's milk is contained in "Composition of Foods," Agricultural Handbook no. 8, U.S. Dept. of Agriculture:

> GOAT MILK is one of the most healthful and complete foods known. It is easy to digest and is often recommended for people with digestive, intestinal, or allergy deficiencies. Compared with Cow's Milk, Goat's Milk contains twice the amount of iron and over four times the amount of niacin. It is higher in food energy, calcium, phosphorus, thiamine, and Vitamin A, and is lower in sodium.

Energy required

7   It takes a lot of energy to raise a goat or cow. The rewards can be fulfilling. Both goat and cow must be milked twice a day. The average goat gives four quarts of milk a day, which is ideal for a small family. The milk cow produces ten to fifteen quarts. This amount can become overbearing unless you plan to make a profuse amount of butter, cheese, or ice cream.

Food required compared to yield

8   To receive milk, you must offer food. For one goat to produce both milk and garden manure, you must feed her 600 pounds of hay and one-quarter ton of grain per year. A cow is a much less economical animal at two tons of hay and one ton of grain per year. The perfect balance between one goat and one cow would be two goats. Whichever you choose, there will always be enough garden manure.

Fencing required

9   To protect your garden from shifty goats or intimate cows, a fence is necessary. Goat fencing must be high and strong for goats are agile jumpers. They require less than one acre of pasture and thrive on brush and shrubs. A cow needs more fencing because one or two acres of lush pasture land is essential. Cow fencing, however, does not have to be as high and strong as goat fencing because they are rarely, if ever, seen pirouetting over them. It had to be a goat that jumped over the moon!

Conclusion

10   "Children of the harvest, join the celebration. Ahhh, milk beautiful milk!!!" Now you have a choice. To guzzle cow's milk or to sip goat's milk, that is the question.

—Anne Hansbrough

Questions on "The Poor Man's Cow"

1. How do the writer's word choice and use of references as well as her facts sway the reader's choice in favor of goat's milk?
2. Why does the writer combine the areas of cost and nutrition?
3. Which structural approach does this paper employ? Is it the best choice for this topic?

Example Papers Comparing Two People

TWENTY YEARS BETWEEN

Thesis

1   An aging woman, soft-spoken and gentle, and a youthful woman, bouncy and energetic, both language gourmets, with opposite but equally effective teaching styles, taught me to appreciate and become comfortable with written communication.

Supporting areas

2   Coming from different generations, different lifestyles, and separated by years of antiquated teaching methods, these ladies stand out as unique. The first, named "Teacher of the Year" several times in her small, native Minnesota town, taught eighth grade children the basics of English grammar. Aunt Viola's warm, personal teaching manner ranged from patience, to more patience, to extreme patience. Each important point was tenderly stressed over and over. She nicknamed her style, "Let's do it again with love."

Aunt Viola's style

Meeting Aunt Viola

3   Recalling the first night we met, I continue to feel remorse she could not have lived longer to guide more disenchanted children to the wonders of expression. The night father brought her into our home for a week's visit so long ago, compassion for her suffering engulfed me. Walking with the assistance of crutches, face etched in pain, she smiled affectionately and greeted family members with a warm embrace. Each agonizing movement her lower limbs managed revealed the constant suffering she endured every waking minute. Mother explained later the cause of her pain was cancer of the leg and hip. After enduring countless operations, the cancer continued to waste her body.

Her suffering

4   Following dinner, Aunt Viola, comfortably propped up in the only overstuffed chair in our modest home, spoke of former students. Many enjoyed fruitful lives engaged in occupations ranging from farmers to state senators. Some benefited so immensely from her guidance, they followed in their mentor's footsteps and entered the field of education, specializing in English. Others utilized their newfound ability to good advantage in their chosen field of business. Fascinated with the prospect of such success for myself, I asked for and received her promise to tutor me in grammar.

5   Our first study session began and ended uneventfully as Aunt Viola, obviously in a great deal of pain, grew tired quickly. The next evening, intrigued with this sensitive woman's innate ability to imprint knowledge in the mind, I feverishly sought to please her. In a few hours, I listed verbs, adjectives, and adverbs as my friends. "Without lovely adjectives," she explained, "nouns remained meaningless, empty words. Every single essential part of language unites and creates a completely beautiful whole." She continually linked elegance with these modifying words. Without "emphasizing words," Mark Twain's writings collapse; the Bobbsey Twins and Nancy Drew mysteries lack substance; and all the other fantastic stories written reduce to emptiness. Patient moment by patient moment, the puzzle pieces slowly came together, and I experienced the same joy she felt. Soaking up every smidgen of information, my brain added commas, semicolons, exclamation marks, and periods to its repertoire. With each new addition, I became more enthusiastic. In two more sessions, I ably mastered mechanics, demonstrated by my English grades throughout the remainder of my school days.

6   Today I am grateful to an extraordinary woman for a wonderful legacy. Because of my brief but rewarding association with this remarkable woman, I feel qualified to recognize a second educator who shares the same love and gift for expression. Using a different technique, modern by design and more determined and demanding, she accomplishes the same goal. Her students learn through her enjoyment of English and passion for words.

7   Mrs. Susan Gibson-Breda glided into class the first session and slapped a huge mountain of dittos onto the table. "Hi, guys," she greeted us. Her shoulder-length, light brown hair cascaded dramatically along each cheek as she bent to take roll. "Let's see who's alive." She informed us "today was one of those days" and pointed out several deficiencies in her clothing and stockings. Dressed casually but quite appropriately in a blue, soft-flowing dress, she did not fit my interpretation of the "normal" English instructor. Chalk in hand, she briskly diagrammed, while orally interpreting, her personal "pyramid" style of teaching. This bubbly, young English master, at least ten years

Susan's pyramid approach

my junior, stood in front of us and confidently predicted we would put down on paper by quarter end such brilliant thoughts as the ones she now tenderly read to us. By acquiring writing skills and building on them one at a time, as carefully as a carpenter builds a splendid house, we would be limited in our final products only by our own imagination. I reacted to her words with genuine doubt. How could I ever do that? Since Aunt Viola's tutoring, I understood language mechanics, but stylistics evaded me. When I attempted to create papers containing expressive and and communicative words, I felt foolish and ridiculous. Would I measure up to her expectations? Her goals for our achievement loomed higher than I thought possible to attain.

Introduction to style

Assignments and success

8   Embarrassed by their amateurish content, I struggled endlessly with the first two assigned papers. This doctor of the English language praised my second paper and my first "masterpiece" returned to its owner stamped with positive feedback. Perhaps I could write after all. In the short weeks that followed, one skill was added to another until my writings showed marked improvement. Her "pyramid" method worked effectively. The motor of my imagination ran full rudder as self-confidence overcame self-consciousness. Words I previously felt embarrassed to use floated off my fingertips as though penned by a great writer. "No paper will ever reach perfection," she informed us. Comforted by the fact that even great novelists revise and revise, I revised and polished until I felt satisfied with the content of my writings. She kept her promise; she convinced me I could write.

Conclusion

9   In similar and brief encounters, two women, one old and suffering, the other young and vibrant, opened doors I thought would remain closed forever. Through Aunt Viola's patience, I grasped the mechanical aspects of writing, and through Susan's determination, I gained the courage to use words to their fullest advantage. Together, they influenced my attitude toward written communication, and because of them, I gained insight into myself and my abilities.

—Diana Brown

Questions and Exercises on "Twenty Years Between"

1. How does the opening paragraph effectively introduce the basic differences between the two teachers? What did they have in common?
2. How are the two personalities re-created through dialogue?
3. Find examples of colorful verbs and good parallelism.
4. What techniques are used in concluding the paper?
5. Explore the structural format of this paper and comment on its effectiveness.

THE INFLUENCE OF TWO MEN

Thesis

Support areas

Mr. Boltin's
physical
description

First
conversation

Entering his
world

Lessons

1   The learning process is experienced not only through a scholastic education, but also through personalities of people one comes in contact with "accidentally" in life. Two men, Mr. Boltin, and Mr. Wiles, both of different character, professional fields, and teaching methods, individually shared with me an important part of their knowledge, while giving me their friendship.

2   Mr. Boltin was an immigrant from Sweden. His short stature was well developed with bulging muscles from his constant exercise and weight lifting. His weatherworn facial features were hidden by an abundant growth of heavy black whiskers. His bushy eyebrows almost concealed his blue eyes. These eyebrows were very expressive and often I could tell his mood by the way that he held them.

3   Mr. Boltin was recommended to me through my symphony conductor. At the time, I was a young violinist struggling with the fundamentals of my instrument. After several tries, I finally managed to find the courage to call Mr. Boltin for an appointment. I was unprepared for the abrupt voice which greeted me; the "good morning" rang loudly through my head. From unknown resources within my body, I gathered strength and replied in one long breath, "Hello, my name is Denise. I wish to take violin lessons from you. Is that all right?" I blushed as a long slow chuckle slowly filled the following silence. "Dat's fine" was his only reply.

4   This first conversation was the beginning of one of my most fascinating friendships. From the moment I entered through his solid oak door until I exited down his plunging stairs, I was introduced to a whirlwind education of music, philosophy, and people. I never quite knew what to expect as I timidly rang his doorbell. Many times the bell would ring and ring until I grew impatient and absent-mindedly began to knock my instrument against my leg. From the archives of the mansion would float down a voice from nowhere—"Denise Kristine Ronnestad, dat is not gut!" The reprimand was not only startling, but also petrifying. The unwieldly door would be ferociously flung open, and I would find myself facing a thunderous pair of eyebrows.

5   My lessons unofficially ranged anywhere from two to four hours. Within those hours, my meager understanding of music was slowly enriched with concepts of music theory and fundamentals. My music repertoire dramatically broadened with each session. For countless lessons, I perched on the edge of a stiff mohair chair and watched as the small instrument came alive with personality under Mr. Boltin's massive fingers. Whenever my mind began to wander to other places and times, an outburst of Swedish lashed my thoughts. Exasperated,

Mr. Boltin would fling down his instrument and stomp from the room. My lesson was over.

6   With his stubborn Swedish influence, Mr. Boltin germinated within me a new hunger for understanding the world around me. In his thoughtful moments, he shared with me his love for flowers, trees, and animals. Through his eyes, I was introduced to the life systems of these small wonders.

Introduction to
Mr. Wiles

7   Feeling courageous at the beginning of high school, I decided to seek a formal understanding of nature through a biology class. When I entered the class for the first time, I was unprepared for the formidable instructor rigidly facing the class. Somewhere in my past day dreams, I had envisioned my new teacher as Mr. Boltin wearing a white lab coat.

Physical
description

However, while Mr. Boltin was short, muscular, and whiskered, this man was tall, wiry, and clean shaven. His lanky frame was stiffly carried as he introduced himself as Mr. Wiles.

Entering his
world

8   While the class labored through the required lab experiments, the hidden, kind heart of Mr. Wiles was slowly exposed. My own fingers fumbled with the unaccustomed equipment in my excitement and often Mr. Wiles looked over my shoulder and helped me readjust the needed knobs. Once I was able to actually observe small animals, my curiosity overwhelmed any fear, and I besieged my instructor with endless questions and inquiries.

9   My interest in the class material opened a comradeship between myself and Mr. Wiles. Many times the two of us stayed after class for several hours, working on special projects. Throughout the entire year, Mr. Wiles's patience with my scientific clumsiness never faltered. In a

Extra lab
sessions

steadfast, quiet manner, he slowly guided my inexperienced hands into the practice of lab work. In our many sessions, Mr. Wiles introduced me to numerous scientific names and information. These innocently given facts gradually were added to the skeleton of interest produced by Mr. Boltin.

10   Although Mr. Boltin and Mr. Wiles came from two different family backgrounds, lifestyles, and education, they shared with me part of their hidden selves as well as a part of their knowledge. Both of them

Conclusion

were totally opposite in character, Mr. Boltin was dramatic and intense, whereas Mr. Wiles was calm and patient, yet both of them were blessed with tender and willing hearts for those people, like myself, who desperately wanted to learn. Through the willingness of both of these men to aid me in understanding music, people, and science, I have come to an unusual understanding of friendship and many "wonders" within our world.

—Denise Ronnestad

Questions on "The Influence of Two Men"

1. How does the writer successfully incorporate specific scenes to capture the effect of each teacher?
2. Which physical details best reflect Mr. Boltin's personality?
3. What organizational format is used in this paper? What advantage does it have in presenting this topic?
4. Which paragraph functions as a transition from one man to the other? What techniques does it employ?
5. How does the paper's conclusion integrate the findings on both men?

THE DEVELOPMENT OF TWO PROFESSIONAL BASKETBALL PLAYERS: PETE MARAVICH AND SPENCER HAYWOOD

Thesis

Supporting areas

1   Pete Maravich and Spencer Haywood are both highly successful professional basketball players, but each came from different backgrounds and reached success in different ways.

Pete's background

2   Pete was born in a rambling, middle-class town in South Carolina. From the time that he was thirteen years old, his dream was to play pro-basketball. Pete's father was a college coach, and he taught Pete many things about basketball. Pete was a loner; his best friend was his basketball, and he practiced with it eight or nine hours a day so he could one day realize his dream.

Spencer's background

3   Spencer was born in the poor section of Detroit. Like many other black youths, he belonged to a gang. He looked extremely old for his age. He hung around nightclubs, made time with women, snatched purses, and generally beat up on "whitey." At this time, he was fifteen years old and six-feet, six-inches tall. Spencer learned his basketball on the playgrounds of Detroit and later used it as a tool to escape from the ghetto.

Reversals for both

4   Because of his poor grades, Spencer attended a small college in Colorado, while Pete went to highly rated Louisiana State. Pete set many records and was acclaimed as the hottest shot in the land. But when the 1968 Olympic team was chosen, Pete Maravich was by-passed. Because of a boycott of the Olympics by most of the good black ballplayers, little known Spencer Haywood made the team. Spencer suddenly became a star as he led the U.S. to a Gold Medal.

Both receive pro contracts

5   Spencer was such a success that he was offered a pro contract by the Denver Nuggets of the A.B.A. He signed this contract while he was still in college, which violated the rule which prevented pro teams from signing a player until his college class had graduated. Meanwhile, Pete finished a career as his college's all-time leading scorer and

signed with Atlanta for an astronomical sum of money. Pete was heralded as a savior in the world of basketball, but Spencer was looked down upon as a troublemaker.

Both end with success

6   Now both Spencer and Pete are two of the most valuable players in the N.B.A. They are leaders, and both have gained respect from their teammates as each has been voted team captain at some time in his career. Both play the same style of basketball. Their job is to score points, and each has a gifted shooting touch that makes them both capable of breaking a game wide open with a quick flurry of baskets. Both Spencer and Pete have reached the same summit in the basketball world, even though they took completely different roads to reach it.

—Ann Lehoczky

Questions on "The Development of Two Professional Basketball Players: Pete Maravich and Spencer Haywood"

1. Why did the writer choose to combine her presentation of both players in paragraphs 4 and 5?

2. How does the structure of this paper differ from the previous two example papers, which compare two people? What are the advantages and disadvantages of each approach as reflected in these papers?

Example Paper on Two Jobs

WORK, WORK, WORK

Thesis
Supporting areas

1   The menial labor of sorting tomatoes on a harvester and the responsibility of supervising children at a playground appear to be very different. Differences in several aspects, environment, work, and pay are plain. However, similarities in other areas, boredom and satisfaction, also exist.

Sorter's environment

2   Tomatoes are sorted out in the fields aboard a giant machine—the harvester. The fields are huge expanses of flat land covered with row upon row of two-foot high tomato plants. The dirt-encrusted, rusty red harvester ambles down the rows hauling up the plants. It is actually a complicated system of conveyer belts. The first is made of metal and chains. It shakes all the fruit off the vines and takes it to the second belt, which spits the empty vines off the back and passes the heavier tomatoes to the last belt. The sorters stand in a row and pull everything that is not a red, ripe tomato off the waist-high belt and drop it down a chute to the ground beneath. "Everything" includes green tomatoes,

rotten tomatoes, dirt clods, and, occasionally, mice and snakes. It is dirty, dusty work.

Playground leader's environment

3   On the other hand, Sunset Playground is a big, old building. It is a single cement floored, grey-green walled room with double doors in opposite walls. Sunset contains a ping-pong table, a few tables and benches, games, balls of all kinds, and a cupboard full of arts-and-crafts materials. The leader's first job is to maintain a semblance of order. This is not easy. The children run, scream, fight, and whiz in one set of doors and out the other on their bicycles. Leaders are expected to interest this chaotic crowd in such arts-and-crafts projects as making paper bag puppets, gluing sticks and leaves to burlap covered boards, or coating old bottles with starch-soaked tissue paper. The two of them are also required to plan and lead organized games when the day's projects have been completed. It is difficult, demanding work.

Sorter's and playground leader's hours and pay

4   The hours and pay are different in the two jobs. Tomato sorters work ten hour night shifts from 7:00 P.M. to 5:00 A.M., six days a week which, at $2.50 an hour, earns them $150.00. Since tomatoes have a short harvest season, the sorter can only expect to make about $500.00. The playground leader's hours are as flexible as the sorter's are rigid. They work for an hourly wage of $2.30, usually five days a week from 12:00 P.M. until 5:00 P.M., but, at the boss's discretion, they receive extra assignments at any time. Recreation leaders earn sixty to seventy-five dollars per week. They work the entire summer and can expect to be seven to eight hundred dollars richer in the fall. Sorters earn a little less money quickly, spend almost all of their time in work and sleep during the season, but have much of the summer free. Leaders earn a little more money slowly, spend almost all of their summer working, but have much of each day free.

Transition to similarities

5   Despite the differences in working conditions, an employee of Gill Harvesting and one of Coalinga-Huron Parks and Recreation District share many of the same feelings of boredom as well as satisfaction.

Sorter boredom

6   The sorter sees multitudes of tomatoes pass endlessly in front of her. Tomatoes all look basically alike. They are red and roughly spherical, or they are green, round, and hard, or they are soft, putrid, and squishy. A dirt clod also looks just like a dirt clod. Each foot of conveyor belt looks like every other foot of conveyer belt. If the sorter steals a glance away from the belt and out to the fields, all she can make out through the darkness is a row of tomatoes stretching out before her and a few rows on either side. She is trapped in an ocean of tomato plants on the island harvester. She is trapped on the harvester too. Her back touches a confining metal bar. Her elbows bump the busy sorters next to her, and always her hipbones press against the rail between her and the million rushing tomatoes.

7   At first tomato sorters relieve their boredom by talking with their neighboring sorters. The rows seem to pass by more quickly when one

Sorter's devices for relieving boredom

is engaged in conversation or gossip. A myriad of subjects ranging from school to home to future plans to tomatoes to the foremen to men in general to couples to childhood memories to current problems are discussed. After a few ten hour nights, there is nothing left to say. The sorters' only recourse is to act slightly crazy. They start out singing—top forty songs, old Beatles and Beach Boys songs, camp songs, movie theme songs, patriotic songs, and even holiday songs. By this time they have the reputation of "that weird bunch who sing all the time." They then change the words of the songs to fit their situation. For example, "I've Been Working on the Railroad" becomes "I've Been Working in Tomatoes." They may make-up songs about their foremen and machine drivers. Their reputation among their foremen is now "those weirdos—hey, let's go see what they are up to." The singing and the attention help, but the last few days are the hardest, and more drastic measures may be taken. Some sorters come to work dressed exactly alike; some sorters wear surgical masks to keep out dust and some sorters "bark" at passing machines and trucks. This temporary loosening of inhibitions and immaturity acts as a safety valve to protect the sorter's sanity.

Playground leader's boredom

8   The playground leader also sees multitudes. Children pass endlessly through her building, and after a few days, most of them look alike. The boys all wear jeans, T-shirts, and high-top sneakers. They invariably need hair cuts and face washes. The girls wear shorts, matching tops, and bare feet. They are all growing out their bangs and painting their finger and toe nails. The arts-and-crafts projects are terribly predictable too. They are messy, and all involve the same paper, paint, glue, and crayons. Occasionally, a novel project presents itself and turns out to be an even greater mess. If the leader looks away from the children and their projects, all she sees is more children playing games, inside and out. She may feel that she is awash in an ocean of children marooned at her arts-and-crafts table.

Playground leader's devices for relieving boredom

9   Playground leaders likewise talk to each other to relieve their boredom. The projects and games seem to run more smoothly when they are talking. They speak of much the same type things that sorters do. Their conversation does not run out as quickly because they work fewer hours, are more actively involved in their work, and add the children, projects, and games to their list of topics. Leaders seldom sing unless it is as part of a game such as "Old MacDonald," but their inhibitions do become lessened. Normally shy leaders will yell out the doors at acquaintances because they are so eager for new intelligent conversation. Normally controlled leaders will scream at children because they are so frustrated. Normally "adult" leaders will resort to childishness because they are so in need of amusement. When they get bored enough, children's games become fun. The leaders may get more excited and involved in ball games, relay races, and contests than the

children. Arts-and-crafts may be a creative challenge rather than a chore. Leaders are often surprised when friends don't appreciate their paper bag Dracula puppet, or their paper plate clown mask, or their spooky swamp shadow box complete with rickety hut and moss-draped trees. These same friends are often incredulous when the leader describes the drama and exictement of that afternoon's ping-pong tournament. The temporary childishness protects the leader from the dullness of being an adult in a child's world.

Sorter's
satisfactions

10   Despite the boredom, satisfaction also plays a part in working "in the tomatoes." Sorters make friends with people they otherwise might never have spoken to. Ties between old friends are strengthened. A common bond of mutual suffering and laughter unites them. The "remember whens" often arise years later. Lasting the whole season gives a great feeling of accomplishment. Not being defeated, as many are, by the heat, pain, and dirt leaves the survivor feeling competent, strong, and able to do just about anything. Sorting is often a first job for fourteen- and fifteen-year-olds, and they grow up a lot in a few weeks. "Hard work" may have been mopping the kitchen floor, "dirty" may have been sliding into home plate, and "responsibility" may have been remembering their homework and lunch money. Sorters gain a deeper insight into these words and may even apply them after the season is over. Sorting tomatoes changes a person, usually for the better.

Playground
leader's
satisfactions

11   Satisfaction is also gained by recreation leaders. They make new friends at training seminars and departmental meetings. They become very close to their partners. Their shared frustrations, near emergencies, and joys bond them tightly. "Remember whens" are even more common among leaders than among sorters. A leader gains insight into children. She may learn that she doesn't really want eight kids. She may learn that they are not just "sweet things" but real little people. She may learn that winning respect from an incorrigible brat is often more touching than getting hugs from an "angel." Completing each day without a major crisis and establishing stronger rapport with the children gives the leader a feeling of accomplishment. The feeling grows as the quiet moments increase, as "no" causes effect faster, and as the children begin to help out spontaneously. It reaches a peak when the boss drops by unexpectedly and finds a quasi-quiet room full of happily busy children. Responsibility for young children makes the leader grow up. She must set an example for the children, so she may have to give up a few of her pet vices—including procrastination, messiness, and foul language. She should use reasonably correct grammar and make an effort to control her temper. Most of all, she has to turn her attention away from herself and toward the children, to become other-centered rather than self-centered. Many, but not all, leaders carry their "grown-up" attitudes out of the playground and into the world.

Conclusion 12 The labor of sorting tomatoes and the work of running a playground have different advantages and disadvantages, but they are both growing experiences, preparing the employee to leave the world of summer jobs and enter the adult job market.

—Becky Payne

Questions and Exercises on "Work, Work, Work"

1. This paper combines a point by point approach with a grouping by differences and similarities. Discuss the effectiveness of this approach.

2. The paper's strength is its details. Find examples of humor created through its specific descriptions.

3. Find examples of statements on the sorters reflected in parallel statements on playground leaders. How is parallelism used to increase the paper's unity?

4. How does verb choice add to this paper's interest and specificity?

Example Paper on Two Countries

A BRIEF LOOK AT ICELAND AND AMERICA

Thesis with supporting areas 1 The Icelandic and American cultures have many similarities in their Christmas celebrations, engagement customs, forms of transportation, household furnishings, merchandising products, politics, and seasons. Within the similarities, however, are variations that distinguish the unique character of each country.

Christmas celebrations 2 The celebrated holiday of Christmas is much the same in both countries. People go all out for Christmas, buying presents, and putting up trees. Children are the focal point and wait in anticipation for Santa to fulfill their Christmas wishes. When it comes to the holdiay feast, however, the Americans usually select turkey to adorn their tables, whereas, the Icelandic people prefer a fully cooked sheep's head.

Engagement customs 3 In both cultures, it is common practice for people to get engaged. It is an intent of marriage and a public announcement of that commitment. Rings are also exchanged. In Iceland, as soon as a couple get engaged, they start living together; it is fully accepted and expected. When they get married, their wedding rings are worn on the right hand. American couples use the period of engagement to make future plans and to look for a place to set up housekeeping. Once married, the rings are worn on the left hand.

Transportation

4   Both countries share most of the same modes of transportation: taxis, cars, busses, and aircraft. The United States has a multitude of different cab companies and types of cars for taxi service. The word "taxi" is usually written on the doors. In Iceland, there is only one type of taxi cab—a Mercedes Benz. The only way to tell if it's a cab is to look on the license plate, which would have a yellow L printed on it. The price of a car in Iceland is about double the cost of one in America, and the government controls the buying and selling of the cars, in contrast to the competition of car sales by various companies in the United States. Unlike America, Iceland does not have railroads. People use busses as their main means of traveling long distances within the country.

House furnishings

5   Icelandic women take pride in their homes just as American women do. In the American home, you are apt to see a conglomerate of furniture made of various types of materials. The beds usually have heavy blankets or electric blankets on them in the winter time with bedspreads covering them for the finished look. The Icelandic home contains a modest amount of furniture made primarily of teak wood. The only blanket on the bed is a huge, down-filled comforter; bedspreads are rarely seen.

Merchandising

6   In both countries, the grocery stores are somewhat alike; both have an array of various items and brands arranged on shelves in long rows, displayed to catch the eye. America pushes the large economy packages to the customers. The shoppers are used to having their purchases placed in brown paper bags for easy carriage home. In Iceland, just enough is bought day by day for what is needed; there is very little waste of food. The women carry their own knit bags with them for their purchases. Many of the bakery products and loose goods are wrapped in butcher-type paper.

Products: beer

7   Beer is manufactured in Iceland just as in America and brings in a substantial amount of revenue. Unlike the United States, however, where the people consume most of the beer they manufacture, Iceland exports all her beer in order to keep the younger people from obtaining it.

Sheep

8   Iceland and America both raise sheep and use the wool for clothing and various other items. The Icelandic sheep, however, have very long, straight hair, in contrast to the sheep raised in America. The long hair is made into beautiful rugs, which are sold through the country and exported.

Politics

9   A president presides as the head of both countries and is looked to as a figurehead for explaining a country's position. The ultimate power, however, rests in the Parliament, called the Althing in Iceland and the Congress in the United States.

Seasons

10   With regard to the seasons, America and Iceland have four distinct seasons. The Icelandic winters don't get much colder than the

coldest states in the continental United States, but because of the chill factor (wind), it tends to feel twice as cold as the particular temperature actually shows on the thermometer.

Conclusion

11   While many likenesses between the two countries exist, the slight differences in their customs gives each country a distinctive personality of its own.

—Nancy Mercer

Questions and Exercises on "A Brief Look at Iceland and America"

1. Explore the different supporting areas used in this paper. Can you come up with larger categories to combine some of these areas? Would larger categories give the paper a more unified effect?

2. How might you rework the ending of this paper to make it seem less abrupt?

Example Paper on Two Forms of One Sport

TWO TYPES OF PROFESSIONAL SKIING: RACING AND FREESTYLE

Background facts

Thesis and supporting categories

1   Snow skiing is one of the Pacific Northwest's favorite outdoor pastimes. Every weekend from November to May, thousands of skiers head for the Cascades. Hundreds of thousands of dollars are exhausted yearly as skiing is the most expensive participation sport in the United States. Professional skiing is also growing with the expanding popularity of recreational skiing. Two basic types of professional skiing are alpine racing and freestyle or "hot dog" skiing, which can be compared in the three categories: style, requirements, and competition.

Styles

2   The styles of racing and freestyle are totally different in that racing involves skiing in a straight-forward direction, while freestyle involves skiing over the whole slope and part of the time being airborne. Racing is determined on a time basis, while freestyle uses a point system, points being given by judged techniques. There are three types of racing: slalom, grand or giant slalom, and downhill. They all involve skiing through a given course in the fastest time possible. The basic difference is the length of the course, with slalom having the shortest course, and downhill, the longest. Freestyle also involves three basic types: moguls, aerial, and stunt-ballet. Mogul skiing consists of skiing over and through bumps or moguls in the fastest and best looking way (flair)

achievable. Aerial skiing is skiing in the air where maneuvers are executed by skiing off a ramp or jump made of snow. Stunt-ballet skiing is composed of ice skatinglike movements, the basic difference is the bulky boots and skis attached to each leg. The techniques for racing and freestyle, therefore, are quite different, but the basic elements needed to participate are somewhat equal.

Requirements

Equipment: type and cost

3   The requirements for racing and freestyle play a crucial role in the performance of the skier. The proper equipment is one of the most important factors in a skier's success or failure. Most boots, bindings, and poles will suffice and can be used for either type of skiing, but the skis are extremely important. Racing skis are long and usually on the stiff side; conversely, freestyle skis should be short and stiff or long and soft, the choice depending on individual preference. The cost of this equipment is rather expensive, $600 being a conservative estimate for a complete outfit.

Conditions needed

4   The terrain and snow conditions for both types of skiing ideally would be a smooth, moderately pitched slope (30°–40° angled hill) with a hard packed snow surface. Mogul skiing, however, requires different conditions. Its ideal slope should be very steep (45° angled hill) with monstrous bumps and a soft to medium hard packed surface. However, it is the speed or technique of skiing that composes the main difficulty and not necessarily the quality of the hill being skied.

Expertise and training needed

5   The skier should be an advanced expert with an ability to ski almost any slope, since the difficulty in skill involved in these types of skiing could only be executed by an accomplished skier, and the danger involved in these types of skiing is too much for a recreational skier. To be sufficiently accomplished, the skier should take various training programs to ready himself for the skiing involved. This is especially important for freestyle because of the aerial maneuvers and various leg and body-straining techniques. After the skier has bought his equipment and trained and practiced his skiing specialty, he is ready to compete.

Competition: obtaining eligibility

Cost

6   Actual competition is the true test for the skier. The skier's competitive background is very important in obtaining eligibility to compete, more so in racing than freestyle. Background is used for seeding or predicting a skier's performance in competition. The growth of racing and freestyle is tremendous, especially in the past few years. The growth rate could be much higher, but the cost of training and actual competition is extremely expensive. The entrance fees for competing range from $25 to around $50 per race for starting-out racers or hot dogs. This amount goes down as the skier establishes a name for himself with a few first place showings. Until then, a skier can spend quite a lot of money trying to get started on the way to the big time. Unlike racing, freestyle competitions demand insurance for the skier because of the high injury risk to the skier. The future of freestyle is a little better

Location

than racing because of the European domination of the racing scene, which has dampened domestic enthusiasm. Freestyle is purely American, the training, money, and contests are all at home.

Opportunities

7   In terms of the opportunities for making money, the outlook is excellent, but only for the accomplished competitor. Freestyle skiing puts up well over a half-million dollars in prize money yearly. A good pro racer can take $20,000 to the bank in one season: the top money winner in racing can take home a respectable $70,000 in six months of work! All this money isn't including the endorsements paid to the skiers for the use and advertisements of the various manufacturers' products. These endorsements can add substantially to the skier's earnings.

Conclusion

8   Racing and freestyle have many differences as well as similarities. This is to be expected since the two types of skiing aren't really the same sport. As to which is better, it is purely an individual preference. Either way a skier chooses to compete, if he's good enough, he can make a lot of money in a very short time.

—Art Funamori

Questions and Exercises on "Two Types of Professional Skiing: Racing and Freestyle"

1. The categories within categories in this paper at times become confusing. Can you restructure paragraph 2 for greater clarity?

2. Can you rework the opening of paragraph 6 to better prepare for the points within it? Find sentences that introduce new points in paragraph 6 that need to be connected to the controlling idea.

3. Does the paper's conclusion redirect its focus?

Example Paper on Past and Present Adaptations of a Lifestyle

GYPSIES—THEIR 20TH CENTURY ADAPTATIONS OF AN ANCIENT LIFESTYLE

Background information

Thesis and supporting areas

1   For a long time, a group of people known as Gypsies lived their life outside the static, safe, and predictable life of the society around them. Their life has been a romantic one of high mobility (staying just ahead of the law) and adventure. They have long made their living by stealing, trading, and fortune telling. Conditions of modern life, however, have made some adaptations necessary in the areas of transportation, shelter, and means of livelihood.

2   Long ago, the Gypsies (who are a tribal people) traveled in caravans. Their horse-drawn covered wagons provided their transportation

Past means of obtaining transportation, shelter, and livelihood

as well as their shelter. In these self-contained units, they cooked, raised their families, and carried on their traditions. Their chosen life-style always remained outside the society they were passing through, and the peripheral relationship they did have (tricking and ripping off the local community) only served to reinforce the separation. Their means of livelihood were traditionally stealing and trading horses, stealing fruit from farmers' orchards, pickpocketing, and fortune telling. From these unorthodox business practices, the word "gyp" was coined.

Stability

3   Although the gypsies had no permanent home, they maintained stability through their strong tribal and family structure, and through the fact that wherever they were, their home and community was always with them. When they stopped to camp, the tents and covered wagons formed a circle surrounding a campfire in the center, which was shared by all.

Personal reaction to old image

4   As a child, the stories of Gypsies that I heard and read always contained images of a people, wild and untamed, dancing and singing around a campfire. Dashing, dark men playing guitars and violins; women with black flashing eyes, bright, whirling skirts, and jewelry that caught the firelight as they danced; children, barefoot and untamed, playing near the fire; grandmas and grandpas too old to dance, sitting by the fire telling stories; a people who loved children so much that they occasionally stole them—these were some of the images the word "Gypsy" evoked for me.

Modern concessions and changes

Personal example no. 1

5   I first became aware of some of the Gypsies' concessions to modern living when a group of them moved into an apartment adjoining my friend's. Even though it was rumored that they were leaders in a "hot" car ring from Pittsburgh, they looked pretty tame to me. The campfire, violins, and guitars had been replaced by a fireplace and transistor radio. When a sign appeared in their front window saying "Palms Read," I was reassured that they hadn't completely given up their culture. But the feast they held shortly before they left completely affirmed their unconquerable and incorrigible freedom of the spirit. The roast lamb they shared had been stolen the previous day from The Woodland Park Zoo.

Specifics of departure

Personal example no. 2

6   A few years later, I had another chance to see some modern day Gypsies. While traveling across the country, I stopped at a Howard Johnson rest stop. This is an East Coast abomination providing gas, food, and a gift shop with gaudy, bizarre trinkets at an equally bizarre price. Just after I arrived, a caravan of five campers, one house trailer, and three Winnebagos pulled into the parking lot single file. As the Gypsies got out of their vehicles, they worked efficiently as a group. The men followed an older man, obviously the leader of the clan, to the row of telephone booths in the lobby of Howard Johnson's. They all huddled together talking in low, excited voices, while the older man

Specifics had a long intense conversation on the phone.

7   Out in the parking lot, children ran, women shook out blankets, and one woman bathed her baby in a pink, plastic wash tub on top of the hood of a pickup. Inside Howard Johnson's, other women, their small children close beside them, used the restrooms and looked over trinkets in the gift shop. The personnel reacted as though under seige. Every available clerk, as well as the management, circled anxiously around the Gypsy women and children.

Departure 8   Abruptly, but with no appearance of haste, the Gypsies left the building. As I walked out to the parking lot, I saw Gypsies coming from every direction and getting in their cars. The woman, who was bathing the baby in the pink tub, quickly handed the child to an old woman. As the old woman wrapped the baby in a blanket, the young woman whooshed the water out over the hood of the truck onto the parking lot. Within five minutes, everyone had been collected, and the caravan, once again, left the lot single file and headed on down the highway.

Conclusion 9   Ten minutes later, four state patrol cars arrived. The patrolmen seemed disappointed as they looked around the Gypsy-less lot. I was disappointed too, because even though the Winnebagos lack the charm of horse-drawn carriages, and transistor radios lack the romance of guitars and violins, the Gypsies, themselves, lack neither charm nor romance, and have adapted to the 20th century only enough to survive it.

—Jeanne Wartes

Questions on "Gypsies—Their 20th Century Adaptations of an Ancient Lifestyle"

1. How does the writer incorporate personal experience with more objective information?
2. What structure is repeated in the two personal examples?
3. How might the writer have incorporated her personal involvement into the paper's opening to keep the paper's tone more consistent?

Example Paper on Two Therapies

COMPARISON AND CONTRAST OF BIOFEEDBACK TRAINING AND MEDITATION

Thesis 1   The inability to cope with stressful situations, anxiety, and tension are common complaints of people in our technological society. Presently, two popular methods are available to decrease anxiety and/or tension. These two methods, biofeedback training and the art of meditation, are growing in popularity with individuals attempting to cope with daily, stressful situations. Many similarities can be found between these two methods. However, the application and consistency of each method varies, and the long-term effect of either one depends on the individual and his or her ability to cope with stressful situations.

Supporting areas

2   In biofeedback training, various machines are utilized to help teach a person to relax. The use of audio and/or video feedback assists the individual in monitoring alpha waves, muscle tension, heart rate, body temperature, and galvanic skin responses. Electrodes are connected to appropriate body points to relay feedback on physiological and brain wave activity, thus determining the anxiety level. Through monitoring brain wave activity, an audio or video message is relayed to the connected person, which indicates the alpha level. In order to achieve a relaxed state, the person must focus on the output of alpha waves because the two are directly related. Through constant feedback, the participant learns to realize the state that produces the greatest level of alpha waves, and thus recognize the most relaxed, tension-free state.

Biofeedback's use of machines

Alpha level and tension

3   Scientific studies and research show high output levels of alpha waves in yogis, gurus, and other meditators during their meditative state. When a meditator's alpha wave level is very high, his anxiety level is nonexistent. This centuries-old art of meditation has taught emotional and physical health through internalization and contemplation. This art, which sometimes takes yogis and gurus a lifetime to master, is one of the seeming wonders of the biofeedback machine. What once took years to learn can be learned in hours or months; however, the effects may not be as long lasting. It is still too soon to know the lasting effects of biofeedback since this discovery is relatively new.

Alpha levels in meditation

Machine producing similar results sooner

4   The art of meditation has never utilized machinery to achieve relaxation because meditators believe internal control is reflected in external control. A meditator's subjective states, significantly associated with abundant alpha-wave patterns, are rest, relaxation, and relief from tension and concentration. The yogis and gurus interpret the subjective states as an experience of being into the "here and now" or as "becoming one with yourself."

Meditation's lack of machinery

5   The control of mental and physiological processes is demonstrated in both biofeedback training and meditation; however, Western technology has classically conditioned people to believe in only those things that can be proved scientifically, making Westerners skeptical about meditation. Due to the novelty of the biofeedback machine and the sparse research available on the subject, many people are still leery of this contraption, too; yet being a machine is in

Control of mental and physical processes

its favor. Most Westerners believe we have the capability to improve the function of our minds, but they avoid developing this potential due to the lack of a structured, step-by-step method, or "paint by numbers" approach. On the other hand, yogis, gurus, and lamas have developed this potential for mental/physical control over thousands of years and are somewhat taken back by, and unsure of, the biofeedback machine.

Western skepticism versus Eastern skepticism

Clinical studies

6   Clinical studies examining the usefulness of alpha biofeedback in treating neurosis of a high anxiety level are encouraging. Most meditators agree biofeedback training has potential, significant medical possibilities, and does enable an individual to minimize anxiety. However, the long-term effects of continuous biofeedback training may create a dependency on instantaneous feedback through audio and visual aids, not unlike television and radio. To feel normal and able to cope with daily living, a person would hook up to a machine, another external extension. On the other hand, meditators feel the stress-reducing effects of meditation are long lasting, ensuring a healthier and longer life.

Long-term effects

7   The contrasts between biofeedback and meditation are waning as the comparative research becomes more extensive. The many similarities between biofeedback training and meditation emphasize the important role of alpha waves in reducing anxiety and assisting individuals in coping with stressful situations. The few differences between the two methods are more a matter of semantics and a fear of the unknown on both sides. The meditators view biofeedback training as a limited method in self-awareness, self-control, and potential development. On the other hand, clinical researchers of biofeedback claim alpha feedback is an entity they can recognize and talk about. As stated in *Psychology Today*, "Biofeedback is the alpha wave of brain electrical activity, not an experience of being into 'now' or 'becoming one with yourself.'" Whatever the interpretation is of alpha brain waves, the fact remains that the potential of humans has not yet been reached by any means, and stressful situations continue to produce much anxiety and tension in Western societies today.

Summary and Conclusion

—Gregory Brown

Questions and Exercises on "Comparison and Contrast of Biofeedback Training and Meditation"

1. How might the supporting areas in this paper have clearer labels?

2. Rewrite the openings for some paragraphs in this paper so they state their controlling idea more openly.

3. How might the writer have defined the importance of alpha waves earlier in his paper and used them in his opening thesis?

4. Revise the last half of the paper's conclusion to keep its focus on the two techniques compared.

Example Paper on Same Theme in Two Works and Two Media

SIMILAR DREAMS IN *MIDNIGHT COWBOY* AND *OF MICE AND MEN*

Thesis

1   The movie *Midnight Cowboy*, directed by John Schlesinger, and the novel *Of Mice and Men*, by John Steinbeck, deal with people in interdependent relationships, in both cases searching for their own idea of Utopia to conquer lonelinesss. Both deal in dreams, and both end in tragedy.

Comparable relationships between main characters

Each meets the other's needs

2   Rico Rizzo's relationship with Joe in *Midnight Cowboy* parallels George's relationship with Lennie in *Of Mice and Men*. Joe Buck is dependent upon Rico as Lennie is dependent upon George, but this dependence is a need for Rico's and George's mental guidance rather than a physical dependence. George looked after Lennie when Curly bullied him, and Rico gave Joe Buck the "lowdown" on getting along in New York City. Still, the dependent characters made up for what was lacking in their partners: Lennie, with his bigness, was like a dog that could be sicced on someone like Curly whom George disliked; Joe Buck with his good health became nurse to Rico when Rico contracted tuberculosis. In each case, the buddies stuck together until the death of one partner, because each met the other's needs.

Comparable dreams

George and Lennie

3   The dreams each man had are also comparable. Each dream dealt with security and finding a spot in the world to call one's own. George and Lennie wanted their own farm: Lennie mainly so he could have his own soft and furry rabbits to care for and pet without anyone stopping him, and all the ketchup he wanted; George for the purpose of simply having his own land where he could "bump off" anyone who trespassed on it.

Joe and Rico

4   Joe Buck and Rico had the same goal: to go to Florida. But Rico (now at the end of the story, helpless, and more like Lennie) wanted his "complete food," coconuts; he desired to be somebody—to be called "Rico" (not Ratso), and to be "useful on his legs." It was important to Joe to have the security of a job—something that would pay for the place he would share with Rico and also to have his own bathroom.

Lennie and Joe's dreams based on memories from the past

5   Lennie's and Joe Buck's dreams traced back to a kindly relative. Lennie often thought of his Aunt Clara who once gave him a piece of soft velvet to stroke, which was security and comfort to him. Joe remembered the care of his grandmother, Sally Buck, and how she

doted over him, and this memory affected his yearning for cleanliness—the washroom, a symbol.

Titles reflect dreams

6   Titles of *Of Mice and Men* and *Midnight Cowboy* deal indirectly with a main character's dream: Lennie loved soft things (rabbits, velvet, a woman's hair, mice), and Joe Buck wanted to spend his cowboy life in what he supposed were the rich pastures of admiration from women in New York. In each case, the dream led to the character's downfall. Lennie's passion for soft things resulted in his murder of Curly's wife. In the same way, Joe Buck's attempts at hustling in the big city caused him to kill a man. Both dreams, as reflected in both titles, led to tragedy.

Endings: Lennie and Rico die happy, thinking of their dreams

George and Joe both left defeated and alone

7   While both of the partners who died ended their lives with visions of their dream, the hope for the survivors died with their partners. Lennie died happy, dreaming of the farm and the rabbits, and Rico died cheerful and optimistic on his way to Florida. For George and Joe Buck, however, the end was a doubtful and frightening experience: their hopes were deflated, their buddies were gone, and each was left completely alone in a world without dreams.

—Jean McVay

Questions and Exercises on "Similar Dreams in Midnight Cowboy *and* Of Mice and Men"

1. Is the point by point approach handled effectively in this paper or does the intermixing of characters from the two works become confusing? What is gained in this approach?

2. Find examples of this paper's condensing many examples to support a single point.

3. How does the paper's ending bring both works back to its opening thesis?

Chapter Five

Thinking Logically

Need for Rational Objectivity in a Commercialized World

Clear writing depends upon clear thinking. To be sure that you are using a logically sound approach in your thinking and writing, you need to be aware of the commercial pressures that invade almost all aspects of our lives—of the approach that asks you to "buy" an idea emotionally rather than analyze it intellectually.

You live in the age of the Big Sell. Advertising slogans are part of your language; advertising techniques manipulate your life. Children recognize cartoon figures on cereal boxes before they can read. Mass media creates instant folk heroes. A national survey to determine the heroes of American young people found that seven out of the ten top choices were figures created or popularized by the media.

Since the early 1950s, the nation's top advertising agencies have hired social scientists to apply "motivational research" to the buying habits of the American public. Motivational research systematically probes your deepest needs, fears, hopes, and anxieties to find out what really makes you buy. In supermarkets, hidden cameras record shoppers' eye blink rates to see which situations or displays produce or release stress. Studies linking men's automobile buying habits to their view of cars as "wives" or "mistresses" created the successful marketing of hardtop convertibles, which combined the unconscious appeal of both images. Research equating cake-making with mothering warned cake-mix producers of the hidden guilt or deprivation involved in overly easy instant mixes. The makers reintroduced the illusion of creativity to the mix by letting the consumer add the egg. Researchers are currently determining the optimum length of time and movement an image must have on screen in order to hold a child's attention.

Mass media and motivational research combine as powerful tools for mass manipulation. Children spend more time watching television than going to school. Adolescents see more movies than they read books. More people watch television news coverage than read newspapers. In recent years, sophisticated advertising techniques have been applied to selling you presidential candidates as well as products, in trying to win your mind as well as your money.

Being human, you have both rational and emotional needs. While you buy to satisfy both of these needs, advertisers have increasingly opted to capitalize on just the emotional ones. Producers, convinced that irrational needs rule people, fail to give your rational side its just due. Ads present entertainment rather than facts; candidates deal with slogans rather than issues; the evening news telecast presents complex news issues as condensed and canned as your orange juice.

The emotional approach has pervaded too many areas where you need a rational discussion of facts. Newspaper editorials, political debates, letters to editors, campaign pamphlets, and various interest groups increasingly appeal to fear and other emotions while failing to clarify or even examine the ideas behind the issues.

You need to sharpen your rational know-how to protect yourself from emotional manipulation. You need to learn how to remain objective in the face of subjective appeals. If you aren't aware of the insult inherent in an emotional approach, these appeals to your irrational side will remain effective, and you will find it harder to acquire the solid information you need to make rational decisions in our complex world.

You can increase your rational awareness by becoming more aware of logical fallacies or false arguments that are used to support ideas or arguments. The following section acquaints you with some of the fallacies you are likely to encounter. Learn to recognize them in others' arguments as being patently false or misleading and studiously try to avoid using them in your own thinking and writing.

Logical Fallacies

> **Logical fallacy** A counterfeit argument; an argument that sounds convincing but does not hold up under rational scrutiny; an argument that diverts attention, distorts evidence, or uses false association, causation, or authority in presenting its case.

Logical fallacies are unconsciously or intentionally false arguments that either lack support or contain faulty, erroneous, or misleading support. These fallacies have five traits in common:

FIVE MAIN FALLACY TECHNIQUES:

1. *Diversion*
2. *Distortion*
3. *False association*
4. *False causation*
5. *False authority*

Diversion Techniques

Diversion techniques distract an opponent or audience away from the actual argument. The following fallacies all use some side-tracking technique to draw your attention away from the valid issues and arguments.

Name-calling   Labeling your opponent with negative terms.

Name-calling labels your opponent with negative terms that discredit him in the eyes of the audience.

Examples:
Hippie, Communist, chauvinist pig, wild-eyed liberal, atheist, bigot, radical, red-neck.

Argument ad hominem ("argument at the man")   Attacking a person's characteristics, marital status, origins, religious beliefs, or home life instead of his or her arguments.

Argument *ad hominem* focuses on the arguer rather than on the argument. Such attacks are fallacious whenever the personal information has no direct bearing on the issues; thus while a person's alcoholic problems might be pertinent to his or her performance in an elected office, past marital difficulties would not. While "name-calling" can be part of an *ad hominem* attack, it need not always be present. For example, to claim a person is unfit to serve on a school board because he or she has no children is a form of *ad hominem* arguing that does not resort to specific labels.

Examples:
She shouldn't be allowed to teach because she's an atheist.
She shouldn't be elected governor because she's divorced.
He has too squeaky a voice to make a good president.

Tu quoque ("You're another")   Responding to an accusation with a counter-accusation.

In a *tu quoque* argument, nothing gets answered or settled, for rather than responding to a specific criticism, the arguer counterattacks. Even if the counterattack presents a valid point, the person has not answered the original accusation and has changed the topic.

Examples:
A husband complains about his wife's inability to budget money; the wife responds by attacking his ability to earn an adequate wage.

A father admonishes his son not to smoke marijuana; the son returns with observations on his father's drinking habits.

Justification by side issue   Arguing that your opponent's wrongs justify your own.

While a *tu quoque* argument answers an attack with a counterattack, the "side issue" argument falsely assumes that two wrongs make a right. Just because your opponent has slandered you doesn't make it legal, necessary, or right for you to slander him in return.

Examples:
I stole from that store because it overcharges its customers.
I cheated on the test because the teacher grades unfairly.

The United States should not criticize our dictatorship, since it suppresses its own minorities.

Red herring   Sidetracking an argument to a different topic.

Red herring is a highly pungent smoked fish whose presence is hard to ignore. The fallacy label "red herring" probably goes back to the old folklore that you can stop a bloodhound from tracking you by dragging a red herring across your trail. The bloodhound will stop and follow the herring's scent and forget all about you. A "red herring" strategy sidetracks an argument to a different subject that is less controversial or enables the sidetracker to look better or have a better chance of winning.

Examples:
In a debate over whether the state should fund all basic education, a speaker suggests that since the juvenile crime rate is increasing, young people no longer deserve our tax dollars.

In a debate over whether the phone company should base local charges on the number of calls made, the speaker suggests that with this pay system parents could keep track of whom their sons and daughters were calling.

In Camus's *The Stranger*, the prosecutor argues that Meursault should be found guilty of an Arab's death, because witnesses reported that Meursault did not cry at his own mother's funeral.

Ad misericordiam ("To the pity of the heart")   An appeal based on sympathy.

The *ad misericordiam* argument plays on sympathies rather than dealing with relevant information. A lawyer, for example, may appeal to the jurists' sympathy for the hard life his client has led rather than focus on the crime his client has supposedly committed.

Examples:
You must give me the job for my family is starving.
You can't flunk me; my parents would disown me.

Distortion Techniques

Distortion techniques put an argument out of perspective by falsely limiting the available choices, playing up similarities while ignoring differences, basing conclusions on insufficient evidence, omitting negative information, or prejudicing an audience so it refuses an opponent a fair hearing. Each of the following fallacies uses a distortion technique to mislead an audience.

False dilemma (also known as the Black/White or Either/Or Fallacy) Arbitrarily limits a person to two opposing choices when more possibilities exist.

A "false dilemma" distorts by oversimplifying a complex conflict into an either-or choice. It's a form of the old argument, "You're either for me or you're against me," used to convince people to join some group.

Examples:
"America—Love it or Leave it."
"Factories or Clean Air"
"Capital Punishment or Crime in the Streets"
"Better Dead than Red"

False analogy   A figurative comparison presented as proof.

An "analogy" stresses correspondences between things that are otherwise dissimilar. Writers often use such comparisons to clarify points or to add interest to their writing. Such comparisons become fallacies, however, if they are presented as proof. If two things are alike in some respects, it does not follow that they must be alike in all respects. A false analogy distorts by omitting differences, and unless one situation is an exact replica of another, what happened in one cannot logically predict or prove what will happen in the other.

Examples:
A slogan in the 1932 presidential election: "Don't change horses in the middle of the stream."
If you buy a new car, you should use it; therefore, since we've de-

veloped a new weapon system, we ought to try it out.
If you're old enough to fight, you're old enough to vote.

Hasty generalization   An all-encompassing conclusion based on too
little evidence.

Hasty generalization gives the illusion of providing proof but actually has insufficient evidence for the scope of its conclusions. It distorts by overstating its case. Words like "all," "every," and "no one," should be suspect in generalizations presented as proof, since absolute cases are extremely hard to verify. A valid conclusion states no more than its evidence allows. If 40 percent of the people surveyed choose one option, for example, the survey summary should report "Forty percent of the surveyed group chose . . ." and not falsely claim "most," or "a majority" in its findings.

Examples:
You're the second person I've talked to who went to that concert; it must have been a sell-out.
He stood me up; men are so unreliable.
She wrecked the car; women can't drive.

Stacking the deck (also known as "loading the dice" or "special pleading")   Presenting only the facts in your favor, ignoring or omitting negative evidence.

"Stacking the deck" distorts by omission. While it doesn't falsify information, it presents only a one-sided version of a complex argument. Usually the arguer's points would be seen in a different perspective if all the facts were known.

Examples:
A company takes credit for putting money into oil research; whereas, it did so only when forced to by new laws.
Arguing only the good points of a particular political system without realistically assessing its drawbacks.

Poisoning the well   Prejudicing or coloring an audience's view of material before it is presented.

"Poisoning the well" assumes that if a well is poisoned, no one will want to drink from it. In Shakespeare's *Othello*, the villian, Iago, not only leaves false clues suggesting Desdemona's unfaithfulness, but so prejudices Othello against her, that all her explanations are in vain.

Examples:
My opponent, Mr. Smith, a red-neck from down South, will now give his views on segregation.
You can't trust what Judy tells you. She lies to make herself look good.

False Association Techniques

False association artificially joins two unrelated things in an audience's mind to create a carry-over effect. Fallacies using this technique appear widely in advertising approaches.

> **Transfer**   Artificially linking two unrelated things to effect a positive carry-over of approval or prestige.

The "transfer" technique assumes that positive feeling associated with people or images can carry over to things associated with them. A company, therefore, hires a well-known personality to advertise its products, creating an association between this person and its product for the carry-over effect. Sometimes advertising relies on images or pictures alone. Thus, one cigarette features ads with nature scenes to reinforce its "menthol fresh" approach, another pictures outdoor "he-men" to influence a masculine audience, and a third stresses "You've come a long way, baby" in its appeal to emancipated women. Commercials for medical products feature men wearing white coats creating the illusion that a doctor is speaking to you. Manufacturers pick a positive image like "youth," "back to nature," "sex appeal," "snob appeal," or "individuality" and then create a "personality" that connects their products with that image. Consumers buy the promised illusion as well as the actual product.

Examples:
"Catherine Deneuve for Chanel no. 5"
"Dorothy Hamill introduces 'Short and Sassy,' the conditioner for short hair."

"Chris Evert for New Everynight Shampoo."
"You and me, babe, Arm in Arm, naturally, babe. . . ." Arm in Arm by
Helene Curtis—"the natural way to stay fresh when you're close."

Glittering generalities   Associating positive "cliché" words with a
product or idea.

"Glittering generalities" use transfer on a word level. The politician who equates his or her candidacy with "patriotism," "law and order," "honesty," "reform," and "American ideals" is using this approach. Glittering generalities usually refer to abstract qualities. Although generalities may "glitter," actual gold is not always present. What a person actually does in office more concretely measures performance than any attempt to associate himself or herself with unearned "virtue" words.

Examples:
"Joan Prudent for Honest Government."
"First Mutual—A Bank You Can Trust"
"American Products—for those who love America."

Argument *ad populum* (Argument to the people)   Appealing to an
audience's particular prejudices and fears.

Argument *ad populum* plays to an audience's emotional fears and desires. It appeals to positive feelings toward God, home, and country and awakens fears of Communism, atheism, or big government depending on the biases of the group addressed. In using it, the arguer identifies with the audience's position on issues and opposes whatever the audience fears. Argument *ad populum* is an elaborate form of transfer that associates the speaker with the image the audience has of itself. Politicians using the *ad populum* argument in speaking to divergent special interest groups are beginning to find themselves in trouble since instant media not only pick up but provide a record of contradictory stances and statements made in trying to "be all things to all people."

Examples:
A politican speaking to a group of large corporation presidents states, "I, too am against big government and for private enterprise. My oppo-

nent, however, supports a welfare state and will let corporate taxes pay for it."

The same speaker talking to union workers states, "The working man has given more than his share; it's time big business stopped getting all the breaks. Why should the poor subsidize the rich?"

False Causation Techniques

False causation claims an erroneous cause and effect relationship based on invalid evidence. The following fallacies link an effect with unprovable or nonapplicable causes.

Post hoc, ergo propter hoc ("After this, therefore because of this")   Using a time sequence to suggest a causal relationship, that is, because event B followed event A, claiming that A caused B.

A simple time sequence is never adequate proof of cause. Just because you received an "A" on your chemistry test after attending a party the night before does not mean that the party caused the good grade. You were probably on top of the material under any circumstances. In time related events, too much can be pure chance to suggest a causal relationship. Politicians often suggest that because an event, like war, occurred during the opposing party's administration, that administration caused the war. Advertisers often rely on a kind of projected "post hoc" argument. They suggest that first you try their product and then you, too, will look like the person in the ad; first you buy the car, then you, too, will have instant popularity; first you take their correspondence course, then you, too, will have instant success.

> *Examples:*
> Don't go to movies; that last time I went to one, I caught a cold the very next day.
> The volcano stopped erupting after the virgin jumped in: our sacrifice worked.
> I took a good stiff drink, and my nose stopped running: alcohol cures colds.

> **Non sequitur** ("It does not follow")   Suggesting a conclusion that has no logical connection with the evidence.

While most logical fallacies might be seen as a form of *non sequitur* reasoning, since their conclusions do not logically follow from their evidence, the term *non sequitur* is reserved for extreme cases where an illogical leap attempts to claim a cause and effect relationship where none actually exists. *Non sequitur* arguments have a startling effect, the logical breakdown is so glaring!

Examples:
I am against labor unions, since my ancestors came over on the *Mayflower*.
Women should have different dorm hours from men, since they get social security at an earlier age.
Alcohol is made from grain, so teetotalers should avoid bread.

False Authority Techniques

People often base their arguments on some form of "authority." If the authority is unsound, chances are, so is the argument. You can't draw any supportable conclusions from unreliable or faulty information. A tainted source produces tainted findings.

Check the reliability and credibility of all your sources. Just because words are published does not make them true. Some disreputable magazines welcome the prospect of a lawsuit from a famous person for the free publicity it would give them. They often make in increased sales far more than the suit costs them. Famous people often ignore false publications rather than give these publishers that free publicity.

A. Transfer Forms of False Authority

Transfer is used as a false authority in the following situations:

1. An expert in one field supports ideas or products in an unrelated field.

Athletes supporting cosmetics.
Physical scientist giving political views.

2. The name of an important person from the past is linked to a contemporary idea or movement.

Examples:
If Abraham Lincoln were alive, he would support urban renewal.
George Washington would be pleased with our bicentennial celebration.

3. Person poses as an authority.

Examples:
Actors dressed up as doctors, educators, or housewives to give testimonials for certain products.

B. *Faulty Premise Forms of False Authority*

The following fallacies start with false, distorted or unprovable premises, posing as true statements, and then attempt to use those false premises to predict behavior or to support untenable conclusions.

Dicto simpliciter ("Oversimplified saying")   Arguing from an unqualified generalization; using an unqualified generalization to make a specific prediction.

Dicto simpliciter starts with the equivalent of a "hasty generalization" and then uses it to predict a specific case or to make a specific application. Since its premise was faulty to begin with, its prediction also has no guarantee of correctness.

Examples:
Dieting to lose weight is good for people; therefore, Mr. Jones (who is extremely underweight) should diet.

The last three fish I caught were trout; therefore, the fish on my line now must be a trout.

> **Hypothesis contrary to fact**   Using a false or unprovable premise to support your argument.

If a person starts with a false premise, of course, the conclusions will also be false. "Hypothesis contrary to fact" not only applies to statements that can be proven wrong, but also applies to statements presented as fact, which in reality are unprovable. Such arguments take the form of "If it weren't for _____, we would never have known about _____." While it's true that a certain discoverer is credited with certain findings, it cannot be proven that if this discoverer had not existed, his or her discoveries would never have been made.

Examples:
If it weren't for Einstein, the world would never have learned about relativity.
If it weren't for this book, you never would have learned about logical fallacies.

> **Genetic fallacy**   Believing that a person's origins or genes will predict his or her behavior.

The "genetic fallacy" uses stereotypes about a given race, sex, nationality, or even hair color to predict behavior. A stereotype is actually a hasty generalization that assumes all members of a given group have the same characteristics. Genetic fallacies are the basis of much prejudiced thinking.

Examples:
He's a black so he must be a good dancer.
She's Irish so watch out for her temper.
She's illogical because she's a woman.
He must be intelligent, since his father's a doctor.

C. Other Forms of False Authority

> **Bandwagon**   The belief that if the majority does something, it is right, or if the majority believes something, it is true.

"Bandwagon" arguing was named after the old political custom of hiring a band and driving it through town on a wagon to advertise a candidacy. People literally hopped on the bandwagon of the candidate they supported, which implied that the best candidate had the most crowded wagon. "Bandwagon" or "popular appeal" arguing sounds impressive, but it does not constitute proof, since the majority can be wrong. At one time, the majority of people believed the earth was flat, but their belief did not make it so.

Examples:
Most of my friends smoke pot; therefore it's O.K. to do so.
Most women prefer Brand "X"; therefore, it's the superior brand.

Hypostatization   Treating an abstract or diverse field as if it were a uniform entity with consistent beliefs.

Hypostatization personifies entire fields or disciplines that, in reality, contain contradictory theories or multiple beliefs and presents them as a unified whole supporting a single viewpoint. Such arguments usually take the form, "History proves . . .," "Education has shown . . .," "Psychology claims . . .," "Medicine has proven. . . ."

Examples:
History proves that man will always indulge in war.
Psychology has found that people are programmed from infancy.

Begging the question   Assuming the truth of what you're supposed to be proving is true.

Begging the question assumes what it's supposed to be proving is already accepted fact. It usually takes the form of the *cocksure fallacy* or *circular reasoning.*

Cocksure fallacy   Stating an unproven assumption as if its truth were too obvious to need proving.

The "cocksure" form of begging the question is like an overly confident bluff. It usually begins "It's obvious that . . .," "Of course we all know that . . .," "No one doubts that . . .," "Everyone would agree that. . . ." This fallacy is so overly sure of itself that it offers no support or evidence at all.

Examples:
Everyone knows that capitalism is the best form of economics.
It is obvious that Mr. Jones is the man for the job.

Circular reasoning (Also known as "rabbit reasoning") Assuming that repetition of an argument constitutes proof.

Just as a chased rabbit runs in a circle, so does a circular argument circle back on itself. The arguer who is "begging the question" assumes the truth the argument should be proving and believes that repetition of the same points in slightly different words constitutes adequate support.

Examples:
Gentlemen prefer blonds because they are attracted to women with light hair.
I like Porsches because they're my favorite car.

Logical Fallacy Exercise

Find the fallacy or fallacies that best pinpoint the breakdown in logic in the following examples. Support your choices.

1. Most dogs prefer Beefchow, the best dogfood on the market.
2. Cats are smart because they have a natural intelligence.
3. Schools don't teach the basics anymore so vote against the school levy.
4. I cheat on my income tax. Why shouldn't I? Officials cheat on theirs.
5. Socrates would have approved of experimental schools.
6. That's the third new Chevelle I've seen today. Their sales must be really booming.

7. Try this author. You'll either love him or you'll hate him.

8. Hire me. I need the job more than he does. I have a huge family to support.

9. Jones has divorced his third wife; now what kind of senator would he make?

10. Don't listen to that egghead's fancy ideas.

11. Medical studies show that our aspirin is the best.

12. Our pantyhose makes even Joe Namath's legs look good.

13. Quarantining prevents the spread of disease; therefore people with arthritis should be quarantined.

14. Ghettos are the cancers of our cities; so let them burn.

15. He kissed me after I cracked my knuckles. I'll have to crack my knuckles more often.

16. Why should I be punished for abusing my authority? All the presidents before me did the same thing.

17. If it weren't for Madame Curie, the world would never have learned about radioactivity.

18. "Pepsi—for those who think young."

19. She's a redhead. I'll bet she's got some temper.

20. So I don't keep a clean house; your workshop isn't exactly tidy either.

21. He took office and prices went up. That's the last Democrat I'll vote for.

22. Of course I'm for nuclear power. Isn't everyone?

23. My opponent, who's full of false promises, will now present his platform.

24. A communist society is like an ant hill; each member works for the good of the entire group.

Story for Review of Terminology

Read and enjoy Max Shulman's whimsical story "Love Is a Fallacy" as a final review for types of fallacies.

LOVE IS A FALLACY[1]

MAX SHULMAN

Cool was I and logical. Keen, calculating, perspicacious, acute and astute—I was all of these. My brain was as powerful as a dynamo, as precise as a chemist's scales, as penetrating as a scalpel. And—think of it!—I was only eighteen.

It is not often that one so young has such a giant intellect. Take, for example, Petey Bellows, my roommate at the university. Same age, same background, but dumb as an ox. A nice enough fellow, you understand, but nothing upstairs. Emotional type. Unstable. Impressionable. Worst of all, a faddist. Fads, I submit, are the very negation of reason. To be swept up in every new craze that comes along, to surrender yourself to idiocy just because everybody else is doing it—this, to me, is the acme of mindlessness. Not, however, to Petey.

One afternoon I found Petey lying on his bed with an expression of such distress on his face that I immediately diagnosed appendicitis. "Don't move," I said. "Don't take a laxative. I'll get a doctor."

"Raccoon," he mumbled thickly.

"Raccoon?" I said, pausing in my flight.

"I want a raccoon coat," he wailed.

I perceived that his trouble was not physical, but mental. "Why do you want a raccoon coat?"

"I should have known it," he cried, pounding his temples. "I should have known they'd come back when the Charleston came back. Like a fool I spent all my money for textbooks, and now I can't get a raccoon coat."

"Can you mean," I said incredulously, "that people are actually wearing raccoon coats again?"

"All the Big Men on Campus are wearing them. Where've you been?"

"In the library," I said, naming a place not frequented by Big Men on Campus.

He leaped from the bed and paced the room. "I've got to have a raccoon coat," he said passionately. "I've got to!"

"Petey, why? Look at it rationally. Raccoon coats are unsanitary. They shed. They smell bad. They weigh too much. They're unsightly. They—"

[1]Max Shulman, "Love Is a Fallacy," from *The Many Loves of Dobie Gillis*. Copyright 1951 by Max Shulman, reprinted by permission of Harold Matson Co., Inc.

"You don't understand," he interrupted impatiently. "It's the thing to do. Don't you want to be in the swim?"

"No," I said truthfully.

"Well, I do," he declared. "I'd give anything for a raccoon coat. Anything!"

My brain, that precision instrument, slipped into high gear. "Anything?" I asked, looking at him narrowly.

"Anything," he affirmed in ringing tones.

I stroked my chin thoughtfully. It so happened that I knew where to get my hands on a raccoon coat. My father had had one in his undergraduate days; it lay now in a trunk in the attic back home. It also happened that Petey had something I wanted. He didn't *have* it exactly, but at least he had first rights on it. I refer to his girl, Polly Espy.

I had long coveted Polly Espy. Let me emphasize that my desire for this young woman was not emotional in nature. She was, to be sure, a girl who excited the emotions, but I was not one to let my heart rule my head. I wanted Polly for a shrewdly calculated, entirely cerebral reason.

I was a freshman in law school. In a few years I would be out in practice. I was well aware of the importance of the right kind of wife in furthering a lawyer's career. The successful lawyers I had observed were, almost without exception, married to beautiful, gracious, intelligent women. With one omission, Polly fitted these specifications perfectly.

Beautiful she was. She was not yet of pin-up proportions, but I felt sure that time would supply the lack. She already had the makings.

Gracious she was. By gracious I mean full of graces. She had an erectness of carriage, an ease of bearing, a poise that clearly indicated the best of breeding. At table her manners were exquisite. I had seen her at the Kozy Kampus Korner eating the specialty of the house—a sandwich that contained scraps of pot roast, gravy, chopped nuts, and a dipper of sauerkraut—without even getting her fingers moist.

Intelligent she was not. In fact, she veered in the opposite direction. But I believed that under my guidance she would smarten up. At any rate, it was worth a try. It is, after all, easier to make a beautiful dumb girl smart than to make an ugly smart girl beautiful.

"Petey," I said, "are you in love with Polly Espy?"

"I think she's a keen kid," he replied, "but I don't know if you'd call it love. Why?"

"Do you," I asked, "have any kind of formal arrangement with her? I mean are you going steady or anything like that?"

"No. We see each other quite a bit, but we both have other dates. Why?"

"Is there," I asked, "any other man for whom she has a particular fondness?"

"Not that I know of. Why?"

I nodded with satisfaction. "In other words, if you were out of the picture, the field would be open. Is that right?"

"I guess so. What are you getting at?"

"Nothing, nothing," I said innocently, and took my suitcase out of the closet.

"Where you going?" asked Petey.

"Home for the week end." I threw a few things into the bag.

"Listen," he said, clutching my arm eagerly, "while you're home, you couldn't get some money from your old man, could you, and lend it to me so I can buy a raccoon coat?"

"I may do better than that," I said with a mysterious wink and closed my bag and left.

"Look," I said to Petey when I got back Monday morning. I threw open the suitcase and revealed the huge, hairy, gamy object that my father had worn in his Stutz Bearcat in 1925.

"Holy Toledo!" said Petey reverently. He plunged his hands into the raccoon coat and then his face. "Holy Toledo!" he repeated fifteen or twenty times.

"Would you like it?" I asked.

"Oh yes!" he cried, clutching the greasy pelt to him. Then a canny look came into his eyes. "What do you want for it?"

"Your girl," I said, mincing no words.

"Polly?" he said in a horrified whisper. "You want Polly?"

"That's right."

He flung the coat from him. "Never," he said stoutly.

I shrugged. "Okay. If you don't want to be in the swim, I guess it's your business."

I sat down in a chair and pretended to read a book, but out of the corner of my eye I kept watching Petey. He was a torn man. First he looked at the coat with the expression of a waif at a bakery window. Then he turned away and set his jaw resolutely. Then he looked back at the coat, with even more longing in his face. Then he turned away, but with not so much resolution this time. Back and forth his head swiveled, desire waxing, resolution waning. Finally he didn't turn away at all; he just stood and stared with mad lust at the coat.

"It isn't as though I was in love with Polly," he said thickly. "Or going steady or anything like that."

"That's right," I murmured.

"What's Polly to me, or me to Polly?"

"Not a thing," said I.

"It's just been a casual kick—just a few laughs, that's all."

"Try on the coat," said I.

He complied. The coat bunched high over his ears and dropped all the way down to his shoe tops. He looked like a mound of dead raccoons. "Fits fine," he said happily.

I rose from my chair. "Is it a deal?" I asked, extending my hand.

He swallowed. "It's a deal," he said and shook my hand.

I had my first date with Polly, the following evening. This was in the nature of a survey; I wanted to find out just how much work I had to do to get her mind up to the standard I required. I took her first to dinner. "Gee, that was a delish dinner," she said as we left the restaurant. Then I took her to a movie. "Gee, that was a marvy movie," she said as we left the theater. And then I took her home. "Gee, I had a sensaysh time," she said as she badé me good night.

I went back to my room with a heavy heart. I had gravely underestimated the size of my task. This girl's lack of information was terrifying. Nor would it be enough merely to supply her with information. First she had to be taught to *think*. This loomed as a project of no small dimensions, and at first I was tempted to give her back to Petey. But then I got to thinking about her abundant physical charms and about the way she entered a room and the way she handled a knife and fork, and I decided to make an effort.

I went about it, as in all things, systematically. I gave her a course in logic. It happened that I, as a law student, was taking a course in logic myself, so I had all the facts at my finger tips. "Polly," I said to her when I picked her up on our next date, "tonight we are going over to the Knoll and talk."

"Oo, terrif," she replied. One thing I will say for this girl: you would go far to find another so agreeable.

We went to the Knoll, the campus trysting place, and we sat down under an old oak, and she looked at me expectantly. "What are we going to talk about?" she asked.

"Logic."

She thought this over for a minute and decided she liked it. "Magnif," she said.

"Logic," I said, clearing my throat, "is the science of thinking. Before we can think correctly, we must first learn to recognize the common fallacies of logic. These we will take up tonight."

"Wow-dow!" she cried, clapping her hands delightedly.

I winced, but went bravely on. "First let us examine the fallacy called Dicto Simpliciter."

"By all means," she urged, batting her lashes eagerly.

"Dicto Simpliciter means an argument based on an unqualified generalization. For example: Exercise is good. Therefore everybody should exercise."

"I agree," said Polly earnestly. "I mean exercise is wonderful. I mean it builds the body and everything."

"Polly," I said gently, "the argument is a fallacy. *Exercise is good* is an unqualified generalization. For instance, if you have heart disease, exercise is bad, not good. Many people are ordered by their doctors *not* to exercise. You must *qualify* the generalization. You must say exercise is *usually* good, or exercise is good *for most people.* Otherwise you have committed a Dicto Simpliciter. Do you see?"

"No," she confessed. "But this is marvy. Do more! Do more!"

"It will be better if you stop tugging at my sleeve," I told her, and when she desisted, I continued. "Next we take up a fallacy called Hasty Generalization. Listen carefully: You can't speak French. I can't speak French. Petey Bellows can't speak French. I must therefore conclude that nobody at the University of Minnesota can speak French."

"Really?" said Polly, amazed. *"Nobody?"*

I hid my exasperation. "Polly, it's a fallacy. The generalization is reached too hastily. There are too few instances to support such a conclusion."

"Know any more fallacies?" she asked breathlessly. "This is more fun than dancing even."

I fought off a wave of despair. I was getting nowhere with this girl, absolutely nowhere. Still, I am nothing if not persistent. I continued. "Next comes Post Hoc. Listen to this: Let's not take Bill on our picnic. Every time we take him out with us, it rains."

"I know somebody just like that," she exclaimed. "A girl back home—Eula Becker, her name is. It never fails. Every single time we take her on a picnic—"

"Polly," I said sharply, "it's a fallacy. Eula Becker doesn't *cause* the rain. She has no connection with the rain. You are guilty of Post Hoc if you blame Eula Becker."

"I'll never do it again," she promised contritely. "Are you mad at me?"

I sighed. "No, Polly, I'm not mad."

"Then tell me some more fallacies."

"All right. Let's try Contradictory Premises."

"Yes, let's," she chirped, blinking her eyes happily.

I frowned, but plunged ahead. "Here's an example of Contradictory Premises: If God can do anything, can He make a stone so heavy that He won't be able to lift it?"

"Of course," she replied promptly.

"But if He can do anything, He can lift the stone." I pointed out.

"Yeah," she said thoughtfully. "Well, then I guess He can't make the stone."

"But He can do anything," I reminded her.

She scratched her pretty, empty head. "I'm all confused," she admitted.

"Of course you are. Because when the premises of an argument contradict each other, there can be no argument. If there is an irresistible force, there can be no immovable object. If there is an immovable object, there can be no irresistible force. Get it?"

"Tell me some more of this keen stuff," she said eagerly.

I consulted my watch. "I think we'd better call it a night. I'll take you home now, and you go over all the things you've learned. We'll have another session tomorrow night."

I deposited her at the girls' dormitory, where she assured me that she had had a perfectly terrif evening, and I went glumly home to my room. Petey lay snoring in his bed, the raccoon coat huddled like a great hairy beast at his feet. For a moment I considered waking him and telling him that he could have his girl back. It seemed clear that my project was doomed to failure. The girl simply had a logic-proof head.

But then I reconsidered. I had wasted one evening; I might as well waste another. Who knew? Maybe somewhere in the extinct crater of her mind a few embers still smoldered. Maybe somehow I could fan them into flame. Admittedly it was not a prospect fraught with hope, but I decided to give it one more try.

Seated under the oak the next evening I said, "Our first fallacy tonight is called Ad Misericordiam."

She quivered with delight.

"Listen closely," I said. "A man applies for a job. When the boss asks him what his qualifications are, he replies that he has a wife and six children at home, the wife is a helpless cripple, the children have nothing to eat, no clothes to wear, no shoes on their feet, there are no beds in the house, no coal in the cellar, and winter is coming."

A tear rolled down each of Polly's pink cheeks. "Oh, this is awful, awful," she sobbed.

"Yes, it's awful," I agreed, "but it's no argument. The man never answered the boss's question about his qualifications. Instead he appealed to the boss's sympathy. He committed the fallacy of Ad Misericordiam. Do you understand?"

"Have you got a handkerchief?" she blubbered.

I handed her a handkerchief and tried to keep from screaming while she wiped her eyes. "Next," I said in a carefully controlled tone, "we will discuss False Analogy. Here is an example: Students should be allowed to look at their textbooks during examinations. After all, surgeons have X rays to guide them during an operation, lawyers have briefs to guide them during a trial, carpenters have blueprints to guide them when they are building a house. Why, then, shouldn't students be allowed to look at their textbooks during an examination?"

"There now," she said enthusiastically, "is the most marvy idea I've heard in years."

"Polly," I said testily, "the argument is all wrong. Doctors, lawyers, and carpenters aren't taking a test to see how much they have learned, but students are. The situations are altogether different, and you can't make an analogy between them."

"I still think it's a good idea," said Polly.

"Nuts," I muttered. Doggedly I pressed on. "Next we'll try Hypothesis Contrary to Fact."

"Sounds yummy," was Polly's reaction.

"Listen: If Madame Curie had not happened to leave a photographic plate in a drawer with a chunk of pitchblende, the world today would not know about radium."

"True, true," said Polly, nodding her head. "Did you see the movie? Oh, it just knocked me out. That Walter Pidgeon is so dreamy. I mean he fractures me."

"If you can forget Mr. Pidgeon for a moment," I said coldly, "I would like to point out that the statement is a fallacy. Maybe Madame Curie would have discovered radium at some later date. Maybe somebody else would have discovered it. Maybe any number of things would have happened. You can't start with a hypothesis that is not true and then draw any supportable conclusions from it."

"They ought to put Walter Pidgeon in more pictures," said Polly. "I hardly ever see him any more."

One more chance, I decided. But just one more. There is a limit to what flesh and blood can bear. "The next fallacy is called Poisoning the Well."

"How cute!" she gurgled.

"Two men are having a debate. The first one gets up and says, 'My opponent is a notorious liar. You can't believe a word that he is going to say.' . . . Now, Polly, think. Think hard. What's wrong?"

I watched her closely as she knit her creamy brow in concentration. Suddenly a glimmer of intelligence—the first I had seen—came into her eyes. "It's not fair," she said with indignation. "It's not a bit fair. What chance has the second man got if the first man calls him a liar before he even begins talking?"

"Right!" I cried exultantly. "One hundred per cent right. It's not fair. The first man has *poisoned the well* before anybody could drink from it. He has hamstrung his opponent before he could even start. . . . Polly, I'm proud of you."

"Pshaw," she murmured, blushing with pleasure.

"You see, my dear, these things aren't so hard. All you have to do is concentrate. Think—examine—evaluate. Come now, let's review everything we have learned."

"Fire away," she said with an airy wave of her hand.

Heartened by the knowledge that Polly was not altogether a cretin, I began a long, patient review of all I had told her. Over and over and over again I cited instances, pointed out flaws, kept hammering away without letup. It was like digging a tunnel. At first everything was work, sweat, and darkness. I had no idea when I would reach the light, or even *if* I would. But I persisted. I pounded and clawed and scraped, and finally I was rewarded. I saw a chink of light. And then the chink got bigger and the sun came pouring in and all was bright.

Five grueling nights this took, but it was worth it. I had made a logician out of Polly; I had taught her to think. My job was done. She was worthy of me at last. She was a fit wife for me, a proper hostess for my many mansions, a suitable mother for my well-heeled children.

It must not be thought that I was without love for this girl. Quite the contrary. Just as Pygmalion loved the perfect woman he had fashioned, so I loved mine. I decided to acquaint her with my feelings at our very next meeting. The time had come to change our relationship from academic to romantic.

"Polly," I said when next we sat beneath our oak, "tonight we will not discuss fallacies."

"Aw, gee," she said, disappointed.

"My dear," I said, favoring her with a smile, "we have now spent five evenings together. We have gotten along splendidly. It is clear that we are well matched."

"Hasty Generalization," said Polly brightly.

"I beg your pardon," said I.

"Hasty Generalization," she repeated. "How can you say that we are well matched on the basis of only five dates?"

I chuckled with amusement. The dear child had learned her lessons well. "My dear," I said, patting her hand in a tolerant manner, "five dates is plenty. After all, you don't have to eat a whole cake to know that it's good."

"False Analogy," said Polly promptly. "I'm not a cake. I'm a girl."

I chuckled with somewhat less amusement. The dear child had learned her lessons perhaps too well. I decided to change tactics. Obviously the best approach was a simple, strong, direct declaration of love. I paused for a moment while my massive brain chose the proper words. Then I began:

"Polly, I love you. You are the whole world to me, and the moon and the stars and the constellations of outer space. Please, my darling, say that you will go steady with me, for if you will not, life will be meaningless. I will languish. I will refuse my meals. I will wander the face of the earth, a shambling, hollow-eyed hulk."

There, I thought, folding my arms, that ought to do it.

"Ad Misericordiam," said Polly.

I ground my teeth. I was not Pygmalion; I was Frankenstein, and my monster had me by the throat. Frantically I fought back the tide of panic surging through me. At all costs I had to keep cool.

"Well, Polly," I said, forcing a smile, "you certainly have learned your fallacies."

"You're darn right," she said with a vigorous nod.

"And who taught them to you, Polly?"

"You did."

"That's right. So you do owe me something, don't you, my dear? If I hadn't come along you never would have learned about fallacies."

"Hypothesis Contrary to Fact," she said instantly.

I dashed perspiration from my brow. "Polly," I croaked, "you mustn't take all these things so literally. I mean this is just classroom stuff. You know that the things you learn in school don't have anything to do with life."

"Dicto Simpliciter," she said, wagging her finger at me playfully.

That did it. I leaped to my feet, bellowing like a bull. "Will you or will you not go steady with me?"

"I will not," she replied.

"Why not?" I demanded.

"Because this afternoon I promised Petey Bellows that I would go steady with him."

I reeled back, overcome with the infamy of it. After he promised, after he made a deal, after he shook my hand! "The rat!" I shrieked, kicking up great chunks of turf. "You can't go with him, Polly. He's a liar. He's a cheat. He's a rat."

"Poisoning the Well," said Polly, "and stop shouting. I think shouting must be a fallacy too."

With an immense effort of will, I modulated my voice. "All right," I said. "You're a logician. Let's look at this thing logically. How could you choose Petey Bellows over me? Look at me—a brilliant student, a tremendous intellectual, a man with an assured future. Look at Petey—a knothead, a jitterbug, a guy who'll never know where his next meal is coming from. Can you give me one logical reason why you should go steady with Petey Bellows?"

"I certainly can," declared Polly. "He's got a raccoon coat."

Connotation and Denotation

Connotation   The associations a word brings to mind, the images it
    evokes, the feelings it produces.
Denotation   The dictionary definition of a word.

An article or advertisement can slant your feelings toward a subject or product by using connotative words. Words that describe the same trait can be rated on a connotative scale from positive to negative without changing their denotations or actual definitions. Look at the following list that rates terms describing fatness on such a scale:

"Fat" Connotation Scale

Positive +	Husky, Stocky, Matronly Figure
	Full Figured—Big Bones
	Queen Size
	Pleasingly Plump
Neutral 0	Overweight
	Obese
	Chubby
	Fat
	Tub of Lard
Negative −	Fatso

Make a similar scale for words that describe being underweight. Note that meaning does not change (you don't call a "fat" person "thin"), only tone does. Also note how scientific words often lack tone and are neutral and how negative terms often resort to slang.

Connotation Exercise

Discuss the connotations each of the words in parentheses evoke in you. Circle the words with the greatest "snob" appeal, which sound the most refined or "classy." Underline the words which sound the most scientific. Then write a version using the most appalling or disgusting words (either use words in the parentheses or introduce your own.)

At last! Put an end to (corpulent, fat, overweight, blubbery, stout, unwanted, unhealthy) figures. No need to (diet, starve, count calories, suffer, deprive yourself).

Get (Reducto, Fat-off, Decrease, Skineroo, Slim-line), a new (find, formula, product, substance, blend) guaranteed to (wipe out, remove, reduce, eliminate) (ugly, bulging, extra, needless, additional, excess) pounds.

Try it and your (weight, fat, lard, poundage) will (be soon out of sight, disappear, fall off, vanish, be gone forever, decrease remarkably).

Assignment Options, Format Suggestions, and Possible Material for Analysis

> **Type of writing** Logical fallacy analysis
> **Approach** Objective
> **Purpose** To present, define, and analyze the use of logical fallacy techniques for a reader unacquainted with the terms.

Logical Fallacy Assignment Options

Choose one of the following options:

1. Find examples of logical fallacies in advertisements in magazines, on television, in letters to newspapers, in propaganda pamphlets, or in other sources, and write an essay analyzing the techniques used.

2. Define a single technique such as transfer, and write an essay analyzing its different uses in various magazines (such as *Cosmopolitan, Reader's Digest, Playboy, The New Yorker, Newsweek, Woman's Day*) according to the audience it's trying to reach.

3. Write a horrendous example of your own, presenting an argument using every fallacy you can work in. Then write an essay analyzing the fallacies in your own bad example.

4. Create an ad or series of ads that incorporate various logical fallacies. Write an analysis of your created examples.

Format Suggestions

Write the paper for someone who does not know about fallacies. Define each fallacy before you present examples of it, and clarify what makes each example guilty of that fallacy. If, for instance, your example uses transfer, identify what positive qualities are being carried over to the product.

Write in essay and paragraph form being careful to write definitions as complete sentences. Pick an informative title that describes the focus of your paper such as "Logical Fallacies in Magazine Advertisements." Your opening paragraph might include a definition of fallacies as well as a framework sentence listing the terms you will analyze in your examples. Wait to define each term, however, until you are presenting examples of it. The paper itself can then be organized either by grouping examples under terms or by following the order of the material you are analyzing (for example, paragraph by paragraph if you are analyzing an essay).

You might want to number and attach magazine ads to your paper for easy reference, but always describe the fallacy in the advertisement you are discussing rather than force your reader to flip from paper to ad. You may also attach original letters or essays, numbering their paragraphs for easy reference.

Focus on fallacies and arguments; pinpoint them and clarify how they are being used. Once you have defined a term, you may use it without repeating its definition.

Be aware of tone in your article or letter so you are not taken in by irony or satire and falsely criticize an intentionally written "bad" example. Keep your own tone neutral, objective, and analytical. You need not indicate your own position; your function in this essay is to analyze, not to persuade or to judge. Be careful that you don't lapse into subjective or judgmental statements and use fallacies such as "cocksure" or "name-calling" yourself. Also avoid irony and sarcasm, since it might mislead your reader.

Your ending might be a simple concluding statement of the effect that fallacies have on the article's credibility.

Possible Material for Analysis

The following material came from a pamphlet opposing the use of fluoridation. You can use prominent examples to illustrate various logical fallacies or do an in-depth analysis of a single short segment of the material.

WHO ARE THE PROPONENTS OF FLUORIDATION??
—AND WHAT KIND OF PEOPLE ARE THEY?

They are a motley group of well-meaning technical experts, so-called new liberals, part-time Americans, welfare state promoters and social experimenters who generally favor Big Government getting Bigger. Many of the well-meaning have for most of their adult lives been drawing milk from The Great Federal Breast, and thus they find concepts of alternative existence for themselves or others quite alien and hard to understand. Others of the proponents are less elegant and more dangerous; these are the tireless apologists for criminals and crime, they clamor for the abolition or reduction of penalties attached to the unlawful use of narcotic drugs, they snicker at American ideals, standards and religious precepts, they regard the present flood of literary and filmed obscenities as an indication of cultural "progress" and "sophistication," and they cry crocodile tears over the gradual destruction of traditional America, which we now witness.

Taken collectively, these are permissive, "progressive" parents, who, unwilling and unable to effectively discipline and set standards for their children, understandably are inclined to vest authoritarian responsibility in an irresistibly powerful Central Government. A "society as rich as ours," such persons often explain, can afford anything, whether guaranteed annual incomes for all, or the time consuming and costly bussing of our *public* school children, like cattle, to meet the demands of endless racial experimentation.

Specifically, and according to sworn testimony, a high official of the Division of Dental Health, Washington State Department of Health attempted to snatch away handfuls of literature being distributed in downtown Seattle by a fluoridation opponent; still another proponent dentist attempted to pick a fight with a fluoridation opponent after first misrepresenting himself as a Police Officer and demanding a "Political Information Distribution Permit." Widows with children who have worked vigorously in opposition to fluoridation have been harassed and intimidated at night and by telephone for daring to assume the responsibility of active citizenship. All these anecdotes furnish finally but a quick glance behind the smiling mask of many fluoridation proponents.

But Why Not Fluoridation?

In America, the U.S. Constitution authorizes exercise of police power by the State for compulsion ONLY in those areas relating to the general welfare in which the individual citizen cannot reasonably be expected to act alone. Instances of this are the raising of armies, the certification of drugs and food dyes, or the establishment of traffic regulations. But since our nation was first established there has been NO PRECEDENT LEADING TO THE FLUORIDATION OF PUBLIC WATER SUPPLIES!

Not by the use of smallpox vaccine, because except in an epidemic you choose to use or not use the opportunity to vaccinate your child against the *communicable disease* smallpox by means of the permission slip which he or she brings to you from school.

Not by the chlorination of public water supplies, because chlorine destroys *communicable disease* germs in the water supply, thereby purifying the water rather than being added to it as a (fluoride) drug.

Not by the addition of Vitamin D to milk, because the vitamin is an officially recognized essential of human nutrition, which fluoride is not, and even should you choose not to use vitamin-fortified milk there are realistic alteratives, BUT THERE IS NO ESCAPE FROM FLUORIDATED WATER!

If the State can presume to compel in the personal matter of oral hygiene and *non-communicable disease* (tooth decay), stop for just a moment and ask yourself what single liberty you value that could not similarly vanish! Let those who wish to use fluorides *obtain them from their physicians, or dentists,* from fluoridated drops, toothpastes, vitamins or pills, as do many opponents of fluoridated public water.

The dispersal of riot control drugs by means of the public's drinking water has been discussed on page 33 of April 21, 1968 *Seattle Times*, and by CBS-TV reporters Mike Wallace and Harry Reasoner during the presentation "60 Minutes" on KIRO-TV at 10:00 P.M. October 8, 1968. The high precision metering and pumping devices essential for the controlled distribution of highly toxic fluoride are similarly required for the water supply distribution of powerful and dangerous anti-riot drugs. The present administration within our federal government is therefore convinced that all "large cities" must soon have fluoridation equipment and assists "local" proponents in whatever way it can.

It is claimed by a few that the benefits from compulsory fluoridation are so great that "on balance" these benefits outweigh any slight threat to the ideals of a free and democratic society. But the folk legends are rich with instances describing the dangers of making such a "pact with the Devil." We remember the Devil and Daniel Webster, Faust and the Devil, or the Rhyme of the Lady and the Tiger, and how in each instance the persons involved were unable finally to master the awesome forces that they had unleashed—they always got more than they "had bargained for." Accepting fluoridation despite its threat to democratic ideals is rather like teaching one's daughters that prostitution is moral only if the wages are good enough.

The membership of Seattle For Fluoridation reads like a Who's Who in Seattle pill-rolling and social liberalism: it is significant that the group boasts no persons of outstanding and widely acclaimed credentials in Constitutional Law, American Political Science, or American History, since such men or women would instantly perceive the anti-democratic nature of this compulsory fluoridation scheme. It was the Cuban revolutionary and guerilla warfare expert Dr. Che Guevara who decided that "the treatment and curing of entire peoples and nations" was more important than the time honored Hippocratic tradition of treating individual patients in privileged confidence; it seems unlikely that his life and fate was an example suitable to most of us.

What is the similarity among those persons who will compel the use of drugs by entire populations as a matter of course? It is quickly found that this type is contemptuous of what they refer to as "the masses" (of people) and that they are hungry for the "efficiency" which is forbidden them by our democracy: these mass medication proponents often privately speak the elitist, anti-democratic language of South American dictatorships in which "simple, happy, and unarmed peasants" are ruled by an iron military. It is by way of similar reasons that every effort was made by pro-fluoridationists to pass fluoridation at the Seattle City Council level without a vote by the people, because they knew it had twice been defeated! This contempt for the voters is clearly demonstrated by the "LOOK JANE, SEE DICK RUN" nature of the principal publication of the proponents. The use of Big Printing, Short, Simple Sentences, Comic Book-Like Pictures showing Big Stacks of Quarters, and Glasses of Water receding into the distance is an insult to the American public. Check to see whether you agree when you examine the proponent's newspaper-like publication picturing a lovely little African-Caucasian-Asian girl staring sadly at you from the front cover.

REMEMBER:
**Minority rights cannot presently be abridged lawfully in the United States. Such abridgement of rights led to present-day Greece, the Soviet form of government, and the Nazi Germany dictatorship that exterminated six million people and laid waste to a continent.
**Democracy is not the easy way, but it is stronger in the long run. Democracy demands more responsible individual contribution because it is less "efficient" than dictatorship.
**Fluoridation has been outlawed nationally in numerous advanced European nations which have no riot-control problem.

**Fluoridation is not simply communistic or nazi-istic. First of all it is NOT AMERICAN!

**One cherished right of free people is the confidence between a chosen physician and the family. LET'S KEEP IT!

**Americans have enjoyed freedom so long as to "take it for granted." DOUBLE THE GUARD!!

Vote NO Social Experimentation   Vote NO More Creeping Dictatorship
Vote NO More Excessive Federal Influence
VOTE NO FLUORIDATION

Responsible Citizens League

Student Example Paper on "Who ARE the Proponents of Fluoridation??—and What Kind of People Are They?"

LOGICAL FALLACIES OF THE FLUORIDATION ARTICLE

1   In the fluoridation article "Who Are the Proponents of Fluoridation??—and What Kind of People Are They? " many logical fallacies can be found. These include name-calling, argument *ad hominem*, hasty generalization, false authority, and *ad misericordiam*. The two most prevalent fallacies are name-calling and argument *ad hominem*.

2   Name-calling is labeling with a derogatory term. The proponents of fluoridation are described as: "a motley group of well-meaning technical experts," "so-called new liberals," "part-time Americans," "welfare state promoters," and "social experimenters." These terms have negative connotations used to alienate the reader from the proponents.

3   The other frequently used fallacy is argument *ad hominem*, which, translated from Latin, means "argument at the man." This is an argument attacking the person's background and personal life instead of his ideas. The proponents of fluoridation are said to: "generally favor Big Government getting Bigger," "clamor for the abolition or reduction of penalties attached to the unlawful use of narcotic drugs," "snicker at American ideals, standards and religious precepts," "regard the present flood of literary and filmed obscenities as an indication of cultural progress and sophistication," and "cry crocodile tears over the gradual destruction of traditional America which we now witness." The proponents are also called "tireless apologists for crime and criminals." These statements don't have anything to do with the fluoridation issue. They are all concerned with personal viewpoints completely outside

the issue. The personal statements are used to arouse people's feelings against the proponents.

4   Within the second paragraph is an example of hasty generalization. Hasty generalization is a conclusion backed up by too little evidence. The example is ". . . permissive, 'progressive' parents, who, unwilling and unable to effectively discipline and set standards for their children, understandably are inclined to vest authoritarian responsibility in an irresistably powerful Central Government." Although permissive, progressive parents may give responsibility to the central government, the specific fact that these parents cannot control their children is not enough evidence to support the conclusion.

5   Another logical fallacy found in the article is false authority. When an expert is used to back up a claim and the expert is unreliable or doesn't pertain to the specific issue, false authority has been committed. In the third paragraph, "Specifically and according to sworn testimony, a high official of the Division of Dental Health, Washington State Department of Health attempted to snatch away handfuls of literature," nothing is said about whose sworn testimony the facts are based on. You don't even know if the testifier is a reliable, unbiased source.

6   The last logical fallacy is *ad misericordiam*. This is another Latin term that translated means "to the pity of the heart." It is an emotional appeal to sympathy rather than to ability. In the last paragraph, "Widows with children who have worked vigorously in opposition to fluoridation have been harassed and intimidated at night and by telephone for daring to assume the responsibility of active citizenship." The reader sympathizes with the widows instead of concentrating on the fluoridation issue.

7   As shown by the logical fallacies, this article is an emotional appeal rather than a logical one. The author has discredited the article even with his title, "Who Are the Proponents of Fluoridation??—and What Kind of People Are They?" It doesn't matter what kind of people they are or what their personal beliefs are. The issue itself should be analyzed, but it was avoided completely.

—Marion Todd Lemon

Questions and Exercises on "Logical Fallacies of the Fluoridation Article"

1. Tighten this paper's opening paragraph.

2. Find effective examples of defining a term, presenting examples of the term, and clarifying the examples in this paper.

3. Do you feel that "hasty generalization" is the best label for the fallacy described in paragraph 4 of this paper? What labels would you suggest?

4. How effective is the paper's ending?

Another Article for Analysis

"No Redemption Via Socialism" appeared in a column written by Eric Hoffer in *The American Statesman*. As you read it, analyze the various arguments he presents for possible fallacies. Then read the student example paper that follows it and compare your analysis to its.

NO REDEMPTION VIA SOCIALISM[2]

ERIC HOFFER

1   There is no evidence that socialism has worked a perceptible improvement in man's nature. No one would maintain that the present-day population of Russia is more honest, decent, tolerant, or humane than were the Russians 50 years ago. A Britain subjected to socialist influence for years seems as prone to racial prejudice as any other country. There is more antisemitism in Russia than in any capitalist country.

2   It is also highly doubtful whether socialism can release new creative energies in literature, art, music, science, and technology. There can hardly be a more striking contrast than that between the cultural aridity of Communist Russia and the rich creative ferment of Russia's pre-revolutionary days.

3   As to happiness: The Scandinavian countries, with a high degree of socialism, have some of the highest suicide rates. Russia has already exceeded the 40 years Moses needed to bring the Israelites to a promised land, and the good life is still a dream. Socialization has become synonymous with greyness and joylessness.

4   As molders of new humanity the socialists and the Communists are remarkably uninterested in the fantastic alchemy of man's soul. They expect "history" to do this and that and their task as they see it is to drive the masses up the steep incline of the future.

5   Are there groups anywhere in the Occident at present dreaming of socialism as a redemption and a new birth? Socialism has become a shabby thing. Everyone now knows that when a country goes socialist it loses its sparkle and zest. The intelligentsia and the politicians usurp the privileges of the rich while the common people are condemned to meagerness and boredom. . . .

6   The real dividing line which is now opening across societies everywhere is that between experimenters and "experimentees." The

---

[2]Eric Hoffer, "No Redemption via Socialism," *American Statesman* (6 July 1968).

socialists and the Communists strive with all their might to strap humanity to an operating table, and the truth is now abroad that these social
surgeons are maniacal quacks who would operate on us with an ax.

Student Example Paper on Eric Hoffer's "No Redemption Via Socialism"

LOGICAL FALLACIES USED IN "NO REDEMPTION VIA SOCIALISM"

1   In the essay "No Redemption Via Socialism," the author, Eric Hoffer, uses the logical fallacies of begging the question, name-calling,
glittering generality, *post hoc*, hasty generalization, and false analogy.

2   In the first paragraph, he employs a form of begging the question.
He uses as proof a statement that itself needs to be established as
fact, when he says that "no one" would see any improvement when
comparing Russian life styles over a fifty-year period. Further, he is
also guilty of hasty generalization when he draws too broad a conclusion based on too little data. Specifically, he denies that socialism has
any worth, because two countries that have been subjected to its
influence are plagued with the problems of racial and ethnic prejudices. Also present is the implication that a causal relationship exists
between these prejudices and socialism because of the time sequence involved. This is an example of the logical fallacy known as
post hoc reasoning.

3   In the second paragraph, Hoffer uses glittering generalities or
positive clichés as well as name-calling or negative labeling. He does
this by referring to contemporary Russian culture as -"arid" and pre-
revolutionary culture as full of "rich creative ferment." This paragraph
also contains hasty generalization and *post hoc* fallacies. The broad
generalization that "new creative energies" have not been released is
based upon a comparison of lifestyles over a fifty-year period. Once
again the implication is that this lack of progress is due to socialism.

4   In the third paragraph, Hoffer uses a *non sequitur* by equating the
suicide rate in Scandinavian countries with the amount of happiness
that can be derived from a socialist form of government. This is an effort to provide proof through the use of unrelated data. Also by comparing the situation in Russia with Moses leading the Israelites to a promised land, he indulges in false analogy or presenting a figurative comparison as proof.

5   The fourth paragraph contains another example of begging the
question, when Hoffer refers to the "alchemy of man's soul." The very

existence of such a concept is in itself debatable. He also uses false analogy when he compares the goal of the "molders of new humanity" with an attempt to push a body up a steep incline.

6   In the fifth paragraph, Hoffer once again uses name-calling and glittering generality. He refers to socialism as a "shabby thing" and the qualities it denies a population as full of "sparkle and zest." In addition, he once again begs the question when he says that "everyone" realizes how bad socialism is.

7   In the final paragraph, he again uses name-calling when he refers to socialists and Communists as "maniacal quacks" attempting to strap humanity down and operate with an axe. This is another example of a false analogy as well. He also introduces a false dilemma by boiling down human existence to a conflict between experimenters and experimentees.

8   In conclusion, Hoffer bases his condemnation of an entire school of philosophical thought on man's inability to implement it. This is, to a degree, a *non sequitur*. Finally he employs card stacking by pointing out several negative aspects of socialism while totally omitting any information regarding advancements that have come about in Russia and China under socialist rule.

—Brad Horrigan

Questions on "Logical Fallacies Used in 'No Redemption Via Socialism' "

1. What organizational format does this paper employ? What are the advantages and disadvantages of this format?

2. Find definitions or examples in the paper that need further clarification or elaboration.

CHECK LISTS

CHECK LIST FOR LOGICAL FALLACY PAPERS
1. *Use standard essay format.*
2. *Choose a clear organizational pattern.*
3. *Keep a neutral, objective tone.*

> 4. *Give clear and accurate definitions.*
> 5. *Use a "sandwich" approach on examples.*
> 6. *Include a brief summary ending.*
> 7. *Check your mechanics, especially use of colons (:) and semicolons (;).*

Expanded Check List for Logical Fallacy Papers

1. *Use standard essay format.* Write your analysis as an essay complete in itself. Start with an informative title that reflects your paper's focus. If you are analyzing outside sources, identify those sources in your title. (See student example papers for title ideas.) Even if you attach the ads you are analyzing to your paper, your paper should describe the ads clearly in context so referrals to the attachments are unnecessary as the paper is read. Use clear paragraphs and write in complete sentences, being especially careful to avoid fragments in definitions and run-on sentences in examples.

2. *Choose a clear organizational pattern.* Choose one organizational approach and stick to it. In analyzing a longer work, you might want to organize various examples under the fallacy they have in common to avoid repetition. To analyze a shorter segment in depth, you might want to go paragraph by paragraph or even line by line, depending on the complexity of the material.

3. *Keep a neutral, objective tone.* Since fallacies appeal to emotions rather than to facts and the purpose of your analysis is to expose this tactic, be sure that you keep your tone objective. Avoid getting caught up in the style of the work you're analyzing. To earn your reader's trust, you need to retain a cool, analytical detachment. Keep yourself and your own position on the topic out of the paper. Your purpose is to analyze logical formats, not to ridicule, counterattack, or argue a position.

A way to test your objectivity is to select a fallacious argument supporting something you believe in. It's easy to find fallacies in arguments you disagree with anyway. The truly objective person can also spot faulty arguments on the side he or she supports.

Be alert to deliberate use of irony and sarcasm in the material you investigate; an ironic example may have been used deliberately to expose false thinking.

4. *Give clear and accurate definitions.* In defining terms, keep the following defining rules in mind:

Defining Rules

A. *Don't use a term as part of its own definition.*
Example:
Don't say "Transfer is the act of transferring . . .," say "Transfer is the act of carrying over. . . ."

B. *Avoid introducing definitions with the expressions "is when," "is where," or "being."*
Example:
Don't say, "Transfer is when a famous person advertises a product," say "Transfer is the false carry over of positive feelings between two unrelated things."

C. *Don't feel a literal translation of a Latin term alone provides an adequate definition.*
Example:
Don't merely say that *post hoc ergo propter hoc* means "after this, therefore because of this"; clarify that *post hoc* reasoning imputes a causal relationship between two events because one followed the other in time.

D. *Don't use an example as a definition.*
Example:
Don't say "Transfer is Joe Namath selling pantyhose," for a reader unfamiliar with the term still wouldn't have a clear idea of it. Give a definition before you give an example.

E. *Define in complete sentences.*
Example:
Don't say "transfer, falsely attaching prestige from a person to an unrelating product" or you create a fragment. Be sure to include a valid verb in your definitions such as "Transfer falsely attaches . . ." or "Transfer carries over. . . ."

---

5. *Use a "sandwich" approach on examples.* First define, then quote key parts, then explain. "Sandwich" examples between explanatory materials. Don't assume they speak for themselves.

The following paragraph from a paper analyzing the fluoridation article illustrates this approach:

Definition   Argument *ad hominem* is the practice of attacking an individual's character or background to divert attention from a discussion. The general topic of the pamphlet is an argument *ad hominem* because it is directed at certain people and never answers a specific point of dis-

agreement. Specifically, reference is made to the fluoridation support-
ers as "tireless apologists for criminals and crime . . . clamoring for the
abolition or reduction of penalties attached to the use or narcotic drugs
. . . . snickering at American ideals, standards and religious precepts. . . . ." The pamphlet further states that an individual involved
with promoting fluoridation "attempted to snatch away handfuls of literature being distributed in downtown Seattle by a fluoridation opponent." Both examples attack the character of these persons while ignoring the real issues: both are *ad hominem*.

6. *Include a brief summary ending.* Include a brief summary ending suggesting the effect fallacies had on the validity or credibility of the
argument. Wrap up your presentation so it sounds finished.

7. *Check your mechanics, especially use of colons (:) and semicolons (;).* Since fallacy analysis often includes lists of terms or fairly complicated sentences, double check your use of colons (:) and semicolons
(;).

A *colon* introduces a list within a sentence only when the material
preceding the colon itself is a complete sentence.

Correct example:
The article uses the following fallacies: bandwagon, transfer, hasty
generalization.

A *colon* never comes between a verb and a list in a short sentence.

Incorrect example:
Examples of fallacies are bandwagon, transfer, and hasty generaliza-
tion.
Correct example:
(No internal punctuation is necessary, take the colon out.)
Examples of fallacies are bandwagon, transfer, and hasty generali-
zation.

Once a *colon* is used, you cannot return to your original sentence.

Incorrect example:
The article uses many fallacies: bandwagon, transfer, hasty generalization, which distort its argument and weakens its validity.
(Reword and take the colon out or make the added material into a
separate sentence.)
The article uses many fallacies such as bandwagon, transfer, and
hasty generalization, which distort its argument and weaken its validity.

The article uses many fallacies: bandwagon, transfer, hasty generalization. These fallacies distort its argument and weaken its validity.

A *semicolon* (;) is used to separate complete sentences or to clarify larger breaks within lists that have internal commas in the items listed.

Correct examples:
Bandwagon appeals to a majority opinion; it claims that popularity constitutes proof of validity.

Fallacies occur in the following examples: bandwagon, in the ad for Gaines Dog Food; transfer, in the ad for "Short and Sassy" conditioner; hasty generalization, in the ad for Maytag washers.

Group Exercises

Possible Group Exercises for Logical Fallacy Review

1. Bring in examples of articles that contain fallacies. Divide into groups. Set a time limit. Have each group analyze its examples to produce a thorough list of the fallacies present. Compare lists and see which group produced the most thorough and accurate list within the time allotted.

2. Have each group write a joint "bad example" to give to another group. After examples are switched, each group presents an analysis of the example to the originating group, and that analysis is compared to the group's intention in producing the example.

3. Have two or more members stage a "horrible example debate" in front of the class on a given topic, trying to use as many fallacies as possible in presenting their case. The class writes down the examples it hears and keeps score on who produced the most horrible example within the presentation.

LOGICAL FALLACIES IN MAGAZINE ADVERTISEMENTS

1   Many people today are obsessed with looking beautiful and being sexy. Advertisers know about this obsession and are capitalizing on it. Magazine advertisements are using logical fallacy techniques such as transfer, bandwagon, name-calling, and glittering generalities to sell everything from cosmetics and cars to oven cleaners and cigarettes.

2   The most common logical fallacy employed in advertising is transfer. Transfer is the carrying over of the prestige or approval of one person or idea to a different idea or product. An example of the use of transfer is in the ad for Hanes Alive pantyhose. Lola Falana (a sexy, pretty, rising star who has had a few television specials) is shown wearing a pair of Hanes Alive pantyhose. This is transfer because the idea of Lola's slim, sexy, well-known legs is carried over to the pantyhose. An ad for Eve cigarettes shows a beautiful, provocative woman smoking a cigarette, and it reads, "There's a little Eve in every woman." The idea transferred in this ad is that if one smokes Eve cigarettes, the beautiful, sexy side of her will become apparent. Transfer is also used to sell cars. The idea of being a "sport" and being surrounded by women is transferred to a car in the ad for Buick Regal. A man is standing next to a Buick on which five good looking girls in shorts and snug T-shirts are leaning. The first line of the text of the ad says, "So that beauty in the picture caught your eye, huh?" This ad's play on sex and popularity is just one more example of how advertisers use transfer.

3   Another logical fallacy technique is bandwagon. Bandwagon is an attempt to persuade someone by the use of popular opinion. The ad for Mr. Muscle oven cleaner uses bandwagon because of the statement that "women all over the country are switching." It also uses transfer and name-calling, which is the placing of a negative label on someone or something to discredit it. The Mr. Muscle ad uses name-calling when it says that the daytime method of cleaning an oven is "old-fashioned." The transfer part of the ad is the use of two women; one uses the "old-fashioned" cleaner and is very worn out looking, and the other, who uses Mr. Muscle, is all smiles and fresh looking.

4   Another ad that uses more than one type of logical fallacy is the ad for Wella Balsam. Farah Fawcett, an actress with long beautiful hair, provides the transfer escape. The bandwagon part is the words, "more women choose Wella Balsam than any other conditioner in the country."

5   Magazine ads for cosmetics almost always picture a beautiful young lady with the advertised cosmetic on. People reading the ad transfer the looks of the model to the product and think (the advertisers hope) that if they used the product, then they will look like the model. Cosmetic ads often use glittering generalities along with transfer. A glittering generality is a form of transfer; it identifies a product by using positive words, phrases, or clichés. An example of a glittering generality is in a Max Factor ad that came out of a *Seventeen* magazine. "Silky, clingy, rainbow colors" describe eye shadows that come in "exciting single compacts." The words "silky," "clingy," "rainbow," and "exciting" could be done away with and the sentences would make sense, but these words are gently persuading the reader to buy Max Factor cosmetics.

6   The ultimate example of transfer and glittering generalities is an ad for "Intimate" fragrance by Revlon. It pictures a woman sitting up in a bed with satin sheets pulled up around her. The ad reads, " 'Intimate.' It's really a man's fragrance. (And lasts as long as a girl needs it.)" The ad doesn't really say anything when taken literally, but the connotation of the two sentences along with the picture spells "sex." The transfer in the ad is the picture, and the glittering generalities are the sentences that say nothing, but at the same time imply "Wear 'Intimate' if you want to be sexy."

7   Through the use of logical fallacies, magazine advertisers try to make a buyer think that a product will make him or her beautiful, popular, and/or sexy.

—Cathy Russell

Questions on "Logical Fallacies in Magazine Advertisements"

1. What organizational framework does this paper employ? How does it change slightly in the second half?
2. What ties the beginning and ending of this paper together?

Logical Fallacies in a Letter to an Editor

The following "letter to an editor" is analyzed by the student paper which follows it.

WHAT ENERGY PROBLEM?[3]

1   I am completely disgusted when I hear our so-called experts expound on the so-called energy crisis.

---

[3]W. H. Wilkes, "What Energy Problem?" *The Seattle Times* (14 November 1976).

2   The only energy crisis we have is that which these people are creating themselves. Furthermore, if they keep up this utter nonsense, they will upset the whole natural balance of things and raise havoc with industry and our whole economic system.

3   Any knowledgeable college professor will tell you that one of the basic laws of physics is that you cannot destroy energy. You merely convert it from one form to another.

4   All of the energy that was on this earth 5,000 years ago is still here in one form or another, except possibly that which has radiated from earth into outer space in the form of heat loss—and that is probably compensated for by absorption from the sun.

5   Man will use the energy form that is the cheapest to produce in his respective period in history.

6   Throughout the years, he has used wood, whale oil, coal, wind, etc. The change has taken place very gradually and with no "help" from politicians, Congress or other experts. . . .

7   No one really knows what form of energy will replace oil 50 or 100 years from now. But when that time comes, we will know. And private industry will make it available during the natural sequence of events and not due to committees of Congress or laws or other acts which merely upset the natural balance of things.

8   Oil is the cheapest source we have in this era in history, so let's use it, and I say the more Arab oil we use the better. What better way to conserve our own oil supply?

9   All of the various suggestions for trying to make the people conserve energy are nonsense. People will buy what they can afford, and that's what keeps our economy in balance, be it gasoline, television sets, or automobiles.

—W.H. Wilkes
Seattle

Student Example Paper Analyzing Logical Fallacies in a Letter to a Metropolitan Paper

LOGICAL FALLACIES IN "WHAT ENERGY PROBLEM?"

1   In the letters to the editor section of the *Seattle Times* dated Sunday, November 14, 1976, there was a letter from Mr. W. H. Wilkes entitled, "What Energy Problem?" Mr. Wilkes's letter was very emotional and contained many logical fallacies. Logical fallacies are arguments that seem correct but which prove, upon examination, not to be so.

2   Mr. Wilkes's premise, although not clearly stated as such, is that

there is no energy crisis because there is plenty of energy. He uses the fallacy *dicto simpliciter*, an argument based on unqualified generalization, by saying energy cannot be destroyed; therefore, it is always available to use. "Any knowledgeable college professor will tell you that one of the basic laws of physics is that you cannot destroy energy. You merely convert it from one form to another." This statement has no bearing on the argument because the fact that energy is present doesn't mean it is in a usable form.

3   He then uses *post hoc, ergo propter hoc* which is assuming a causal relationship between two events simply because one follows the other in time. Mr. Wilkes is saying since a new source has always been found when it was required, a replacement will be found for oil. "Throughout the years, he [man] has used wood, whale oil, coal, wind, etc. No one really knows what form of energy will replace oil 50 or 100 years from now, but when that time comes, we will know."

4   While these two primary fallacies alone cast doubt upon the validity of his argument, Mr. Wilkes includes examples of several other fallacies as well.

5   In paragraphs one and nine, he uses name-calling. Name-calling discredits someone's judgment or reliability by labeling him or her with a name that has unfavorable connotations. "I am completely disgusted when I hear our so-called experts expound on the so-called energy crisis." He has doubts about the experts and the energy crisis. In two and nine, he says that all of the various warnings and suggestions are "nonsense."

6   In paragraph three, he uses false authority, persons, or institutions in one field used to support something in an unrelated field. "Any knowledgeable college professor will tell you that one of the basic laws of physics is that you cannot destroy energy." He is using the prestige of "college professors" as a class to support his thesis, regardless of whether their expertise is in english, history, physics, or theology.

7   In paragraphs two and eight, he uses hasty generalization, a conclusion based on insufficient evidence. Mr. Wilkes concludes that "The only energy crisis we have is that which these people are creating themselves." He gives no evidence to support this statement. He also says, "Oil is the cheapest source we have in this era in history, . . ." Here again, he gives no supporting evidence.

8   Last of all, Mr. Wilkes uses the fallacy *non sequitur*, presenting a conclusion not justified by the evidence or reasons given for it. In paragraph seven, he states that, "No one really knows what form of energy will replace oil 50 or 100 years from now. But when that time comes we will know." Can we afford to wait until then to find out?

9   Because Mr. Wilkes includes so many fallacies in his arguments, he makes it difficult to accept the validity of his premise.

—Faye Morris

Questions on "Logical Fallacies in 'What Energy Problem?' "

1. How does this writer organize her material?
2. What additional labels can you find for some of the fallacies in the article which the paper does not mention?
3. How does the ending relate to the paper's opening analysis?

LOGICAL FALLACIES UTILIZED BY SOME MEMBERS OF THE AMERICAN FUNERAL INDUSTRY

1   Some members of the funeral industry attempt to manipulate the public through their frequent use of logical fallacies both in their advertising and sales techniques. An undertaker's selling plan is subtle and manipulative since a "hard sell" approach would be inappropriate. The funeral transaction is influenced by a combination of circumstances: the disorientation caused by bereavement, the lack of standards by which to judge the value of the commodity offered by the seller, the need to make an on-the-spot decision, general ignorance of the law as it affects the disposal of the dead and the ready availability of insurance money to finance the transaction. These factors predetermine to a large extent the outcome of the funeral transaction and make the buyer vulnerable to the logical fallacy techniques of the funeral industry.

2   One of the most blatant logical fallacies employed by the funeral industry is known as the "false association technique." This technique attempts to artificially join two unrelated things in a buyer's mind to create a carry over effect. This is exemplified in a quotation from Jessica Mitford's *American Way of Death*: Burial footwear demonstrates "consideration and thoughtfulness for the departed. The closed portion of the casket is opened for the family, who on looking see that the ensemble is complete although not showing. You will gain their complete confidence and good will." *The Catalogue of Practical Burial Footwear* of Columbus, Ohio, quotes "the No. 280 reflects character and station in life. It is superb in styling and provides a formal reflection of successful living." In these examples, the attempted association is between positive, unearned "virtue" words and the product—burial footwear. "Consideration," "thoughtfulness," "character," and "successful living" are all glittering generalities falsely associated with the product of burial footwear.

3   Another example of this false association technique is found in another quotation from Mitford's book: "The latest in casket styles includes something to please everybody. The patriotic theme comes through very clearly, finding its eloquent expression in Boyertown Burial Casket Company's 'Valley Forge.' " This one is "designed to reflect

the rugged, strong, soldierlike qualities associated with Valley Forge. Its charm lies in the warm beauty of the natural grain and finish of finest maple hardwoods. A casket designed indeed for a soldier—one that symbolizes the solid, dependable, courageous American ideals so bravely tested at Valley Forge." Here, the logical fallacy involves another example of glittering generalities which attempts to associate coffins with unearned virtue words such as "soldierlike," "dependable," "charming" and "courageous."

4   The funeral seller, like any other merchant, is often preoccupied with price, profit, and selling techniques. One of these techniques is another logical fallacy termed distortion. One type of distortion, called "Hasty Generalization" is created by stating sweeping conclusions based on insufficient evidence. This technique is exemplified in the words of the *National Funeral Service Journal:* "The focus of the buyer's interest must be the casket, vault, clothing, funeral cars, etc.—the only tangible evidence of how much has been invested in the funeral—the only real status symbol associated with a funeral service." This hasty generalization by the funeral director-seller stereotypes all bereaved customers as status seekers. This unflattering appraisal is too all-encompassing a conclusion based on too little available evidence. The American funeral industry is all too accustomed to telling the customer what sort of funeral he wants or must have and does so by playing on the buyer's emotions and guilt rather than on his rational judgment.

5   A second example of the distortion technique is described as a false analogy. In this type of logical fallacy, a figurative comparison is presented as proof. As presented in *The Principles and Practices of Embalming* by Frederick and Strub, "a funeral service is a social function at which the deceased is the guest of honor and the center of attraction. . . . A poorly prepared body in a beautiful casket is just as incongruous as a young lady appearing at a party in a costly gown and with her hair in curlers." The only corresponding analogy between these two areas is the incongruity of the situation involved. While a comparison between an unembalmed dead body and a lady with rollers in her hair at a party may add interest to the argument, this false analogy presents a figurative comparison as proof for embalming, yet does not mention the illogical incongruity of a funeral service and a social party.

6   These same writers, Frederick and Strub, commit another logical fallacy known as a "false causation technique." This technique erroneously claims a cause and effect relationship based on invalid evidence. A specific category under this logical fallacy is known as *"post hoc, ergo propter hoc,"* "after this, therefore because of this." In other words, a time sequence (which is inadequate proof) is used to suggest

a causal relationship. To quote Frederick and Strub: "It is a significant fact that when embalming was in its infancy, the death rate was 21 to every 1,000 persons per year, and today it has been reduced to 10 to every 1,000 per year." This writer goes so far as to attribute the falling death rate in this country to the practice of embalming and its sanitation benefits. This false causation suggests that because event B (reduced death rate) followed event A (improved embalming methods), then A caused B, which is inadequate proof of a causal relationship. This erroneous claim was in fact stated in a panel discussion among funeral directors, and the purposeful manipulation involved was exposed. As reported by the National Funeral Service Journal, Dr. I. M. Feinberg said, "Sanitation is probably the farthest thing from the mind of the modern embalmer. We must realize that the motives for embalming at the present time are economic and sentimental, with a slight religious overtone."

7   To return to the previously discussed distortion technique, there is another form of this logical fallacy incorporated by the funeral industry known as an argument *ad populum* (argument to the people). This technique appeals to an audience's emotional fears and popularly held prejudices. Also from Mitford's book, this quotation concerns cremation. "Characteristically, funeral directors seek to counter the trend towards cremation by playing on the emotions of the survivors, portraying the procedures as hideous and horror-filled." A funeral director, writing in *Mortuary Management*, describes how this can be done: "When anybody asks me about cremation, I simply tell them the truth; that it can be the cheapest way of disposing of a body, but that anyone who ever witnessed a cremation wouldn't cremate a pet dog." This argument prejudices a customer so he refuses his opponent (the owners of a crematorium) a fair hearing by appealing to the popular fear of cremation—the horror of burning a loved one. On the contrary, the owners of crematoria and the niche and urn salesmen, do not, of course, see it this way.

8   The owners of crematoria employ this same type of a logical fallacy known as an *ad populum* distortion. As Mitford states, they say, "Cremation is the clean, beautiful method of resolution by incandescence rather than the unspeakable horrors of decay—We think of our loved one as in his ethereal body, as 'robed in his garments of light.' " They too appeal to the popular fear of death, being buried, and decaying.

9   As illustrated, the American funeral industry utilizes logical fallacies to con the public into paying for costly funerals, and one is even made to feel guilty for not having spent more money than he or she did. While the current American funeral, burial, and memorialization practices are largely pagan and wasteful, the grief-stricken and unedu-

cated person is vulnerable to exploitation. Recognizing the logical fallacies involved in the funeral industry is one of the first necessary steps toward changing the high cost of dying.

10   Undertakers are often persuasive and incorporate logical fallacies to manipulate a customer's emotions rather than offering down-to-earth advice. A funeral director can be even more pushy than a used car salesman because with him, there's only one to a customer!

—Gregory Brown

Questions and Exercises on "Logical Fallacies Utilized by Some Members of the American Funeral Industry"

1. Which incorporation of an example with a definition comes across clearest in this paper?

2. Find some sentences that use the verb "is" and see if you can rewrite them with different verbs.

3. Try to shorten some of the longer sentences in this paper.

Student Created "Bad Examples" Plus Analyses

Deliberate Bad Example

WHAT HAPPENED TO DISCIPLINE IN OUR SCHOOLS?

1   Many years ago, teachers had a strict upper hand in the classroom by being forceful over the students. After the beginning of the 1950s, disciplinary action by the teachers was curtailed. From that time on, students have risen to power to create utter chaos in the school system.

2   It is obvious that students need to be kept in line by their teachers, just as dogs need to be well trained by their handlers. A dog will often turn against its handler, if it is not properly trained. Because discipline was forced out of the teacher's hand, students have turned against their teachers.

3   Since discipline in our schools was the only moralizing impact on students, it is no wonder that we now have nuts running around our country like "Ted," the sex murderer. Most people agree that unruly, disrespectful students become the focal point of school unrest. Even school employees such as janitors and bus drivers have trouble with the school system.

4   Statistics show that three out of every five students that are educated in undisciplined schools have problems adjusting into their environment. Why, if it weren't for discipline in our schools, we would never have had men like George Washington, Thomas Jefferson, or Abraham Lincoln. Instead, our schools are producing riotous, disrespectful students who are really ripe for rebelling against the entire country.

5   It's about time we give the poor, suffering teachers a break from these riotous students. We need to go back to the peaceful, well-mannered schools that kept our country running. We must either return discipline to the teachers, or suffer the consequences of student rebellion. . . .

LOGICAL FALLACIES IN "WHAT HAPPENED TO DISCIPLINE IN OUR SCHOOLS?"

1   In the "bad example" article "What Happened to Discipline in Our Schools?" many logical fallacies are presented. Logical fallacies are invalid arguments that do not hold up under analysis. The entire article is based on the logical fallacy, propaganda. Propaganda is an argument that appeals to an emotional rather than a rational response. The article is filled with many emotional statements and ideas that are intended to sway the reader's opinions and distort the actual issues involved.

2   In the first paragraph, the article uses circular reasoning, *post hoc ergo propter hoc*, and begging the question to support the argument. Circular reasoning, a form of begging the question, is an argument that uses repetition of the same argument as proof of itself. The first sentence says, in essence, that the teachers were strict with the students because they were strict. *Post hoc ergo propter hoc* is an argument that states that because B follows A, that A has caused B. The remainder of the paragraph says that because student unrest followed the abolition of discipline, the abolition of discipline caused the student unrest. Begging the question is an argument that uses as proof something that needs to be proved itself. The first paragraph uses begging the question in stating that utter chaos resulted from lack of discipline as if it were an accepted fact.

3   In the second paragraph, cocksure fallacy, false analogy, and begging the question are used as proof to support the argument. Cocksure fallacy, a form of begging the question, states a position in need of proof as if its truth were obvious. The first sentence uses cocksure fallacy by saying "it is obvious" when it is not. False analogy is a comparison used as proof to support an argument. The argument compares the student's disobedience with that of a dog and its handler. Although the two examples have similarities, they also have differ-

ences making it impossible to use one as proof of the other. The last sentence uses begging the question by saying that the students have rebelled against the teachers as if it were a proven fact.

4   In the third paragraph, *dicto simpliciter*, name-calling, bandwagon, and *non sequitur* are presented. *Dicto simpliciter* is an argument that supports a specific point based on an unqualified generalization. The first sentence says that "Ted" and people like him are a direct result of disciplinary neglect. Name-calling, a form of red herring, is a technique of negative labeling to discredit a person or idea. Red herring is a diversionary tactic that pulls attention away from the main focus. Name-calling is presented in the words, "nuts," "unruly," and "disrespectful." Bandwagon is the argument that because everybody does it, it is right or because everybody believes it, it is true. The article says that the majority believe that undisciplined students cause school unrest. *Non sequitur* is a conclusion that has no connection to the premise it follows. Unsatisfied janitors and bus drivers have nothing to do with lack of discipline in the schools.

5   In the fourth paragraph, hypostatization, *post hoc*, hypothesis contrary to fact, name-calling and argument *ad populum* are given. Hypostatization, a form of false authority, uses a concept or idea as an authority. The article uses statistics as the false authority. *Post hoc* is again used by stating that because undisciplined students follow lack of discipline, lack of discipline caused this type of student. Hypothesis contrary to fact is an argument based on a premise that is already proven false. There is no way to prove men like George Washington or Abraham Lincoln would never have come along if it weren't for discipline. Name-calling is again used in the words "riotous" and "disrespectful." Argument *ad populum* is an argument that appeals to people's popular prejudices. The fear of national student rebellion is used in the article as an example of *ad populum*.

6   In the final paragraph, the article presents *ad misericordiam*, name-calling, glittering generality, false dilemma, and argument *ad populum*. *Ad misericordiam* is an argument that appeals to sympathy rather than fact. The article talks about "poor suffering teachers" and again uses name-calling with the word, "riotous." Glittering generality is a transfer of positive labeling. An example is the phrase, "peaceful, well-mannered." False dilemma is a technique of limiting a person to only two choices when there are really more. The article uses "either-or" reasoning and limits the reader to returning discipline to the schools or suffering the consequences.

7   The article, "What Happened to Discipline in Our Schools?" contains numerous logical fallacies that support its argument. The statements at first sound logical until a person examines them closely. Fal-

lacious arguments are used to appeal to the reader's emotions and distract his attention away from the actual issues under debate.

—Debra Lermond

Questions on "Logical Fallacies in 'What Happened to Discipline in Our Schools?'"

1. How does following a paragraph by paragraph organizational format allow this paper to be extremely thorough in its analysis?

2. In paragraph 5 of the analysis paper, the writer calls the George Washington and Abraham Lincoln references examples of hypothesis contrary to fact. What other labels would be appropriate for these examples?

AN EXAMPLE OF LOGICAL FALLACIES

1 "Mom," I cried, as I ran through the door, "You've got to let me go to the movie with Mike tonight; everybody's going to be there."

2 "No," she announced, "You know how I feel about that crazy roughneck. Everywhere he goes, he causes trouble. Besides, the last time you went somewhere with him, you got caught drinking, so I know he's a bad influence on you."

3 "Oh, Mom," I answered, "everybody knows he's not as bad as you make out. It's just that all the parents are against him, and no older people like him. He never gets a fair chance with your friends. They either pretend he isn't alive, or they cut him down behind his back."

4 "That's not true," she argued. "It's just that he's been in trouble before, so it's a sure thing he'll get in trouble again. Those kinds of people always cause problems. Besides, I don't like his looks. Those long-hairs are all rebelling against society."

5 "You've got it all wrong," I replied. "I've been best friends with him for years, and I'm not bad, so how could he be?" Then I said, "He's really different than you think. He's smart, ambitious, witty, and fun to be with. Anyhow, some of your friends aren't so great either."

6 "I don't care what you say," my Mom responded. "His mind is like a stagnant pool, and Dr. Smith told me Mike would never be any good after quitting school."

1   In the preceding example, eighteen logical fallacies are used. In the first paragraph, the first sentence is an example of the bandwagon fallacy, which is the argument that because everyone is doing it, it's right.

The second sentence, with the words "crazy roughneck," is using the name-calling fallacy, which is the technique of labeling a person negatively to discredit him. The third sentence is an example of *dicto simpliciter* because the mother is basing her argument about Mike's causing trouble on an unqualified generalization. The fourth sentence shows the *post hoc* fallacy, the belief that because B followed A, A caused B. The next sentence, "everybody knows . . .," is assuming as true something that needs to be proven and is known as the cocksure fallacy, one form of the begging the question fallacy. The sixth sentence is appealing to sympathy rather than facts and is an example of the *ad misericordiam* fallacy. The last sentence in the paragraph is a false dilemma because the older people are being limited to two choices when they actually have many more.

2   The first part of the fourth paragraph shows the hasty generalization fallacy, because the mother is basing her sweeping conclusions about Mike on insufficient examples. It can also be seen as another example of *dicto simpliciter*. The mother's statement that "those kind of people always cause problems" is a genetic fallacy. She thinks that because she knows a person's origin, she can predict his behavior relying on false stereotypes. The last sentence contains three fallacies: (1) stereotyping, not allowing for differences within a group (in this case long-hairs); (2) propaganda, using an emotional, one-sided argument; and (3) bandwagon, claiming many other adults take her stand.

3   In the fifth paragraph, the boy is trying to take the approval he has and carry it over to Mike. This is called the transfer fallacy. Then he uses the glittering generality fallacy by describing Mike in positive words, along with the card stacking fallacy which shows only one side of an argument. The last sentence is a *tu quoque* fallacy because the boy counters his mother's attack by attacking in return.

4   In the last paragraph, the mother is using a false analogy by using a comparison as proof: "His mind is like a stagnant pool. . . ." She then uses a person with a reputation in one field to support her argument in an unrelated field, which is the false authority fallacy. Also in the last sentence is the argument *ad hominem* fallacy since she directs her argument at the person, not his ideas.

5   On first reading, the example may seem like a typical family fight, with good points brought in by both sides. It's not until the logical fallacies are pointed out that the reader realizes that both sides are trying to prove their arguments by using false logic or name-calling. Analyzing logical fallacies can provide a reader with a more objective understanding of which side, if either, is using supportable evidence as opposed to emotionally loaded or distorted arguments.

—Doyle Whiting

1. What are the eighteen fallacies used in the example? Are there any that the writer has missed or that you would relabel?

2. What sentence pattern repeatedly introduces paragraphs in this paper? Suggest other wordings.

LOGICAL FALLACIES IN A HYPOTHETICAL PUBLIC ORATION

1 Faulty logic has instilled itself deeply in our communication. We have to learn to be aware of it in order to separate fact from emotional appeals.

2 The following is a hypothetical situation consisting of a small town city council meeting. They are debating the question of whether or not to eliminate parking meters in their downtown district:

3 "Mr. Councilman, I would like to introduce Mr. Thomas J. Fitzmoore, President of the McDerfy's Drive-In Restaurant chain. I have asked him to speak on behalf of the citizens against parking meters."

4 "Thank you, Mr. Peterson. I have been asked to speak out against those ridiculous parking meters which that Communist revolutionary, Simmons, has proposed. We all know what the papers have been saying about his contributions to that student radical group. I'm for removing the meters because they are a thorn in the citizen's side, and thorns are a real pain. Everybody is against parking meters downtown. When the meters are removed, Pumpkin Center will once again become a great town."

5 When this oratory is dissected, the logical fallacies become evident. First of all, the use of Mr. Fitzmoore is an example of transfer, the prestige or approval attached to one idea or person being carried over to another by association. The prestige of a famous restauranteur is used assuming that his experience in drive-ins extends to the use of parking meters.

6 Fitzmoore's opening statement about those "ridiculous parking meters" is an example of name-calling or using words with negative connotations to prejudice one's opinion. Name-calling is also used in the opening sentence when Fitzmoore called Simmons a "Communist revolutionary."

7 Fitzmoore goes on to refer to Simmons' past contributions to a student radical group. This attack against a person rather than his ideas is called argument *ad hominem*. Comparing the meters to a thorn in the citizen's side is a false analogy. When offered as logical proof, all analogies are false. Thorns and parking meters may have

superficial resemblances, but by no means does the comparison validate the argument to remove the meters.

8 Another logical fallacy, bandwagon, is used when Fitzmoore claims that "everybody is against [the meters]. . ." Bandwagon is an attempt to persuade by appealing to popular opinion.

9 Mr. Fitzmoore's closing statement that Pumpkin Center will be a great town once again, after the meters are removed, is an example of *post hoc, ergo propter hoc*, which literally translates as "after this; therefore, because of this." *Post hoc* assumes a casual relationship between two events simply because one follows the other in time.

10 Since much of everyday communication is clouded by logical fallacies, it is important to be able to recognize them. If a person is unaware of these fallacies, he might be misled by false arguments that distort or direct attention away from valid information.

—Steve Smith

Questions on "Logical Fallacies in a Hypothetical Public Oration"

1. Write an extension of the hypothetical debate.
2. Find examples of paragraphs with definitions or examples that could use further clarification.

Chapter Six

Toward Complete Objectivity

Subjective versus Objective Writing

Following the assignments in this book, you have produced both subjective and objective writing. One type of writing is not superior to the other; each has its own purpose and effect. Subjective writing enables you to both communicate and actually re-create your feelings in others. Objective writing lets you focus on ideas and minimize your personal involvement. Powerful writing can result from either style. Your purpose for writing determines which approach you should use.

Exploring the Concept of Objectivity

To illustrate the difference in styles, the assignments in this book have moved you progressively toward more and more objectivity. You might wonder, however, how objective can your writing actually become? Is complete objectivity possible?

The answer is "no" since the world is always viewed through your subjective mind. Different degrees of objectivity, however, are possible. To push this concept to its practical limits and explore its effects on writing approaches and style, read the following definitions of "objectivity" in writing. Experiment with the "objective" approach to writing and analyze the significance of your results.

Clarifying Degrees of Objectivity Obtainable in Writing

Objectivity refers to anything external to or independent of the mind. One school of philosophy suggests that no objectivity exists, since all is perceived through one's mind. Putting that extreme position aside, however, the various characteristics of objectivity are best clarified by constrasting them with the qualities of subjectivity.

Chart of Objective and Subjective Traits

Objective External landscape

Subjective Internal landscape

Objective	Subjective
1. Something perceived as distinguished from something existing only in the mind of a person thinking.	1. Produced by the mind, resulting from the thoughts and feelings of the person thinking rather than the attributes of the object thought of.
2. Having verifiable existence or reality through observation.	2. Incapable of external observation.
3. Determined by and emphasizing the features and characteristics of the object or thing dealt with rather than the thoughts and feelings of the artist, writer, or speaker.	3. Determined by and emphasizing the ideas, thoughts, and feelings of the artist, writer, or speaker.
4. Uninfluenced by the emotion, surmise, or personal prejudice of the writer or speaker.	4. Reflecting the emotion, feelings, beliefs, and personal prejudices of the writer or speaker.

Objectivity, then, is a matter of focus, intention, distance, and control. Writing objectively, your focus is outside yourself, your intention is to clarify or to describe that outside focus, your aim is to achieve distance by maintaining a neutral stance, and your tone and descriptions are controlled by that stance.

Most writing combines the objective with the subjective. If you were to try for complete objectivity in writing, you would be acting like a verbal motion picture camera with sound track. A camera cannot think, judge, or interpret; it only captures and records sights or sounds. However, even a camera has an element of subjectivity because the photographer deliberately selects and chooses what the picture will record. For the degree of objectivity that can be achieved in writing, the following chart clarifies what can be put in and what must be left out.

OBJECTIVITY CHART

Can put in:
1. Descriptions that are physically observable such as facial expressions, actions, facial coloration changes, gestures
2. Statements that are made and accurate condensations or summaries of those statements
3. Descriptions of tone of voice and voice pitch changes, pauses, noises that another observer could also hear

Must leave out:
1. Words that interpret what gesture and tone might mean

2. Reactions

3. Value judgments

4. Emotions or feelings
5. Thoughts
6. Anything taking place inside your head that is not observable by others

Group Exercises

Exercise to Produce Writing Samples for Analysis

Since writing conditions can influence not only what we write about but also how we write, this exercise provides different viewpoints for describing the same incident.

Directions: Split the class into three groups (encourage volunteers for the first group), and give each group one of the following assignments:

Group no. 1 (volunteer group)—Stage a "happening" in front of the class that all group no. 1 members can participate in for a short period of time. For example, recite something in unison, march in circles, clap out a rhythm, play a simple game.

Group no. 2 Carefully observe whatever group No. 1 does.

Group no. 3   Observe group no. 2's reactions to group no. 1's performance. Take notes as you observe.

After group no. 1's performance, each person in all groups spends five to ten minutes writing what he or she did and observed. Each person labels that writing sample with the group number and turns it in.

Alternative Exercises to Produce Writing Samples

Class members bring in writing samples from sources that show various degrees of objectivity ranging from romance magazines to newspaper editorials to textbook explanations.

Class members do a focused freewrite (see chapter 1) on a given topic such as: My Favorite Place, Meal, Activity, Person, Movie, Book, or Television Character.

Analysis of Group Writing Samples

Analyze some of the writing produced in the group exercises above for subjective and objective content, justifying your analysis as you go. (Note: A single statement can contain both objective and subjective parts.)

> *Paragraph from Group no. 1*
> *Objective (Verifiable act)*
> I volunteered to be in group no. 1.
> *Objective (Verifiable fact)*
> We were told to stage a "happening" in front of the class and decided to play
> *Objective (Verifiable fact)*
> the game "London Bridge is Falling Down."
> *Subjective (Feeling)*
> I felt foolish. When we entered the
> *Subjective (Feeling)*
> room, I felt everyone was looking at me.
> *Subjective (Feeling)*
> I was sorry I volunteered. I formed one
>
> *Objective (Verifiable act)*   *Objective (Verifiable act)*
> half of the bridge.   After catching one student, we
>   sat down.
>
> *Subjective (Feeling)*
> I was glad it was over with.

Paragraph from Group no. 2

Objective (Verifiable observation)
Ten students came into the room and started playing "London Bridge."
Subjective (Feeling)
I couldn't believe my eyes.

Subjective (Judgment)
Boy, did they ever look dumb.
Objective (Verifiable observation)
but not all of them joined in.
Subjective (Judgment)
I thought the whole thing
was pretty silly.

Objective (Verifiable observation)
They sang the song as they played,
Objective (Verifiable observation)
Some laughed a lot.

Paragraph from Group no. 3

Objective (Verifiable fact)
I watched a girl in the back row.
Subjective (Interpretation)
When group no. 1 came in, first she looked surprised,
Objective (Verifiable observation)
then she started to laugh.
Objective (Verifiable observation and actual quotation)
She started commenting to the girl next to her saying, "I don't believe it."
Objective (Verifiable observation)
When she noticed I was looking at her and taking notes, she got quiet and turned red.
Subjective (Interpretation)
I think she was embarrassed.

Questions for Discussion on Analysis of Group Writing Samples

1. Were some groups or examples more subjective than others? If so, which ones?

2. Did the extent of personal involvement affect the degree of subjectivity?

3. What types of subjective comments appeared most frequently? What types of objective statements appeared most frequently?

4. How did note taking, topic choice, or writer's purpose affect the degree of objectivity present?

5. What did the exercise show you about factors affecting subjective and objective responses?

Overall Questions for Discussion on Subjective and Objective Writing

1. Can objective writing portray emotion as effectively as subjective writing?

2. What techniques do subjective and objective writing have in common?

3. In what ways is objective description writing like personal experience writing (the most subjective form of writing you did)?

4. Which aspects of analytical writing are objective? Which subjective?

5. How do subjectivity and objectivity affect tone?

6. Which type of writing is most effective for which type of writing situations?

7. What factors determine whether a piece of writing is loosely labeled subjective or objective?

8. What do you see as the advantages and disadvantages of each approach?

Suggested Writing Assignments

> **Type of writing** Objective description or interview summary
> **Approach** Strict objectivity
> **Purpose** Write a detailed description with no subjective statements to gain a clearer idea of the difference between objectivity and subjectivity.

1. *The Objective Interview Summary.* Interview someone on a topic that you know will elicit an emotional response. Choose highly controversial, explosive topics. Retain an objective stance yourself throughout the interview. Make no evaluative or judgmental statements, and give no indication of your own position on the issue. Ask probing questions in the areas that elicit the strongest response. Have some prepared questions with you, but feel free to make-up and expand on others as you go. Take notes on actions and responses.

Write a summary of the interview in essay form, re-creating the scene in elaborate detail and restricting yourself to *only objective* statements.

2. *The Objective Description*. Unobtrusively observe an argument or emotionally charged scene. Listen carefully, not only to words but also to tone of voice, and watch the expressions on the participants' faces. Take notes if you can do so without attracting attention.

3. *The Reaction to a "Happening."* Stage a "happening." Attempt to convince passersby to join in a game of jump rope, sign an unusual petition, volunteer for a clean-up squad. Write a strictly *objective* description of their responses.

4. *The Interview of Contrasting Groups*. Interview five or more people on a controversial topic. Select areas that would have different interest groups like the campus lunchroom, a construction site, a suburban neighborhood, a church group. Write a completely *objective* summary of their responses and reactions.

Check Lists

CHECK LIST FOR OBJECTIVE WRITING ASSIGNMENTS
1. *Use standard essay form.*
2. *Eliminate all subjective statements.*
3. *Add concrete, observable details.*
4. *Make sure your paper sounds finished.*

Expanded Check List for Objective Writing Assignments

1. *Use standard essay form*. Whether you are summarizing an interview, collating the responses of different groups to a given situation, or writing an objective description, keep your paper in essay form. Present information in descriptive paragraphs rather than merely writing down the questions and answers presented in an interview. Change paragraphs to reflect a change in focus or speaker. (See student papers at the end of this chapter for examples.)

2. *Eliminate all subjective statements*. Limit yourself to observable actions and verifiable information. (Review the charts describing objectivity in this chapter for specific ideas.) Leave out interpretive, judgmental, or emotional remarks. For example say, "She turned red

and started tapping her fingers," rather than "She became embarrassed and made nervous gestures with her hands."

3. *Add concrete, observable details.* Enliven your objective writing by adding physically observable detail to your descriptions. (Review the "Objectivity Chart" in this chapter for specific ideas.) The student example papers at the end of this chapter use details to excite interest and produce impact. Descriptions like "His dark brown eyes pierced out beneath thick grey brows that just about met over the bridge of his nose" from the "Interview with Mr. S_____," and "His words were coming faster now, so close together they almost blended, and he didn't pause to swallow so that white spittle flecked his lips," from "Willy on the Government" are specific and dynamic and objective.

4. *Make sure your paper sounds finished.* Prepare your reader for the end of an interview with comments like "His final words were . . . ," or "We ended the interview by. . . ." By identifying comments as closing remarks or labeling actions as completing an interview or scene, you help your paper end gracefully.

Student Example Papers

INTERVIEW WITH MR. S

1   I interviewed Mr. S. of Duvall. Mr. S. is a fifty-one-year-old farmer, who is married and has six grown children.

2   Mr. S. was standing looking out the window when I asked him, "What do you think about people living together who are not married?"

3   "Well, I call that shacking up, if they're not married," he replied as he shifted his weight to his right foot and tucked his plaid shirt further down below his worn belt.

4   "How do you feel about it?" I asked again.

5   "Well, I can tell you, I'm not supporting none of my kids while they do that. If they go off and live with someone, that's it." He waved his big knuckled hand in the air, back and forth in front of him, and added, "I'm not responsible for them anymore." He walked to a nearby chair and sat down.

6   "Then you really don't object to them living together as long as they are self-supporting?"

7   The smooth shiny spot in the center of his balding head turned pink-red. "I didn't say that," he said. His dark brown eyes pierced out beneath thick grey brows that just about met over the bridge of his

nose. He continued in a louder voice. "You kids want everything without the responsibility or the work that goes with it. It takes work to stay married. Living together without being married is just like everything else today—lazy and the easy way out." He wiped the back of his hand across his mouth.

8   "Did you and your wife live together before you were married?" I queried further.

9   "No such thing." His face reddened. "In my day, we were different." He took a large wrinkled handkerchief from his rear pocket and blew his nose. As he replaced the handkerchief, he continued, "We didn't do any of this tomfoolery. We had to work too hard." He uncrossed his legs and slid further in the chair using his hands on the arms of the chair.

10   "Have you ever felt you didn't know your wife well enough before you were married?"

11   "Oh, I knew her well enough. She lived on the farm next to us all her life, and we went to school together." He spotted some lint on his right pant leg and swatted it off.

12   "I meant, was she the same after you were married as you thought she was going to be before you got married?"

13   "We all change," he said and again his hands swept the air in front of him. "I had to work very hard, so I didn't have time to worry about such things." He squinted one eye at me and leaned closer. "We had a farm, and that takes a lot of work, you know." He took a pipe from his shirt pocket and fingered it.

14   I then asked him, "Were there times in your married life that you thought about divorce or wished you had married another woman?"

15   He cleared his throat and as he spoke his head leaned slightly to one side. "Sure, I don't think there's anyone in life who doesn't have their quarrels and fights. You can go out and get divorced every time you fight, if that's what you want. People should spend more time thinking about how to get along better instead of whether or not they should get a divorce." He raised his arm and shook his forefinger at me. "You kids today just don't work hard enough at anything. You just want everything in life to be easy, but that's not the way things work." He continued to look at me.

16   I then asked, "Well, do you think living together is harmful?"

17   He began to answer before I finished my question, "Of course I do," he shouted. His face reddened and his right hand, holding the pipe, wagged at me while his left one clasped his knee to help him lean forward. "You kids don't stop to think that when you break up it's just as hard on you as if you were married. You just don't have to pay an attorney, that's all."

—Laurel Elledge

1. Was the paper completely objective throughout?
2. Find examples of particularly detailed descriptions.
3. How do you pick up the man's emotions without the writer interpreting or evaluating the scene for you?
4. How might the writer have ended her paper to make it sound more finished?

WILLY ON THE GOVERNMENT

1   Willy was leaning forward in the chair, his legs slightly spraddled and his hands clasped between his knees. His eyes stared straight at grandpa, and the light sparked them when he tilted his head.

2   "The government, a big wheel like that," he was telling grandpa, his slight southern accent becoming more pronounced. "You let him get away with it and what the hell kinda respect is any kids gonna have for law and order, or anything else?" Straightening up, he put one arm on the chair arm. He rested the hand of his other arm on his knee. His words were coming faster now, so close together they almost blended, and he didn't pause to swallow so that white spittle flecked his lips. His brows were drawn down, shadowing his eyes from the light, but his voice never raised, "I don't care what. That guy," he paused a moment as he was forced to draw a breath so that his next words came out clear and ringing, "They should've slammed him in for life! I'd throw the . . .," he paused again, then pronounced each word carefully, "I'd throw the key away!"

3   Willy leaned back in the chair, crossed his legs, and picked up his coffee cup from the table beside him. After taking a sip, he continued, his accent fading and his eyebrows held high above his eyes, pushing the skin on his forehead in wrinkles up to his hair, "I don't care what party he's in." He began to emphasize each word with a slight gesture of his coffee cup. "I mean he's a Republican who got caught. There's probably a Democrat across the island doing the same stupid thing."

4   Willy plunked the cup back on the table and leaned forward, his brows again drawing down over his eyes, "And all that crap about him losing his job being punishment enough!" He shook his head, the lines bracketing his mouth became deeper, "I know, I know this guy right down town here who got arrested for not paying his income tax, and they slapped him in jail for three years, and him with two kids and a wife to feed!" Willy slowly shook his head, and he again picked up his coffee cup and leaned back in the chair. Sighing slightly, he concluded, "I'm telling you, this government is going to hell!"

—Judy Marrs

Questions on "Willy on the Government"

1. What kind of person is Willy? How do you know? How does this objective description characterize him without evaluating him?
2. Find examples of concrete use of detail and close observation.

WALTER'S LAMENT

1   Walter Brown settled his slender frame into the overstuffed chair. The lines in his face were noticeable as he stared at the small fire flickering in the fireplace. He took a deep breath as he reached for the coffee cup. It shook slightly as he picked it up to drink. The steam from the hot liquid fogged his wire-rimmed glasses as he first blew then sipped the contents. A drop or two spilled out as he returned the cup to its saucer.

2   "What will you do now?" I asked.

3   "Guess we'll have to sell the place," he said quietly. "That last operation took everything we had in the bank. Your Grandmother and I thought maybe we'd be able to live out our years out here on the lake, but that just don't look possible now." As he spoke his eyes gazed around the room.

4   "It took us almost twenty years to build this place—every nail and every piece of wood was put there by me—me and your grandmother. Now it's got to go. Just don't seem right." He smacked his lips and shook his head as he reached again for his coffee.

5   "Well, doesn't Medicare help out?"

6   "Oh sure, it helps out some," he said. "But by God when you're out of money, it sure won't put no food on the table. No sir!"

7   He wiped his mouth with the palm of one hand, moved it down over his chin, and back onto his lap. "'Sides, we can't afford these taxes they got us payin.' "

8   He leaned his head on the back of the chair and started rocking slowly.

9   "The problem here, my boy, is nobody cares. No one wants nothin' from me 'cept my taxes so's some shirker can get him some more free food. Let some fella my age who's worked all his life, let him try and live off a what he's saved. His money ain't gonna last no time at all, prices what they are today."

10   "Well maybe there will be something done about lowering taxes for the aged. Maybe you won't have to move," I said.

11   His head jerked back slightly as he chuckled. A grin appeared on his face.

12   "Hell, I might be dead tomorrow or next week or next month some-

time. Ain't no politician gonna waste his time and not get a vote for his trouble."

13   The grin was gone as he stared back into the fire.

—Brad Horrigan

Questions on "Walter's Lament"

1. What details re-create Walter for you?
2. How does the writer retain objectivity in the descriptions?

INTERVIEW ON WOMEN IN SOCIETY

1   I interviewed a girl in my Biology class, Sue G. Her major is art, and she's transferring to the University of Washington in two years. I asked her questions about some of the problems women are facing in our society today.

2   The first question I asked was, "What do you think about men who believe the woman's place is in the home?"

3   Sue's eyes went to the side, and she had a smile on her face. After a few seconds elapsed, she answered, "It depends on the man and the woman." Her head tilted to one side, and she swiveled back and forth in her chair. Her right arm went out to the side, and she said, "It should be a mutual agreement between the man and the woman, never one-sided." She ended by saying she wanted a husband and a home to take care of. She threw her head back and put her hands under her legs.

4   The second question was, "Do you think a woman should be called a whore or prostitute because she enjoys sex with a variety of men?"

5   Sue jumped out of her chair and said, "No, no, absolutely not. That makes me furious." Her hands were clutched, and she said, "Society puts all the responsibility on the woman. She should be able to control her sexual drives, but it's all right for the man not to control his." She kicked her legs up and down and turned around in her chair. Her eyes opened widely as she said, "It takes two to tango," then scratched her arm. She was humming and wrote something in her notebook. She snapped her fingers and slapped her legs saying, "Mercy, mercy, mercy."

6   "Do you think there should be nude go-go men in nightclubs?" was the third question.

7   She bent over, laughing loudly, and clapped her hands. Her eyes widened as she answered, "If women, by law, can dance in the nude in

certain states, men can. There's just as many men with good bodies as there are women." She kicked her legs and threw her hair behind her shoulders.

8   The last question was, "What do you think should be done to rapists?" She threw her hands up and dropped them between her legs. "They should be sent to an institution for rehabilitation." She swerved in her chair and folded her hands. "Rapists have a psychological problem not a criminal tendency, and they should be helped." She had a smile on her face and said that she hoped she never would be raped.

—Toni Maness

Questions on "Interview on Women in Society"

1. How are the writer's questions geared to elicit strong responses?
2. How does the writer capture the emotion in the interview and yet retain an objective stance?

Appendix

How To Write a Paper (When You Really Don't Want To)

You can't always wait for inspiration before you begin to write. Unfortunately, you often have to produce important papers when you are most tired and least in the mood. Even though you have probably heard that papers should be written far ahead of due dates and carefully revised for best results, you may find yourself still waiting and writing frantically at the last minute, using running out of time as an excuse for doing less than your best.

If getting started is your greatest problem, and you want to break your old bad habits and take the fear out of writing, the following techniques are guaranteed to help.

Write a Paper in Steps

A task always seems largest and scariest if you think you have to do it all at once. Instead of thinking, "I must now sit down and write my entire paper," break the writing process into steps and begin with the easiest and least threatening. This approach has many advantages. First, it gets you started. Second, it enables you to think about ideas and clarify them before you commit them to paper, and finally, by the time you've completed the beginning steps, the final steps become that much easier to do.

For example, you might try writing your paper using the following six steps, or you might combine steps or create a workable pattern of your own. At any rate, see the completion of each step as reaching a subgoal and reward yourself in some way. If you can, complete the steps on different days, but if you are short on time, at least take a break between steps. Eat a favorite food, read a magazine, go for a walk, or in some fashion reward yourself each step of the way.

Six Suggested Writing Steps

1. *Sketching out ideas step.* In this step all you do is think of various topics and sketch out ideas for them. You may try freewriting on various parts if you wish, but you do *not* actually write the paper. You may also write out various ideas for beginnings and endings. If you are writing an analytical paper, you might try to formulate various thesis statements.

2. *Adding details and supporting examples step.* In this step, you add specifics that will complement or support the main ideas in step no. 1. For example, if you are writing personal experience papers, you might list sensory details you could add to specific scenes. If you are writing an analysis, you could list possible examples that would prove or illustrate each of your ideas.

3. *Writing a rough draft.* Using your working sheets from steps 1 and 2, write a complete rough draft. Mark areas that are rough and that you might want to rework later, but don't stop writing until either your draft is complete or you have reached a point where you know exactly what you will write next.

4. *Reading your draft out loud and reworking trouble spots.* Read your draft out loud. If some places seem awkward, reword them the way you might explain them to someone you were reading your paper to. Rework each area you have marked in the previous step.

5. *Rewriting the entire paper.* During this step, pay special attention to verb choice and tightening techniques for the type of writing you are doing. (See suggested Style Exercises in the chapters that explain each type of writing.)

6. *Checking for mechanics.* Now go over your paper carefully for spelling and punctuation. Look up words. Ask for help if you're having trouble.

Use Psychology on Yourself

If you still have trouble getting yourself even to begin the six writing steps, try some proven psychological techniques to get yourself started. David Premack of the University of California has developed a technique known as the "Premack Principle" that can easily be applied to writing.[1]

In simple terms, Premack's Principle takes something you enjoy

---

[1]Premack's Principle is described in detail in Dr. Frank J. Bruno's book, *Think Yourself Thin* (New York: Harper & Row, Publishers, 1972), pp. 69–74.

doing and normally do and makes it contingent on something you are less likely to do. For our purposes, you would take an activity you normally do and enjoy each day such as eating an after school snack, reading the paper, watching a television program, or listening to a favorite record and make yourself complete one writing step before you allow yourself to do the favored activity. You don't have to do the writing step, but until you do it, you don't let yourself do the other activity. The technique may sound simple, but it's effective, and it works.

Glossary

Active voice   starting sentences with subjects that perform the action indicated

Ad misericordiam ("to the pity of the heart")   an appeal based on sympathy

Analysis   breaking a whole into its parts; exploring the relationships of those parts to the whole

Argument ad hominem ("argument at the man")   attacking a person's characteristics, marital status, origins, religious beliefs, or home life instead of his or her arguments

Argument ad populum ("argument to the people")   appealing to an audience's particular prejudices and fears

Bandwagon   the belief that if the majority does something, it is right, if the majority believes something, it is true

Begging the question   assuming the truth of what you're supposed to be proving is true

Black/white fallacy   see "false dilemma"

Circular reasoning (also known as "rabbit reasoning")   assuming that continual repetition of an argument constitutes proof

Cliché   a wornout expression that has lost its originality, specificity, and impact through overuse

Cocksure fallacy   stating an unproven assumption as if its truth were too obvious to need proving

Connotation   the associations a word brings to mind, the images it evokes, the feelings it produces

Deadwood   unnecessary words that take up space but add no meaning

Denotation   the dictionary definition of a word

Dicto simpliciter ("oversimplified saying")   arguing from an unqualified generalization; using an unqualified generalization to make a specific prediction

Dramatic irony   a situation in which what a fictional character says or stands for is the opposite of what the author believes

Either/or fallacy   see "false dilemma"

False analogy   a figurative comparison presented as proof

False dilemma (also known as the black/white or either/or fallacy)   arbitrarily limiting a person to two opposing choices when more possibilities exist

Focal point   the incident that pinpoints your paper's main idea

Focus   a writer's emphasis or center of attention

Focused freewriting   writing on one idea, memory, thought, or reaction as long as the words come; remaining free from mechanical concerns but limiting yourself to a chosen subject or area

Fragment   part of a sentence written as if it were a complete sentence

Freewriting   writing done as rapidly as possible without worrying about grammar or mechanical correctness; to record your normal speaking or thinking voice rather than a more self-conscious or premeditated writing style

   focused freewriting   freewriting on one idea, memory, thought, or reaction as long as the words come; remaining free from mechanical concerns but limiting yourself to a chosen subject or area

   unfocused freewriting   freewriting without a controlling subject or thought, putting down anything that comes to mind; skipping from topic to topic, thought to thought; having no subject limitation

Genetic fallacy   believing that a person's origins or genes will predict his or her behavior

Glittering generalities   associating positive "cliché" words with a product or ideas

Hasty generalization   an all-encompassing conclusion based on too little evidence

Hypostatization   treating an abstract and diverse field as if it were a uniform entity with consistent beliefs

Hypothesis contrary to fact   using a false or unprovable premise to support your argument

Irony   a situation in which a writer says or has a character say the opposite of what is meant (Irony is communicated through tone and in deliberately contradictory details. Example: a character praises someone he hates)

   dramatic irony   situation in which what a fictional character says or stands for is the opposite of what the author believes

   situational irony   a situation where one expects one thing to happen and the opposite actually occurs

   verbal irony   a situation in which what is said is the opposite of what is meant

Justification by side issue   arguing that your opponent's wrongs justify your own

Loading the dice   see "stacking the deck"

Logical fallacy   a counterfeit argument; an argument that sounds convincing but which does not hold up under rational scrutiny; an argument that diverts attention, distorts evidence, or uses false association, causation, or authority in presenting its case.

Name-calling   labeling your opponent with negative terms

Non sequitur ("It does not follow")   suggesting a conclusion that has no logical connection with the evidence

Objective   writing that focuses outside of you; writing in which you seek to eliminate or at least to minimize any show of personal bias or emotion as you present your material

Parallel construction   presenting ideas in the same sentence structure, repeating the same connecting words, parts of speech, and word endings

Passive voice   starting sentences with subjects that receive action or are acted upon

Point of view   whose head you're inside of in viewing an event; the person whose mind re-creates an event

Poisoning the well   prejudicing or coloring an audience's view of material before it is presented

Post hoc, ergo propter hoc ("after this, therefore because of this")   using a time sequence to suggest a causal relationship, that is, because event B followed event A, to claim that A caused B

Red herring   side-tracking an argument to a different topic

Run-on   two or more sentences written as one

Satire   exposing and ridiculing a situation in hopes of reforming it

Situational irony   a situation where one expects one thing will happen and the opposite actually occurs

Special pleading   see "stacking the deck"

Stacking the deck (also known as "loading the deck" or "special pleading")   presenting only the facts in your favor, ignoring or omitting negative evidence

Stereotype   an oversimplified portrayal based on exaggerated clichés that falsely assume that all members of a given race, sex, nationality, religion, age, body build, hair color, or any other group are alike

Style   how something is told. Style includes word choice, sentence structure (long, short, complicated, simple), tone (happy, sad, tongue-in-cheek) rhythm, and sound. Style is a reflection of a writer's distinctive voice

Subject   what a work is about

Subjective   writing that focuses on and inside of you, the writer; writing in which you reflect and emphasize your feelings and emotions as you present your material

Tag line   the identification of who is speaking or thinking in a direct quotation, indicated by expressions such as "I said," "he replied," "I thought to myself"

Theme   abstract concept, message, moral, or idea implicit in a work; feeling or interpretation of life presented by a work

Thesis   a paper's position statement; the central idea or framing concept which controls a paper

Transfer   artificially linking two unrelated things to effect a positive carry-over of approval or prestige

Tu quoque ("you're another")   responding to an accusation with a counteraccusation

Unfocused freewriting   writing without a controlling subject or thought, putting down anything that comes to mind; skipping from topic to topic, thought to thought, having no subject limitations

Unity   the effect achieved when related parts join to create a single harmonious whole

Verbal irony   a situation in which what is said is the opposite of what is meant

Verb tense   any of the forms of a verb that show the time of its action; English has six tenses: present, past, future, present perfect, past perfect, and future perfect

Response Sheet

To the Users of this Book

For a book to be useful, it must continue to meet its readers' needs. Please comment freely on any or all of the following questions or add new categories of your own; then mail this page to:

> Pauline Christiansen, English Department
> Bellevue Community College
> Bellevue, Washington   98007
> I look forward to your responses.

Name _____

Student or instructor _____

School _____

Course title _____

Instructor's full name _____

    1. Which parts of the book were most useful? (topic ideas, check lists, example papers, discussion questions, group exercises, style exercises)

    2. Which parts would you change? (eliminate, add more materials to, refocus)

3. What might be added to the book to increase its usefulness?

4. What reactions or suggestions do you have on the book's format?

5. Which selections would you keep or drop?

6. Additional comments:

7. May you be quoted on any of the above?

Date
Signature
Mailing address